TALKING POWER

The Politics of Language in Our Lives

ROBIN TOLMACH LAKOFF

BasicBooks
A Division of HarperCollins*Publishers*

The author gratefully acknowledges permission to reprint excerpts from the following material:

"Personals" by Leah Garchik, © 1989 *San Francisco Chronicle,* reprinted by permission.

"Doctors Denying Women Pain Killers," reprinted with the permission of United Press International, Inc., © 1989.

"President 'Apologizes' to Mrs. King," © 1983 *Los Angeles Times.* Reprinted by permission.

"Me and My Family," 1981, reprinted with the permission of Ann Landers/Creators Syndicate.

"Spin-Doctors" by Lynn Ludlow, © 1988 *The San Francisco Examiner,* reprinted with permission from *The San Francisco Examiner.*

"At China's Ministry of Truth, History is Quickly Rewritten," by Richard Bernstein, © 1989 by The New York Times Company. Reprinted by permission.

Library of Congress Cataloging-in-Publication-Data
Lakoff, Robin Tolmach.
    Talking Power: the politics of language in our lives/Robin
Tolmach Lakoff.
        p.   cm.
    Includes bibliographical references and index.
    ISBN 0–465–08358–7
1. Languages—Political aspects.   I. Title.
P119.3.L25   1990
306.4'4—dc20   90-80247
                                                                CIP

For Butterscotch, Antoine Meillau,
Portnoy, Oedipus, Tobermorey,
and (currently) Catiline, all Practical Cats:

Cum tacent, clamant

CONTENTS

PREFACE

I PROBABLY found my way into the academic world, some twenty-five years ago, as an escape from the anxieties of the real one. The study of language—two removes from that disturbing reality—seemed particularly suitable for this purpose. At first I thought I could play it safe as a transformational syntactician, whose only concern was the arrangement of words in sentences. But in time, several of my colleagues and I were forced to recognize that sentence structure was not autonomous: you had to know who was speaking, under what social circumstances, and what their assumptions were, before it was possible to assign appropriate form to a sentence, or relate a sentence's form accurately to a meaning. No longer, then, was language a safe refuge.

But we didn't know how far we had to go: how much of real experience had to be encoded in linguistic rules. We had to proceed by trial and error, case by case, looking for evidence. It didn't take long to find some examples in which a speaker's role or assumptions figured in the determination of syntactic form, but it was equally clear that not everything we knew or could discern about the real context of language use was explicitly encodable into specific linguistic choices.

This was in the late 1960s and early 1970s, when the women's movement was becoming a significant force. I began to wonder whether one particular part of our physical identity—namely, gender—figured in syntactic decisions. (My colleagues generally thought it a silly question, but I was as stubborn then as now.) I found, rather to my surprise, that it did indeed, in many ways. Most importantly, I realized that—unlike most of the linguistic choices with which the field concerned itself—these possibilities transcended the ivory tower. They arose out of, and gave birth to, disparities in power between the sexes, restricting the options of both.

Since that epiphany, I have tried from time to time to retreat to the safety of the academy, only to find that whatever facet of language caught my interest was ineluctably entangled with real-world politics. I am sure this coincidence arises because I tend to get interested in linguistic behavior only after I have been thrust, generally willy-nilly, into direct experience of it. So I got interested in therapeutic discourse because of my involvement in that process; in the language of the courtroom out of a stint on jury duty; and in the discourse of academe, through being around universities for all my adult life, as student and faculty member.

It is as well, I think, that I have chosen topics such as those to work on. It seems clearer and clearer to me that we cannot understand language except through direct experience, using it or having it used to us. Unless our words make a difference in the outcome, we cannot make valid judgments. Too often the sociolinguist or pragmaticist still attempts to play the games of the ivory tower, to study some aspect of real language use "objectively." If it's a form of language with which we are all familiar anyway, like conversation, there is probably no harm done. But when the researcher ventures into foreign territory, like the courtroom, it is essential to be engaged, to get a whiff of the adversariality in the air by joining the game, not standing on the surface decorously jotting notes. True, one loses "objectivity" by taking one side or another, by being involved crucially in the outcome; but only thus is it possible to truly know why certain choices were made, whether change is possible or useful.

What follows is my attempt to put together some ideas, observations, and experiences that argue for the political nature of communication. Of course, as an effort to change our ways of thinking about what we tend to take for granted, this book is itself an exercise in the politics of language.

Berkeley, California
November 1989

ACKNOWLEDGMENTS

I T would be satisfying, but impossible, to thank everyone who, over many years, in one way or another, has contributed to the thinking that has resulted in this book. Let me try, however, to express my gratitude to those who have played especially important roles.

First, there are my friends and family, who have helped me get this done by their support and encouragement: Mandy Aftel, Elizabeth Bader, Andy Lakoff, Deirdre Lashgari, Herb and Liz Simons, Deborah Tannen, and Vivian Wilson. Additionally, some of them have read this manuscript as a whole or in part, and to those particularly I give heartfelt thanks.

I want to mention my students, past and present, who continue to give me a reason for doing the work I do, and remind me that there is a future in it. Being forced to clarify my ideas in order to make them intelligible to students is always invaluable.

Parts of the book have come about through the impetus of being invited to present my ideas at various professional forums. In particular, I would like to thank Joanna Bankier and Gabriel Berns, organizers of the NEH Summer Translation Institutes at the University of California at Santa Cruz, during the summers of 1987–89, and their students. Chapters 12 and 13, as well as material in several of the other chapters, developed out of the lectures I delivered during those years, and the discussions with faculty and students during and after. Much of the subject matter in chapters 5 and 6 was developed for presentations during the 1985 Linguistic Institute at Georgetown University, directed by Deborah Tannen. Some of the topics discussed in these and other chapters were also given impetus by invitations to speak, in 1985 and 1987, at the California Attorneys for Criminal Justice conferences at Asilomar, California. Finally, during the month I spent as a guest lecturer at the Universitad Autónoma de Barcelona in

May and June 1988, I had a chance to think about and discuss, with students, faculty, and staff, many of the topics of the book.

Next, and perhaps most importantly, there are the people who have allowed me access to the workings of their professions by sharing their working experience and their wisdom with me. This book would not have been possible without their intelligence, clarity of understanding, patience, and good humor in explaining the obvious to a neophyte: Mandy Aftel, Judge Stanley P. Golde, Liz Krainer, Deana Logan, Michael Millman, Charles O. Morgan, Doris Treisman, Harriet Verben, Pauline Weaver, and Richard Zimmer.

Finally, deep thanks and appreciation are due my editors at Basic Books, Inc., Jo Ann Miller and Phoebe Hoss, whose ideas and advice have improved this work immensely; and my agent, Frances Goldin, whose support and encouragement are, now as ever, greatly valued.

INTRODUCTION:

The Politics of Language

W E feel ourselves at the mercy of language and its manipulators, the slick professionals—advertisers, politicians, televangelists—who use it with cynical skill to entice us, innocent amateurs, into their webs of words. We blame the professionals who bamboozle us; our anger doesn't stop them from trying it again, nor prevent us from being taken in by still more polished tactics next time. It might make better sense to blame ourselves: we all have access to the same repertoire of linguistic strategies and could become consumers of language as sophisticated as the merchandisers, attacking the "demand side" as they say. A close look at the naïve, "innocent," and spontaneous ways we use language in our everyday lives, in our conversations with friends and intimates and at work, would reveal, inchoate perhaps but definitely present, the same strategies of persuasion and manipulation the professionals have at their disposal. In communicating, no matter what the level or the function, we all have the same basic needs, which we try to meet through our linguistic interaction. We want to be liked, first of all; the rest follows: we want to be authoritative, to have our instructions or advice followed, to be admired (to name but a few needs). But from the most intimate tête-à-tête (micropolitics) to a speech aimed at millions (macropolitics), the aims are the same, and the techniques closely related.

We are reluctant to examine our conversational gambits; first, we get nervous when we have to examine closely behavior that has become habitual and unconscious. Don't try to figure out how you tie your shoes, or you'll never be able to do it again; the same holds for conversation. Then, too, especially in the area of interpersonal behavior, we like to see ourselves as guileless, our actions as spontaneous. To recognize that we are following set patterns, sometimes engaging in strategies to achieve something at the expense of someone else, is to be forced to see ourselves and our motives in an ungenerous light. But it is the logical first step to divesting professional users of their illegitimate tricks.

Special tactics need not be illegitimate, and it is important to distinguish between situations where professional and persuasive ways of using language are necessary and valid, and those where they hide impure motives. Language can certainly be used for mystification. Everyone who has ever entered a courtroom in a lay capacity (as witness, juror, defendant, or spectator) has seen it. The rituals of the courtroom, the formalities of the discourse, are intimidating in themselves, let alone in terms of the vital matters transacted in these places. But if we understand that the arcane uses of courtroom discourse are not generally malign in intention and that the form of the discourse to a considerable degree reflects and arises appropriately out of its function, we will be less awed and more able to sift the meaningful ceremony from the self-protective mystique, to discount the latter, and to utilize the former. Knowledge of special language is power, normally reserved for the professionals; but there is no law that prevents the power from being spread around the larger community through greater understanding.

There are many special languages, or *codes,* professional and otherwise: we all have access to one or more.[1] We develop special languages for communication with intimates, with special names for one another, words that have private significance, deep looks, little sighs. We can think of these mini-languages as reinforcing the power of the relationship to hold its members together by its obscurity to the outside world. Every kind of discourse has its own specialized forms, rules, and strategies, based at least in part on the functions it serves. "Dr. John Brown" talks one way to his colleagues, staff, and patients at the hospital (professional code), but at home he's "Jack" to his wife and "Daddy" to the kids, and (one hopes) puts on another way of talking (intimate code) along with his slippers when he gets home. As children, we first acquire competence in that intimate code with our parents and siblings, and that code therefore serves as the model against which we compare everything else we encounter: the language of classroom and office, for almost all of us; perhaps the church as well, the court, the therapeutic consulting room. Each code shares some features with other types, but finally each is unique in the way its form serves its function and must be learned when first encountered just like another language.

The trick for all of us is to grasp the generalizations, the larger picture. What is the connection between the form of a communication and the power it provides to its user? What is the relation between the subtle exercise of political strategies in friendly conversation, the more obvious clout special language gives the doctor or the lawyer, and the persuasive blandishments of the political or commercial great communicator? All language is political; and we all are, or had better become, politicians.

Because we all speak and comprehend it, everyone has some intuitive understanding of the workings of language. Many people have more—whether because they paid attention to their high school English teachers, or just because they are interested in it and have developed a sensitive ear for its nuances. People can sense, more or less intuitively, when language is being used well and poorly, legitimately or not. But our pleasure or indignation tends to be unfocused: we recognize the effect on us, but can't say how it came about. The first step in becoming a skilled consumer is taking the product apart, seeing the stuff of which it is made. Consumers' Union dismantles the appliances it tests, seeing how the efficiency of the whole is created or compromised by the integrity of each component and the smoothness with which they work together. A consumerist stance toward language can do no better.

But Consumers' Union doesn't just invite people in off the streets and supply them with sledgehammers. Techniques for dismantling and for reassembling provide illumination beyond the intuitive realization that this car's a lemon. The same is true of language: there are special techniques for analysis and synthesis. Those are the province of linguistics.

Linguistics by this name, and with its current concerns, is a relatively new development, dating back to the early years of the twentieth century, and in roughly its present form to the late 1950s.[2] It isn't surprising that people are puzzled when I introduce myself as a "linguist." "How many languages do you speak?" they ask, thinking of the older sense of *linguist*, that is, "polyglot." But modern linguists are not necessarily fluent in many languages (though most of us do know more than one); rather, the field is concerned with understanding the underlying patterns that create language, the mechanisms that give it structure and allow it to be used as a vehicle of communication. Linguists are interested both in the strategies of particular languages and in those shared by all languages: both tell us something about the organization of the human mind and the way it perceives and comes into relation with the world external to it.

Linguistics is an amalgam of many older disciplines, taking from all and creating its own coherent synthesis, essentially working toward a definition of language (we don't yet have one that would satisfy all of us, or perhaps any of us). Perhaps the oldest field to focus on language was *rhetoric*, developed in ancient Athens and concerned with the persuasive use of language: which forms best serve specific functions, specifically those of public life. Some centuries later, scholars turned from the public arena in a time of authoritarian governments to the private and inward, from the here and now to the links between past and present. Out of this work arose *philology*, which looks at texts and tries to determine how they are put together: the significance of choices of words; issues of style. There is often a focus on using those findings to determine the genesis of a particular version of a text that has come to us from ancient times, determining which of several alternate texts is genuine based on what is known about its author's use of language.

Grammar focuses on deciding the right way to use language and correcting what is presumed to be wrong. The prescriptive grammarian tells us not to split infinitives or say *irregardless*—sometimes providing "reasons" for the prohibition, as often legislating language by fiat. Prescriptive grammarians hope to keep control over language, to keep its forms constant. They are not interested in why English sentences take the form they do, and not other forms: in why, for example, we say, "John picked up the garbage and threw it out," but not "John picked up the garbage and threw out it."

The prescriptive grammarian is not concerned with the nonexistence of the second form, which is precisely what occupies the linguist. Why doesn't that form occur? Is there a generalization? What is the most economical way to describe the fact that forms like "throw out it" (including, as a partial list, "look up it [an address]," "turn on it [a light]," "put back it") don't exist? The linguist's jobs here are, first, to set up the category of verb + particle in which those forms don't exist, as opposed to similar-looking others (for example, "He looked up the street," which can be shortened to "He looked up it"), and then to write a rule that covers just the items in the first category and no others. The rule is *predictive* and *descriptive*, not prescriptive: it is an attempt to predict what kinds of utterances are ever used by fluent speakers of English, not to tell them not to say things they might otherwise say.

Modern linguistics is also allied to several of the social sciences, most closely anthropology. The first people who called themselves linguists in the modern sense were anthropologists. Beginning in the late nineteenth century, they went into exotic locales and studied peoples whose ways were strikingly different from those of Westerners. They found that statements philologists had confidently been making for centuries about the way language has to be, and how its forms are related to human mental processes, were rendered invalid by the vast profusion of ways in which non-Indo-European languages express meaning. The introspective techniques used by rhetoricians and philologists (equivalent to, "What would I mean if I said this? How do I react to this?") were useless in the encounter with languages whose forms were totally unfamiliar, whose world view as captured by language was totally unfamiliar. Back from the field, anthropologists began to develop linguistics as a *science:* that is, the techniques of objectivity and uninvolvement that had yielded rich results in the physical sciences over the last century were applied to the analysis of language. In this approach, one could study patterns and structures that could be discerned from inspection of superficial data (what came out of the field notes and, later, the tape recorder). Questions like, "Does sentence A mean the same thing as sentence B?" or "When would you use A, when B?" were out of bounds as requiring *mentalism,* a dirty word: the observer uses his or her own mind as an interpretive tool, as an astronomer uses a telescope or a physicist, a cyclotron.

At the same time, but without any formal connection, philosophers of language were becoming increasingly concerned with the relation between language form and the mind it represents. If the anthropologists' underlying question is, "What is a human being, considering the varieties of surface form that comprise human behavior?"; the philosophers' is, "What is a human being, based on what we can tell about the human mind?" But just as the anthropologist found it hard to get at the needed answers because of the variety of superficial human patterns and the difficulty in understanding those that were very different, the philosopher ran into problems because the mind is too deep, abstract, and inaccessible. Needed was a window to the mind: surface form that clearly reflects underlying psychological process. Language was that window. But these philosophers were introspective: assuming, with Descartes, that logical processes are universally the same, they assumed that any mind could function reliably as the prototype of all minds; therefore the investigator could use his or her intuitions about language exclusively as the instrument. That assumption enabled philosophers to develop theories of meaning and intention, ways of connecting form and function, which were off limits to the antimentalist linguist. Each, therefore, variously scorned and ignored the other, and many still do.

The field of linguistics has, then, evolved out of many fields, more or less explicitly deriving its methods, theories, and assumptions from all. We take from the philologist and the philosopher the use of introspection as a tool, the idea that (as long as we confine ourselves to languages with which we are fully familiar) our own minds are the most reliable interpreters (an essential assumption if we are to understand meaning and intention, yet fraught with perils). From these disciplines and from mathematics and the hard sciences generally we borrow many of our methods: the insistence on rigorous, predictive rules; the need to test hypotheses with data; notions of universality based on commonality of thought processes. We borrow from the anthropologist and social science in general the recognition that the range of possibilities is broad and that ethnocentric (or other) value judgments are not the business of anyone seeking true understanding. From these fields we derive other methods and techniques: the gathering of natural data by the recording of actual utterances; a suspicion of the use of the investigator's own mind, at least as sole tool; a wish for quantification, not often reliably fulfilled. From these fields, too, we have been encouraged to progress from looking at the "sentence" in a vacuum as artifact, since sentences do not exist by themselves, free of context. Language may demonstrate quasimathematical regularities, but it is not like numbers, existing on its own, without reference to the creatures who create and use it. The anthropologists noted the importance of context, social and psychological, and pioneered (along with small-group sociologists) the analysis of real discourse, particularly conversation.

Linguists enter the field with a wide array of agendas, explicit and otherwise, and are trained within a variety of traditions, including those I have mentioned. As with many academic fields, underlying prejudices and assumptions are seldom examined; depending on where and by whom a linguist is educated, he or she will reach scholarly maturity with various unexamined prejudices about what language is and how it should be studied. When groups collide (and ours is numerically a tiny discipline!), hostilities erupt. It is a contentious field, its members too often eager to plant their flags on some piece of turf ("We declare that ours is the only correct method and theory"), rather than trying to pool their knowledge and see how much really is compatible.

Those who are mathematically inclined see the discovery of rigorous dichotomous rules as the field's true function. Any interest that detracts from that concern is, ipso facto, declared beyond the concern of linguistics. Those who are anthropologically inclined see the comparison of the surface traits of diverse groups as our mission; hence, any introspection is taboo. Both, therefore, have grounds to be suspicious of what I am trying to do here, which is to begin to suggest informal generalizations (the precursors, perhaps, of formal rules; perhaps not) to cover a wide array of human behavior, patterns discernible across cultures and across discourse genres. I would argue that the time has come that the field can peel off its blinders; that its factions may by now be able to pool their resources and modify their prejudices. One reason is that both extremes seem to be wandering off into separate and pointless solipsisms: the mathematicians into the more and more formal analysis of less and less actual language, less and less connected to the context of its use; the anthropologists into the decoding of more and more and increasingly diverse data, without the ability to tell us what is really going on, why these forms and not others, what subjects actually think they're doing. So I am trying these projects here as an exercise in breaking stated and unmentioned barriers.

Since everyone, maybe even linguists, can agree that people use language to achieve certain aims, the broad topic of the politics of language provides a way of investigating how the forms of language facilitate its function, and how they are created to serve specific functions. Until we have ways to ask and investigate those questions, I don't think we will have much understanding of language, no matter how many formal rules we produce, how many recorded conversations we transcribe. I think the fundamental question of linguistics is "How are the forms of language related to the use we make of it?" I also think it's exciting and fun, and maybe even a little dangerous.

Over the last twenty years, two subfields have been developed within linguistics, pragmatics and sociolinguistics, which have devised methods of investigating variation and function.[3] They give us opening wedges, more or less precise ways of asking the questions we need to ask and evaluating potential answers about topics like these: the relation between speaking directly and indirectly; the forms and functions of politeness; the relation between one's social group and the way one speaks; the analysis of conversation, both in its externally visible forms and its deeper logic; definitions of style; public and private ways of talking. It is these issues I address in part I: the power tactics in ordinary language use by individuals in small and generally egalitarian groups. In part II, I move to the linguistic strategies of three selected institutions—the law, psychotherapy, and the university—to see how the professional members of institutions develop their own ways of speaking, and to examine the political consequences of that. In part III, I examine the ways in which membership in different cultures entails different linguistic strategies: different notions of logic, different ways to achieve persuasion; and the advantages and disadvantages of our tendency to devise linguistic categories of *we* and *they* to separate one society from another. And finally, in part IV, I turn to what is most traditionally thought of as the politics of language: the usurpation of language by the powerful, in one way or another, to create, enhance, and justify their power.

Language is politics, politics assigns power, power governs how people talk and how they are understood. The analysis of language from this point of view is more than an academic exercise: today, more than ever, it is a survival skill.

I

THE POLITICS OF EVERYDAY LANGUAGE

CHAPTER ONE

Language, Politics, and Power

T HE trial lawyers are selecting a jury for a capital case. The defense attorney is trying to discover whether a prospective juror is capable of voting either for death or for life imprisonment without parole in this case. The juror knows only the bare outlines of the case; what she might do *now* is less germane than what she might eventually be able to decide at the end of the trial. At the same time, the judge has cautioned against "speculative" questions, which are apt to elicit meaningless responses.

The defense tries: "Can you envision any mitigation outweighing the fact of two women having been killed?" The prosecutor objects to "envision" as encouraging "fantasy," meaning speculation: it's in his interests to constrain the form of this question as much as possible. The two go back and forth rancorously; the judge threatens contempt; finally, the prosecutor remarks that he doesn't see why the defense is insisting on this form of the question: "It's just semantics."

In other words, give me the decision, since it really doesn't matter, it's only words. But he and his adversary have just spent most of fifteen minutes wrangling over that very choice of words, wasting valuable time and trying the judge's temper (always inadvisable). Either he believes that language counts enough to justify the time and the risk, or he's behaving totally irrationally. Since he is a professional and since trial lawyers with any competence (and even his opponents acknowledge out of his hearing that he's pretty good) calculate their every move, we have to assume he has a good idea of what he's doing and has concluded that depriving the defense of this choice of phraseology is worth risking the judge's displeasure. But his remark does cause both the judge and the defense attorney to cool down and step back; and the latter agrees that, well, the words don't really matter so much after all, and tries something else.

Lawyers are particularly dependent on language; their success is a measure of their linguistic proficiency, their recognition of the ability of language to create, highlight, and distort reality, their power to force language to do their will. At the same time, they know that actual evidence—the blood-stained garment, the eyewitness identification—has potency where mere words fail. Their ambivalence, then, is not surprising. But they are not alone in taking a dual position on the relation between language and power.

Politics and power is a smoother juncture than *language and power.* The words belong to the same semantic realm. *Politics* is the game of *power;* politics allocates power and utilizes it. The promise of power makes politics worth the effort. Power in particular is vibrant, the very word conjuring up images of strength, force, action. Whether positive or negative, those images are strong. Power is physical: it changes reality, it gets things done or undoes what exists. It creates effects that can be seen, felt, and measured. Power is the engine of the 747 that lifts the behemoth off the runway; it is the "plow that broke the plains"; the firing squad; the nuclear bomb under discussion at the conference table; the parent who can give or withhold the keys to the car; the boss who can hire or fire at whim. All of these operate to change reality for better or worse. We may admire power or resent it, but we can see its operations and feel its physical effects on us. Politics distributes that power, determines who has it and how it can be used; it is the handmaiden of power—or better, its parliamentarian.

Politics, we might say, is the physicality of power made psychological, power as sentient humans experience it and use it. It is applicable to every form of human interaction. International politics concerns large and abstract entities: countries forming alliances; competing for trade or influence, determining war and peace. National politics allocates the perquisites of power (wealth, influence, comfort) among competing groups and convinces those who control that allocation that one choice rather than another represents their best interests.

Politics also works at an individual level, as we have come to realize recently. Families have political structures, like businesses and friendships.[1] As in the larger contexts, there are winners and losers: winners get the power, the means to do as they choose and to define their own actions and those of others. Losers get destroyed or devalued or otherwise reduced in status. In one form or another, power informs all human relationships and politics is the instrument by which power creates and defines those relations. Both are real; both have physical forms and effects.

But how does language, the third member of the triad, fit in alongside the other two? Not very well, it might seem. Language is as abstract as power is concrete; it is impalpable, an artifact of the mind rather than the body. Only metaphorically does language *strike* us or *move* us, and it changes us only in indirect ways. But as politics brings the brute physical reality of power into the sphere of the human mind and heart, language is the means of that transformation. Language drives politics and determines the success of political machinations. Language is the initiator and interpreter of power relations. Politics is language.

At the same time, language is politics. How well language is used translates directly into how well one's needs are met, into success or failure, climbing to the top of the hierarchy or settling around the bottom, into good or bad relationships, intimate and distant. Language allocates power through politics, defines and determines it, decides its efficacy.

When societies of humans confront ideas and realities that are profoundly moving and disturbing, they do something uniquely and essentially human: they create culture around them—myth, religion, art, and eventually science. By such means what feels chaotic and beyond control is reduced to the lawful and understood, the predictable. And around language all of these explainers have flourished, as culture after culture has sought ways to make sense of the intrinsic duality: language as rooted, one foot in the real and tangible, the other in the airy world of imagination; language as powerful and as powerless, and in fact, improbably, both at once.

One way we come to terms with unsatisfactory dichotomies like these (that is, dichotomies that are psychologically comforting but not accurate representations of observed fact) is to construct systems, mythological, legal, or artistic. Society after society offers two distinct views of language, its role, its power, and its tangibility, coexisting necessarily if uneasily. As advanced as we believe our culture is, as far as we have transcended, as we think, the rationalizations of myth and superstition, we enshrine those dualities as surely as anyone else.

THE TWO FACES OF LANGUAGE

Language is powerful; language is power. Language is a change-creating force and therefore to be feared and used, if at all, with great care, not unlike fire. Change itself is frightening, as is that which creates it (especially in abstract and undetectable ways).

Particularly evident in less scientifically advanced cultures (but by no means absent even from the most sophisticated) is the use of language in ceremonials, *as* ceremony: language as the maker of a mood, and thereby a force for efficacy. In fairy tales we encounter magic words: say "abracadabra" or "shazam!" and *something happens,* by the utterance of the words alone. But they must be just those words: slip on a syllable, misplace a word, and nothing happens, or worse. In old Roman law, for a contract to be valid the contracting parties had to pronounce a set of words (some so archaic they were no longer understood) precisely right, or it was null and void. Today contracts must be written according to specific and rigorous legal rules that do not necessarily contribute to clarity of meaning; if not, they can be broken.

Many fairy tales and legends center around the power of language for good or evil, the dangers of an ill-considered word, the value of silence. The Fisherman's Wife intemperately uses the last of her wishes to grow a sausage to her husband's nose. The young queen is warned that her brothers will be released from enchantment as geese only if she can spend seven years without saying a single word. Misunderstanding of language brings disaster. Odysseus tells the Cyclops, "My name is No-man." When he puts out the monster's eye, the latter's friends ask him who did it, against whom shall they seek revenge? "No-man injured me," says the creature; and his fellows reply that, if no man injured him, there's nothing to be done, it was his own fault. By learning Rumpelstiltskin's name, the princess achieves power over him.

Finally, like other societies we have proverbs and other guiding expressions that warn us to be careful what we say, that language is potent:

Silence is golden.
The pen is mightier than the sword.
The tongue is the hangman of the mouth.

And, like other societies, we identify and reward those persons whose use of language is especially skillful. "From his tongue fell words sweeter than honey," says the *Iliad* of Nestor, who would otherwise, as an old man in warfare, which values youth, be a man without a role. Today we speak bemusedly of the "Great Communicator," wondering how Ronald Reagan's use of language seemingly rendered him impervious to criticism.

Along with testimony to the very real powers of language, we also find a collection of reverse folklore: tales, customs, and proverbs that use magical thinking to deny the potency of language by stressing its differences from the reality of deeds. Language, in this view, is weak, empty air: by itself, without the force of reality behind it, it counts for nothing, accomplishes nothing. So, for instance, when it is important that language be forceful, we attempt to buttress it in some tangible ways. Thus, since treaties are no more than words on paper, cultures have from ancient times required backups: hostages exchanged between the negotiating parties to guarantee that they meant what they said. Often, too, under these and other solemn conditions (in courtrooms to the present day), oaths are exacted of those whose words must be truthful for the procedure to "work." Nowadays we often think of these oaths as mere words themselves, *pro forma* declarations. But they originated as dire threats: to swear by a deity, take the name of a god in vain, was to invite vengeance. Not only was lying ruinous to the perjurer, but the ruin, and its cause, were obvious to all. The very words *testify, testimony* recall one ancient link between words and reality. They are derived from the Latin *testes,* its meaning the same as in current English. In swearing, the Roman male (women were not allowed to participate in these procedures in the earliest times) placed his right hand upon his genitals; the implication was that, if he swore falsely, they would be rendered sterile—a potent threat. The need for such desperate measures suggests a fear (or hope) that words alone are not enough.

We have proverbs and sayings to the same effect, from "No woman was ever seduced by a book" (in Federal Judge John M. Woolsey's 1933 opinion overturning the obscenity laws to allow the importation of James Joyce's *Ulysses* into the United States) to the more traditional:

Talk is cheap.
Words are feminine, deeds masculine.
Sticks and stones may break my bones, but words can never harm me.

And when we wish to undermine another person's political use of language, we call it "mere words," "empty rhetoric," "just semantics."

So we are continually faced with the paradox that those words, pure air, that have no physical reality and that we are encouraged to disparage, have potent consequences in the real world every day: in the decisions of courtrooms, the actions of governments, the pronouncements of institutions, and the relationships with our nearest and dearest.

> "The question is," said Alice, "whether you *can* make words mean so many different things."
> "The question is," said Humpty Dumpty, "which is to be master—that's all."[2]

The paradox is not unsolvable. Words can be powerful or not. They can affect reality or not. Words become powerful because they can be used as tools: like a hammer or a gun, they don't make changes by themselves, but through a human being's use of them, skillful or clumsy. Guns don't kill people, the National Rifle Association likes to say: people kill people. By the same token, words don't change reality, people change reality. But like guns, words make it possible for people to achieve the effects they seek.

Language is a symbol, not a reality; the map, not the territory, as Alfred Korzybski, the general semanticist, put it many years ago. But symbols have tremendous potency, often more than the reality they stand for, because so much volatile emotion attaches to them. We all agree, for instance, that the American flag is a "symbol" of this country and its ideals: freedom, democracy, justice, and so forth. But as recent history demonstrates, the same people who are ready to rise up, in arms if necessary, in defense of "the flag" are quite willing to stand by uncaringly as blatant nonsymbolic injustices are perpetrated.

THE LANGUAGE OF PUBLIC PERSUASION

If we agree that language can be a source of power, we tend to see that as true for those people with special access to both language and power. If "they" choose, they can use language so skillfully and deceptively that we—the rest of us—will be helpless against them and their stratagems. They know something we don't; they have training we don't. We are the helpless and passive recipients of manipulative communication; they are the users of it and, through it, of us.

We put those special people into two or three major categories: economic persuaders, on the one hand, advertisers and salesmen; and political persuaders, on the other. Sometimes we divide the second into two groups: those who use language especially effectively but legitimately, "politicians" (or "statesmen" if we want to be respectful or they are dead); and those who use it in some illegitimate way, or for some illegitimate purpose, or both—"propagandists." We try from time to time to draw clear lines between the legitimate and the illegitimate persuaders, but too often these lines distinguish those with whose message we are in basic agreement from those whose appeal threatens us. Such a definition, based on the personal preferences of the definer, is not valid. Moreover, advertisers and politicians are not the only skilled users of powerful language: we all have some persuasive skills.

It is true that there are special, learnable skills that give those who have mastered them an advantage over amateurs. But the difference is quantitative, not qualitative. It is not that they know things of which we are totally innocent, but that they are better at the tricks we all know. After all, those smooth persuaders don't require that their audiences be specially trained and prepared, so the strategies they use must be ones we already know how to appreciate, even if we can't use them as effectively. There are some clever new strategies, but they are not ironclad or guaranteed: in fact, one thing both advertisers and politicians know too well is that the public becomes wise to their tactics remarkably fast; they have to keep replacing techniques to keep them working at all.

It is equally true that the twentieth century has provided a host of techniques, tactics, and strategies that render language more potently persuasive than it used to be. The development of modern psychology and the explicit discovery of the unconscious and its mechanisms, on the one hand, provide one route of access; and the development of new media provides another. The two go hand in hand. Freudian concepts, defenses, repression, sexual symbolism, and the rest can be used to get at us where we are not accustomed to being consciously manipulated; television provides a way to bring those messages home to us, where we feel safest and most protected. One of the century's pretty ironies is that public relations, perpetrator of some of the cleverest manipulative techniques, was pioneered by Edward L. Bernays, a nephew of Freud's on both sides of his family (his mother, Freud's sister, married Freud's wife's brother). But the human mind is if nothing else ingenious: no sooner does the therapist, or the propagandist, find a way to undermine the barrier of the defenses, than the mind finds a new and stronger defense. We can fight back, even if this version of who uses language and how is correct.

We construct worst-case scenarios, like Newspeak in Orwell's *Nineteen Eighty-Four:* a manipulation of language that not only empowers its creators but renders them unassailable. But that scenario is only an exaggeration of our fears about the way it really is now. There is an amorphous *them* out there who know all the tricks and use them to play us like violins. Without our realizing it, we are moved to do as they say. Some years back Vance Packard's *The Hidden Persuaders* gave substance to those fears with the concept of subliminal advertising. Later research showed the fear to be exaggerated: subliminal advertising had only the most limited range of usefulness, if any, and claims for its effectiveness were greatly overrated. But we were left with the vague sense that *they* were using language in ways that *we* could neither fathom nor defend ourselves against; they had all the good words and the bad words; we were marionettes on their strings.

This kind of thinking has its comforting and its frightening aspects. It comforts us to divide the world in two, *them* versus *us.* It is comforting to think of ourselves as virtuous and innocent; and when we make stupid or dangerous decisions, to attribute that to *them* and their illicit persuasive techniques. But at the same time, that division makes us feel helpless and reinforces any tendencies we already have toward passivity. We don't try to be intelligent consumers: why bother? It's beyond us, utterly foreign, totally mysterious. We can't stop those sneaky communicators by heading them off at the pass with equal and opposite analytic strategies. Rather, we demand that the lawmakers protect us with legislation that covers each imaginable case. Since each case is different, such legislation is a patent impossibility, but we continue to hope and be outraged when we keep getting taken in and nobody steps in to prevent it.

EVERYBODY IS A POLITICIAN

This scenario, attractive though it may be, is inaccurate. We are not mere passive recipients of manipulative communicative strategies. Orwell and other worriers ignore the truth, whether unpleasant or happy: we all manipulate language, and we do it all the time. Our every interaction is political, whether we intend it to be or not; everything we do in the course of a day communicates our relative power, our desire for a particular sort of connection, our identification of the other as one who needs something from us, or vice versa. Often, perhaps usually, we are unaware of these choices; we don't realize that we are playing for high stakes even in the smallest of small talk. We may enter the transaction knowingly or not, we may function mainly as manipulator or manipulatee—but we are always involved in persuasion, in trying to get another person to see the world or some piece of it our way, and therefore to act as we would like them to act. If we succeed, we have power. Mostly we are without formal training, we work by intuition, and some of us have better instincts in language use than others. But we are all trying to do it, all the time.

Even the most innocent and well-intentioned conversational gambits entail power strategies. Most of us have participated, in one role or another, in dialogues similar to the following ones. On their face, most look guileless; no one is using finely honed Orwellian methods. But what is really going on in each?

> HE: Wanna go to the movies?
> SHE: Oh, I don't know. . . . Do you?

This is one traditional form of the male-female game (although others can play as well). He has made a suggestion, and it's up to her to take it or propose another. Either course would entail self-assertion. She would be stating and taking responsibility for a personal preference. Particularly if she makes a counterproposal, she has to worry if it doesn't work out well. She will feel guilty. If she is deficient in self-esteem, she is likely to be fearful of that outcome—better, then, to avoid any sort of assertion and leave the decision making up to him. But then, she never does get to do what she wants; and if the decision is good, it proves to both of them that he's smart and she's not. It's a form of linguistic politics, to be sure: she is trying to retain what power she has by never being proved incompetent; by leaving the decision up to him, she gets him to make the commitment and run all risks. Women are often castigated for this sort of behavior, but it arises out of deep fears of incompetence that societies too often foist upon female children.

> SHE: Tell me how to fix this Xerox machine.
> HE: Oh, don't you worry about that, honey. Leave it to me.

Now the shoe is on the other foot. This vignette illustrates one way that men maintain control over women, by reducing their self-confidence (and thereby leading to scenes like the first example). What is happening on the surface is different from the meaning at a deeper level. On the surface, he is being polite and considerate: he's saving her time and energy by doing the job himself. The "honey" offers intimacy and caring. But look again. The hidden message he is conveying is that she would not benefit from being told how to do it herself (which would give her power in the future: she wouldn't need to keep asking him for help). She probably couldn't do it anyway; fixing machinery is a man's job.

Her only hope is to be able to cajole him into helping her each time she encounters a snag: she has to rely on him; her functioning is dependent on his goodwill. His words convey to her that she *should* lack self-confidence; she isn't really competent. And if she knows what's good for her, she'll remember to be deferential to him, now and in the future. He has set up their future relationship with himself in charge. The "honey" only helps in this: he assumes an intimacy that is not reciprocal (she probably can't call him "sweetie-pie" back), and this puts them in a relation analogous to adult-child (an adult can call a child "honey," but not vice versa). It does not matter whether the woman in the first case, and the man in the second, openly acknowledge that these were their intentions, or passionately deny it; this is the function of such language uses. They are strongly political; power is the topic under discussion.

Gender is not the only battlefield where struggles for power are waged:

A: Have some of this chocolate mousse.
B: I *told* you I was on a diet!

This colloquy can be perfectly innocent conversation on both sides, but it can also be treacherous. The interpretation depends on just how the sentences are said (as is generally true, bare words on the printed page tell us little). Much depends, too, upon what has preceded them: If A has been "complaining" about his or her inability to gain weight, then we might read into the offer some invidious intent. On the other hand, if A is the well-meaning hostess, it would be unreasonable to draw any negative inference. Now consider B's rejoinder: If it is accompanied by the marks of resentment and outrage—tears, a raised voice, a reproachful expression—it might signify, "You don't really care about me," or even, "I bet you want me to be fat." Since neither is said aloud in so many words, A is effectively helpless. A's possible hostility is not asserted by B, but presupposed, meaning that A cannot fend off the attack by saying, for instance, in response to B's outburst, "Of course, you are important to me," or "I like you just the way you are." The use of implications such as B's is an old and effective way of playing conversational politics: B wins the point because A cannot counterattack or defend. Nothing has been *said* that requires a defense, so that anything A says runs the risk of seeming to protest too much, getting the unfortunate A into still hotter water.

The games are not necessarily face to face. Imagine this telephone conversation:

A: So, I was wondering if you were free on Saturday, because I was thinking———
B: Oh, excuse me, there goes my other line. [*Hangs up.*]

With each innovation in communicative technology, the political possibilities are multiplied, and the more savvy and well-equipped the communicator, the more numerous the opportunities. The telephone has always allowed us to invent excuses for getting out of a conversation that, in person, would be impossible ("Oops, there's the doorbell!"). The phone is also good for making demands and accusations, since it's hard for most of us to behave badly to someone else while making eye contact. (It's probably also easier to lie on the telephone, and harder for the hearer to spot.) The initiator of the phone call is in a position of power: the caller chooses the time, has the facts ready, and normally terminates the call. (Clever people learn to play "telephone tag" to their advantage: when you're up to something, never allow the other person to call you back.) The recent advent of call-waiting has only added fuel to the fire. Advice columns not infrequently print letters from people outraged by being put on hold and hung up on by others, especially when the latter initiated the call. "Well," says B, when confronted in the preceding example, "what was I to do? The phone beeped! I had to answer!" True enough, but alongside the perfectly practical reasons for B's behavior and call-waiting in general, the innovation allows the user ingenious political manipulations and, at worst, convinces the victim on the other end that some political game is being played. The covert message that B may or may not intend, but A is likely to receive, is: "Let me see if it's someone more interesting on the other line." And if B "has to hang up" on A, the latter will be sure that someone more interesting is, in fact, waiting.

It is equally possible to play power games in person, in relatively public settings:

A: I have an appointment with Dr. Snarf at eleven forty-five.
B: Oh, Doctor's running late. Please have a seat.

Like call-waiting, being kept waiting by professionals engenders furious reactions, from private grumbling to letters to advice columnists. Tales are prevalent of people billing their doctors for time wasted sitting in offices, or even suing them in small claims court for compensation. It is not so much the actual time spent sitting there, nor the dog-eared copy of *Today's Health* that galls; it is the attitude and, specifically, the subliminal message: "Doctor is more important than you. You'd better be subservient, because you need us more than we need you." Salt is rubbed in the wounds (dubious medical procedure) by the receptionist's use of the honorific title "Doctor." Under few circumstances in this culture are people referred to (not addressed) by title alone; my secretary, for instance, does not tell callers, "Professor's fighting her computer. Call back later." In fact, professors are addressed as "Professor" only by non-academics—a mark of outsidership. The practice is most common in the rigid stratifications of the courtroom:

a lawyer may be referred to (as well as addressed) as "Counsel," a judge as "His Honor" (though this is relatively uncommon). But in the egalitarian world of every day, most of us aspire to a general, at least superficial, *pro forma* equality. In fact, the only ordinary-world analogue to the receptionist's "Doctor" is "Mommy" and "Daddy" with children. ("Hi there, dear. Is Mommy home?") Even this may seem patronizing to some children if used by those outside the nuclear family. "Doctor," like "Mommy," presupposes a strongly unequal relationship and thus both justifies the enforced wait and makes objection to it more difficult, just as you'd better not talk back to Mommy. The polite imperative ("Please") that follows may make matters even worse: "What choice do I have?" the patient wonders. The politeness may be as fake as the aspidistra in the corner.

In each of the preceding imaginary dialogues, at least one of the participants uses linguistic form to achieve political ends, to create or reinforce a power imbalance that would, in turn, lead to further advantages. The linguistic politician may have worked the other into a position of responsibility for a past or future course of action; of inadequacy on any of various societally agreed-upon grounds; or of inferiority, requiring one to take what is offered however unsatisfactory it is. And, in most of the cases examined, the game is won by hidden means. No receptionist says, "I want you to know that Dr. Snarf considers you vermin, and you should be glad he lets you wait in his office at all." No, that is actionable. "Doctor is running late" has much the same subliminal effect, but if you are miffed, any attorney you consult will tell you it's in your mind, not in anything that was said. You bear the responsibility for the invidious interpretation. Politics is piled on politics.

MICRO AND MACRO

Whether speaking as a professional or in everyday life, one still plays the linguistic game according to hidden agendas, the unsaid being far more potent than the said. Furthermore, power drives power: those who already have it (advertisers and politicos) parlay it into authority, and their superior status enhances the credibility of their message, which in turn enhances their power over us. It is the use of our deepest and least-acknowledged fear, shame, desires, by speakers whose authority emanates from their apparent transcendence over those base needs, that allows linguistic power games to work between intimates and colleagues, in dealing with professionals, from higher-ups to lower-downs, and from powerful individuals to groups.

We can call one kind of power-oriented discourse *micropolitics;* the other, *macropolitics.* The first involves the development and use of strategies that create and enhance power differences among individuals; the second, strategies of group management. Micropolitical tactics tend to be personal, hinging on the establishment of a relationship and determining its rules: how close will the participants be? Who will make the decisions? Who will be dominant in which areas? How direct or indirect will communication be? Usually these negotiations are unconscious and implicit: participants are not aware that they have taken place; the relationship just seems to fall into a pattern. To bring these issues into the open, to articulate them, is to *metacommunicate,* to communicate about communication. This metacommunication is fraught with perils and, therefore, generally avoided. But the achievement of honesty in intimate relations, and the getting of satisfaction in more distant ones, is often contingent upon running those risks; otherwise, the games will continue.

Macropolitical discourse determines power relationships within and between groups, individuals functioning in cohesive units: nations, religions, races, and institutions, for instance. It may concern a struggle for power between two or more such groups, or the assertion by an individual of authority over a group. Linguistic power tactics are most apparent in struggles over a nation's choice of an "official" language as in Quebec. The frequency with which such issues develop into armed conflict demonstrates that they are more than a matter of administrative efficiency; the decision, by implicitly calling into question the individual identity of speakers of the nonchosen languages, thereby suggests that some identities are more valuable and valid than others. Macropolitics also covers the special languages of institutions: If your doctor tells you what your illness is in language you don't understand, or if laws and trial procedures are so cumbersome that only a lawyer can negotiate them, as an outsider you are rendered powerless over your fate; the institutions, by their development of and insistence upon special languages, both justify and underscore their authority and legitimacy and shield their members from scrutiny by the larger community. In this way they perpetuate the status quo, as official languages do, and are intended to do. Language can be a force for change; but, if controlled by those entrenched in power, it is a force for conservatism.

There are mixtures of micro and macro. For instance, women in most cultures use language differently from men, who, typically, hold political, social, and economic power. Therefore, women's ways of using language are disparaged as illogical (since men define logic according to their own practices). Therefore, it makes sense to deny women power, since they would not use it well. Therefore, too, women tend to get short shrift at all levels: in ordinary conversation, they are interrupted and the topics they broach ignored; in groups, they are not called on to speak, and if they are, their contributions are unrecognized or incorrectly attributed to others (men); women who seek power at the highest levels are seen as "shrill," "strident," "bitches," or slaves to raging hormones—often all the above. To change this and other situations where the linguistically proficient dominate those who are not, we must understand how we and others use linguistic politics.

ANALYZING THE LANGUAGE GAME

Whether in power or out of it, one plays the language game. Even one who has the upper hand and is an abuser of others will in turn be abused by someone still higher or more skilled, or by someone who possesses particular expertise. Only by learning how power is assigned and determined through linguistic structure, and what power is equitable, what not, can we work to develop fairer ways of communicating. Then, at last, we can stop being mystified and victimized by those who wield the power inherent in language. Then we can decide, in Humpty Dumpty's words, "which is to be master."

CHAPTER TWO

Talking about Language

MANY of us agonize over the so-called rules of language and what others will think if we get them wrong. *I* before *e* except after *c*. *Irregardless* is not a word. Never end a sentence with a preposition. Should a letter to an unknown person begin, "Dear Sir," "Gentlepersons," "To whom it may concern," or "Dear Sir or Madam"? We fear the very real effects of language choice on reality: use the "wrong" form and be marked as an ignoramus. At this level, language is concrete, if still mysterious. It is clear that there are rules and, as with rules elsewhere, penalties for disobedience. But who makes up the rules, and why? Are these the real rules that put a language together, or just some sort of superficial etiquette?

THE DESCRIPTIVE RULES OF LANGUAGE

In their attempts to explain language, linguists talk about rules, structures, and systems. But the rules they try to capture are not those of the grammarian who warns about spelling and diction in red ink on school compositions, but those all fluent speakers of a language use without conscious reflection: rules that are ingrained in the mind, learned effortlessly in infancy. These rules are "descriptive," meaning that they tell us how language actually is, rather than "prescriptive," like the rules in handbooks of style, which dictate how authorities think language should be.

The descriptive grammarian is interested in what people actually do: what are the general principles that describe most succinctly what one observes? The linguist notices that sentences like the first of the following two examples are found in English, but never any like the second:

Two hours elapsed.
Two boys elapsed.

And like the first of these, but not the second:

John admires sincerity.
Sincerity admires John.

Even someone who has never encountered any of these four can tell at once that the first member of each pair is a possible sentence of English, the second not. There must be some overriding principle speakers follow, so that they know intuitively that certain structures are permissible and others, also constructed of English words, are not. Those principles are the descriptive rules of English grammar.

Knowing those rules, speakers confidently form and understand sentences they have never heard before. If they know intuitively that the organizing principle in the first set of examples is that the verb *elapse* requires a noun representing an extent of time as its subject, they can form sentences like:

Two hours and five minutes elapsed.
The two hours that I shall always recall with horror as the worst in my
life up till that time elapsed.

Although the second example may be stylistically awkward, it is understandable; but not so "Two boys elapsed," which, however elegant, is unintelligible. Once we understand the rule for the use of *elapse*, we can form a potentially infinite variety of sentences using it, and always be sure we are speaking grammatically. In this way, the rule-governed properties of language allow its speakers to be creative in their use of it.

To the despair of prescriptivists, the rules of the descriptive grammar are not etched in stone. The forms of language are continually changing. Even the English of a hundred years ago sounds a little strange to us. Part of the fascination of studying language is seeing what can change and how language shifts its form over time. Some rules are in flux right now, before our eyes. For example, most speakers would unquestioningly accept the following sentence as a grammatical and stylistically unexceptionable sentence of informal English: "The party last night was fun." Dictionaries classify *fun* as a mass noun (one that occurs without an indefinite article and not in the plural: we don't say, "I had a fun," or "I had fun, but Mary had two funs"). But adjectives can also occupy the position in the sentence occupied by *fun* in the preceding example: "The party last night was neat." Unlike nouns, adjectives can be compared: *neater, neatest.* They can be placed before the nouns they modify: "a neat party." *Fun,* as a noun, does not have these options.

Now decide how you feel about each of the next three examples. Are they grammatical? Are they "right"? Would you say them? Have you ever heard any of them?

> Bob sure knows how to throw fun parties.
> This party is fun, but Mary's was even funner.
> This is the funnest party I've ever been at.

Monitor your reactions closely, but guard them carefully: they reveal your age. The older you are, the more conservative you are likely to be about these sentences. Younger people, teenagers especially, tend to accept all of them without question. Older people, those over fifty or so, like none of them. People in between might like the first of the last set of examples, but not the latter two, or the first two but not the third. What's going on?

This little corner of the grammar of English is currently in flux. *Fun,* which used unequivocally to be a noun, is turning into a word that can be either a noun or an adjective—a change made easier because *fun* is a mass noun. Like adjectives, but unlike count nouns, mass nouns do not occur with articles and do not have distinct plural forms. So *fun* can readily shift its allegiance, but a count noun that occurs in the same position cannot: "Mary's party was a drag." Nobody is going to say, "This party is a drag, but Mary's was even a dragger"—because the indefinite article stops the speaker from moving the expression *a drag* into adjectival status. So the grammar can change in ways existing structure permits. The linguist notes the changes but, as a descriptive grammarian, makes no value judgments on them.

THE UNITS OF LANGUAGE

The structure of language is complex: it starts from a small set of concrete units, combining these into ever larger, more abstract forms. The smallest units are the sounds: vowels and consonants. These are meaningless in themselves, acquiring meaning only in combination. Every language has a unique inventory of sounds, its *phonology;* some are found in all or almost all languages (the *a* sound in *father,* for instance); some occur much more rarely (the *th* in English *thick*). A language has a relatively small number of such sounds to work with—say, between fifty and a hundred. Languages are generally resistant to adding more. When we adopt foreign words into English, we generally, sooner or later, give them "English" pronunciations. We do not, for instance, palatalize (precede with *y*-like sounds) the *e*'s in *perestroika,* although a speaker of Russian does.

Sounds are combined to form meaningful units we call *words* (linguists like to call them *lexical items*). The number of words in a language is, though finite and countable, much larger than the number of sounds. While it is relatively easy to count the sounds in a language, knowing the number of words in it is tricky. What is a word? Is *glasnost* a full-fledged word of English in 1989? Is *archiphoneme,* a linguistic technical term, a word with the same status as, say, *word?* Is *fuck* a word, and if so, why isn't it in my dictionary, and if it's not a word, why not? How about compounds? When, if ever, do they become words in their own right? *Cost-effective? Junk bond?*

Words, in turn, combine to form *sentences,* larger, more abstract entities. Unlike sounds and words, the number of potential sentences in a language is infinite. Out of a pair of sentences, I can create a new, third one by combining them in any of several ways. In order to tell which strings of words are grammatical sentences of a language and which are not, speakers refer (unconsciously) to the rules I have just discussed. The number of rules is finite; the number of sentences they allow to be created is not.

Sentences themselves combine into still larger, more amorphous structures. In writing, we build sentences into *paragraphs.* In conversation, sentences comprise a speaker's conversational *turn.* As these forms are larger, they are also less precisely structured. There are fewer precise rules for the organization of paragraphs and turns than sentences.

THE TRIANGLE OF LINGUISTIC STRUCTURE

The essential properties of language are form, meaning, and function; and their relationship can be represented by an equal-sided triangle (see figure 2.1). Of course, none of these three points can be seen in isolation: the idea of representing language as a triangle is that just as a triangle from which a point is taken away not only is no longer a triangle, it isn't anything; so language is a composite of all three aspects, and none can be studied in isolation without incurring distortion or creating nonsense. As in architecture, form *is* function, and is meaning as well.

The formal aspect of language structure, the first point, includes the inventories of sounds and words, phonology and lexicon, as well as the set of syntactic rules that specify what words can occur together, in what order, to form grammatical sentences.

But form is empty by itself. Forms have *meaning:* they refer to entities

FIGURE 2.1
Properties of Language
FORM
(phonology, syntax)

MEANING/REFERENCE   FUNCTION/INTENTION
(semantics)   (pragmatics)

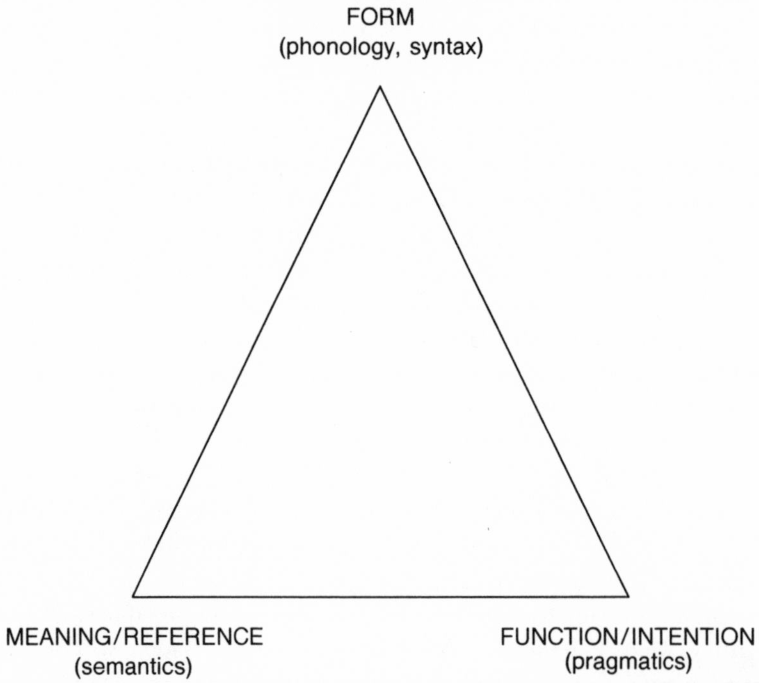

outside themselves by agreement among speakers. Language works because you
and I agree (implicitly) that, as speakers of English, we will mean, when we say
table, an object of furniture with legs supporting a horizontal surface.

Semantics, which links form and meaning, applies both to the meanings of
separate words (what is a *table?*) and to their combinations in sentences (Does
"John admires sincerity mean the same as "Sincerity is admired by John"?). It
also is concerned with larger structures: how is an English paragraph constructed,
as opposed, perhaps, to the analogous unit in Arabic discourse?

Pragmatics, the third point of the triangle, is crucial to the subject matter
of this book. Pragmatics sees language as communication—that is, in terms of
function. It attempts to discover both the principles regulating speakers' intentions as well as hearers' understandings, and the reasons the first and the second
too often are not identical (we call this *misunderstanding,* although *misspeaking*
might often be at least as accurate). While syntax connects words to other words
and semantics words to things, pragmatics connects words to their speakers and
the context in which they are speaking: what they hope to achieve by talking,
the relation between the form they choose and the effect they want it to have
(and the effect it does have), the assumptions speakers make about what their
hearers already know or need to know. Pragmatics offers reasons for the multiplic-

ity of forms speakers use to say, apparently, semantically equivalent things (*doctor* and *physician*; *Shut up!* and *Could you please try to be a little more quiet?*).

Pragmatics includes the functions and forms of indirectness; politeness strategies; and the relation between language form and the type of discourse in which it occurs (a topic that I shall consider in the next chapter).

Directness and Indirectness

Like many of the concerns of pragmatics, indirect expression may arouse strong feelings of anger or fear. We feel ambivalent about it, sometimes thinking that a good and sincere person should say exactly what she or he means and not pussyfoot around, beat about the bush, or any of a host of other depreciatory terms for indirectness. But as often we take umbrage at blunt expression, bemoaning the lack of tact and savoir-faire, not to mention manners and civility. The columns of Miss Manners, Ann Landers, and Dear Abby often become running arguments between proponents of the two camps. Perhaps the best way to discuss the alternatives is to point out the virtues and flaws of each; and to say that fully competent communicators have access to both, actively and passively, and know where and why to use each according to the rules of their culture.

The intention to communicate indirectly is reflected in the form of an utterance. Indirectness may (depending on its form) express avoidance of a confrontational speech act (say, an imperative like "Go home!") in favor of a less intrusive form like a question ("Why don't you go home?"); or avoidance of the semantic content of the utterance itself ("Go home!" being replaced by an imperative that makes its point more circumspectly, like "Be sure and close the door behind you when you leave"); or both ("Why don't you take these flowers to your mother on your way home?") It is possible to be indirect in several ways and to various degrees.

One type of avoidance is speech act substitution. A *speech act* (as defined by the philosopher of language, J. L. Austin) is a linguistic form, which, by being spoken, alters reality.[1] To say "I promise to pay you tomorrow" creates a relationship of obligation between speaker and addressee—a new reality. The many types of speech acts can be classified into a relatively few general categories. One large set, for instance, includes *assertions,* in which a speaker is providing information to an addressee. A second set includes *commissives,* which, as the name implies, commit a speaker to a course of action: promises and offers are examples. A third, *injunctions,* commits an addressee to a future action and includes orders, suggestions, and requests. Other categories include questions; apologies, congratulations, and the like; and accusations. There are conditions under which each set is used appropriately, and conditions determining whether the speech act has been carried out successfully. One way in which speech act classes differ is in the power relationship between participants that each assumes, as well as the power differential created by the performance of the speech act. Asking a question is, in general, less troublesome than giving an order, and providing information is perhaps the least interactively difficult of the three. Giving a direct order implies a power relationship where the speaker has both the right to give the order and the expectation that it will be carried out, even though the recipient of the order would not have performed the action had it not been imposed. Asking a question, on the other hand, places the speaker in a position of inferiority, one of needing something from the other person—information. But questions do restrict a hearer's possibilities for action. One is normally expected to respond with a germane reply; to do otherwise is rude or bizarre. An assertion is less onerous than a question in that no specific response is demanded of the addressee; but the latter is placed in an inferior position as the recipient of needed information from the person making the assertion. (If it were not needed, the assumption is that it would not be offered.) Numerous hedges, restrictions, and caveats must, to be sure, be placed upon this bare-bones description of a complex theory, some of which I shall clarify later.

Since speech acts involve different amounts of interactional risk, it is clear why one is sometimes substituted for another, though clarity is thereby lost. There are in ordinary conversation higher obligations than clarity. One of our culture's basic beliefs is that good communication consists in making oneself clear and getting to the point. One should be honest, direct, and straight from the shoulder. But no one lives by that precept alone and survives. In fact, most of us actually live by a more complex precept: try to be honest and direct and make your point clearly; but when doing so would infringe on manners or taste, or be actually or potentially hurtful to one or both participants, mitigate your utterance—make it harder to understand in order to make it gentler and kinder.

Philosophers of language, starting with Austin, have engaged in much discussion about the relationships, formal and otherwise, between the intended force of an utterance (its *illocutionary force*) and its superficial form, which is often mitigated. To utter a direct order is not kind or gentle, since it makes it brutally obvious that the speaker outranks, and has the power to control the actions of, the hearer. But the speaker who chooses a different speech act, one that does not set up a sharp power imbalance and makes the participants equal or even exalts the addressee, will make the future interactions of the participants smoother, saving the face of both speaker and addressee. If the speaker were to give a direct order and be disobeyed, that defiance would be a serious loss of face. But if the order is mitigated, there is no problem. It's also true that (a bit paradoxically) hedged orders are more likely to achieve compliance (except where the power difference really is sharp and unquestioned), because the addressee feels more cooperative toward a speaker who has behaved with solicitude.

Mitigated orders take many forms, in English and elsewhere. (Languages and cultures have different mitigation strategies and forms, but all have some means to achieve mitigation.) Other types of speech act may also have indirect equivalents, but orders seem to have the most, because they are the most confrontational. So if I want you to open the window, I have such choices as:

It's hot in here.
Won't someone open the window?

or

Please open the window.
Could you open the window?
Open the window, won't you?
You look strong enough to open the window.

Most of these mitigations take the form of questions; a few are declaratives; and there is also the possibility of the imperative itself, softened by "please," which turns the order into a polite request: the speaker is not requiring the addressee to act, but the latter is seen as being able to choose to do something for the former, reordering their power relations. In the other cases, a less problematic speech act replaces the direct form. Though theoretically intelligibility is impaired, practically speaking it is uncommon for someone who is asked, "Can you open the window?" to flex an arm experimentally, reply, "yeah, guess I probably could," and not act. (Such a response would make the other person pretty angry: it would seem a willful distortion of the situation rather than an innocent misinterpretation.)

So the absolute certainty of being understood, while a conversational desideratum, is overshadowed for most people in most kinds of discourse by the desire for protection, both self-defense and solicitude for the self-esteem of others. Naturally, the heavier the imposition placed on the addressee, the more elaborately it will be disguised. If I want you to make me a loan of a large sum of money, I will be likely to adopt all sorts of roundabout verbal strategies; and you would be annoyed if I didn't. But if all I want is the correct time, and you're plainly wearing a watch, it would be strange for me to frame my request elaborately: "I wonder if it wouldn't be too much trouble for you to give me the correct time?"

Besides finding a gentler speech act replacement, indirectness is also achieved by putting the message into other words: circumlocutions or euphemisms. For instance, if I have to tell you something I don't think you will want to hear, I have no speech act options other than an assertion. But I won't say it flat out; for instance, the usual letter of rejection doesn't begin: "Grunch University has rejected you as a member of the Class of 2001." Rather, writers employ any number of dodges to distance themselves from the unpleasant act itself or to disguise the message. One can achieve both distance and the appearance of sharing the recipient's pain. For example, in the phrase "I regret to inform you that Grunch U . . . ," the painful information is syntactically embedded beneath two layers of sentences ("I regret something," and "I inform you of something"). Or, the bad news can be put in the passive, so that the speaker (or the institution he or she represents) no longer bears the responsibility for doing the dirty work: "You have been rejected. . . ." And there are such other impersonal mechanisms as: "It is the painful duty of the President and Fellows of Grunch U. . . ." While none of these greatly improves the spirits of the rejected candidate, at least they let the writer of the letter feel like a decent human being.

Power and Directness

Indirectness works as I have described particularly when both participants are on an approximately equal footing, but not one of true intimacy, so that both need protection and feel a need to protect each other. In an intimate relationship, where participants have gotten beyond such needs and anxieties, and no longer fear that the other might hurt them or think ill of them, people use direct and unmitigated imperatives and make less effort to soften the blows of difficult communications. But if one person has something to say that may be unusually distressing to the other, or wants to make an especially burdensome request, indirectness is still likely. Problems arise in close relationships first, because the partners have different ideas about how close the relationship is, and therefore about whether the usual rules are in effect or not; second, because they have different personal calibrations of how severe the imposition is; and third, because the scale of directness-to-imposition is different for each partner. These differences can arise out of nonshared cultural backgrounds, differences in gender, or simply different personality styles.

The rules also work differently for the powerful. For the nonpowerful, directness is dangerous in part because it involves responsibility both for an utterance and for getting a proper response to it. But indirectness is dangerous because it can be misunderstood. For the powerful person, both dangers are lessened. The powerful have less to fear through directness: they don't have to worry so much about being rude (who cares what underlings think of them?), and they don't have as much reason to worry about being found to be in error. But the fear still exists, at least if the power is not absolute (and even if it is, heads do occasionally roll). So we might expect the powerful to speak exclusively in direct forms, thereby preventing misunderstanding. Sometimes they do—but the risk is still there, however lessened. What is really nice about having a lot of power is that the danger of misunderstanding is lessened as well. We are willing to go to much more effort in order to interpret powerful people's utterances: their wish is our command.

Examples abound in history and literature in which those with power have taken advantage of the willingness of others to interpret, thereby saving themselves from the responsibility for a particularly loathsome act. In Shakespeare's *King Richard II*, Richard, the king, has been deposed and imprisoned by a group of nobles led by Henry Bolingbroke. Though Henry has been crowned king, he must worry as long as Richard is alive about the possibility of another coup. What happens next is told indirectly in a bit of dialogue between Exton, a member of Bolingbroke's entourage, and a servant:

> EXTON: Didst thou not mark the king, what words he spake,
>   "Have I no friend will rid me of this living fear?"
>   Was it not so?
> SERVANT: These were his very words.
> EXTON: "Have I no friend?" quoth he: he spake it twice,
>   And urged it twice together, did he not?
> SERVANT: He did.
> EXTON: And speaking it, he wistly look'd on me;
>   As one should say, "I would thou wert the man
>   That would divorce this terror from my heart;"
>   Meaning the king at Pomfret [Richard]. Come, let's go:
>   I am the king's friend, and will rid his foe.
>
> [5.4]

What Henry wants, of course, is for Exton to kill Richard; but even though he is king, Henry cannot quite bring himself to say it. He frames his desire as a request for information, theoretically satisfied with a simple yes (or no). If Henry were not king of England, his interlocutor would no doubt understand that the question was more than it seemed, but interpret it (openly at any rate) as no more than a request for reassurance: "Yes, of course you do. No need to worry—there, there." But, since Exton is anxious to please, he interprets the king's question further: not only is it a wish, it constitutes a command. Henry underscores the sincerity and importance of his speech act (without clarifying for Exton exactly what it is) by repetition and nonverbal language, which Exton again takes special pains to interpret. But Henry has not *said* in so many words what he wants. Exton carries out what he believes to have been Henry's command and later enters Henry's presence along with Richard in his coffin.

> EXTON: Great king, within this coffin I present
>   Thy buried fear: herein all breathless lies

The mightiest of thy greatest enemies,
Richard of Bordeaux, by me hither brought.
BOLINGBROKE: Exton, I thank thee not; for thou hast wrought
A deed of slander with thy fatal hand
Upon my head and all this famous land.
EXTON: From your own mouth, my lord, did I this deed.
[5.6.30–37]

By assuming the privileges of royalty, Henry has it both ways: his enemy is dead, and he is not responsible (at least officially).

Politeness

Indirectness can function as a form of politeness.[2] Politeness is a system of interpersonal relations designed to facilitate interaction by minimizing the potential for conflict and confrontation inherent in all human interchange. We like to think of conversation as conflict-free, with speakers normally being able to satisfy one another's needs and interests. But, in fact, we enter every conversation—indeed, every kind of discourse—with some personal desideratum in mind: perhaps as obvious as a favor or as subtle as the desire to be likeable. For some of these needs, participants can accede to each other, and both gain their desires; but with others, one must lose, however minimally, for the other to win. One person must tell another something that the other doesn't want to hear; one person must refuse another's request; one person must end a conversation before the other is quite willing to go. In such cases, there is the danger of insult and, consequently, the breakdown of communication. If societies did not devise ways to smooth over moments of conflict and confrontation, social relationships would be difficult to establish and continue, and essential cohesion would erode. Politeness strategies are the means to preserve at least the semblance of harmony and cohesion.

Politeness is most necessary when the interaction is an end in itself. Friendly conversation is the clearest case. In the many kinds of discourse in which we engage for other motives, we may still employ conflict-reducing strategies, but forms of communication designed to achieve clarity may supersede them if there is a conflict between the two. In the courtroom, for instance, uncovering the truth is considered more relevant than not offending someone (at least, unless that someone can hurt you if they take umbrage: the judge or the jury). So one excuse for the peculiarities of legal language is that it must be extremely clear and explicit, lacking the usual dodges we have come to expect in ordinary conversation, which help us make sense of it. When these are absent we feel adrift, as if we were communicating with faceless interlocutors. As long as an interchange is its own excuse for being (or a principal reason), politeness will supersede any other strategy, even at the cost of intelligibility.

As long as all parties in a communication agree about the type of communication (whether politeness- or information-oriented), all will be able to understand the reasons for clarity or lack of it (as long as they are all competent in the particular discourse genre). As long as everyone knows that they are engaged in friendly conversation, they will adjust their grammatical expectations to allow for indirectness and the need to do a certain amount of interpretation. On the other hand, listeners at an academic lecture properly expect information to be the point, and will misunderstand and miss a veiled reference, both its purpose and its meaning. A problem can arise if not all participants agree about the nature or the goal of the discourse in which they are engaged—interaction or information. If participants belong to different cultures, these discrepancies are especially apt to arise.

More common, both cross- and intraculturally, are confusions that arise because participants, while implicitly in agreement that politeness is appropriate to the discourse, have different definitions of how to be polite. This discrepancy is possible because there are three basic strategies of politeness. Every culture adopts one as its dominant mode. If members of cultures with different assumptions are in conversation, each may unknowingly insult or confuse the other by utilizing the wrong system. (Furthermore, cultures, as well as individuals, have different ideas about what is likely to produce conflict or unpleasant confrontation, and will therefore resort to politeness strategies under different conditions.)

These strategies are *distance, deference,* and *camaraderie.* Distance politeness is equivalent to what most people in our society consider "polite" behavior, since it has been our standard form of politeness for about a millennium, and we are used to it. It is the behavior associated with formal etiquette, courtesy, and rigid rules of deportment. Though it uses formality, it is not the only meaning we attribute to the use of formal devices.

Distance cultures presuppose that conflict and confrontation are inevitable as long as they are possible, and that they are dangerous. The aim of the strategy is to prevent (conventionally and symbolically, if not actually) participants from coming into direct contact with one another, for if they did, conflict would result and relationships would break down. Distance politeness is the civilized human analogue to the territorial strategies of other animals. An animal sets up physical boundary markers (the dog and the hydrant) to signal its fellows: My turf, stay out. We, being symbol-using creatures, create symbolic fences. Introductions are required before conversation can start; conventional forms begin and terminate conversations; we are careful, except with intimates, not to "get personal" and intrude on another's "space"—emotional or physical. Cultures have different definitions of what constitutes "my space" and what is an intrusion of it, both concretely and symbolically. But every culture has taboos, topics that cannot be broached in a "polite" conversation, because they would risk a dangerous confrontation. For some cultures, it's money; for many, sex; probably for all, death. Likewise, for some societies, twelve inches is considered the appropriate distance to stand apart in a conversation; but for others, it's up to two feet. If another person fails to observe the territorial boundary, we feel "invaded" and will probably try to escape as fast as we gracefully can, unless we are inspired to start an argument. Anything personal tends to be perceived as forcing interaction, and therefore confrontation, on an unwilling other. Therefore formality, the avoidance of individual or personal references, is characteristic of distance politeness.

Distancing cultures weave remoteness into their language. The attribution of responsibility represents an intrusion of the personal: it suggests that individuals with different interests are involved in the discussion. So grammatical devices that minimize a speaker's personal involvement are favored—for instance, passive verb forms and impersonal forms like *one*. Words that threaten to convey or evoke dangerous emotion are replaced with safer ones, which suggest that no emotion is involved. This formal language is the language of diplomacy, bureaucracy, and the professions. Diplomats speak of an *incident* when they mean that their countries are in a virtual state of war; bureaucrats talk of *revenue enhancement* when they renege on a promise of no new taxes; doctors discourse on *iatrogenesis* when they mean they did something that made the patient sick. These words provide a buffer between pure denotative meaning and its emotional wallop: the hearer, in all probability, knows perfectly well what the speaker intends; but the latter has chosen deliberately Latinate words from a sector of the vocabulary not rich in emotional connotations, so as to lessen the danger of collision. Speak of *war, taxes,* and *disease,* and our hair stands on end; we demand redress, revenge, or at least explanation. But use the technical terms, and your hearers, being properly brought up ladies and gentlemen, know that the only appropriate response is a genteel "tsk-tsk."

Another culture might avoid the danger of conflict by adopting a strategy of deferential politeness. If a participant decides that whatever is to happen in a conversation—both what is said and what it is to mean—is up to the other person, conflict can easily be avoided. It takes two to have a fight. With deference as with distance, there is a sense of danger in interaction; but deference denies the existence of interaction by removing the speaker from the action. Where distance politeness more or less assumes equality between participants, deference works by debasing one or both (depending upon whether the deference is mutual or unilateral).

Where distance is impersonal, deference is indecisive: it uses questions and hedges in profusion. But the questions typically are not really information-seeking (since the speaker is using them for reasons of politeness), and therefore they tend to occur in forms that signify to the hearer, "I really know this, but I'm just leaving the final judgment up to you." Very frequent in deferential style are utterances that are syntactically declarative but end with the rising intonation characteristic in English of questions designed to be answered with "yes" or "no," and tag questions:

> He's the one in the red shirt? (Meaning, "He's the one in the red shirt, if you see what I mean.")
> Bill's an archconservative, isn't he? (Meaning, in deferential use, "I think Bill's an archconservative, but I hope that's OK with you, that you agree and aren't offended.")

When uncomfortable topics arise, the deferential way out is to resort to *euphemism* and circumlocution. Euphemisms differ in feeling and effect from the technical terms that are characteristic of distance. The latter are denotatively and cognitively unambiguous, merely denying their emotional implications. Euphemisms preserve the latter but avoid direct mention of the offensive concept itself. For instance:

> Max and Mary were *doing it* in the elevator. (= "having sex")
> Mr. Oglethorpe *passed away* last month. (= "died")
> They are *in comfortable circumstances*. (= "rich")

Hedges are another means of expressing deferential politeness. They qualify and dilute both what is intended and the speech act involved.

> It was sorta stupid of you to buy that bridge for $22.95. (Meaning, "It was very stupid.")
> Don't you find it hot in here? (Meaning, "Open the window.")

While distance politeness has been characteristic of the middle and upper classes in most of Europe for a very long time, deference has been typical in many Asian societies. But it is also the preferred mode of interaction for women in the majority of societies, either always or only when talking to men. As long as all participants are following the same system, all will understand that their interlocutors are using polite forms conventionally: the standoffishness of distance and the uncertainty of deference are not taken literally as expressions of character or intellect. But all politeness forms have, alongside their conventional understanding, a literal sense (from which the convention was derived). In other words, it is possible to be *actually* distant and standoffish, instead of (or in addition to) using those attributes to express conventional distance. It is possible to be really indecisive and fuzzy-minded, as well as conventionally deferential. But as long as all participants are operating within the same system, they will tend, if at all possible, to interpret an interlocutor's behavior as conventional within that system. So if we expect distance as characteristic of ordinary good behavior, we won't draw back in indignation when someone persists in calling us by title and last name (a sign of distance). But if we're in a different system, we might sniff, "Who's he think he is?" In other words, we are normally unable to interpret as conventional conventions that are not our own: we take them as literal.

This has been the problem with female reliance on conventional deference. In societies in which deference is used by both sexes, men do not attribute stupidity to women on the basis of their interactive behavior. But in Western society, men (from the perspective of distance) see deferential behavior as literal: indecisiveness and hesitancy are not ways of avoiding the appearance of aggression, but rather indicate one does not know one's own mind (or have one) and thus does not expect to be taken seriously. Women, on the other hand, see male distance as literal coldness and lack of interest, and react accordingly (and inappropriately). Misinterpretation is mutual; but since men have the power, women get the worse end of the deal. Yet nobody really profits.[3]

Both distance and deference work on the assumption that the avoidance of involvement is essential if relationships are to prosper. Once a relationship is firmly cemented in trust and intimacy, the conventions may be discarded or modified. A third strategy that has recently emerged in this culture makes a different assumption: that interaction and connection are good in themselves, that openness is the greatest sign of courtesy. Since signs of trust and intimacy indicate that the user means no harm, their presence signifies that confrontation need not be feared. This conventional camaraderie is rapidly taking over as the preferred form of politeness for both sexes in many parts of the United States and appears to be making inroads in Europe as well.

It is essential to realize that camaraderie can be conventional as well as the other two strategies. But as with those, someone unaccustomed to conventional camaraderie will take it as genuine, arising out of long acquaintance and the development of mutual liking and trust. Modern camaraderie probably began in California as an outgrowth of the human potential movement of the 1960s and 1970s. For a while it was a bane to visiting Easterners, who were confounded by the Californian's appearance of good fellowship and deep caring: the immediate first-naming, touching, looking deep into the eyes, and asking *truly caring* questions: "Are you really happy with your life?" To the properly brought-up Easterner, such behavior was permissible only after years of earning it, and maybe not then. Easterners fell into one of several schools of thought about the character of Californians: either that they had the simplicity of children and should be patronized; or that they were rough frontier sorts, probably raised by wolves (and you know how wolves are); or that they were truly wonderful people who could get to know you as well after two seconds as would take most of us a lifetime. All of these attitudes assumed, of course, that the camaraderie was real rather than conventional. Those who held the last attitude were particularly subject to disillusionment when they presumed upon the "intimate" relationship to ask a big favor: the Californian acquaintance of a day, acting just like his or her New York counterpart, refused the stranger. "Have a nice day," indeed! California was *fer sure* a state of hypocrites.

Those who had embraced camaraderie, in turn, who had achieved becoming *mellow* and *laid back* (the terms for the virtuous human being in a camaraderie system, as *mannerly* and *civil* are for the distance person), saw the Easterner as pushy or "uptight"—probably both.

In a camaraderie system, the appearance of openness and niceness is to be sought above all else. There is no holding back, nothing is too terrible to say. There are no euphemisms, no technical terms; there are only four letter words. (The medical man speaks of "copulation"; the deferential, of "doing it"; but the Californian "screws"—or worse.) It is illegal or at least antisocial to have a last name in public (restaurant reservations are typically made by first name alone). There is a lot of touching. Speech act qualification, to the extent that it exists, seems to occur mostly to indicate, "I trust we're understanding each other": a lot of "y'know's" and "I mean's."

Politeness systems may seem cumbersome drags on communication to those who believe that the function of the latter is the most efficient exchange of information, and that this goal is directly related to the speed of the communication. But if communication is defined as necessarily including and indeed stressing the interpersonal relationship, then politeness strategies become crucial for many forms of discourse. They are parts of a conversation, of course, not the whole of it—facilitators of interchange rather than the interchange itself. To understand how politeness and indirectness function politically in informal conversation, we must turn next to an examination of the forms and workings of conversation itself, and to a consideration of the different types of discourse of which conversation is only one.

CHAPTER THREE

Talking Politics

MEMBERSHIP in a culture entails a great deal of sophisticated implicit knowledge. Among the forms such knowledge takes is the expertise necessary to participate in, and recognize, several forms of discourse. All members of a culture have some degree of competence in ordinary conversation; some being, of course, better than others—a distinction sometimes based on Johnsonian epigrammatic skill, sometimes on telling good stories, sometimes on being a "good listener." Furthermore, in any society there will be experts conversant in one or another particular type of talk. This might be learned in childhood, like classroom discourse, and, like the latter in this culture, eventually acquired by almost everyone. Or it might be the special forms of the courtroom, which relatively few of us master actively, though many more acquire a smattering, whether through jury duty or through watching "Perry Mason" reruns. When we encounter something new, we compare it, consciously or not, to ordinary conversation. To the degree that we understand how its special forms reflect new functions, we can achieve competence and, even as passive observers, make sure the arcane form is being used to accomplish necessary business, not to keep us out by decreasing or impeding our understanding.

This chapter explores the nature and properties of ordinary conversation, as well as briefly surveys a few other types of discourse for contrast. What follows suggests that—far from being either rule-free or apolitical as we tend to think it—conversation is rigorously structured, and that its structures can be used for purposes of dominance and control. So power and structure go together, and by learning to recognize the underpinnings of ordinary conversation, we can appreciate (and avoid misusing) its complexities.

Most attention to the regularities of language has been in the areas of sounds, words, and sentences. It is reasonable to see the context that determines the range of possibilities of these structures as largely or even purely linguistic: other sounds or words in their environment. At these levels, language can be seen as a self-sufficient and all-inclusive system (although many linguists would argue that that perspective leads to distortion and serious theoretical error). What happens to notions of systems and predictions when larger and more abstract units are under inspection—units whose form, meaning, and function are crucially dependent upon the social and psychological context in which they occur? Linguistic theorists can talk about "words" and "sentences" without acknowledging that they are used by people to effect changes in reality. But we cannot begin to discuss intelligently the many larger abstract units—"conversations," "lectures," "literary essays," to name a few—without reference to the circumstances in which they occur: How many participants are involved? What is the role of each? What is the aim of each? How does the form chosen succeed or fail in its purpose? In trying to understand these units, we must understand the forms of language as arising out of human social and psychological needs, influenced by speakers' real-world positions and in turn influencing those positions. Among the rule systems we would like to understand for these reasons are those underlying conversation and other discourse types. (I use *discourse* to cover all linguistic interactions that follow predictable patterns known implicitly or explicitly to participants and have a discernible function.)

CONVERSATION ANALYSIS

The analysis of discourse types has proceeded more slowly, and by other means, than the analysis of sentences. Structures have been discovered not by the mentalistic and introspective procedures of the syntactician, but by the empirical methods of the social scientist, who finds natural data and subjects it to dissection and analysis. Investigators first record real conversations on audio tape and examine them to see what structures recur. Just as at the sentence level, regularities of co-occurrence emerge: certain forms occur together; others do not. There are regularities of ordering: one form always precedes another, never the reverse. With such regularities persuasively demonstrated by the data, scholars agree that conversation, and discourse in general, is rule-governed.

I have been speaking mainly of "conversation" for a number of reasons. Since ordinary conversation is our basic and most common mode of oral communication—the one we learn first, the one with which we are most comfortable—this form of discourse has been subjected first, and most thoroughly, to analysis, with the expectation that once it was deciphered, the method could be adapted to other types.[1] At the same time, conversation might seem the hardest case for predictability: it involves the active and spontaneous collaboration of at least two people, so that any claims to regularity must take into account their competing interests and styles. It makes intuitive sense to see sentences, or single-person discourses like lectures, as the product of a grammar located in the speaker's mind. But where is the grammar of conversation to be found? In each participant's separate mind (in which case, how do they cooperate to form a seamless whole?) or somewhere in the space between (and what might that mean?). However vexing the question may seem, we can say that speakers use their individual grammars with the expectation that other participants have similar grammars that will produce forms intelligible and functional for all.

The structures of discourse are discoverable through the application of two analytic techniques. First, it is useful to construct taxonomies: What properties distinguish one type of discourse from another? What are the properties of a conversation as opposed to a classroom exchange, a trial, or a psychotherapeutic interview, to list just a few possibilities? How are variations of form related to differences in function?

One can also attempt to determine the superficial regularities of each type of discourse: How do participants begin? What can participants do in response to the actions of others? At what point, marked by what explicit signals, do speakers determine that the business of the interchange is satisfactorily concluded, or that it will be impossible to reach a good conclusion? How do they terminate the interchange? Several properties are helpful in establishing categories and making predictions.

Ordinary conversation is *reciprocal*; most others are not. In a reciprocal discourse, participants have equal access to all possibilities of action and interpretation. Usually, in ordinary conversation, if A can ask a question, so can B; if A can ask a personal, intrusive question ("Have you put on some weight?") and expect a responsive answer, so can B. (If this proves false, the conversation may well be felt to be unsatisfactory if not anomalous—probably by B.) All participants enjoy the same range of possible interpretations for their contributions. If A can explicitly "decode" B's utterance, B should be able to do the same for A's. If A can ask, "What's THAT supposed to mean?" so can B. If A's questions are open to interpretation by B as "really" declaratives (for example, "What are you doing on your vacation?" being taken to mean, "I'm curious about your personal life," and therefore capable of receiving from B the response, "Why do you want to know about my personal life?"), then B's utterances may be subjected by A to the same (explicit or implicit) interpretive procedures.

By contrast, most other discourse types are either completely or partially nonreciprocal. In the classroom, one participant holds the floor and controls both topic choice and participation by others. In the courtroom, each active participant has a sharply distinct role to play.

Ordinary conversation is generally *informal*: that is, it assumes true interaction between individuals. Therefore, linguistic forms will refer to the persons present: expressions of emotion will be favored, as will overt reactions to the contributions of others, as well as self-assessments; there may be interruptions and silences (which remind speakers of one another's presence). In many cultures, people may touch one another and call each other by first name, recognitions of their status as unique and responsive individuals.

In many other types of discourse, *formality* is the rule. In courtrooms, for instance, law and custom minimize direct interaction; language is stylized; titles of address and reference substitute for people's own names ("Your Honor," "Counsel," "Juror Number Five"). There are physical as well as symbolic impediments to direct contact (the jury box, the judge's bench, the witness stand).

Some kinds of communication have *public accessibility:* they are intended to be open or accessible to all. Others are private, intended to be intelligible only to those directly involved, and therefore make use of language not accessible to all: telegraphed and highly colloquial forms of speech ("Hiya!" "Whatcha doin'?"); nonstandard forms of the language if the individuals participating all speak it; implicit reliance on prior communication between speakers. Ordinary conversation, as a private form, emphasizes such strategies. Private discourse is not supposed to be available to people outside the immediate conversation or even to participants after their actual encounter. People often resist the efforts of conversation analysts to get permission to tape conversations: they are puzzled and disturbed by the request, as it turns private discourse public—like putting love letters in print.

In public types of discourse, speakers are careful to spell things out, and often there are formulaic ways of speaking to ensure full explicitness. There is an established, explicit order of business to ensure that everyone can follow what is going on. Proceedings may be published, or otherwise accessible to the community, present and future. Courtrooms are particularly good examples; classrooms and lecture halls somewhat less so.

In ordinary conversation, we properly assume that—aside from a few moments at the beginning and end ("openings" and "closings")—what occurs in a conversation is *spontaneous* (unscripted and, by and large, uttered as it springs into the minds of participants). In part because several active participants are involved, it would be unthinkable for anyone to enter a conversation by pulling out a script or even notes: no one is supposed to have that sort of control. Hence ordinary conversation makes much use of devices that signal, "I'm making this up as I go along": repetitions, corrections, hesitations, and "fillers" that play for time to compose one's thoughts. In part, these are literally necessary because speakers are constructing their talk as they go along; but they also figuratively signal, "This talk is spontaneous, you can trust me."

Nonspontaneous discourse makes much less use of these devices, and they are often aesthetically frowned upon. In mixed discourse types like TV news interviews, the hearer is often unpleasantly struck by the quantity of "y'know's" (one sort of filler) in an interviewee's speech, which would go largely unnoticed in casual conversation. But an interview is semiscripted, and hearers come to it with the expectation of more organization than is possible or proper in conversation. Ritual or ceremonial forms are also characteristic of, and symbolically mark, nonspontaneity. In courtrooms, such forms abound; among the several purposes they serve is to signal that a trial is a special activity, where behavior must be different from the everyday.

In some forms of discourse, *power allocation* is egalitarian. There is at least the conventional expectation of parity among participants—if not social real-world equality, at least equality of linguistic opportunity. In ordinary conversation, each participant has (theoretically) equal access to the floor, and equal right to introduce topics. If this expectation proves false, the slighted participant may feel frustrated and even cheated.

Participants enter other forms of discourse with differing amounts of real-world power, authority, and status, and these are translated into differences in permissible linguistic behavior. In lectures, speakers are allowed to hold the floor, select topics, and control the participation of others (amount and type), because they possess special authority which allows them to lecture in the first place. In some types of discourse, power shifts: in the courtroom, the judge has most of it while the trial is in session, but the jury (which enjoys none of the observable signs of discourse power) ultimately is the most powerful participant. Here those who do the most talking and determine topics (the attorneys) arguably have less power than anyone else, and their linguistic options are severely constrained.

These five properties are clearly not independent of one another: a discourse type that is reciprocal is likely to be spontaneous, and one that is public, to be formal as well; formal types often employ ritual and other marks of nonspontaneity since the impersonality of ritual is closely related to the uninvolvement of formality. Power goes along with formality, nonspontaneity, and nonreciprocity. Nor are these characteristics all-or-nothing phenomena. Courtroom and classroom discourse are both formal relative to conversation, the former much more so than the latter.

RITUAL AND SPONTANEITY IN CONVERSATION

A complementary approach to discourse is to examine each type by itself, to see what recurrent patterns make it cohesive. What forms may and may not occur in a conversation and in what order? It turns out that while there are indeed rigid rules, many variants are possible within the system. Besides, topics and responses are up to the speakers (although in this area there also exist constraints, which we call variously "tact," politeness," or "appropriateness").

Like many forms of discourse, ordinary conversations are more heavily ritualized at their beginnings and ends than in the middle.[2] This pattern seems to be the case in almost all cultures; although the degree of ritualization and the length of ritual necessary, differ from one group to another.

It makes sense that the ends of conversations are more stylized than the middles. Beginning and ending an encounter are psychologically and socially tricky moments. At the start, all participants need reassurance that the others *want* to engage in talk with them, are glad to see them, and value their company. At the end, at least one speaker must both make known a desire to terminate the encounter and communicate that desire to the others without suggesting that leaving is desired or that the conversation was not pleasurable. When difficult tasks are to be undertaken, it is comforting to have a prearranged, stylized procedure for doing them, acceptable to all, so that at least the form of the difficult utterance is unexceptionable. Moreover, when one's emotions are tense, it helps not to tie up the intellect thinking up clever and novel ways of doing the job. Hence, cultures develop a few stylized ways of beginning and ending, generally (at least in origin, though over time the form and meaning may become obscure) conventional expressions of caring, reassurance that the conversation will go well or did go well: at the start, *greetings* ("openings"), statements of recognition and assurance that the speaker is glad to be in the encounter and wishes the other well: "Hello, how are you?" At the end, *farewells* ("closings"), suggestions that the speaker will continue to be concerned about the other's well-being: "Goodby (from "God be with you"), See you soon, Take care." Ending is, emotionally speaking, even harder than beginning and typically takes longer. Often, especially on the telephone (where there are no nonverbal signals of reassurance), there is a whole ceremony of winding down: "Well, I'd better get back to work. . . . Been good talking to you. . . . We'll have to have lunch soon. . . . Give me a call sometime. . . . 'Bye now!" Farewells stress the speaker's unwillingness to depart, offering it as a necessity imposed by cruel circumstance rather than the speaker's desire. We say, "Gotta go!" not, "Wanna go!"

But the central part of a conversation is not so constrained in form. Topics are freely brought up and changed. Yet there are rules: some combinations of possible utterances exist; and others do not or, at least, are much less likely to occur. Students of conversation sometimes describe it as a "game" and sometimes as "work" (terms that are not, in this usage, contradictory). A game is a form of interaction whose rules have been agreed upon by participants. The progress of the game determines whether they win or lose. Game theorists further distinguish those games in which one person must lose for the other to win, from others in which everyone can win. Conversation, ideally, is of the latter type (though we do speak of "scoring points").

Conversation (like other forms of group behavior) is also work. Participants must accomplish certain tasks in order to get the sustenance they require (in this case, mostly emotional). In this work, cooperation is necessary: the whole, the conversation is equal to more than the sum of its parts, and everyone must play a part correctly to satisfy the needs of all.

The Universality of Conversational Structure

A problem in any attempt to discover the universal attributes of conversation is that its forms are not identical in all cultures. Should a definition reflect the Western origin of most of the people instrumental in its development, or try to encompass conversational behavior universally? The social scientist's answer would ordinarily be the second; but, in fact, a disturbing amount of conversational theory sees conversational possibilities through ethnocentric Western eyes.

One example is the basic rule of conversational structure: "No gap, no overlap." Ideally there should never be a point in a conversation where no one is speaking (a gap, or silence), or a point when more than one is competing for the floor (overlap). In fact (as the analysts note), these departures from the norm do occur frequently in conversation, since they are ideals rather than necessities, and when they do, participants experience distress: they shift posture, make jokes, begin again, apologize. But the distress itself makes clear that these situations are not normal; that when they occur, special allowances must be made.

In other cultures than our own, "No gap, no overlap" seems much less stringent a requirement. In many societies, silence truly *is* golden: participants in conversation will sit for minutes—sometimes hours—saying nothing at all; and when the encounter is over, all will feel perfectly content. This is true in many American Indian and Asian cultures. In others—such as Mediterranean groups— it often happens that, in conversations involving several speakers, two or more conversations will be going on at once. Not only will there be pairs, each holding its own conversation; but members of the pairs may move into one conversation and out of another, from topic to topic. To an American, this may seem as chaotic as the first example sounds chilling; but to Italians or Arabs, it is perfectly acceptable.

Within our own system, it is a little deceptive to consider as having the same meaning all moments when no utterance is occurring or when more than one speaker is holding the floor. Technically all of these are violations; but depending on the relationship among the speakers and their cultural expectations, as well as the actual form of the violation, a variety of responses is possible.

There is a difference between a silence that goes on and on, for more than a few seconds, and one of briefer duration, which is much more tolerable and more easily repaired (the longer a silence continues, the more awkward will be any attempt to begin the talk again); a silence that a speaker inserts into his or her own turn, and one occurring between turns; and a silence that falls just because a topic seems to be exhausted, and one that communicates that the unspeakable has been spoken. Silences can be cold or companionable.

Likewise, there are interruptions and overlaps. An interruption is partially defined by form: one speaker attempts to take over a turn before a prior speaker has given any indication of reaching the end of it. An interruption also typically shifts the topic. An overlap, on the other hand, occurs when a speaker is clearly about to finish and generally reinforces that speaker's point or amplifies the topic. While interruption is usually seen as aggressive, overlap tends to be understood as supportive and exciting—an adornment to the conversation rather than an act of boorishness. But not every culture utilizes overlap, and someone to whose culture it is foreign will see all speaking out of turn as interruption and, therefore, as verbal aggression.

Turns and Sequences

In the formal analysis of any behavior, the basic units must be discovered, compared, and contrasted. In conversation analysis, the basic unit is the *turn*. This is defined not on the basis of what it contains (since that is variable), but in terms of its physical boundaries: a turn is the period during which one speaker holds the floor, from the time the previous speaker relinquishes it to the time the next one takes it over. A turn can be as short as a grunt or a smile and as long as an interminable harangue. It is possible to shift topics as the turn changes (that is, at the *transition relevance place,* or TRP), to modify the topic, or to merely embellish a prior speaker's topic.

A speaker's options are restricted by *preference organization:* that is, there are "preferred" and "dispreferred" responses to a prior turn (*seconds*); by uttering one kind of speech act rather than another, one sets up and implicitly announces one's expectations for a reply. While it is possible for speakers to violate those expectations, violations are marked, so that there had better be a good and obvious reason for them if the rhythm of the conversation is not to be awkwardly disrupted.

For example, if A asks a question, B's response is expected to take the form of a declarative statement responsive to the content of the question. If A issues an invitation, B's response must be acceptance or rejection, preferably the former; if the latter, it is better if accompanied by some excuse. (That is, an acceptance is "preferred"; a refusal, "dispreferred." Dispreferred seconds require some mitigation.) So if, in response to A's invitation, B begins a turn with anything other than acceptance, A will tend to interpret it as preparation for a dispreferred form. An invitation like, "Come to dinner next Friday," can be refused with, "That's awfully nice of you, but I'm taking my cat to the vet that night," or any other reasonable prior commitment, but not just by "No." Similarly a request is preferably followed by an indication of compliance ("OK"), a bet by a sign of acceptance ("you're on!"). It is useful, too, to distinguish between dispreferred responses, violations (like "No"), and altogether impermissible responses (neither acceptance nor rejection of the invitation).

Dispreferred turns are disturbing, both to speakers and to the flow of the conversation. So speakers may take pains to shield themselves by the use of *"pre-sequences"*: forms giving the other advance warning and a chance to dissociate themselves from the interchange before the problem is actually on the table for all to see. For example, there are pre-invitations, like A's opening gambit:

A: Are you busy Saturday?
B: No, why?
A: Well, I'm having a party, and . . .

The pre-invitation makes life easier for A, who gets the chance to avoid a direct turndown, but is tricky for B, who has to make an advance commitment before knowing what lies in store. (It's bad form to suddenly "remember" a prior engagement when A's offer turns out to be undesirable.) There are also pre-offers ("Hungry? . . . Then how about some lunch?"), pre-requests ("Have you ever done any bricklaying? . . . Well, then, maybe you could help me. . . ."), and many other pre-sequences.

A response need not follow directly upon the turn eliciting it. As long as it can be construed as working cooperatively, an "insertion sequence" is permissible, as in this invitation sequence:

A: Wanna go to the Aardvarks concert this Saturday?
B: How much are tickets?
A: Twelve fifty.
B: OK.

The insertion (B's first response and A's reply) must be completed before the speakers can return to the major sequence.

The Politics of Conversation

These analytic devices, while illuminating in themselves as underpinnings to a theory of conversational mechanisms and structures, also demonstrate that conversation is a political activity. The savvy conversationalist can achieve power, as the inept can lose it, in the playing of the "game."

In conversation, power is demonstrated by the holding of the floor. In general, the one who has the floor the most, and/or is responsible for more successful topics than anyone else, has the most power at least for the purposes of the conversation. Most often, people who come into a conversation with the most real-world power tend to display the signs of power within the conversation: they monopolize floor and topics. ("But enough about me. . . . Let's talk about you. What did you think of my book?") Exceptions do exist, though a person must be aggressive to create one. In general, men have more conversational power than women, even women of greater real rank. Indeed, it has been demonstrated that men do much more interrupting of women than women of men, than men of men, or than women of women; and that if topic choice is charted in mixed-sex conversation, men generally contribute the lion's share of "successful" topics.[3] (A topic "succeeds" when others take it up; an unsuccessful topic is one that is broached and left to die. Women are responsible for an unusual number of these, largely because neither men nor other women are eager to take up women's topics, but everyone is more responsive to men's.) A speaker who has been made to feel powerless by the devices mentioned will tend to become progressively more silent as the conversation goes on, or at least will take shorter and less assertive turns, thereby diminishing her power still further.

Silence, like interruption, can be powerful, but mostly where the silent one has real power or in a conversation with only two participants. (In other cases, the conversation will simply go on without that person.) To respond to someone's topic signifies approval of both the topic and its originator; to say nothing can convey the worst kind of disapproval or lack of interest. Frank disagreement with a statement is generally less pleasant than agreement, but at least it shows an interest in the topic and a feeling that it is permissible and worthwhile. But silence conveys the opposite and (unlike verbal disagreement) cannot be challenged without creating a breach of etiquette. (To someone with less power, one can sometimes snap, "What's the matter? Cat got your tongue?", but this retort is not advisable as a challenge to equals or superiors.)

Conversational Style

Besides conversational structure and rules, power allocation makes use of participants' individual styles of interaction, which both lend variety and interest to conversations and enhance or diminish access to power. Two such patterns have been identified as *involvement* and *considerateness*.[4]

A speaker who uses involvement employs devices suggesting emotional connection, interest, concern: variety of pitch and speed; colorful vocabulary; variety in syntactic form; touching, address by name, frequent change of topic; a lot of overlapping and back channels ("Um-hm, yes, I see, yeah . . ."). Considerateness uses the opposite strategy: long waits before taking a turn; relatively steady and unremarkable articulation, conventional expression; no touching or addressing by name; few back channels, little overlap or interruption. Where involvement is exciting, creates interaction, but is often aggressive, considerateness is blander, less involved in the conversation but more receptive to other speakers' needs.

In same-style interactions, there is no difficulty: speakers know how to maximize the utility and minimize the problems of their own stylistic patterns, and they do not make characterological interpretations based on others' use of the same stylistic forms. But when a conversation includes both types of speaker, each tends to make derogatory assessments of the other: to a considerateness user, an involved speaker is aggressive; and indeed, the former may have trouble getting and keeping the floor in company with involved speakers. On the other hand, involvement users often see considerate speakers as boring and uninterested, and if the former perceive themselves to be riding roughshod over them, rationalize that the latter didn't have much to say anyway. In such mixed groups, involvement users certainly hold a conversational advantage: they do most of the talking and choose most of the successful topics. But in the long run, they may lose power because they are perceived as not good people, as too difficult to deal with. On the other hand, considerate people may lose twice, the second time because they are seen as unintelligent or unconcerned. Involvement works best in power relations that are unilateral and hierarchical, where control is the object of competition (which the involved speaker will win). But if power is understood as collaborative, the considerateness style is likely to be more productive, if less exhilarating.

Power in conversation, then, is related to but not directly dependent on power in the external world. The interactive and reciprocal forms of ordinary conversation lend themselves better than other discourse types to egalitarian behavior; yet even in this most egalitarian realm, there is power to be had, and people will compete for it. The forms of ordinary conversation can be turned to one speaker's advantage in power acquisition, as can differences in personal interactive style.

OTHER DISCOURSE TYPES

While ordinary conversation has been subjected, in the last twenty years or so, to intensive study by linguists, anthropologists, sociologists, psychologists, and other social scientists, other types of discourse have attracted far less attention. One reason is practical: it is relatively easy to get hold of ordinary conversations in the forms of tapes and transcripts; it is much harder to find examples of most other types. Even when those are accessible (as with trial transcripts), the peculiarities of the language itself and the special assumptions of experts have been daunting to linguists. We are all equal as "experts" in the understanding of conversations. But professionals have special expertise in the courtroom, in the psychotherapeutic consulting room, and even in the classroom. So those scholars whose expertise is based on linguistic knowledge alone have been hesitant to tread on the feet of real experts in each of these areas; and when they have tried, either their work has been ignored (which is bruising to the ego) or dismissed by professionals as not really understanding the discourse in its milieu: you have to be there, you have to be one of us.

But with the tools and intuitive methods developed in the study of smaller units (like the sentence) and the techniques of conversation analysis, linguists can have insights about other discourse types, different from those of professionals in the field, but valuable precisely because observers are disinterested in the outcome, and their egos are less dependent on a favorable assessment. Our questions may be dismissed impatiently as impractical or irrelevant by the professional: we don't give them much advice about how to do their work better (win trials, cure neuroses), but we can provide some insight into how each type of discourse fits into the larger scheme of linguistic behavior. Our main focus is on what the existence of all the many ways people have of communicating shows about the nature of humankind.

Literate Discourse

Literate discourse includes all modes of linguistic communication in writing, from the most casual to the most serious, including memoranda, letters, diaries, poetry, fiction, and expository essays. A grouping so disparate is hard to categorize; yet, all forms of writing have commonalities, distinguishing them as a group from oral forms.

Linguists have always seen spoken language as basic, writing as secondary. Speech historically preceded writing; it is developmentally prior; while virtually all hearing human beings acquire spoken language with little difficulty, the same cannot be said for writing. Many individuals even in highly literate cultures fail to master writing or achieve only a low level of competence (*functional literacy*). And many societies have been and are nonliterate, using other means than writing to transmit information, culture, and history. People who are comfortable with literacy tend to assume that its achievement is a necessity for a sophisticated culture, as well as an unqualified good; but students of literacy and its acquisition have uncovered evidence challenging both of these assumptions. It is certainly a disadvantage to have less than full literacy in a society that uses literacy to transmit information. But there have always been highly successful cultures that achieve the same ends at least as competently by oral transmission, cultures whose members often demonstrate powers of memory and narrative skill far superior to ours. Often, too, when writing is introduced by well-intentioned First World agencies to pre-literate cultures, the new technology is co-opted by men. Women, who previously had an important and valued role in the culture as transmitters of ancient but still precious wisdom, are disempowered: old (pre-literate) wisdom itself becomes worthless, its bearers rendered superfluous, as new technological knowledge made accessible by literacy is given higher value.[5]

While writing takes many forms and serves as many functions, it can be generally contrasted with the equally diverse oral genres. First, and probably most significant, is the fact that writing of all kinds is intended to be preserved and therefore is considered consequential. Writing is mechanically harder than talking, it requires special equipment, and it leaves a record. Therefore, one does not embark on the task of writing unless there is good reason to do so: the communication *matters*. There is lots of small talk but little small writing.

Since writing is of consequence, efforts are generally made to be clear and precise, to a greater extent than is true for most kinds of talking. Writing may, on the other hand, be more circumspect than talking, since one takes legal responsibility for the written word as one cannot for the spoken. (The shredder is an attempt to obviate some of this risk.) It is, at the same time, harder to be unambiguous in writing than in oral communication, since most of the devices with which we habitually disambiguate the latter (intonation and gesture) are unavailable in writing. Some writing systems have ways to incorporate these disambiguating devices, like italics and exclamation points, but they are pallid substitutes for the real thing. In writing, we often resort to more complex syntax than we do when speaking, for two reasons. First, simple syntax is easier both to encode and decode in speech, where we can't check back to the beginning if we get confused, as we can in writing; and second, complex syntax is a way of making the relationships among the items in a sentence explicit, analogous to the intonation contrasts and pauses available in speech.

Writing is also mostly nonreciprocal. Even letters, which are technically reciprocal, are so only after a delay. One writes, another reads, and generally there is no direct contact between the two. Therefore misunderstanding is more likely, and clarity even more crucial, than in oral discourse. Writing is nonspontaneous: the reader's assumption is that the writer has had the opportunity to correct and perfect, so that there is no excuse for sloppiness or misleading expression. In speaking, we can claim that our words were misrepresented, that we misspoke in our haste. In writing, it is possible to give exact quotations (though one can always plead, "It was taken out of context!"), and one can't expect much sympathy for the argument that "I miswrote"—if that is even a possible excuse.

Because of these requirements, writing tends to be more formal than speech:

since it is not directly interactive, formality is an intrinsic part of written communication. Although writers may try to minimize the distance from their audiences by writing "informally," this course is full of dangers. Slang and colloquialism, so winning in speech, must be handled with extraordinary skill by a writer who does not wish to sound foolish.

Telephone Conversation

Telephone talk is a special type of ordinary conversation, but significantly different in that the speakers cannot see one another. Face-to-face talk makes use of extralinguistic devices: gesture, posture, facial expression. None of these are available on the telephone. This lack can be a blessing or a curse, so that some people enjoy telephones more than direct contact, others the reverse. In the absence of extralinguistic signals, it is difficult for one speaker to judge when the other has reached the end of a turn, so that there are more interruptions, apologies, and awkward pauses. For this reason, conference calls involving several speakers are tremendously hard for the uninitiated to negotiate: it is nearly impossible to keep track of who's talking, who said what, and when to jump in for a turn. Children often have difficulties grasping the nonvisible nature of telephone conversation: ask a small child if her mommy is there, and you may well get silence. If you were in the child's presence, you would see her nod; but she doesn't know you can't see her, or at least hasn't figured out why that should make a difference in the way she communicates.

TV Commercials

For purposes of comparison, I shall consider here just the subgenre of television commercial which purports to represent a real conversation between two real people: one in some sort of quandary ("I have a headache!" "What can I feed my family?" "What to do about dishwasher spotting?" and the thousand other ills the flesh is heir to); the other with the means to solve it ("Take X!" "Give them Y!" "Try Z!"). Although these look like bits of reality, honest-to-goodness conversations, their patterns are strikingly different from the template, because their functions are different.

The main difference is that, in ordinary conversation, the participants and the intended audience are one and the same, and the format is reciprocal. If participants A and B are friends, there are things they both know about each other, things each knows the other knows: hence the informality of ordinary conversation. Many things will not have to be spelled out; and, in fact, it would be bizarre to do so. At the same time, in ordinary conversation, participants have all the time in the world, or at least the pretense of it: they can carry on a topic as long as they desire: Since there are typically no external constraints on the length of a turn, a topic, or the conversation as a whole, there is lots of room for back channels, clarifications, hesitations, hedges, repetitions, and other signals of spontaneity.

Commercial conversations are just the reverse. However cozy the parties are shown as being, the real intended recipient of the discourse is the viewer behind the TV monitor, whose intimacy with the conversants cannot be presupposed. So things must be spelled out as they would not be in real life: "How's my favorite mother-in-law?" to identify the relationships of the participants quickly to an observer; "You know the doctor told us to cut down on cholesterol!" At the same time, there are severe constraints on the length of commercial chats: no more than thirty seconds, often less. So the devices that anchor real conversational gambits must be dispensed with: few back channels, repetitions, or hesitations are found, except to express nervousness. And while fragments are not uncommon in informal talk, they are used in commercials much more frequently and in many more situations: "Company's coming! What to serve!" where the ordinary conversation equivalent would be something like, "Oh golly, did I tell you that, y'know, I'm having company for dinner. I just can't imagine what to serve them." The fragments are meant both to impart verve and spontaneity when the real-world devices that signify the latter are unusable and to help keep the skit within the thirty-second limit.

The Classroom

There are many sub-versions of classroom interchange[6], and its format changes substantially from kindergarten to graduate seminar. Yet there are significant commonalities. Nonreciprocal power distinguishes the classroom from ordinary conversation, even in those manifestations (like the seminar) where it might appear that everyone has equal access to the floor and the topic. A teacher's questions are different in function, if not form, from the students': the teacher generally knows the answer desired (at least in the early grades) or has a general idea of an acceptable response. And should the teacher call on someone, that person is required to answer; to fail to respond appropriately is to fail. Students' questions, on the other hand, genuinely request information, and the teacher is free not to answer, on any of several pretexts: "We'll get to that next time"; "I answered that last time—weren't you in class?" "Well, that might just be on the final—think about it!" The teacher selects and controls topics, as well as controlling who gets called on. It is a position of considerable discourse power, buttressed by considerable real-world power in the form of grades, recommendations, and the like.

In explaining the reason for the different types of discourse and how their forms relate to their abstract functions, I have tried to demonstrate their innate coherence. It doesn't work to make courtroom talk look more like informal chatter, nor is it helpful to teach children to write with the premise that writing is just talk put on paper. Furthermore, the reasons behind the structure of ordinary conversation can help us understand communication in such formal areas as the psychotherapy office, the courtroom, and the university.

II

LANGUAGE AND INSTITUTIONS

CHAPTER FOUR

The Talking Cure

O F all forms of communication, psychotherapy takes language the most seriously. All forms of "talking therapy" use language as the major means of transmitting information from client to therapist and from therapist to client. Additionally, psychological distress is manifested in linguistic difficulties, so the therapist's discovery of confusion or unclarity is diagnostic. Finally, the therapist uses language as an instrument of healing: interpretations— the right understanding in the right form—create change.

But therapy is a double-edged sword—or rather, to employ the medical analogies much favored by the profession, a two-edged scalpel. The very linguistic properties that set therapeutic discourse apart from the conversation of intimate friendship and make it a force for change make it, in the wrong hands, a weapon capable of doing great damage. Instrumental in determining how the process will turn out is the therapist's attitude toward the work and the client: How important is unilateral power? If it is too important to the therapist's psychic satisfaction, the relationship is virtually certain to be abusive for the weaker party, the client, often in ways the latter is unable to perceive. The problem has plagued the field from its inception.

FREUD'S ABUSE OF THERAPY: THE DORA CASE

In the fall of 1899, an acquaintance and former patient brought his eighteen-year-old daughter, known as Dora, to Freud.[1] She suffered from a constellation of minor hysterical symptoms, which were making life annoying for her family and, in particular, her father. The latter's directive to Freud: "Bring her to reason." From the start, then, Freud was acting at the father's behest, not in his patient's interests, in accepting the former's assignment at its word. Freud saw it as his job to persuade Dora that—however correctly she might have analyzed her family situation—she had to admit that her own self-induced neurosis was at the root of her troubles; and that, in order to be "cured," she must renounce her own perception of things (though it might be correct) in favor of her father's and Freud's.

Dora's family was enmeshed in a Victorian phantasmagoria of secrets, passions, and fantasies. Nothing was said; everything was suggested. Dora, an intelligent and articulate girl, had gathered years earlier that her father had contracted syphilis and transmitted it to her mother, and that she herself had probably been congenitally infected as well. Her mother (the perspicacious Freud never made the connection) was now obsessively dedicated to household cleanliness. Both Dora's father and brother, and Dora herself, had only contempt for the mother.

For many years now, Dora's family had been friends with another family, the K's. Herr K. was very like Dora's father (and, curiously, Freud): ambitious and successful men in their forties, described by Freud as "passionate smokers." (In this case, though, a cigar is apparently only a cigar.) Frau K., a much younger woman, had two children. She and Dora, not yet out of childhood, became confidantes in sexual and other matters. Dora came to realize that her father and Frau K. were having an affair, and that the families were making vacation plans to facilitate it. No one, of course, wanted Dora's mother, so Herr K. was odd man out.

From the time Dora was seven or eight, Herr K., the busy successful businessman, found the time to take long walks with her and the money to buy the child expensive gifts. No one, apparently, thought anything of it. At the age of fourteen, Dora went by invitation to Herr K.'s office to watch a festival from the window; Frau K. and the children were supposed to be there, too. When she arrived, she discovered that Herr K. was there alone, and the curtains were drawn. He grabbed the child as she came up the stairs and gave her a deep kiss. She felt his erection. She pulled away in disgust and horror, and ran. Freud's analysis: her reaction was neurotic, a reversal of her "true" feelings, which were love and desire for Herr K. ("This was surely just the situation to call up a distinct feeling of sexual excitement in a girl of fourteen who had never been approached"[28].) Her symptoms began with this incident. There were a couple of other incidents, similar though more serious; and with each her symptoms exacerbated. Dora eventually tried to tell her father about the incidents. He confronted Herr K., who denied everything; and Dora was accused of creating fantasies in order to make trouble. (During this period, Herr K. managed to send flowers to Dora at home every day for a year, without arousing the suspicions of her "shrewd" father.) Dora ultimately came to the conclusion that the men were using her as an object of barter: my wife for your daughter. The only problem with the arrangement was that, although the other three were consenting adults, Dora's preferences were never consulted. Freud acknowledged that Dora's perceptions had validity, but he felt that it would be an error for him to tell her that: it would just encourage her in her willful and disruptive ("neurotic") behavior. So three powerful adult men were aligned against one eighteen-year-old girl.

Dora remained in analysis with Freud for three months. On New Year's Eve, at her regular session, she informed Freud that she was not coming any more. Freud was nonplused and disappointed. (Patients weren't beating down his door at this point.) Why had she left him? He offered posterity two explanations. First, she was taking revenge on him for not responding sexually to her: he had not been aware of the transference. Second, she was, after all, homosexual (and hence had not responded to Herr K., who Freud thought was a suitable lover and perhaps eventual husband). Her attraction to Frau K. was the pre-eminent emotion in Dora's life, and therefore she was incapable of forming an erotic transference to Freud, and therefore the analysis was doomed to fail. Choose one or both. It is noteworthy that there is virtually no explicit evidence for either argument in Dora's own recollections or associations.

This long case history exhibits considerable evidence of abuse. First of all, Freud saw himself not as his patient's advocate or agent but as her father's (who was paying the bills), and his task was not to make Dora happy or productive, but to "bring her to reason"—that is, to induce her to stop pestering her father and his friends. We may ask to what degree Dora was seeing Freud voluntarily. She would not have come except at her father's insistence; but on the other hand, she felt free to leave when she chose. To the extent that therapy was imposed on Dora, we must consider it abusive.

I have two reasons for going back nearly a century to this appalling example of the abuse of power in therapy. First, for the first half of the twentieth century, *psychoanalysis* and *psychotherapy* were virtual synonyms. The latter might some-times be pressed into service to describe a process that was briefer and less intense than the orthodox, Freudian method. But it still employed most of the latter's theoretical and many of its methodological assumptions: the importance of the unconscious, the role of repressed early traumatic memories, the transference and the necessity of its interpretation. Since then, other schools have arisen making sharply different assumptions: most important among them, in making the sharp-est break, is the one most often called *brief therapy*, based most directly on the work of Gregory Bateson and his collaborators.[2] Their work is focused less on the dynamics of the individual, internal psyche; more on interpersonal communica-tion. In analytically oriented therapies, a patient (the word they tend to prefer) who complains of family difficulties is usually seen alone, and his or her problems traced to disturbed relations in the family of origin. On the other hand, practi-tioners of brief therapy will probably insist on working with the whole troubled unit presently constituting a client's (their preferred word) life: spouse, children, or both. Such a therapist will focus, not on communicative difficulties in a client's childhood (the keeping of secrets, the distortion of reality), but on the confused and disturbing communication *now* upsetting the current family's workings. No attempt is made to ferret out underlying motives or causes; the aim is merely to derail the aberrant communicative habits the family has settled into, and to replace them with new, positive ones.

In many ways the antithesis of analysis, brief therapy is actually its lineal descendant. Particularly in respect to my focus in this book, their relationship is more close than distant—all the more so because, like siblings, the two schools squabble and are jealous of each other. Freud's original and brilliant vision embraces both—indeed, all schools of "talking" therapy: the realization that communication is the clue; that bad communication between intimates inevitably leads to individual psychic distress; and that the only way to restore to full competence someone suffering from that distress is to teach ways to communicate directly. Thus communication is the key in both, though psychoanalysis qualifies it "with himself or herself," and brief therapy, "with others in the context."

That is one reason I am concentrating my comments here on Freudian theory and therapy. The other is that over the years it has been far and away the most influential of therapeutic systems, coloring not only the culture's view of how to cope with distress of all kinds, but giving us our peculiar twentieth-century *Weltanschauung,* our view of ourselves and our relationships as individuals and in larger units. Other models surely have much to tell us, perhaps more accurately than psychoanalysis, about our functioning, but none has penetrated deeper into our ways of thought and speech.

Because psychoanalytic theory in all its aspects remains pervasive (even though the orthodox therapeutic method itself may be falling into desuetude), its potential for abuse continues unabated. So the antiquity of Dora's case history can be of little comfort: while inappropriate therapeutic interaction may be mitigated in current practice by today's expectations for male-female relationships, it has not deeply changed. What was deadly then is perhaps potentially more so now, because more hidden and less recognizable. And ninety years ago, psychoanalysis was unproven, not institutionalized, not respected; Freud's name was known to few. So any power he brought into the therapeutic relationship was derived from the outside: his position, gender, and age relative to his patient. Today therapy, and especially psychoanalysis, is a respected institution, it is "science." It permeates the culture. Its dogma is our dogma, our religion. As hard as it was then for a patient who felt she was being mistreated to leave, it is very much harder now to recognize the mistreatment and to dare to challenge it.

COMMUNICATION AS CAUSE AND CURE OF NEUROSIS

Freud's insight was that psychic distress is communicative in origin.[3] What causes neurosis is less a specific action (the seduction, the forbidden sight) than the language surrounding it: the shaming, the terrifying admonition, the worry over what can or cannot be spoken, the guarding of the secret. Ultimately psychic pain arises from what cannot be said, or cannot be said so as to be understood either by another person or by the speaker's own conscious adult mind. Symptoms (illness, dreams, errors) are distorted communication: a way of saying the unsayable, a compromise between what must be spoken and what cannot be; therefore, finally, an unsatisfactory way of communicating. Psychotherapy is the process of figuring out the real message (the interpretation) contained in one's distortions, omissions, and fragments of memory, and then of learning how to make one's "story" coherent again—to give oneself a meaningful history by making everything fit together for the first time.

Then psychotherapy is discourse about discourse, discourse within discourse, discourse for the sake of discourse. To the extent that it succeeds, it does so by pure linguistic understanding, by stretching to their limits the communicative powers of therapist and client.

Symptoms (said Freud) arise because their possessor has repressed an intolerable memory, pushing it out of linguistic awareness or twisting it into a form that will not recall the trauma. But the memory does not go away. It festers where it cannot be reached and dealt with in later life, with adult awareness and intelligence. The secret is not gone, just out of control, and continues to have a life of its own in the unconscious, always striving to penetrate consciousness again. But its path is blocked by repression: it can emerge only in distorted form. Even this offers some immediate relief, but in the long run is not satisfying, and the symptom keeps recurring. The only way out of the cycle of repetition is by remembering: the restoration via interpretation of the original memory, the recollection and reliving of the traumatic event.

For example, Dora had as one of her symptoms a "nervous cough," which Freud traced to her discovery that "there was more than one way of obtaining sexual gratification." "I [said] that in that case she must be thinking of precisely those parts of her body which in her case were in a state of irritation—the throat and the oral cavity. . . . A very short time after she had tacitly accepted this explanation her cough vanished" (47–48).

The client provides the life story, the anamnesis. The therapist listens carefully. Are the events told in chronological sequence, or does the narrative skip chronological steps, making the client's life difficult to follow? Does the therapist get a sharp-focused picture of the client's current daily life and the people within it, or is the picture murky? Do the client's explanations, reasons, justifications make sense, does one event connect logically to the next, or is the listener frustrated with a hodgepodge, a ragbag of irrelevance? True, some people have a gift for narrative and others don't. But when confusion occurs, when the thread of intelligibility snaps abruptly, when the therapist has to suppress a yawn, it is reasonable to suspect a deliberate, if unconscious, distortion. The client is making no sense to the therapist, because making sense is too dangerous: not only because the therapist would see things clearly, but because, for the first time, the client would.

At first the therapist has to grasp at subtle cues. A, followed by B, may not set up a particular scenario, but a leap from A to C offers a tantalizing possibility. Does the narrative make sense? If not, what is missing? If that piece is missing, why? The therapist works as much with what is not there as with what is. Interpretation is inserting B between A and C to make the sequence ABC, or rearranging ACB. And at the same time, the therapist must provide constant, subtle reassurance: it's OK that you aren't making sense (as it would not be in any other kind of talk); it's OK, too, for me to make sense of it: you can trust me with it.

That, in brief, is the therapeutic process—or rather, its semantic aspect. This makes therapy sound rather like the work of the biblical scholar, scanning a text whose meaning is sometimes deliberately obscure, sometimes obscured by historical changes in language and culture. In fact, it makes the client look like a mystic or a poet, and the therapist like a critical reader, working in one sense cooperatively, in another, competitively. Freud liked to think of his field as an "art-science." The art is in the creative intuition that is interpretation. The claim of psychotherapy to scientific status is harder to justify.

PSYCHOTHERAPY AS A "SCIENCE"

Historically psychoanalysis arose out of medicine—neurology, Freud's specialty. It developed in the late nineteenth century, at a time when science seemed to be replacing both religion and humanism as the basis for understanding humankind and its relation to the cosmos. Freud's first project was an attempt to construct a completely formal account of mental processes, based on electromagnetic and hydraulic theory.[4] This aim was soon, thankfully, abandoned, but these ideas linger in Freud's use of metaphor and parable in his later theory. The mind, for him as for us, was a black box whose workings could not be directly perceived or understood but could be made intelligible through figurative language. Repression is likened to the damming up of a rushing stream of water: the water gathers force behind the dam, and eventually the force becomes so potent that nothing can hold it back. Thus symptoms develop. Or the analyst's work is compared to that of the surgeon (another glamour occupation of Freud's period): he must cut and hurt in order to cure. Curiously, these figures are often taken by practitioners as representing a literal truth: not that psychic processes are *like* a rushing stream: they *are* a rushing stream. Therefore, it has seemed necessary for modern developers of analytic theory to "modernize" the metaphor (which they don't recognize as metaphor): substitute for electricity or hydraulics artificial intelligence or cybernetics, and—presto!—you modernize the field. That such discussion is taken seriously enough to be published in the field's scholarly journals is one indication that psychoanalysis is not really scientific.[5]

Whether psychoanalysis is to be categorized as art, science, or faith has important consequences—a realization that was one of Freud's most crucial insights. He himself, born in the mid-nineteenth century and living and writing almost to the middle of the twentieth, stood at the cusp (as another faith-science might put it) of a discourse revolution. Before him, religion was the discourse genre by which authority spoke and truth was transmitted. It was the basis of metaphor about the meaning of life and what it was to be human. It was where one looked to find the answers, all the answers. Toward the end of the nineteenth century, science began to take the place of faith as the discourse of authority and knowledge, a role it has continued to play with ever greater prominence. Now, anyone who wants to tell us where we stand, how to think about ourselves, how to perceive the universe around us and within us, must couch those insights in scientific terms, as *-ologies*, not *-isms*. Freud both made use of the switch and was instrumental in it. So the choice he made, to align his field with science, contributes today to its authoritative power. The metamessage of "scientific" psychoanalysis is, "This field knows the truth, *because* it is a science. As a twentieth-century person, you must listen when we speak or be cast into the hell reserved for scientific heretics—ignorance." In that sense, the co-optation of scientific methods and vocabulary by Freud and especially his followers has a rich potential for abuse: rather than examining whether the field merits the authority of science, it merely adopts it by taking its language.

Bruno Bettelheim, one of Freud's co-workers and disciples, has suggested that Freud "really" intended psychoanalytic theory to have a religious and humanistic, rather than scientific, cast: the science was unwittingly introduced by inept English translations.[6] I sympathize with the spirit of this argument: it certainly seems as if the workings of psychoanalysis owe more to religion and humanism than to science. But Freud's writings provide evidence to the contrary. His metaphors, parables, and other allusions are taken largely from science. He referred to himself and his colleagues most often as medical men, not as clerics or poets. Freud, believing that science was the prestigious discourse of his age (as it is of ours), felt that if psychoanalysis were ever to achieve full respectability, it would be as a medical specialty, mostly science with some admixture of art.

(He had little use for religion, personally or professionally.) He spoke of the "dosage" and "titration" of interpretations, as though these humanistic interactions could be measured out by the technician's pipette.

Bettelheim's strongest argument is that Freud's terminology was mistranslated by A. A. Brill, Joan Riviere, and James Strachey and his collaborators. Where Freud chose vocabulary from everyday, nonscientific German, his translators substituted Greco-Latin formations—as a brief comparison demonstrates:

Freud's German	English
(der) Ich ("I")	ego
(das) Es ("it")	id
Besetzung ("settling on")	cathexis
Verdrängung ("pressing down")	repression
Übertragung ("carrying over")	transference

In each case, the English is a literal translation of the German—but into Greek or Latin elements rather than native English vocabulary. While Bettelheim's facts are correct, I think he misunderstood both Freud's intentions in creating the underpinnings of his field and the requirements of competent translation. Since Freud wanted his field to be recognized as a science, it is clear that he did everything he could to bring it into that category. This was as important for him as it remains for psychotherapy as an institution today. But even Bettelheim's strongest point, the choice of vocabulary, overlooks the fact that every language imposes on its speakers its own view of reality.

Since the Renaissance and until very recently, English-speaking science has constructed its technical vocabulary from Latin and Greek sources, perhaps because of the insecurity of the inhabitants of a small island only recently risen to imperial status. In the Elizabethan period, when England first became a world power, its scholars and public men felt that its language had to be elevated to equivalent status. Until then, there were few English grammars: the language was not considered worthy of close study, as even other modern European languages were. Having no native model of "good grammar," grammarians reached back to the Renaissance status symbol, Latin, often making up rules for English based on the principles of Latin grammar (although English is distinctly different from Latin). This is the reason we are not supposed to split infinitives or end sentences with prepositions: you can't do it in Latin (even if you want to). Science was also on the rise during this period (largely in the forms of astrology and alchemy), and it was natural to base new technical vocabulary on Latin. The practice continued for centuries. Only recently, in the post–Second World War period, have we gained enough confidence to baptize the offspring of our newest sciences with

English names: in computer science, we say *input, floppy, bit, byte;* in genetic engineering, *splicing.* (Only in linguistics, perpetually insecure, like any social science, do we speak of "preference organization.")

German, on the other hand, has always had a tradition of constructing scientific nomenclature out of native vocabulary. Where ordinary language to us has until recently sounded a bit naïve and unserious, that is not so for speakers of German. While speakers of English created *oxygen* in the eighteenth century, Germans constructed an etymologically analogous term out of native elements: *Sauerstoff.* Where Bell created *telephone* from Greek roots, German made *Fernsprecher* with the same meaning ("far" + "speaker").

So Freud's choice of native German elements for his psychoanalytic vocabulary was not a conscious decision to eschew science. He had no other option. When English translators in the first decades of this century created equivalents to the German terminology, they had no rational choice but Latin and Greek, or their translations would have sounded childlike and imprecise. Since speakers of English were accustomed to serious words being Latinate or Greek, other choices would have been confusing, rather than illuminating.

Freud's adoption of scientific terminology is apparent everywhere in his writings, even in the case histories, which might seem the best excuse for humanism. *Dora,* for instance, is explicitly and repeatedly framed as a "scientific" work, one way Freud justified his frank discussion of sexuality. ("It's OK, I'm a doctor.") The very title promises a work of science: *Analysis of a Case of Hysteria.* Chapter 1 is entitled "The *Clinical* Picture." The preface opens: "In 1895 and 1896 I put forward certain views upon the *pathogenesis* of *hysterical symptoms*" (7). Throughout, Dora's symptoms are given names in medicalese, even where ordinary language terms would be more readily intelligible: *tussis nervosa* for "nervous cough"; *perityphlitis* for "appendicitis," *aphonia* for "loss of voice."

Ultimately, though, Bettelheim's arguments miss the point. Freud did indeed, as Bettelheim says, take from the language of faith some of his vocabulary: for example, *Geist* and *Seele,* the words translated into English by "psyche," which in German at least sometimes are much closer to "spirit" or "soul". But he placed these words from religious discourse into his newly formed "scientific" context, thereby explicitly transferring the concepts they represented from the domain of faith to the domain of science. Hence (as Karl Menninger remarked some years ago[7]) it is no longer fashionable to speak of "sin": the concept of the *Seele* gone wrong is reclassified as "illness," a word of science. It is not so much that Freud redefined these terms; rather, he recontextualized them—and so changed the nature of the discourse, allying his field first linguistically, then actually, with the domain of power.

Power was important to Freud, both for his field and within the analytic setting, for the doctor relative to the patient. He also emphasized the medical model because, in his time as in ours, a doctor has a great deal of authority and power—intellectual, social, and moral—over a patient. The minister was losing influence; presciently, Freud saw that the doctor was gaining it. By bringing analysis into the tent of "medicine," Freud ensured that psychoanalysts, and psychotherapists, would be imbued with the prestige and power of the medical profession. All of Freud's specifications—the laws and principles, theory and method, of psychoanalysis—served to enhance the power discrepancy between therapist and client. The reason is that therapy, partly by Freud's fiat and partly arising out of the necessities of the discourse type itself, makes use of a distinct power imbalance between the participants in respect to communication.

IMBALANCE IN THERAPY: POTENTIAL FOR ABUSE

Therapeutic discourse is nonreciprocal.[8] This is patently the case in orthodox psychoanalysis, with the analyst seated in a chair, out of the view of the patient, and the latter supine, visible to the therapist. The therapist is physically higher, in a more adult and protected posture; to see is more powerful than to be seen. More modern versions have both participants sitting in comfortable chairs facing each other. In the same way, many analysts of older generations required title–last-name address ("Dr. Smith") from their patients, and addressed them (especially if female and younger) by first name. This nonreciprocal pattern is characteristic of relations between unequals, especially men and women. More recently, at least in California and among non-analytic and non-M.D. therapists, mutual first-naming has largely replaced this practice. On the other hand, I once had occasion to eavesdrop on the following bit of dialogue in a psychiatrist's waiting room. The doctor was a man in his late thirties; the patient, a man in his twenties.

> DOCTOR: Are you John?
> PATIENT: Yes—and you're Richard [the doctor's first name]?
> DOCTOR: I'm Doctor Smith.

At that moment and with those words, the power dynamic between the two was fixed irrevocably for the duration of their relationship. The doctor didn't object to the first-naming or correct it ("No, I'm Dr. Smith"), but merely confirmed the existence of the power imbalance as an aspect of eternal truth.

More significant, in all forms of talking therapy, nonreciprocity is manifested in the possibilities each participant has for speaking and being understood. The therapist communicates mainly by questions; the client, by declarative statements. That is not to say that each is literally restricted in this way. But therapy is transacted via clients' revelations and musings, which occur as statements and which are most readily elicited by questions. The basic information and the source of all knowledge gained in therapy must be the client's communications; therefore, declarative utterances by the therapist (except for relatively infrequent interpretations) are out of place. Thus, even when a therapist says something that is formally a declarative ("It sounds as if you're afraid of your father," "You've been late three times this month"), it will be—unless intended by the therapist as an interpretation—treated by the client as a question, that is, a device for eliciting information ("Are you really afraid of your father?" "Why do you keep coming late?"). The well-known "therapeutic question" is a compromise: declarative in form, but with the rising intonation of a yes-no question: "You've always felt this way about bagels?"

The client may ask questions as well, but they will likely be treated as informative statements, revelations about the client's psyche:

CLIENT: Why can't you see me on Monday?
THERAPIST: That seems to disturb you, doesn't it?

Here the therapist's comment means something like, "Your question conveys your anxiety about being separated from me."

As the one who alone has the right to make interpretations, the therapist decides what both participants "mean"—a source of tremendous, if implicit, power. Over the course of therapy, ideally the client should be learning how to make interpretations for himself or herself. If the therapeutic process works this way, where the client learns a new way to communicate, the participants become more nearly equal. This ideal scenario assumes that the therapist is able and willing to relinquish power as the client becomes able and willing to assume it. But it is mainly the job of the therapist to make this possible: to teach the client how to do what needs to be done; to judge when a client is ready to move to the next step; to reassure the client that it is safe and feasible. Too many therapists, though, become dependent on power and are reluctant to relinquish it to support a client's growth.

The complexity of the therapeutic relationship makes it hard for both participants to know how to use power and how to let it shift. The major power, the power to interpret, is largely the therapist's. Also belonging to the therapist are most of the physical concomitants of power: possession of the territory, the right to set appointments, the determination of when to begin and end, the ability to keep the client waiting before appointments. The therapist makes the formal rules: whether appointments can be canceled, how much and when clients will pay, whether a client will sit or lie down, often whether a client is "ready" to terminate. Yet there are apparent contradictions, sometimes used by therapists as arguments that they really don't have the power in the relationship: the client "can" come late, leave early, refuse to speak, not pay bills. But these areas are not where the real power lies. They are analogous to the child's "right" to have tantrums and refuse to go to bed. They are not seen by either participant as the free choices of an intelligent and autonomous mind; rather, they are the desperate shrieks of the irrational aspect of the client's mind, a sign of lack of control.

Furthermore, therapeutic discourse mixes forms in a way quite unlike that of ordinary conversation, in which the person holding the floor and selecting the successful topics (most often the same person) is the one with both the real-world power and the power in the conversation. In therapy, the two are separated. Almost invariably the client holds the floor most of the time; and any utterance by the therapist refers to the client's needs rather than the speaker's. Yet the one who in theory introduces the topics, on whom the topics focus, is not the one who defines what the topics are or what they mean. Although the client may hold the floor, she or he does not have the right to decide what the utterances on the floor mean, even what speech acts they represent. So the determination of power must be made by looking below the surface of the conversational structure.

Therapists with whom I have discussed these matters often get upset with such comments on the power imbalance, and hasten to provide the putative counterexamples I have noted. But a power imbalance is not intrinsically evil or undesirable—even though it is in ordinary conversation, which is defined and understood by participants to be reciprocal and egalitarian. In types of communication where one person has skills to impart to another, equality (at least until the latter has begun to acquire those skills) is an impossibility. Unequal power elsewhere is neither undesirable nor problematic unless it is misused, or abused, by the more powerful participant. Though a serious problem in therapy, abuse is not a necessary accompaniment of power imbalance; it is merely a possible outcome, one that can be avoided with sensitivity and understanding. Ordinary conversation would fail in its purpose and feel unpleasant to participants if a power imbalance existed; likewise, therapeutic discourse would become empty if participants were fully equal; and if they pretended an equality that was not there, the whole interchange would become a sham, the discourse teaching the client to live a lie (based on the therapeutic-model discourse) rather than to pursue the truth.

Indeed, it is a real question whether therapy can exist at all if external reality tips the balance of power toward equality: if a client is very wealthy, famous, or powerful. In such cases, the power the therapist holds by virtue of authority and knowledge is countered by the power the client actually wields in the world and brings into the consulting room. The therapist's job may be compromised for any of several reasons: The therapist may be awed into feeling incompetent. Someone as successful as the client (more successful, by many standards, than the therapist) cannot be confused or needy. The therapist may feel intellectually unworthy of contradiction or confrontation. Or the therapist may be seduced, explicitly or otherwise, by the client's offers: secrets of the rich and famous, real gifts, access to others at the client's level. Therapy can degenerate into the divulging of gossip; or the therapist can be so overwhelmed by the client's generosity as to forget to do the job at hand. Finally, the therapist may be blackmailed by the threat, open or covert, that the client will leave if therapy gets too rough. Therapists are seldom happy to lose clients, of course; but the pain is compounded when the client is so desirable, and the loss of income is a small threat compared with the loss of access and privilege.

In cases like these, a therapist may find it difficult to engage in the confrontation that is the soul of therapy. The relationship can be pleasant for both but is likely to be merely self-indulgent—for both. There is no motive for the client to change as long as the therapist does not have a power imbalance to work from.

Truth in Therapy

Truth and knowledge are said to be the objects of the therapeutic discourse, to find out what *really* happened in a client's life, what a client's true story is. That is why everything the client says is considered (intentionally or not) informative: it reveals truth even if (or because) it attempts to obscure it. But "truth" in therapeutic discourse (even more than anywhere else) is a complex matter. A client's story can be retold many times, in many ways, with significant changes in the historical record. In ordinary conversation, one would have to say hearing the whole set that only one could be true, the others "lies," "misunderstandings," "misstatements," and so on. And there would be an assumption that the true story would be the same one for all observers or participants. If there are discrepancies, only one version is the true one, and there should be ways for hearers to determine what to believe: skepticism is valid.

In one sense, this is the case for therapeutic narratives: the client is supposed to produce, as time goes on, "less and less distorted derivatives"—that is (among other things), to retell his or her tale so that it is ever closer to the "real truth." Not that the client is lying, but that the unconscious, to save itself, has distorted the memory or even the original perception. That distortion is, or underlies, the symptoms that brought the client into treatment in the first place. The treatment consists of helping the client both to reach through the distortions to the reality and to confront that reality with courage.

At the same time, and not contradictorily, each of the accounts the client produces over time represents *a* truth, something true for that person at that moment, and informative (therefore "true" within the therapeutic function) for the therapist at that moment. The fact that the client sees a moment in his or her life in this way, at this time, is a truth; anything else at this point, even the historical truth, would be false, would represent an unrealistic picture of the client's psyche. Part of the therapist's work is slowly and patiently to reconcile the client's "truths" into one actual historical reality; but the therapist must be ready to face a client's rejection of actual truths whose time has not yet come. Here, too, the determination of what "truth" is real is up to the therapist, though the latter is expected to make use of signs from the client. But the client's say-so is insufficient.

Through this aspect of the interpretive process, too, the therapist achieves power. To tell someone which part of his or her story is true, or that it is untrue, is to define that person, to make him or her coherent or incoherent for himself or herself and the world at large: it can create or destroy individuals, literally and symbolically. Too often therapists obsessed with power, and unwilling to look hard at the ways of the society that has given them that power have found themselves facing a choice between a client's "truth" that is embarrassing and destructive to the entrenched power structure, and a "truth" that preserves everyone's pretenses and requires no change from anyone but the weakest person, the client. In such cases, the tendency is to discard the client's truth as fabrication, the delusion of a sick person (or why would she or he be in therapy?). This is a most serious abuse of therapeutic power if later it turns out that the client told it the way it was, and was punished for it.

A power imbalance, while essential to the therapeutic process, is full of potential dangers for both participants, especially the weaker member. Interpretation requires a power imbalance, but unilateral interpretability is a great temptation to abuse. The temptation is harder to resist if the therapist is a member of a social group more powerful than the client's: then the power intrinsic to the therapeutic context merges with the power that exists in the outside world to make the therapist especially liable to abuse his or her powers, and the client especially vulnerable to the abuse. It is not that therapy is impossible or always abusive under these conditions, but that special vigilance is essential for both participants.

Therapeutic Discourse as Adversarial

The problem is exacerbated by another aspect of therapeutic discourse: it is covertly adversarial. Ordinary conversation is, ideally, collaborative rather than adversarial: everyone can win; and if all play by the rules, all should win by emerging from the exercise feeling good and competent. On the other hand, courtroom discourse in this society is overtly and necessarily adversarial: for one participant to win, the other must lose. Hence (although courtroom discourse, like therapy, is officially committed to discovering "the truth"), all sorts of deviousness and aggressiveness are permissible and often admirable if they lead to victory for their user. But at least all participants know that they are in an adversarial situation. The language of the courtroom is designed to warn participants of the adversarial nature of their communications. Therapy, on the other hand, is generally seen as collaborative and beneficent for the client—as, in many ways, it certainly is. But it is often not recognized that therapeutic discourse is covertly adversarial. Because this quality goes unremarked and unrecognized, therapeutic language has built in no safeguards for the weaker party—an encouragement to abuse. And if a client feels like the weaker party in an adversarial situation (being bullied like a witness under cross-examination), that feeling will be "explained" by the district attorney of the consulting room as "negative transference" or "resistance"—in other words, as a symptom and a distortion, not a reality.

The adversarial aspect of therapy exists in both intention and form. Much has been written about the "therapeutic alliance" or "working alliance"—the collaboration between the therapist and the healthy or adult part of the client's psyche, the adaptive ego in psychoanalysis.[9] The alliance works for collaboration, for courageously finding truth and attempting change, but at the same time is against what caused the distress that brought the client into therapy. This is often identified as another, less accessible part of the client's mental structure: the unconscious or the id, or the defensive aspect of the ego. For the therapy to be successful, the therapist and the "good" part of the client's ego must wrestle with the "bad" part, argue with it, maybe even seduce or bribe it, but overcome it at any cost. The adversary of both therapist and client, it is also a part of the client and reflected in at least some of his or her behavior. So one aspect of the client's personality must be induced to work alongside the therapist and against another part of the same psyche.

This is never pleasant work, especially for the client. In ordinary conversation, when someone criticizes someone else severely, the latter usually has the option of returning the favor or at least leaving the scene. But in therapy, either of those choices is interpretable as further proof of the client's unreason. The client can escape, but only with a sense of being "bad" for doing so, and is seen as giving up on the chance of mental health and future happiness by so doing. Some would say it takes great courage, some great cowardice, to escape; in any case it takes autonomy, a scarce commodity among those in therapy.

Confrontation is essential to the therapeutic process, since most of us resist change. Non-egalitarian and nonreciprocal confrontation is an exceptionally dangerous weapon in the wrong hands. Perhaps we can take a leaf from Freud's book and see the adversarial stance of therapy as a laser beam. Used with sensitivity and intelligence, it is a vital weapon in the surgeon's arsenal, a way of sparing patients a great deal of suffering. Used by a Darth Vader, it is an instrument of destruction and a reminder of his own superior power. But the presence of the laser beam in the surgeon's hands is overt and recognized, and rules have been devised and agreed to for its proper use. Adversarial confrontation is covert in therapy: no one quite acknowledges its existence, and there are no rules and no protections, no way for therapist or client to be sure it is being used in the right way. Here as elsewhere, the functions of therapy necessitate the adoption of potentially dangerous forms of discourse, but the limitations and risks of those forms are unknown.

Freud's analysis of Dora is therapy at its most adversarial. Freud at several points uses language both to and of his patient that suggests he sees himself as judge and jury at her trial: he "forced her to acknowledge" certain truths; she "confess[ed] that she had masturbated" (76); her objections to his interpretations are "easy to brush aside" (101). She "admit[ted]" (37, 100) that certain thoughts have occurred to her, that she has read forbidden books, that she used to wet the bed. In a collaborative relationship, the two participants would have (as Freud said in other case histories where his patients were men) "discovered" such facts together, or Freud would have "explained" his hypotheses. The discussion would then have had a very different feeling for both participants. Theoretically interpretations are to be offered, and experienced, as teaching strategies; for Freud in this case, they were weapons to "use against" Dora.

The power that psychotherapists have in their relations with clients stems from the belief of both parties that therapy works. Detractors have argued the opposite for many years, often making the claim that therapy is no more than "paid friendship"—ordinary conversation for money. Certainly seen from the outside and understood superficially, therapy looks that way. But for the institution to have survived for a hundred years, it must work at least sometimes, at least to some degree, at least for some clients. Partial success is all we can ask of any institution; and for one as young as therapy, partial success seems a perfectly reasonable accomplishment, although it is to be hoped that practitioners will continue to work for improvement, rather than (as they do now too frequently) deny the existence of serious flaws.

Change

The only thing exchanged, the only medium, in the therapeutic relationship is talk. So if therapy is effective as ordinary conversation is not, therapy talk must accomplish something different from the ordinary, different in a way that creates a specific effect: change.

Different systems at different times have defined in various ways the "change" that is the object of therapy: change in behavior, change in psychic organization, change in worldview, change in relationships and work habits. But evidence of change is the basic proof of the efficacy of the process. Surely by now everyone has heard this version of the light-bulb joke:

How many shrinks does it take to change a light bulb?
One, but it has to really *want* to change.

However familiar, this joke's popularity illustrates the provenance of this definition of therapeutic success.

How can language—abstract, ethereal, ambiguous as it is—create change in palpable experiential reality? Speech act theory tells us that in one sense any use of language affects reality. But the creation of permanent change in a person's psyche is a different and more difficult enterprise. Freud spoke of the "adhesiveness of the libido"[10] as the reason people resist changing even though they know that staying the same is causing them suffering: to change is to dare the unknown, to abandon the comfort (however dubious) of familiarity for a promised reward, but only in the future and at the expense, most likely, of increased present pain of many kinds. So therapeutic discourse must provide a bridge, making the transition more tolerable and the future benefit discernible on the horizon.

Another reason change is elusive is that it is abstract. We cannot, usually, *see* ourselves change; we cannot perceive change happening. Most of all, we cannot observe changes in our minds, since the latter are abstract entities hidden from our direct inspection. To provide that bridge, therapy must somehow make the process visible and its results observable. One way has already been mentioned: the use of allusive language, metaphor, simile, parable. All of these link an abstraction to something more concrete, something never experienced to everyday reality. Freud speaks often of intrapsychic struggle, the fight between ego and id for control: because the id has great power, the struggle in therapy and outside of it must be continuous and often seems futile. But how can we think of ego versus id, when both are invisible abstractions? How to make intelligible the reason therapy is an uphill battle, or why the rational element seems to be winning in one session, only to cave in a few days later? Freud's allusions help. The victory of the ego is analogous to the success of the Netherlands in holding back the Zuyder Zee. The land has been reclaimed, to be sure, but at the cost of continual vigilance and frequent repair. The simile sets up the two sides: the ocean, the wild force of nature, essentially untamable, irrational; versus the forces of reason and civilization, the human products of engineering, scientific observation, memory of the past. The battle that goes on unseen and poorly understood in the patient's mind is linked to humanity's triumph (partial and slow) over the forces of indomitable nature. That makes the struggle of psychoanalysis both grand and winnable and comforts the patient for the difficulties of the process.

A successful therapeutic allusion has three properties. First, it links the client's psychic reality with a larger universal truth. Second, it belongs wholly to the two who create it. The therapist who provides the same warmed-over analogy for everyone is not giving the client something equal in effort to the latter's sacrifice—of comfort and security. Finally, it represents a collaboration between therapist and client, each contributing a meaningful part to its creation. Therapy, in order to be efficacious and non-abusive, must be a partnership in some ways at least. The therapist should not be telling the client, "Here's how you are. This is what you mean"; each must supply pieces of the puzzle. Too often when these principles are overlooked, nothing much happens in the therapeutic encounter. "But this metaphor worked for Freud," muses the therapist afterward. Yes—and that is precisely why it cannot work again.

It is not that the mutual creation must be exactly equivalent on both sides. Each may supply a different kind of piece. The client supplies a bit of history, or a feeling, or an expression of confusion. The therapist says, "It sounds as if . . . ," and the client says, "Oh! That's just right!" That moment of creative joining becomes part of the bond that links the two, a secret code they share. To share secrets is to trust; to trust someone is to be able to count on that person to support you when things get rough. A few such collaborations over the period of therapy are essential if the process is to succeed. If they do not occur, therapy can be comforting and helpful to a client in any number of ways—but will not lead to change.

Interpretations, when effective, are shared constructions. A therapist's role in an interpretation is, ideally, collaborative: the interpretation rests on what the client has brought into the conversation, and its appropriateness is determined by a client's willingness and ability to accept and incorporate it. An interpretation, or a meaningful allusive intervention of any kind, is a gift shared by both participants. The client gives the therapist the materials with which to work; the very supplying of these is an invitation to the therapist to enter the client's privacy and even be dangerously intrusive: it is a statement of trust and hope. The therapist takes the raw materials and fashions from them something that tells the client, "I understand. This is my understanding. Now you understand." The therapist enables the client to make sense. The client enables the therapist to make sense.

By this mutual construction, the therapeutic pair accomplish a number of things. The client "tries on" a new role and a new way of reacting in the world: perhaps for the first time, he or she sees that trusting can bring rewards; that trust can be repaid by trustworthiness; and that, at least sometimes, being open can lead to insight, which need not be as painful as feared. Further, the client sees himself or herself as making sense: what was hidden and confused becomes lucid through allusion. And the client, who may have seen himself or herself as plodding and uncreative, sees the possibility of participating in acts of creativity, *as long as there is trust of self and others.* So the therapeutic interchange is real conversation, an interchange between persons; but at the same time, it is a metaphor of or allusion to conversation in the "real world." The dialogue creates a new reality because it represents a new reality. It is the model and the real object at once.

THERAPY AS PRIVATE DISCOURSE

Other special features of the analytic conversation make it both efficacious and susceptible to abuse. Therapy is the most private of all discourse forms. Client and therapist share not only secrets but also multiple realities, neither of which can be part of a client's "public" record. The allusive language developed between the participants remains for them a private, secret language, both because it is normally not shared with others outside the context and because it continues to be used and built upon by both, for the specific purpose of their shared endeavor. The topics discussed are those that are ordinarily confined to intimate discussion: dreams, embarrassments, strange thoughts and feelings. Over time, the participants recognize that they have built up a stock of shared background assumptions, and in time come to allude to them telegraphically and cryptically: "the cigar dream," "the thing when I was six." Things are said by both to each other that would be tolerated only by intimates on the outside: insults, intrusive questions, unreasonable demands. Therapeutic standards and the law recognize the essential privacy of these communications in the doctrine of confidentiality: it is taken for granted that nothing the client says will find its way outside the shared conversation. To some degree, we have that hope for ordinary conversation, but because gossip exists, we recognize the necessity for discretion. In therapy, however, the client has the right to assume that the conversation is entirely private; gossip is anathema. (If one wants to go on believing this, one should not frequent therapists' parties: names are seldom mentioned, but everything else is.) This doctrine has lately been the cause of some distress in the therapeutic community. The transmission of knowledge of both theory and method in the field has long been aided significantly by published case histories. It has always been the practice of their writers to disguise the identities of the clients and relevant others, sometimes by merely changing names, when necessary by changing details of the subjects' lives (occupation, location, ethnic background, and so on). For nearly a century the practice continued without trouble. But in the litigious 1970s several lawsuits were brought, and won, against therapists on the grounds of violation of confidentiality by former clients who, in reading professional journals, had come across case histories that, however distorted, they recognized as their own. Several courts ruled that (even if the disguise was completely opaque to everyone else) if the subject of a case history could recognize himself or herself in it, confidentiality had been violated and damages could be assessed. At present, the therapeutic community is not sure what that ruling means for the future of the case history. In order to create a history that even its subject would not recognize, is it not necessary to distort the facts so severely that what remains is of no theoretical use? And, further, who has the right to someone's history? The question is more complex since that "history" is in part the creation of the therapist. Those not in therapy can see their histories as belonging to themselves alone; but a history that emerges from therapeutic collaboration is a child of both its parents. Should the relationship end, surely both have the right to custody.

Confidentiality is a crucial aspect of therapeutic discourse. It is essential to preserving its privacy and instilling the client's trust in that privacy. It is the most concrete and observable form of the privacy of the discourse, as its violation instantiates and reifies violation of other essential aspects of the genre. At the same time (the two-edged scalpel resurfaces), that confidentiality, essential to the effective working of the discourse, becomes fertile soil for its abuse. If what goes on in therapy is private, to be shared only by those in the consulting room together, surely that requirement is imposed on both parties. Then if something happens that makes the weaker party uneasy, the latter may feel, though incorrectly, forbidden by the rules to bring the issue outside. Confidentiality becomes the protector not of the weaker, but of the stronger, member.

Even as therapy is extraordinarily private, at the same time it is public—more so, at least, than most ordinary conversation. The talk is done in a public place, an office rather than someone's house. Money is exchanged, as is not characteristic of truly intimate discourse; and money makes relationships impersonal, therefore nonprivate. There are formal (that is, nonpersonal) procedures to be followed: setting up appointments, ending according to the clock rather than the flow of interest. And while every private relationship is unique, in therapy the therapist is the same for all clients, sitting in the same chair as different people occupy other seats in the room. In that sense, all clients are interchangeable; and interchangeability is characteristic of formal, non-intimate proceedings. (In other ways, though, the therapist is different for every client, responding to each according to different needs.) Therapeutic discourse at the same time occupies a space between the truly and utterly private discourse of the self, internal, cryptic to outsiders; and the public conversation that requires no explanation. In therapy the client must learn to make that which is opaque and secret intelligible to one other person, at least: a step toward public expression.

RESPONSIBILITY IN THERAPY

There is one final curiosity about therapeutic discourse. Unlike ordinary conversation and most other discourse types (except courtroom discourse), therapy is *about* personal responsibility. In most discourse, participants attribute to themselves and others full responsibility for actions and consciousness of what they were doing and of the likely results of their actions, and the power to decide whether to act. As a result, we feel perfectly free to criticize and blame, openly or not: He should have known better, Why did you do it, I can't believe she said that. But in therapy the client's full consciousness and responsibility are the topics of the discourse and cannot be presupposed.

Clients come into therapy with varying degrees of personal responsibility and consciousness. But all must eventually face a hard question: "How much of *this*—what is bothering me, the problems I face in living—is of my choosing and doing, and how much just happens to me?" It is a truism of therapy that only by accepting responsibility for one's actions, accepting that one *could* and *can* make choices, can one in fact change internal and external reality. But one is in therapy because, at this point anyway, one feels unable to make those changes; one is, therefore, not fully responsible. And it is another truism of the field that clients (or, rather, patients), are *sick:* that is, they bear no more responsibility for their predicament than do people with ulcers. At the same time, a sick person must be seen as having the ability to make a choice not to have that "illness," to do what it takes to get well. If the client were seen as fully responsible, the therapist would often have to see his or her behavior as reprehensible. But the therapist typically does not (unless it is very bad indeed, and sometimes not even then); rather, thoughtless acts and words are the client's unconscious "acting out": the client had no control over that behavior and thus is in therapy. So at any moment in the process a client is, and is not, responsible for his or her thoughts and actions: unpleasant acts are symptoms and, at the same time, reprehensible behavior. The therapist is by definition fully responsible. The therapist who sees the client as fully responsible, or himself or herself as in any way not responsible for the purposes of the therapeutic relationship, is opening the way to abuse, especially sexual abuse. ("The client seduced me" makes this logical error.)

PARADOX IN THERAPY

In discussing therapy as paradoxical, Jay Haley, the noted family therapist, has argued that it is that very aspect of therapy that is change-creating.[11] The client, to understand what is happening in the process, must go outside of and beyond the therapeutic discourse itself, must understand as true both the A and the non-A of therapy (for example, it is real and it is non-real; it is "deadly serious play"), and be able to tolerate the contradiction. The client must learn a new way of experiencing language, must come to tolerate ambiguity and paradox. If one can acquire this ability in the safe realm of the consulting room, one can continue to learn outside it.

The resolution, or understanding, of these dualities is another way in which therapy models successful dealing with the realities of life. In the outside world, too, language and actions are ambiguous. The client is not "crazy" to understand things differently from the powerful people in his or her life: there really are more than one reasonable option (hence, the "historical" truth may shift according to time and person). What the client first confronts, early in therapy, as intolerable contradiction later on turns out to be perfectly reasonable. In the same way, the distortions and misperceptions of reality with which the client entered the process can be re-understood as partial truths, the rest of which one can recapture without danger.

The adoption of "new" language has other effects in the process. Not only do clients learn a new way to communicate, but they are learning as an infant learns, implicitly and by example, rather than the way we learn new languages in school, with explicit grammatical instruction, books, and exercises. Like babies, clients are on their own for much of this: the therapist, like the parent, provides a model and responds to attempts to make sense of the new language, but does not explicitly instruct. Thus, engaging in therapeutic discourse itself necessarily re-creates for the client the situation of childhood, the infantile parent-child bond with all its intimacy and all its mysteries and dangers. Analysts speak of the creation in therapy of the *transference,* the patients' tendency to experience the analytic relationship as they did their relationship with their parents, treating the analyst irrationally (that is, without evidence from the "real" analyst's personality) as if the latter were behaving or thinking like the patient's father or mother. Psychoanalytic theory relates the development of transference to sexual—that is, Oedipal—fantasies. But it makes at least as much sense to account for it through the misperception, dependency, and confusion that often accompany therapy, and are reminiscent of feelings present as part of the major significant activity of early childhood—the implicit learning of a new language. Not fully understanding language, and knowing that the adults in one's context do, can easily create feelings of love, awe, and dependency for those adults, as well as confusion about reality. So when the linguistic state of infancy is recapitulated, in adulthood, in the therapeutic dialogue, it is not at all surprising that a collection of old emotions will accompany that rediscovery.

The new linguistic experience of therapy is not identical to the language learning of the child. The child, after all, has to learn the rules of ordinary conversation, as well as the permissible patterns of sounds, words, and sentences. The adult in therapy already knows those things. In therapy one does tend to learn new vocabulary, but other aspects of the communicative process are more important: transcending the paradox; creating and unraveling allusion; learning new ways to be direct and open, as well as allusive and therefore private. This new language is a key opening the door to competence, just as the original process of learning was. The re-instantiation of the infantile linguistic experience with its dependency, uncertainty, and helplessness is both an essential aspect of therapy and a potent breeding ground of therapeutic abuse.

ABUSIVE COMMUNICATION

While much has been written about abuse in therapy,[12] therapeutic discourse is not intrinsically abusive, nor is it the only kind of interaction that has abusive potential. But it is equally false to claim that therapy is automatically safe for the weaker party. In fact, whenever it is meaningful to speak of a "weaker party"— that is, whenever there is a power imbalance—the potential for abuse is present. In all such cases, consumers sooner or later become aware of the danger; and in time, with lurid exposés in the various media, pressure grows for protection, generally seen as coming from legislation. Legislative bodies are urged to write laws that will allow abuse to be identified unambiguously, prosecuted, and severely punished. Or, professional societies are urged to create or empower groups to judge colleagues who are accused of malpractice and to censure them in appropriate ways if they are found guilty.

These measures are necessary, but at least for psychotherapy, insufficient. Of the blatant abuses of power that are recognizable and punishable, sexual transgression is a clear instance. But that is just the visible and physical worst-case scenario, and is best seen as the end of a continuum of abusive relations. Others are more subtle and less discernible, and thus more dangerous. While sexual abuse, if proven, can be legally punished, these more subtle forms are not illegal— not even, by society's standards, immoral. For our culture like most has for millennia given the stronger the power to undermine the self-confidence of the weaker: men over women, adults over children. If therapists practice mind control, especially male therapists over female clients, who can complain? It's the way it ought to be—isn't it?

The goal of therapy is and must always be the client's autonomy. Any behavior on the therapist's part that undermines that goal, or makes it harder to achieve, is abusive. Any therapeutic discourse that uses the power of one participant to discourage the other from questioning the therapeutic relationship, or larger assumptions in the society that support that relationship, is abusive per se. This abuse occurs purely through the use of language and nowadays typically makes use of vague implications rather than the explicit prescriptions of the bad, old, strict Freudian days. The women's movement has made it impolitic for therapists to berate their female clientele for "penis envy" if they show any tendency to be ambitious or assertive. But that does not mean the concept no longer exists in therapeutic dogma or the average (male or female) therapist's mind. The bias may have mutated to subtler, and all the more dangerous, forms, which make it harder to identify precisely the source of a client's despair.

How is pure discourse abusive ("sticks and stones . . . ," after all)? Sticks and stones are very well in ordinary conversation, but therapeutic discourse is by definition *efficacious:* it is designed to change one's experience of reality; it is an instrument, a surgical tool as Freud put it. If you go to a therapist, and go in sincerity, you put your mind in the hands of an expert, you expect your attitudes to be challenged, you open yourself to new perceptions and the possibility of change. But you also enter the discourse in some disorganization and distress. Your life isn't coming out the way it was supposed to, there are things you feel unable to handle, and you turn to an expert who can tell you what you're doing wrong and how to make changes. If you aren't willing to adopt that stance, the therapy will not be therapy, you cannot make the changes necessary. But if you do make those assumptions, you leave yourself without protection. If your ordinary good sense and garbage detector must be checked at the door (and renamed, for the duration, "defenses" and "resistance"), you cannot properly evaluate a therapist's interventions. Therapeutic comments must often make the client uncomfortable. But how uncomfortable, and about what? There is no way to legislate this, no way to assess a client's discomfort with a therapist's interpretations, to determine whether the latter are a valid exercise in promoting growth, or a pusillanimous attempt to reduce a client to psychic rubble in order to foster the therapist's megalomania. Most often, the form of the words themselves is beside the point: what is relevant is the state of the client's mind when a suggestion is made; the nature of the relationship existing between therapist and client at that time; and, impossible to gauge but most important, what the therapist really has in mind. What is harmless for a client near termination, who already has a great deal of strength and can tell insight from garbage, can be disabling to someone with a more tenuous hold on self-esteem and more dependency on a therapist's approval. Also important are external factors: the genders and sexual preferences of both parties; their levels of education and social class; their relative articulateness.

The potential for psychic abuse (denial of autonomy) in therapy is great, as I have said; and the means to prevent it relatively few. Appeal to legislation is generally futile (and in the best case, would only redress wrongs, rather than prevent them). The only hope, here as elsewhere when language has potential for abuse or misuse, is in the education of both therapists and clients.

SOME POSSIBILITIES FOR IMPROVEMENT

This education might take the form of a variant of currently existing therapeutic training: the examination of case histories by well-known older practitioners. In psychotherapy, the case history is the means by which knowledge of theory and technique is indirectly transmitted from one generation to another. It is impossible for therapists to set down precise rules: Do A, then say B, but don't say C. Then the client will do D, and you respond with E. Rather, neophytes read case histories to get a sense of how to be responsive, how to make interventions, how to avoid errors should the temptation arise, and how to recoup if they are nevertheless made. The specifics of the case history are understood as generalizations, attitudes to take, stances to adopt. Freud's several long histories have an honored place in this educational method. They are studied, to the present day, as documents not only of historical interest, but of current theoretical and methodological relevance. Although some minor changes in technique might be suggested today, the basic method remains as illustrated; the basic treatment is considered sound. If the results are unfortunate or ambiguous (which happens to be the case in every one of Freud's published case histories), either the fault is the patient's, or the failure results from some ignorance of "technique" which does not exist today.

The case of Dora illustrates the evils of unilateral interpretability at its worst. Freud makes a series of astonishing deductions about Dora's sexual status, intentions, and desires. At some points in his history, he treats Dora as a sexually innocent child (so it is all right for Freud to use suggestive language to her: since she's innocent, she won't understand it, and it won't do her harm); elsewhere, as we have seen, he attributes to a protectively reared fourteen-year-old the sexual responsiveness of a mature woman. Further, he sees Dora's responsiveness and emotions from one perspective only: whether they are beneficial to the men in her environment, including himself. If the young adolescent recoils in disgust when her father's best friend makes abrupt and unprovoked advances, it cannot be because it disrupts her sense of trust in the adults she knows, or because a response is required of her that she is not mature enough to give, or understand. No: she is neurotically denying the fulfillment that, Freud confidently assumes, would result from the proposed liaison. Likewise she denies Freud for neurotic reasons—not because he functions as the third of a series of betrayers, the ultimate proof that men, especially ones like her father, are villains. Thus, Freud systematically and implicitly denies Dora full personhood: her emotions belong to men; "good" ones are those that make men feel good; "bad" ones are neurotic and have to be cured. That Dora might have needs of her own, for self-realization and autonomy, never insinuated itself into Freud's discussion. The therapeutic process described here is, from beginning to end, abusive in intention and in execution.

That process of abuse is apparent at the level of the explicit verbal interchange itself. Freud claimed to be reporting the dialogue as it actually took place—and made no allowance for the difficulty we all have remembering conversation accurately, especially if it is emotionally loaded. But Freud almost certainly captured its emotional tone with accuracy. Since we might expect Freud to have erred, if at all, by presenting himself as kinder or less biased, we can probably take his account of himself as harsh and biased as a reasonable approximation of his true mental state, which was clearly transmitted to Dora.

Dora responded first by becoming more and more combative; then by leaving the analysis prematurely (by Freud's standards). Ultimately, according to later testimony, she married unhappily and led an unsatisfactory life. We cannot wholly blame Freud for this poor outcome (although he was ready in speculations at the end of the history to take credit for an imagined good one), but it does seem appropriate to suggest that, by serving as the third example that proves the rule, Freud left Dora with a permanent sense that men were not to be trusted; and by ignoring the very real needs of an adolescent girl for self-definition, autonomy, and appropriate identification with strong female figures, he failed to meet the basic needs that brought her into analysis: clear malpractice, at least by our contemporary standards. He failed to see that Dora was a victim of her society and her family, and the masculine bias of both, because he was himself a beneficiary of that system. He used the power that his social position, his gender, and his profession gave him to leave Dora more vulnerable than she had been.

It is clear to most contemporary readers of the case history that Freud abused Dora. What may be less clear is that the same kind of thing could happen today. Perhaps a therapist would hedge; perhaps not. But nothing in modern psychotherapeutic theory precludes anything of what Freud said to, or about, Dora. More recent commentators on the case from within the analytic tradition have, with a few exceptions, been only too happy to endorse Freud's analysis of the failure: yes, Freud didn't understand transference in 1900 (but today we do!); yes, Dora was homosexual (so any man would be doomed to fail with her—it's her fault). But, in fact, the cause of the failure is in the expectations of the powerful participant: that he is, and by right ought to remain, powerful; and that "treatment" should support and reinforce the status quo that caused the patient's distress, rather than overturn it.

CHAPTER FIVE

Life and Language in Court

I N the spring of 1988, I spent a month in Barcelona, lecturing at one of its universities. Among the courses and lectures I gave was one for graduate students on language and the law. The students were well educated and articulate in Spanish, Catalan, and English. Just for orientation, at the start of my first lecture I asked them how a trial in Spain proceeds so as to have a basis for comparison with the American trial courtroom procedure I was about to describe and analyze.

Having taught courses and lectured on the same topic in many places in the United States over the last several years, I was confident of getting some response. Ask any American audience over high-school age how a trial unfolds, and you're sure to get an answer. It may be inaccurate in spots, out of order, or reflect misunderstandings of what the various activities mean, what is permissible and why; but you can count on a summary that has some relationship to what actually happens in a real courtroom.

So I was shocked to encounter a total silence, which grew embarrassed as the seconds lengthened into minutes. I tried various pedagogical devices: OK, what happens first? Who are the participants? Can you think of any language special to courtrooms? Questions that, if needed at all, were guaranteed to evoke a response in Americans. Still nothing. Someone finally said, "We've never been in a courtroom."

I was puzzled at that response. Most Americans have never been in courtrooms, yet have little trouble with the assignment. Why?

Something still stranger now occurred. The students (desperate, no doubt) began to tell me what happened in *American* courtrooms—with almost as much accuracy as I'd gotten from Americans. No one in the room but myself had ever been in an American courtroom, yet they had a pretty good idea of what went on in one. "How do you know that?" I asked.

The mystery was promptly solved. They got their information from the same sources Americans do—movie and television courtroom drama. Americans watch "Perry Mason" reruns and "L. A. Law," deriving their knowledge of courtroom procedure from these and other such sources. And (I had already learned from the TV set in my hotel room) these two programs were shown on Spanish television, dubbed into Spanish, and were favorites with many of my students. Spanish television had begun to produce indigenous versions of many American genres—soap opera, game show, adventure—but there was no Spanish equivalent of American courtroom drama. Hence nobody had the faintest idea what went on in a Spanish courtroom.

It wasn't that courtroom procedures in Spain were totally boring: news programs during the time of my stay talked about restrictions on torture in interrogation and other significant legal developments. But the business of the trial court itself, which is sufficiently fascinating to Americans to spawn an unending series of representations in various media, apparently held no such interest for Spaniards. Why?

The answer lies in the difference between the Spanish and the American legal systems. American trial procedure is *adversarial:* the two sides (prosecution and defense in criminal trials, plaintiff and defense in civil suits) present to a jury their own version of what took place; a judge presides, to make sure nothing patently unfair occurs. Evidence is presented by witnesses, under questioning by the lawyers. At the end, the jury considers the evidence and decides in favor of the side that has made the most persuasive case. It is our belief that (although each side may distort the facts to suit its own case) the truth will emerge out of the confrontation between adversaries, probably reflecting neither side's constructions completely, but one more than the other. The jury of lay persons is assumed to be able (through horse sense and street smarts) to pick through the pyrotechnics and razzle-dazzle on both sides in order to determine who is really in possession of the truth. That the adversarial system, including some version of trial by jury, has been in effect in the English-speaking world since medieval times is a testament to our faith in the sense and incorruptibility of ordinary people.

Most other countries have an *inquisitorial* trial procedure. A panel of professional judges listens to the evidence, presented by a state-appointed attorney, and delivers a ruling based on exposure to this one-sided presentation of evidence. The advantage is that there is no competition to produce the most dazzling show, nor is there a susceptible jury to play to. The disadvantage is that a defendant's side may not be fully represented, and also that the judges (generally older men of middle- or upper-class background, with legal training) lack the understanding of ordinary life (and the skepticism about the workings of the law) that can enable an American jury to show mercy to a defendant when there are extenuating circumstances, and sometimes to vote in favor of ordinary fairness rather than strictly legal justice. Lawyers tend to hew to the letter of the law.

There is one more difference. Adversarial encounters are thrilling; inquisitorial, generally tedious. It takes two sides to make a discussion interesting to an outsider. That's why we have courtroom dramas, but not (in this sense) classroom dramas. The American courtroom *is* intrinsically interesting (at least, if poetic license can be taken and the hours of tedium sheared off): two people are fighting tooth and nail, using every rhetorical device dreamed of by Aristotle, along with all the technical expertise money can buy (slides, videotapes, charts, and graphs have all become standard equipment in the American courtroom). Add the human desire to see justice done and truth revealed, and you have all that is needed for gripping drama. So Americans (and the British, too) are courtroom addicts. But countries with inquisitorial systems have no tradition of courtroom drama. Hence nobody, other than the professionals, knows or much cares what happens inside a Spanish courtroom.

In the late summer of 1984, I was a member of a jury in a capital case, a trial that went on for almost six weeks. As a result of that experience and what I learned in it, I volunteered about a year and a half later to help the defense team in another capital case with jury selection. In California, in capital cases, prospective jurors are questioned individually, a total of about six each day for at least a two-month period. (In chapter 6, I will talk more about jury selection.) In that case, the defendant was found guilty, but the jury hung on the question of penalty; when the case was retried about a year later, I helped to select the new jury. Finally, earlier this year I served as an expert witness in a civil case, a slander suit. So I have seen the courtroom from three active positions, as well as observed trials from the spectators' section.

ORDER IN COURT

There is a fixed order of procedures leading up to and constituting an American criminal trial. First of all, suspects are taken into custody after the commission of crimes. They are read their rights ("mirandized") and interrogated—an interesting procedure in its own right. They are *arraigned*—brought before a judge and formally charged, at which time bail is set. Then there is either an *indictment* handed down by a grand jury or a *preliminary hearing,* a sort of mini-trial in a courtroom; each of these is a way of determining whether there exists enough evidence against the suspect to justify a trial. If so, the defendant is bound over and a trial date set; if not, the suspect is freed.

Most of us think of a trial as consisting in its entirety of the procedure before a judge and a jury. We also think that the major participants first encounter each other as the trial opens with the prosecutor's or the plaintiff's opening arguments. So jurors may be surprised at the testiness with which attorneys and judge seem from their apparent first encounter to be addressing each other: an edge in their voices at this early date—won't they (pant, slaver) be literally at each other's throats before it's over? But in fact, the same parties have usually been in contact with each other since the preliminary hearing; encountering each other in pretrial motions and in the process of jury selection, they have acquired a sense of one another's weaknesses, tactical tricks, and eccentricities.

The opening of the trial proper is the empaneling of a jury. A panel (sometimes called a *venire*) is selected from voter rolls and sometimes other records. Many more people are empaneled than the twelve plus alternates (for a criminal trial) who will eventually be needed. The judge is allowed to *challenge for cause* any panelists who show themselves in the questioning (*voir dire*) to be biased or to have too much (read: any) knowledge of the case, or who otherwise might be unable to reach a fair verdict. The judge can disqualify any number of jurors for cause. Then each attorney is allowed a certain number of *peremptory challenges:* the ability to dismiss a prospective juror without giving any reason at all, sometimes because the lawyer believes the juror to be biased, but can't convince the judge; sometimes based on the belief that a juror with certain demographic or personal characteristics is bad for one side or the other (thus, defense attorneys tend not to like political conservatives; on rape cases, they tend not to like women; prosecutors prefer older people to younger, in general).

The courtroom phase of a trial opens with the prosecutor's or the plaintiff's opening statement, which may be of any length and is not (the judge informs the jury) under oath. It is intended as an organizing summary, helping the jury to fit together and make sense of the testimony they will hear from witnesses (and, hopefully, to put them in the right frame of mind for it). After this, the defense may make its opening statement or, more often, elect to put that off until the prosecution/plaintiff's case is completed. Lawyers first question their own witnesses (who have been sworn to tell the truth) in the *direct examination.* Then the attorney on the other side may *cross-examine,* with the aim of showing inconsistencies in a witness's courtroom testimony; inconsistencies between a witness's courtroom testimony and what has been said at a deposition, as shown on a transcript; or inconsistencies with the testimony of other witnesses. The lawyer can also suggest that the testimony is self-serving in one way or another, or is simply not the way things could have happened. Cross-examination is the heart of the adversarial method. The jury has been enjoined by the judge to watch closely the witness's demeanor, to see how reliable the testimony is. (The jury is not, however, told what aspects of demeanor are to be considered meaningful; this judgment is supposed to be part of ordinary people's common sense.) There may be a *redirect* examination by the witness's lawyer, designed to undo any damage done in the cross, and then a *recross*. After the prosecution/plaintiff's case concludes, the defense makes its presentation. Both sides then produce *closing arguments* or *summations*, summing up the testimony, urging one view of it, and asking for a particular verdict. The jury then is instructed, or *charged*, by the judge. The jury is said to be the *trier of fact*, while the judge is the *trier of law:* the jury's job is (strictly speaking) only to determine what actually happened; the judge's, to fit those determinations into the legal code. But for many kinds of crimes, part of the jury's job is determining which specific crime fits the facts as the jurors see them (murder I? murder II? manslaughter?), so they must know the law involved as well. The judge instructs them in this, more or less intelligibly, and also gives them some guidance in deliberation procedure. They go off to the jury room, "a convenient and private place" by California law. Precise details of procedure are up to them. In some states, the foreperson is simply the first juror selected; in most, when the jurors start to deliberate, they select a foreperson by any criteria they wish. With the guidance of the latter, they establish a procedure for deliberating, discuss, vote, and continue till they reach a unanimous verdict (in criminal cases) or ten of twelve (or five of six) in civil cases. The jurors return to the courtroom, and the verdict is read. They are dismissed, let us hope with thanks from the judge. Court is adjourned. In the case of a guilty verdict, some weeks later the judge, having received pre-sentencing reports, sentences the defendant, who is then sent to prison or placed on probation.

That description is the bare bones of the American courtroom exercise. It's hard to see the excitement in these cut-and-dried, legally mandated procedures. But, in fact, despite the appearance that everything about a trial is controlled and codified in advance, there is room for a great deal of experiment and innovation. A trial is, in form, a compromise among its participants and the law. The laws mandate the general format but are vague about specifics. The trial judge determines what evidence will be introduced, what questions can be asked prospective jurors (and what use will be made of the answers), what testimony can be introduced, what objections will be sustained, what instructions will be given jurors, how long jurors may deliberate before a mistrial is declared (that is, the jury is hung), or whether a mistrial can be declared for other reasons, and what sentence will be pronounced. The judge also sets the style for the courtroom: how formal it will be, how much latitude will be allowed each of the participants, what the general "feel" will be for the jury. The lawyers also contribute to the style and mood of things: how contentious each is, how each plays to judge and jury, the quirks and eccentricities of each. So although there is a good deal of prearrangement and stylization, each trial is a drama created as it goes along, and all participants must be on their toes at all times.

The Trial of the Witness

None of the curiosities of the courtroom is fully intelligible without an understanding of its adversarial dynamic, manifest in many ways and covertly present in others. Cross-examination is directly and entirely adversarial. It is assumed that, if someone is put under enough pressure, they will tell the truth, or the truth will emerge despite the teller. Witnesses are warned by the lawyer for whom they are testifying that seemingly harmless questions may be venomous: they are to consider for a moment before making any reply. There are two reasons for this: one, to think things over; two, to give their lawyer a chance to object. (This hesitation makes good sense in the courtroom, but goes against both the witness's and the jury's instincts. The witness is accustomed to the give and take of ordinary conversation, in which quick comebacks mark a desirable spontaneity. Jurors, too, assume that any hesitancy in response masks "something to hide": if the witness isn't trying to conceal something, why not blurt out just what comes to mind?)

Witnesses are warned to answer questions directly and to the point, and to add nothing superfluous, both because extra information may be objected to as "unresponsive" by the cross-examining attorney, thereby arousing the suspicions of the jury or antagonizing the judge; and because any new piece of information may "open the door" to a new round of questioning, allowing questions on topics that the attorney on whose side the witness is testifying wanted to keep from the jury. Ordinary conversation, on the other hand, makes progress and derives much of its pleasure from each participant's carrying the topic a little farther along, adding and embellishing. A witness ought to come across to the jury as a good person, a comfortable person; but many of the ways in which we convey those attitudes in private informal talk are dangerous on the witness stand. Then, too, the cross-examining attorney may resort to tricks designed to entice the witness into a trap—actions that would be considered impolitic and unfair in conversation. The lawyer may repeat a witness's words with ironic intonation or the merest curl of a lip; the witness is naturally nettled but cannot show it. It is a favorite tactic in cross-examination to drive a witness to a show of anger, since a jury is likely to interpret that as an admission of duplicity: if you have nothing to hide, what are you getting so upset about? In conversation, it is unlikely that an interlocutor would engage in such tactics unless he or she were up to something; and then you can turn things around by asking, "What's *that* supposed to mean?" Or even, "What's eating you?" It is difficult for a witness to take control in this way: the lawyer controls the discourse in too many ways. The cross-examiner selects topics, can cut an uncooperative witness off in midsentence, can collude with judge or jury to make the witness look incompetent.

The witness stand is not a place for comfortable conversation. Usually, the giver of information holds power, but a witness does not. A witness cannot control topics or their interpretation and has no say over when the conversation begins and ends. The witness is generally a neophyte in the courtroom; the lawyer, a polished professional. The witness is just one step above the jury; the attorneys are running the show. The lawyer-witness repartee may seem to an outside observer like especially snappy but otherwise normal conversation. But as in therapeutic discourse, its purpose and therefore its rules are different. To the observer, the discourse seems a dyad between lawyer and witness. But in terms of its function in a trial, both are in fact acting together as one participant, the speaker, with the jury as the hearer. Without this understanding, much about the examination procedure would be unintelligible: one partner telling the other, at great length, what the latter already knows. Another difficulty for the witness accustomed to the conventions of ordinary conversation is that testimony is addressed not only to the lawyer; not only to the jury; not only to those present in the courtroom; but, via the court reporter's record, to the public at large, present and future. The court reporter normally makes note only of verbal expression, not back channels such as grunts, nods, or even whispered "Mm-hms." So the witness is admonished to answer aloud and clearly, "Yes" or "No," even though the answer is obviously a foregone conclusion. A witness can feel very stupid (drawing on the assumptions of ordinary conversation) clearly articulating responses that are logically and communicatively unnecessary. For the lawyer, this is old stuff, and lawyers learn how to feel comfortable with it. For the witness, typically in court for the first time—certainly not someone who makes a career of it—the implicit contradictions may be bewildering.

Lawyers say, Never ask a witness a question to which you do not know the answer; you could be unpleasantly surprised.[1] (Sometimes they are surprised despite the admonition, but it improves the odds.) In ordinary conversation, we ask questions *only* when we don't know, and need to know, the answer (aside from rhetorical questions, which these are not). In direct examination, a witness may be asked a question that that witness has answered for that lawyer more than once. This kind of interchange makes no sense by the rules of ordinary conversation. It makes sense only if the intended recipient of the dialogue is the jury. In direct examination, lawyer and witness together create a scenario for the jury's information, a story that fits together as a seamless whole. In cross-examination, they are operating at cross-purposes, the witness trying to preserve the scenario, the lawyer to demolish it. But both are doing so for the jury's edification, not their own.

The Judge

Because the questioning is adversarial, there must be an umpire, a referee, to keep the fight clean and make sure no one's rights are interfered with. That is the judge. The judge plays several courtroom roles, different ones for the various players. For the jury, the "little kids," the judge is the wise parent, on a pedestal, a figure of power, authority, and mystery. What the judge says, goes: the jury sees the judge as nonpartisan, one whose instructions must be the true ones. If one of the lawyers tells the jury about the law, that information could (think the jurors) well be tainted by self-interest. They listen with skepticism. But the judge tells it like it is. So (unless there is patent hanky-panky) juries tend to see judges as embodiments of fairness.

Lawyers have a different perspective. Judges are to them merely lawyers like themselves, in fancier dress and in more comfortable chairs. They know that they have prejudices, so judges must, too: and lawyers who have been practicing in court for any length of time have discovered through their own experience or courthouse scuttlebutt that judges have distinct personalities, quirks, and biases. Judge A goes ballistic at the sight of a beard on a lawyer; B can't tolerate delay; C has a daughter in law school and a soft spot for women lawyers; D believes that anyone charged with a drug-related offense should get the death penalty, sight unseen. As long as these prejudices are not explicitly manifested before the jury, so as to become part of the trial record, they do not constitute grounds for reversal on appeal, so all lawyers can do is learn to work with them or around them. But they all know well that they cannot count on a judge to protect them or their clients from adversarial abuse, though that is one of the judge's major official roles.

FORMALITY

The best protection against the abusive potential of a discourse genre are the rules of the genre themselves. Courtroom discourse is remarkable for its formality and ceremonial character: it is unusually nonspontaneous.[2] These qualities create problems, especially for the nonprofessionals, but they also enable the system to work equitably. Formality and ceremony are anathema to the late-twentieth-century American, as signs of unsociability, stuffiness, probably furtiveness as well. We have taken pains to weed these characteristics out of most of our interactive strategies. We move at once to first-name address; we devise new, "spontaneous" ways of saying hello and goodbye; we try to get our telephone-answering machines to sound like living people rather than disembodied voices on tape. But in the courtroom older ways are preserved. Much of the courtroom is ancient in feeling: the architecture of the courthouse, the dark wood paneling characteristic of courtrooms, exude reverence, or so it is hoped. In Alameda County, California, prospective jurors are warned on the form they receive in the mail that "the courtroom is a formal place: be sure to dress appropriately." Of course, people have different notions of what that means, and show up in everything from Imelda Marcos-style cocktail dresses to *clean* blue jeans and T-shirts.

Dress and architecture are visible signs of formality. The discourse itself incorporates many more. The notion of formality as the nonrecognition of the individual and the personal accords well with the overarching mission of the courtroom: blind justice, dispensed to each according to one general universal standard, unrelated to who one is or how one behaves. To this end, participants lose much of their individual identity on their appearance in a courtroom.

The address terms of the courtroom signal that something special is going on. Although Americans usually go by first names these days, sometimes when we do not anticipate much direct contact, we revert to the greater formality of title plus last name. First names are informal: they distinguish each of us as individuals (however common those names may be). A last name identifies someone as a member of a group: "Mary Jones" is a particular individual, the "Mary" of all the "Joneses"; but "Mr. Smith" is merely one of the male Smiths. Titles used alone are the most formal of all: they identify individuals purely in terms of their positions, interchangeable with all others in the same position. Numbers have the same meaning, and in an informality-worshiping culture nobody wants to be "a number." But in the courtroom, titles are the norm. The judge is "Your Honor," "the Court," or a bit less formally, "Judge"—never (during official proceedings) "Judge Smith." Lawyers are addressed and referred to as "Counsel"; witnesses as "the witness." Jurors become "Juror Number One," and so forth, depending on the seat to which they are assigned.

The avoidance of individual personal reference creates social distance. Everything about everyone but their courtroom function becomes a mystery, a cipher. The less you know about your adversary, the less you can use against him or her. In a perilous situation, one must keep one's distance, and the rules of the courtroom guarantee that one will. At the same time, the existence of such rules reminds participants that they are in an adversarial setting: otherwise, why bother with formalities? So these oddities both arise out of the adversarial nature of the discourse and protect participants against abuse.

There are other formalities as well: the formulaic utterances scattered through trial procedures. One addresses a judge with, "May it please the court," rather than, "Judge, I'd like to . . .";, or requests permission to place matter in evidence: "At this time I would ask that this be marked as People's Exhibit C," meaning, "Let's mark this as People's C."

Among physical formalities, there is no touching between parties in a courtroom. To ensure distance, physical boundaries separate each of the parties: the witness stand, often closed off in front; the jury box; the judge's bench, not only separate but raised; and the long table or tables behind which the adversaries sit. The courtroom is large, its spaciousness keeping everyone symbolically distant even as it suggests the grandeur and significance of their transactions.

Courtroom Ceremony

The rituals or ceremonials of the courtroom also have multiple significance. These include much repetitive language, utterances reeled off in a monotone until they become no more than a chant, an incantation: the bailiff's opening of each session ("Remain seated, come to order, Department——is now in session"); the judge's opening remarks to the effect that this is the case of——, all jurors are present and seated; the swearing in of witnesses (though this has other functions as well); the swearing in of the jury as they are first empaneled, then after they have been selected, and before they deliberate; the judge's warnings to the jury, as they are dismissed after each session, not to discuss the case among themselves or with others, not to read newspapers or watch TV news reports about the case, and so on. Although each of these utterances does contain a bit of informative content, after several repetitions anything ceases to be informative. Indeed, its semantic emptiness and monotonous pronunciation signify that this language is not intended to inform: it is merely language for its own sake, form become content. It has become a formula, an incantation by whose very utterance something magically comes into being. These forms are cousins to "Abracadabra" and "Hocus-pocus," as well as the litanies of the church and the schoolroom pledge of allegiance. They create a sense of group solidarity for all those who hear them and signify that all are bound together as participants in a ceremony. Additionally, they function as definers of circumstances. They demarcate the courtroom (like the church or the school) as a special place. Just as marble steps lead to the courthouse, setting it off from the daily life of street and home outside, so the bailiff's opening incantation makes every hearer a part of the world of the courtroom, sealed off from the reality outside, subject to special rules and special ways of thinking and acting. The judge dons voluminous black robes and sits at a raised bench on a raised dais. (At one trial, a juror, having seen the judge in mufti at lunch, remarked that he seemed smaller out of his robes.) The closing rituals at the end of each session again seal the courtroom off from the world into which participants will shortly emerge: there is to be no contamination between the two. And just as jurors must learn that in the courtroom ordinary concepts like truth and justice have special signification, they must also learn that words familiar in one sense from ordinary life, like *malice* or *negligence*, must be understood here in a different and special way. Reformers have argued that the cryptic, archaic language of courtrooms disempowers nonprofessionals, making jurors feel uneasy and incompetent. To a degree that argument is true. But let us not be too quick to abolish ceremony and formality, since we *want* the courtroom to be hallowed, to be set aside; we want everyone who enters to know that by that entrance they are transformed. Courtroom formality and ceremony are among the last magical rites in our world, and we may need those bits of magic more than we know.

Nonreciprocity in Court

The nonreciprocity of courtroom discourse also contributes to the courtroom's mystique as well as to its difficulties. Courtroom discourse is nonreciprocal not only in terms of the particular speech acts permitted of each participant and the possible ways in which each can be understood, but also because parts of a trial are closed to each participant: no one person sees it all, nor does all the relevant discourse make its way into the trial transcript. No one has a complete record.

At the level of superficial observation, each participant is restricted to certain kinds of speech acts or interpretations thereof. The jury throughout the trial proper has no speaking role. Occasional judges allow jurors to ask questions, usually by passing them to the bailiff in written form after a session; the judge decides whether to answer them or not, usually not. The judge is officially restricted to evaluative statements: sustaining or overruling lawyers' objections, some clarifying of testimony, as well as giving explanations to the jury. (Judges occasionally take over the questioning of witnesses when lawyers seem unable to do it right.) Lawyers may ask questions but may not give witnesses information via declarative statements (if they do, their opposite number is likely to object that "counsel is testifying"). Witnesses, on the other hand, may only answer, not ask, questions and must answer "responsively"—that is, directly to the point. There is considerable latitude for interpretation, though. A lawyer may preface a question with a statement that clarifies it or places it in context; a witness may ask a question to ascertain what the lawyer meant. And judges generally allow some digression, especially if a lawyer can explain the purpose of the anomaly.

The most interesting form courtroom nonreciprocity takes is the secrecy of parts of a trial to one or another participant. Imagine a three-person conversation in which, most of the time, all three are involved, hearing or speaking. But every so often one of the three is obliged to leave the room. The other two carry on the talk without the third, who sooner or later rejoins them. But the third party is not allowed to ask what the others have been talking about; and if he or she should somehow discover it, the conversation as a whole is seriously jeopardized and may well come to an abrupt and unsuccessful end. Additionally, what goes on with only two parties present remains official business, for which all parties are in some way responsible. So there are important pieces of the whole conversation that only two parties know about, and the identity of the two shifts: no one knows everything.

Add to this the fact that the conversation is not ordinary small talk. Its outcome seriously affects the reality of at least one person; and the manner in which the conversation unfolds largely determines the outcome. It helps to some degree that an official written record is being kept of the transaction. Some of the "missing" pieces appear in the record, but others do not: they are in the memory only of those present; and under most circumstances, the others do not have the right, or the means, to compel the forgetful to activate their memories.

It is always this way in a trial, as required by law. The gaps are necessary to protect the fairness of the trial, to make sure that the jury is neither exposed to prejudicial material nor subject to tampering by any of the others. Hence, jury deliberations are always closed to everyone else, including the judge (no one is to be able to influence the jury). If the jury requests evidence or other material from the trial as they deliberate, most often (even if the material could be supplied in writing) they will be summoned back into the courtroom along with everyone else, and the requested testimony will be read orally by the court reporter in open court. The jury room is closed to everyone but the jurors (except the alternates) throughout the trial, and it is forbidden for anyone else to have any contact with jurors for the duration. Yet lawyers know that their success is in the jury's hands, and have a powerful curiosity about what is going on in the minds of individual jurors as well as the jury as a body. The judge, too, has an active interest in what the jury is thinking, but no way of finding out. It is not unheard of for judge and both attorneys to make bets, shortly before or during deliberations, on the eventual verdict. I mean money bets.

Even more is off limits to jurors. They normally aren't aware of some of the restrictions: they occur before the beginning of the session or after it. But sometimes jurors are dismissed from the courtroom on a motion from one of the attorneys (an "offer of proof" to the judge, for instance). Or there is a "sidebar conference" in which attorneys converge at the bench to debate a point of evidence or procedure in stage whispers, just out of the jury's hearing. These bits are tantalizing to jurors: it's always that way if you know there is a secret that is relevant to your work, but you cannot uncover it. The matter might be tedious in the extreme; but the jurors, straining from the sidelines to catch a syllable, are convinced that what is being argued over is *the* single piece of testimony most germane to their verdict. They don't know why it's being kept from them (they are the triers of fact, right? Well, this is a fact) and they resent it.

During a trial, everyone is watching everyone else with wide-eyed wonderment. The jurors look to the judge for cues of all kinds. How should they behave? What should they believe? They scan the judge's countenance, observing nonverbal signals, to see what their model thinks about witnesses and counsel.[3] As is typical of the powerless (and jurors do feel powerless during the trial, although in fact they will ultimately have great power), they overinterpret the powerful: everything the judge does or doesn't do is given meaning, which they will mull over in private or with one another in the jury room. They wonder about the lawyers,[4] their imaginations honed by years of "Perry Mason." They were going at each other fast and furious this morning. Do they really hate each other so much, or is it an act? After the session, or after the trial, do they go out for drinks together? If the lawyers are of different genders, the speculation gets more heated still.

The lawyers return the favor with interest. They scan the jurors individually and as a body.[5] Both lawyers and judges have all sorts of elaborate theories about what kinds of jurors are "good" for particular kinds of cases and the degree to which particular panelists represent desirable options. There are "good" juries and "bad" ones. Was Juror Number Three sleeping during my opening statement, or just bored and uninvolved? Did Number Five wink at me? Wants to sleep with me, I bet. Have her in my pocket. Did Number Four smile at Number Eight, seated behind him? Are they forming an alliance, and if so, who is the more persuasive one and what does that mean? Number Six is always dressed fashionably and carries a Gucci attaché case. Foreman material? Pay special attention to him.

Of course, the jurors scrutinize the witnesses: they're supposed to.[6] They also keenly observe the defendant seated at the table beside one or more attorneys. What was in the defendant's face as the survivor testified: remorse, defiance, apathy? Why was the defendant smiling during the pathologist's report? All this figures in the deliberation and the verdict.

So the trial court is a place of furtive curiosity, mostly unsatisfiable, and as such leads to the growth of speculation and superstition, as is common when people feel their destiny is in the hands of others, over whom they have no direct control. That the superstitions are only occasionally borne out has as little effect in the courtroom as anywhere else in life.

Power in Court

The uncertainty should not obscure the amount of power that is at stake—but just who has it, how much of it, and when are much less clear. In most forms of discourse, whoever comes in with power leaves with it. In therapy, it is true, the balance of power between therapist and client is somewhat evened out by the time of termination, at least ideally. But it is clear at most points who has the power, and it does not switch wildly back and forth (which would be chaotic).

In the courtroom, the assignment of power is ambiguous, unresolved, or simply confusing—at least to outsiders. Most confusing perhaps is that possession of power is not connected to possession of the floor: quite the opposite. Participants can be divided into two groups: those who do a lot of the talking and topic selecting, and those who don't; and two more groups, the powerful and the nonpowerful. Using the rules of ordinary conversation and the classroom, jurors and other outsiders naturally assume that the talkers and the powerful are one group, and likewise the nontalkers and the nonpowerful. Not in the courtroom. The lawyers, who do the talking (by themselves and through witnesses), have the least power, being the ones who need things from the others: from the jury, a favorable verdict; from the judge, favorable rulings; from witnesses, useful responses. To attain these ends, lawyers must fawn, flatter, flirt, and cajole—the traditional tactics of the underdog. And like traditional underdogs, they resent their masters. After hours, secure in their lairs, they grumble about the stupidity of jurors, the venality of judges, the unpredictability of witnesses, the personal quirks of all and how to use them. Lawyers can manipulate, but cannot coerce; they cannot act on their own. Manipulation is the strategy of the powerless.

Judges look powerful enough, from the vantage of the counsel table and the jury box. They sit on high, enrobed; and their word is law. They can compel others to talk and to be silent. They can start and stop proceedings at will. They have the power of authority and knowledge: they *are* the law. Unlike lawyers, they are seen at least by juries as untainted by personal interest, so what they say has weight. Yet judges' powers (unbeknownst to outsiders) are not absolute. They have calendars to keep. In some jurisdictions, judges get a monthly "report card" detailing how many cases they have brought to a conclusion; and reappointment or re-election may hang on this record. As a result, judges tend to get testy at delays: if a juror is late, if a lawyer requests a postponement to track down a witness, if a witness seems to be going on too long. "Order in court" more and more comes to mean, "Let's keep it moving." Judges also have to worry about antagonizing the lawyers, although jurors don't see this. Annoy the prosecutor, and a judge gets a reputation as "soft on crime," the kiss of death for election or reappointment; annoy the defense, and they run the risk of a "reversible error" ruling by a higher court, which looks bad on their record. So although judges look like absolute monarchs in the context of the courtroom, in a wider perspective they turn out to be as constrained as the others.

Even in the courtroom, the judge does not have real power if power means deciding what the discourse is about. Courtroom discourse is about truth and justice, or at least innocence and guilt. The judge can (more or less subtly) influence proceedings in favor of one verdict, but cannot produce that finding. The judge can sentence, thereby mitigating an overly severe verdict, or strengthening one that seems too lenient; but the verdict still is the basis for the sentence.

The real power in the courtroom belongs to the jury, the silent party to the courtroom conversation. Not only is the jury silent, but it is also an outsider uneducated in the law, all of which would normally ensure powerlessness. It is extraordinary when you think of it that we are willing to entrust such a responsibility—even including life and death—to a group of people who are, after all, only *us*. Sometimes the jury rises to the task; sometimes it does not. But what a monumental responsibility to place on ordinary people with no special training, this temporary mantle of nearly absolute power over another person's life and liberty! This is one of the glories of our judicial system. No single participant possesses all the power and the perquisites of power. The jury is truly closer in spirit to the defendant than a judge would be: both are inarticulate nonprofessionals in the courtroom. In a system in which verdicts were rendered by a panel of professional judges, the defense would lose that little edge which is so important in our system.

Both sides have their edges, though the balance is, as it should be, slightly in favor of the defendant. The prosecution starts with a big advantage: it represents the community which is also represented by the jury; society, the decent people, *us*. The prosecutor is protecting *us* from people like the defendant—*them*, who frighten us and make life dangerous and unpleasant. But the defense represents another aspect of *us*: the people who can be victimized by the powerful, who need to have their day in court, who are human and err but perhaps can receive understanding, even forgiveness. The defense is also given advantages by our laws and trial procedures. It has advantages in discovery: it has access to all evidence acquired by the prosecution, which does not have equal access to defense material. The burden of proof ("innocent until proven guilty") rests on the prosecution. And guilt must be determined by the jury "beyond a reasonable doubt." In the presentation of evidence, both sides have advantages. The prosecution normally goes first: it gets to write first on the *tabula rasa* that is the jury. But the defense goes last, and so is able to undo the damage done by the prosecution and leave its message in the jury's mind as it goes out to deliberate.

The Public Nature of Courtroom Discourse

The different understandings and manifestations of power and reciprocity in courtroom discourse are not the only ways in which it is special. Above all else, courtroom dialogue is public, both literally and symbolically—a fact that both requires special forms and uses of language and gives special meaning to otherwise ordinary uses. As psychotherapy is the most private, so the discourse of the courtroom is the most public of all oral types. To be public is to be intelligible to any member of a society: no secrets, no special understandings, no hidden codes. Everything must be spelled out so that everyone can be sure of deriving the same understanding from it: there must be no ambiguities. Justice is contingent on openness, including total accessibility: no secret deals behind closed doors. And the law must be seen as applying to, and accessible to, all in its domain: the language must be understandable to all. These are ideals rather than realities, but they explain much about the oddities of the language encountered in court.

Sociolinguists distinguish discourse intended for public use, *elaborated code*, from the way people speak in private to intimates, *restricted code.*[7] In public, speaking to strangers or distant acquaintances, we cannot draw on shared common experience to clarify vagueness or ambiguity. At all levels of language, in elaborated code discourse, things are spelled out: precise pronunciation, specifically referential words, complex syntax. In restricted code communication, we can count on other participants to catch on quickly, and we are more telegraphic and less careful. We trust the other participant, both to understand the language and to understand us.

Elaborated code not only heightens the intelligibility of public discourse but, secondarily, also signals non-intimacy and all that goes with it. We use elaborated code in private talk in this symbolic way: when we get angry, we enunciate more carefully, we refer to the breakdown of trust ("Read my lips!"). In other circumstances, the use of elaborated code signifies, "This proceeding is public; be on your best behavior. Don't trust anyone: they're not one of you." Restricted code has the opposite symbolic significance. Thus the language of the therapeutic consulting room, as highly restricted, signifies, "We are intimate. You can trust me." And the language of the courtroom, hyperelaborated, warns all participants, "This is public talk. Don't trust anyone here." But even as that hyperelaboration plays a useful role in signaling participants how to behave properly, it can also be confusing to neophytes because elaborated code performs diverse functions.

A hearer is often struck by the overexplicitness of testimony, by normal standards. Normally, that is, we are accustomed to some degree of restricted code in our communication. Ordinarily we attribute overexplicitness to irritation: "Do I have to spell it out for you?" In testimony, things are often spelled out. "Did there come a time when you came to know the defendant, Mr. X, in a capacity other than the one to which you have previously testified?" is translatable into English as, "Did you get to know him in a different way than you said?" Or, "Please tell the jury what you observed on the night of July 24, 1985," is equivalent to, "What happened that night?"

There are other ways in which courtroom procedure is maximally public. A public record (the trial transcript) is available to anyone who requests it (and can pay for it). All aspects of the trial that take place in open court are open to the public, except in extraordinary circumstances: spectators can be present even for sequestered jury selection in capital cases, where other prospective members of the jury are barred.

While court is officially in session, everything is public, formal, and relatively nonspontaneous. The rules of order are fixed; one speaks only when permitted and says only what is permissible. But public formality does not descend on the courtroom all at once. At the start of a session, people begin to trickle in: the bailiffs and the court clerk tend to be there from the start, since it's their job to keep things going. The lawyers mosey in more or less when things are supposed to begin. At this point there is often a lot of informality and camaraderie among those present. They may smoke; they converse with one another, telling jokes that are not for the ears of the others (ribald remarks about the defendant's sexual proclivities are not off limits); they wander around the courtroom chatting with spectators. The defendant is brought in, and things get more sedate; the court reporter usually arrives about now. The judge enters, sometimes not yet robed and sometimes smoking (which never is done on the bench, or in robes); the joking continues, with the judge taking part. When the judge is finally robed and on the bench, the jury is brought in, and court is now really in session. The jury must see only order. The jury is the last to enter and the first to leave the courtroom, which the jurors always do *en masse* from or to the jury room. The message conveyed to all present is that the jury creates the trial.

Because we are attuned to the underexplicitness of restricted code, the hyperexplicit language of the courtroom is marked for us; we expect it to have special meaning. Since in fact it does not (other than, "we are in a courtroom, which is a public place"), the language devised for clarity may instead create confusion. As soon as jurors catch on that the elaborated code marks the specialness of the courtroom symbolically as well as providing literal full public access, everything will be well. But jurors are on their own: nobody warns them about this, and it may take them a while to realize what's going on.

The laws themselves are typically written in highly elaborated (in all senses) language, justified as preventing ambiguities. Yet statutes themselves are notoriously vague or ambiguous. Were this not so, appeals courts would have little work to do. And laws *must* be ambiguous to some degree, since their framers cannot possibly imagine all the cases to which they will, in the future, be applicable. Sometimes, though, the fuzziness of codifications makes trouble for trial courts, both the judges who must interpret the laws for juries, and the latter, who must determine their provenance. It sometimes seems, too, that the more important a law's content, the more elusive its intent.

Ambiguity in High Places

Death penalty legislation is notorious for its lack of clarity. A 1972 decision of the United States Supreme Court requires that a jury in a capital case operate with "guided discretion."[8] It says no more. Trial and appeals court judges have agonized over what the Court intended since 1972. What the ruling means is simple enough: in deciding between life and death, a jury cannot at any point in its deliberations be forced to choose death; it must have "discretion." But it cannot choose one option over the other on capricious grounds: the choice must be "guided." At what point and in what way can "guidance" be given? Is there a point at which "discretion" ends? In California, juries are told that they must "weigh" mitigating and aggravating factors in making their decision. Mitigating factors can be pretty much anything jurors want them to be. They are given a list of some twelve possible aggravating factors by the judge, and cannot use others. If they find mitigation to "outweigh" aggravation, or both to be equal, they must choose life. But if aggravation outweighs mitigation, there is uncertainty, at least at this writing. The original California statute specified that in this case the jury "shall" impose the death penalty.[9] When cases in which this wording had been the basis of instructions given to juries were appealed to the state supreme court, the argument was made that the use of "shall" mandated a choice of death and thus violated the U.S. Supreme Court's requirement of "discretion." The state court's ruling did not help significantly: it ruled that as long as "shall" was taken to mean "must necessarily," it was in violation, but that "shall" could be taken to mean "may" and therefore was legitimate.[10] Juries could be given the "shall" instruction in the expectation that they would (or could) interpret it as "may." The ruling was enough to make linguists blanch. We have had, heaven knows, plenty of trouble determining the meaning of modal auxiliaries. To be told that "shall" could mean "may" didn't help matters at all. Of course, it was "just semantics," as lawyers like to say. But here semantics might be the difference between life and death.

Nor is the deliberate ambiguity of jury instructions restricted to capital cases. All criminal juries are instructed that, to return a guilty verdict, they must find the defendant guilty "beyond a reasonable doubt." Judges frequently amplify this injunction by defining the phrase as "to a moral certainty," adding that 100-percent intellectual certainty is impossible. Within the last several years, there has been considerable discussion of these terms in California jurisprudential circles. The conclusion reached is that, while the terms are vague, they ought to be: jurors must be left with some freedom for individual decision. That is all very well, except that, in the real courtroom, the instruction emanates from robed authority along with many explicit, precise, and concrete definitions of legal terms. This may convince jurors that there *is* a concrete and specific understanding of "reasonable doubt," and they may experience frustration trying to find it. Frustration and confusion seldom lead to good verdicts.

The Logic of Legal Language

Courtroom discourse has a logic of its own, but not necessarily in the sense that philosophers might use the term. Legal language is intended for clarity, but that aim often renders it peculiarly opaque. It is a language devised for and by professionals, but its most important users, the jurors, are amateurs. It is public discourse in which important matters are kept private. It is adversarial, and yet requires a high degree of cooperation to make it work. It is, above all, charged with power and political implications: public language with, ultimately, highly personal consequences.

Aside from its interactive (that is, pragmatic) peculiarities, courtroom discourse is semantically unusual in several respects. Lawyers, when forced to defend the intricacies of their professional language, argue that it is designed for "logic" and general intelligibility. To that end, it is intended to be concrete and literal. Literalness makes sense in an elaborated code discourse genre: allusion implies a sharing among participants of cultural and psychological context, so that everyone can figure out that a metaphor is appropriate, and what it is intended to signify. (This is one reason we often find the poetry of different cultures almost incomprehensible, or at least we have to work especially hard to derive their meaning.) The law deals in concrete reality, we are told: very seldom does it involve itself in psychological abstractions like intention. Guilt is *having done it,* where *it* is something known by everyone to be wrong. There is little room for partialities: an action is a crime, or not; someone does it, or not; it was intentional, or not. The jury's process is seen as an all-or-nothing decision. The defendant is guilty or innocent, not sort of guilty.

This picture is not strictly true. For some actions a jury can reach intermediate judgments. For instance, if it is determined that the defendant has killed the victim, the jury still has to decide what official name to put on that act: murder I, murder II, manslaughter (voluntary or involuntary), self-defense. In theory and according to the judge's instructions, each of these is unambiguous in its representation of the defendant's state of mind: premeditated or not (murder I versus murder II), intended or not (murder versus manslaughter). Technically the jury is given no space for what may, in fact, represent the truth: the defendant sort of had it in mind to kill the victim, but also wasn't really thinking clearly, kind of intended, but not with the full force of his or her intellect. The law does not, strictly speaking, permit such a verdict. But the triers of fact sometimes can arrive at a truer understanding of reality than the law allows. They cut through the logical requirements for dichotomization by crafting among themselves a compromise that splits the differences among them. For instance, in a homicide case, suppose five of the jurors believe the defendant intended to kill the victim (murder I); four think that, while he did it, he did it purely by accident (involuntary manslaughter); three are confused. After some hours of debate, the jurors realize that they will never get out with a verdict totally satisfactory to everyone, and if things go on this way they will hang, which will dissatisfy them and infuriate the judge (whom they want to please). So they compromise, going for the middle. Though no one actually believes that the defendant, while not intending to kill, did intend to commit bodily harm (which would make it voluntary manslaughter), they decide on voluntary manslaughter as a verdict, thereby informally expressing the idea that reality is much more complex than the dichotomous procedures the law demands.

But the laws themselves often sneak nonlogic into the courtroom in hidden form—a most dangerous way to get things done, because people are unaware that language has slipped from literal to figurative. One particularly troublesome instance is in death penalty jury instructions, in which the jury is told to "weigh" the evidence presented in mitigation against that presented in aggravation to decide life or death. Now, in the literal world, "weight" is a property of physical objects: ideas have no "weight," although figuratively we have no trouble attributing it to them. (We even talk of "heavy" ideas in the vernacular.) As long as we are dealing in allusion and metaphysics, we have no trouble with "weighty" notions. But what happens when jurors are told to "weigh" one set of findings against another, and on that basis emerge with a concrete reality: a man's life or death? That is literal, very literal, and jurors often feel that, in order to reach a decision with such stark consequences, they want concrete physical objects to "weigh," they want actual "poundage." The image of the scale occurs throughout the justice system, but here jurors want to know what to put in each of the baskets. From a discourse in which everything was (presumed to be) precise, literal, and concrete, they are suddenly thrust into one that is highly allusive, and are asked to make a decision with concrete consequences on the basis of allusive instructions. It's a bit like trying to choose a wine on the basis of wine writing like the following typical example: "Merlot is less lean, hard and angular than cabernet sauvignon, fuller-bodied in flavor than pinot noir, and more dimensional than zinfandel."[11] But where such flights of fancy may lend depths to the oenological experience, the analogous sort of metaphor mixing can only befuddle in jury instructions.

The danger is not in the normal literalness of the law, or in any particular use of figurative language, but in the mixing of the two without warning, in instructions given to amateurs who already have difficulty figuring out what's going on. Jurors generally do make sense of the metaphor, somehow: but it's not clear that instructions like this follow the Supreme Court's requirement of *guided* discretion.

It is not uncommon for the trial discourse itself to swing giddily between the literal and the metaphorical, leaving the jury to translate as it may. At least sometimes these mixtures are created deliberately to confuse a jury. For instance, in the capital murder case I discuss in the next chapter, *People* v. *Delgado*,[12] the defendant was a Vietnam veteran, and a principal argument in mitigation was "post-traumatic stress disorder" (PTSD)—that is, psychological deterioration and bizarre behavior due to the war experience. Early in the trial, one prosecution witness described a car ride with the defendant in which the latter, two months prior to the murder, described how he would go about it. The witness reported on the stand, "I said to him, 'Are you crazy? Do you know how much time you'd have to do?' " In his cross-examination the defense attorney picked up the remark: "Crazy? You said 'Crazy'?" And got the witness to reiterate the word several times. In the redirect, the prosecutor brought out the point that, in ordinary language, we don't use *crazy* to mean literally "insane." But the possibility of confusion was being dangled before the jury.

The defense strategy was an attempt to mix literal and metaphorical discourse, ordinary language and legal/medical technicality. *Crazy* is a term of colloquial English, with no technical usage in either law or psychiatry. In the vernacular, we frequently use it figuratively to mean something like, "acting foolish." *Insane* shares all the senses of *crazy* in ordinary language; but, unlike "crazy," it has a highly precise (more or less) meaning in legal language and no current use in psychiatry. A third term, *mentally ill*, is a precise (well, more or less) term of art in psychiatry but has no such use in the law; it, too, has come into figurative use in ordinary language, though not to the same degree as *insane*.

Everybody knows, even jurors, that someone who is legally insane is not responsible for the crime—"not guilty by reason of insanity" (NGI). The defense was not, *officially*, making a plea of NGI: there were no grounds for that. They did intend to adduce PTSD, but in mitigation of guilt, not exoneration, in the hope that it would save the defendant from the gas chamber, not substitute a mental hospital for prison. But if the defense could somehow sneak over on the jury the proposition that the defendant was "insane," could that perhaps work in favor of a "not guilty" verdict, or at least confuse a few jurors so as to induce the jury to reach a more lenient verdict by way of compromise? The words *crazy* and *insane* were never explicitly linked, but the defense hoped that the jury would fill in the lexical gap. (One reason they might is that otherwise, the attorney's insistence on the word *crazy* had no point, and juries are loath to see any part of trial procedure as pointless: it devalues their contribution.)

The prosecutor didn't miss a step. In redirect, he remarked several times on the imprecise meaning of *crazy* in ordinary language. But, he said, that didn't mean the defendant was "insane," just "wrapped kinda loose" or "not too tightly wrapped." These terms go beyond the colloquialism of *crazy:* they belong to contemporary slang, a part of language that comes into and out of fashion with dizzying speed and is never used by people when they want their ideas and themselves to be taken seriously. By switching from colloquialism to slang, he suggested that the defendant's purported mental problems were trivial, and that the jury was not to take them seriously.

Later in the trial, the lexical minuet took another turn. The defendant had been found guilty of first degree murder with special circumstances, making him eligible for either life imprisonment without possibility of parole, or death. Now the jury had to "weigh" factors in mitigation and aggravation. PTSD was offered by the defense as one of the former. The defense brought in a psychiatrist as expert witness, testifying to the reality and the nature of PTSD. In cross-examination, the prosecutor went at the doctor's discussion of *stress*, as in post-traumatic *stress* disorder. The psychiatrist had gone through a lengthy explanation of how sufficiently high "stress" could, under some conditions, create psychosis (or "mental illness"). The D.A. strode up to the witness stand, brandishing a copy of DSM-III, the American Psychiatric Association's *Diagnostic and Statistical Manual of Mental Disorders,* like an evangelical preacher waving a Bible at an exorcism. "Stress?" he asked in a voice dripping incredulity. "We all have stress. I have stress. Everyone here has stress," and so on. He went on to suggest that, if all of us experienced this "stress" every day and didn't kill anyone, why was the defendant's "stress" so special? Where earlier the defense had been trying to elevate a colloquialism with the meaning of "silly" to the level of "mental illness," now the prosecutor was doing the opposite: lowering "diagnostically significant technical term" to "word of ordinary language and ordinary life."

All this prestidigitation was for the benefit (for lack of a better word) of one group of hearers: the jury. How they responded to this and other rhetorical techniques would turn the trial in one or the other direction. But what was the jury that heard these words near the end of a six-week trial? Its members were not the same twelve individuals who, as much as three months earlier, had walked into the courthouse to begin jury duty; nor were they the group who had been sworn, six weeks earlier, to serve faithfully and well. Something had happened to each of them over that time; and those individual experiences had now come together for all to create that peculiar instrument of American justice—the jury.

CHAPTER SIX

We, the Jury

I N the spring of 1984, I got a notice summoning me to jury duty in Alameda
County Superior Court. I postponed the inevitable until the end of the
academic year, but in mid-July I found myself ascending the steps to the
county courthouse in downtown Oakland and up one floor to the Juror Assembly
Room. It was my first encounter with jury duty. Up to that time, if I thought
about it at all, I had two ideas about the jury system. First, it was the epitome
of the American Way, Democracy in Action. Second, it was a royal pain in the
butt, a waste of time, exposure to the stupid, the venal, the aggravating.

As I was to learn, it is both, and much more. Over the next several months,
the affairs of Alameda County Superior Court were to occupy large chunks of
my time and my interest; to be the focus of passion, despair, and consternation.
Those weeks were to change my life: the way I saw myself and my society; the
work I did and how I did it.

Jury duty, I came to see, could be a trivial exercise in time wasting, or the
most profound encounter most of us have with representative democracy, testing
us to the limit of our abilities. The explicit job of a juror is, with eleven others,
to hear testimony, comprehend the necessary laws, and thereby produce a just
verdict. The implicit work is more subtle and difficult: to understand a new
language; to persuade and be persuaded; to work with others to create and refine
a narrative that may, unlike the stories we spin for one another in our daily
existences, make the difference between life and death. In short, a jury's job
embodies the politics of language in a peculiarly salient way. To avoid being
manipulated, jurors must be able to follow what is happening in the courtroom.
They must be able to construct a cohesive understanding of complex, often
bizarre, textual material. They must be able both to form an opinion and use

language to justify it to their colleagues, and at the same time to work collabora-tively with those colleagues, remaining malleable without knuckling under. They must be articulate, yet reticent; incisive, yet patient; suspicious, yet compas-sionate.

Jury service is glamorized in civics classes as one of an American's highest and proudest duties. But a juror's introduction to the reality is often less auspi-cious. Jurors are at the disposal of the county for ten working days. Some jurors will serve on several juries during the time of their tenure. Others will be empa-neled but never serve. Some may become part of a long-term trial. Some will never see the inside of a courtroom. All will waste a significant amount of time waiting: at home, in the Juror Assembly Room, in a courtroom, or in a jury room. Waiting is not necessarily what jurors do best, but it is what they do most.

The system is geared to the needs and convenience of judges and lawyers. It is never certain just when a case will come to trial, or how many panelists it will require in order to compose a jury, or how long it will take (and therefore, how long before the courtroom allotted to it will be free for the next trial). So the system must always have a crowd of prospects waiting to serve, to make sure that the creature can be fed when it is hungry.

The Alameda County Juror Assembly Room does little to inspire faith in the American way of justice. The clerk at the front begins the first day of service by taking attendance (the first in a long series of infantilizing proce-dures) and follows with an instructive lecture about the privilege of being a juror, including the information that if you happen to forget to come in when called, a bench warrant will be issued for you. Furthermore, don't try to park in this area, nor do we provide parking for jurors. Jury duty is a precious part of American freedom. Don't come late. Don't leave possessions unattended. If you need proof of service for your boss, the form can be had from the clerk. A brief videotape is shown about what jurors do, though not nearly enough to make courtroom business intelligible. In this jurisdiction there is no juror man-ual, although many others have such booklets; I think all should, both in order to help jurors feel competent and to give them a sense that they are being taken seriously.

Television sets are scattered around the room's periphery, simultaneously blaring soap operas, sports, news, whatever. Card tables are on one side; groups of people sit at them playing board games or cards or talking. In the center of the room, folding chairs are set up, room for about one hundred people. At first most are occupied; as the day goes on and panels are called out, the room is depleted. When the room is full, the noise and crowding are oppressive; when it's emptier, it's cavernous and desolate. Some people sitting in the chairs try to work; others bring knitting, novels, or newspapers, or strike up conversations with those seated around them. It seems to happen not infrequently that people know others in the room. You strain to hear if your name is being called for a panel over the din. All in all, there is not much feeling of the vaunted pomp and seriousness of the judiciary in room 101.

JURY SELECTION

Sooner or later you are called (but you must remember that many are called, few are chosen). A panel may be of various sizes, depending on the court's estimate of how many will be needed to compose a jury of twelve, plus alternates. In a case that has received much publicity—or a capital case in which each side has twenty-six peremptory challenges, and about half the panel will be dismissed by the judge for cause—two hundred may be empaneled in all; in a shorter and simpler case, the number is likely to be closer to thirty. The group files into the specified courtroom, taking seats in the spectators' section. The court clerk reads the names: attendance ritual again. (There always seems to be someone missing, but I have never actually seen a bench warrant issued.) The jurors stand and swear, *en masse,* to tell the truth, the whole truth, nothing but the truth in the questioning, the *voir dire.*

The judge reads the assemblage the *information.* This, the finding of the preliminary hearing, is equivalent to an indictment handed down by a grand jury. (The information will be read again at the start of the trial proper.) The defendant and the counsel on both sides are introduced by the judge, and the judge introduces himself or herself and explains a little about the *voir dire* and other pertinent matters.

As I listened, with the eighty or so others comprising my panel, I heard the words "first degree murder with special circumstances." I knew, with a chill running down my spine, that this jury was being selected for a capital case. The twelve chosen would determine whether the defendant now seated at the table before us was to live or die.

In noncapital cases, the court clerk now picks twelve names at random and those named file, in order, into the seats in the jury box. The *voir dire* then proceeds. Typically cause challenges come first: the judge attempts to discover whether any of the panelists are biased or otherwise unable to render a fair verdict. Any last-ditch attempts to get out of jury service are generally given short shrift. People are automatically dismissed if they claim to know any of the participants, and often if they have prior knowledge of the case. People are asked if they have been the victims of crime; if they have, the defense often requests and sometimes gets a dismissal. They are also asked whether they or other family members have committed crimes. (Remember that they are in open court, with other community members present, and also under oath.) A panelist is not permitted to refuse to answer any question. If someone deems a question too embarrassing, the judge may take him or her into chambers (with counsel, defendant, and court reporter) and ask the question "privately." Refusal to answer is grounds for a contempt citation. On occasion, prospects fail to disclose their criminal history, sometimes from years back and very minor. The District Attorney's Office has (as a law enforcement agency) access to police files. If the D.A. feels that such a panelist is undesirable for the prosecution, she or he may bring that history to the attention of the court. The errant panelist will be haled back into court to be questioned again, threatened with contempt, and then dismissed for cause (perjury), thereby saving the prosecution one peremptory challenge, but creating a nightmare for the juror, who may have misunderstood the question or forgotten a long-ago, minor incident.

When the judge has concluded the cause challenges, the lawyers have the right to exercise a given number of *peremptory challenges*—dismissals for no stated reason. These typically are made because lawyers believe that a particular panelist is likely to be biased, but the judge has not been convinced of that: perhaps the claim is based on something the panelist said, but as probably on grounds of race, class, age, gender, occupation or other demographic facts. Attorneys hold all sorts of superstitious beliefs about how different kinds of people behave; and since they don't have a chance to find out much about what panelists are really like, they must go by these hunches. Some attorneys feel that they could do practically as well by taking the first twelve people called, but most, for various reasons, make drastic efforts to psych out the jury.

Depending on the seriousness of the case, each side will get a given number of peremptory challenges. But they normally will not all be used: lawyers are afraid that if they use up all they are entitled to, the other side will have an edge toward the end. Usually a jury will be completed before the panel runs out; but if the latter occurs, a new panel will have to be assembled, with consequent delay (much to the judge's annoyance). Questioning may go in any of several ways, either questions being put to all the jurors at once ("Is there any of you who feels unable to render a fair verdict?") or directed at one member in particular ("Number Four, you say your cousin is a police officer? Do you think that would affect your ability to render a fair verdict in this case?") When one panelist in the jury box is dismissed, the court clerk calls the name of another from the spectators' seats, who takes the seat of the departed juror. Depending on the length of time estimated for the trial, a number of alternates will be selected (one for each week seems to be a rough rule of thumb). They assemble with the jurors each morning, sit outside the jury box, but are exiled to the Juror Assembly Room during deliberations. (The alternates, strictly speaking, are not jurors, and the law says that deliberations are closed to everyone but the jury.) When the full number has been assembled, the remaining panelists are dismissed back to the Juror Assembly Room; the panel members are sworn as a jury, and the judge tells them when the trial is to start, and where they should go (the jury room connected with the particular courtroom).

Death Qualification

That is the normal procedure. In capital cases everything is more convoluted and difficult, and jury selection is no exception. A much larger panel is assembled and sworn in, and the information is read to all. The words "special circumstances" are a giveaway that the death penalty is being sought. The judge then explains the rules. In a capital case in California, each panelist is examined apart from the others, to keep them from influencing one another (a *sequestered voir dire*).[1] Typically seven are questioned each day, so that it takes a good two months to make up a jury. About half are dismissed for cause: reasons for cause challenges include prior knowledge and bias, and also strong views on the death penalty. A panelist is dismissed for cause in case he or she claims total inability to ever impose the death penalty; or claims that, in a case such as this (based on the information), he or she would always vote for death. The former is obviously easier: you don't get into sticky arguments about whether what you don't know yet might influence your decision; and it might also seem difficult to make the claim with the defendant sitting at a table not ten feet from you. Therefore, it used to be the rule that, of those dismissed for cause, two thirds "Witherspooned out": that is, claimed they would never vote for death (based on a 1968 U.S. Supreme Court opinion called *Witherspoon*,[2] which says that a panelist cannot be dismissed for cause merely for having "scruples" against the death penalty, but must totally reject it); and one third "A.D.P. (automatic death penalty) out." But recently the figure has been closer to fifty-fifty. Those who survive the culling are said to be "death-qualified."

My run through the gantlet came about a month after the original empanelment. I took the indicated seat in the jury box and picked up the microphone lying on it. I took a breath and waited to see what would happen. I wondered what all of us—me, lawyers, judge—would find out in the questioning.

I had never given a great deal of thought to the death penalty. I'd had vague opinions but never had to argue for them. In the month since I had found out I was to be in this position, I'd tried to discover what I really thought and why. But my opinions kept dissolving into a murk of "Yes, but's" and "Well, maybe's." A good thing, I thought, that academics seldom got to serve on juries. Well, I'd sit back and let the experts figure out what I thought.

The judge sat on his raised bench, silver-haired, black-robed, and intellectually fierce—a prototype judge. He teased the lawyers unmercifully but was the soul of courtesy to me. He proceeded with the cause qualification: Could I vote, in a case of this kind, to impose the death penalty? I trotted out some of my uncertainties. Society should have progressed beyond simple retributive justice; deterrence was probably a dubious claim; but, on the other hand, there were crimes so hideous as to shred the fabric of society, breach the social contract. To restore faith and trust, did we not require symbolically monstrous countermeasures? Could you, said the judge, vote for death in a case such as this one? I replied that I had never been in such a situation, so I didn't know whether I could. Then, said the judge (I detected a glint in his eyes), you can't say that you couldn't. No, I allowed. I was death-qualified.

After all panelists have been interviewed in this way (normally for about twenty minutes, though it may be much longer or shorter), those who have not been challenged return to the courtroom. They are seated by twelves in the jury box, and the two sides take turns reading out the names of those who are peremptorily challenged: there is no further questioning. If all the panelists currently assembled in the box are acceptable to one of the attorneys, the latter passes. If each side passes in turn, the jury is declared complete. Alternates are then selected in the same way.

I thought for sure that, though I had slipped through the cause challenge, the two sides would fight to be the first to get rid of me via a peremptory challenge. I knew little about the process and the reasoning then; but I could sense that I was not the meat either side should prefer to eat. As I had revealed in my *voir dire,* I was a pure Berkeley liberal and an academic to boot. The prosecutor should dispose of me in seconds. On the other hand, I was upper middle class and a feminist (the crime involved a rape charge) and had acknowledged considerable suspicion of psychiatric expert testimony (which the defense had indicated its intent to use). So the defense should be uneasy with me. To my surprise, neither rushed to get rid of me; and I found myself in due course taking the oath as a juror in *People* v. *Delgado.* [3]

Science Meets Superstition

Lawyers have superstitions about whom they want, and jurors, as well as rejects, have theories about why they were chosen or not. Lawyers like to feel scientific about jury selection; but when dealing with the complexities of the human mind, science is essentially helpless. Lawyers also have all sorts of theories about what is most important in securing a verdict: selection, rhetorical brilliance during a trial, or (heaven forfend!) a strong case. Since nobody knows the answer (and indeed, all trials and all juries are different), they figure it's best to play safe and bring all that science and superstition have to offer to bear on the business of jury selection.

The "science" is largely the work of the field of jury consultation, which has come into being over the last twenty years. It began as a serious calling during the political conspiracy trials of the late 1960s and early 1970s, in which social scientists often volunteered their services to the defense and brought professional techniques to what had been an intuitive enterprise: demographic analysis, interviewing skills, and the construction of personality profiles of prospective jurors played a significant role. (It is also said that astrologers and handwriting analysts were used in some trials, so perhaps the methodology was not as scientific as was claimed.) Many of these trials culminated in verdicts favorable to the defense, or in mistrials, giving rise to the belief that "scientizing" jury-selection procedures could greatly strengthen the odds for the side using them. Later observers have commented that perhaps consulting was oversold: conspiracy is notoriously hard to prove, so that the verdicts might have come out the same way without the help of social science.[4] In any event, it is impossible to provide scientific proof that jury consulting makes a difference, since it is impossible to set up studies with control juries alongside the real ones.

Jury consultants do many things, depending on the time frame, the seriousness of the case, and the money available. They can focus on selection, or on the conduct of the trial, or both, as well as doing postverdict interviews. Their methods, while not illegal, certainly can be intrusive. They cannot interview panelists themselves, but they do sometimes (if they get the juror list enough in advance of selection, as in a capital case) talk to neighbors. They do "drive-bys" to inspect panelists' neighborhoods, see the houses they live in and the cars they drive (to draw demographic conclusions). They advise on what questions to ask in *voir dire* and how to interpret answers, and provide a ten-level scale for evaluating candidates, based on their estimated favorability to the side; persuasiveness to other jurors; likelihood of being foreperson; and other criteria. During a trial they may set up *shadow juries:* groups culled from jury lists but not currently serving on a jury, otherwise matched as closely as possible to the actual jurors. Shadow jurors sit with the spectators every day, and each evening are debriefed by the consultants about how effective presentations were, and how they are leaning. Consultants also provide advice to lawyers and clients on how to dress; how to present themselves; demeanor on the witness stand; the construction of opening and closing arguments; and so on. (One reason lawyers find it useful to hire these expensive experts is that typically they have had virtually no formal education in trial procedure themselves.) After the verdict, consultants interview as many jurors as will speak to them on the telephone, in person, or via written questionnaire, to find out why they voted as they did. Interviews may be a couple of hours long, and respondents are often paid, though nominally.

The idea of jury consultation and scientific selection of jurors may raise the hair on the neck: can the side with the most money buy a verdict? Theoretically, yes. But fortunately there seems to be plenty of evidence that jurors, as human beings, are more complicated than social scientists would like to believe or can handle by their machinations. I said in my *voir dire* that, although I was troubled by the death penalty, I could envision circumstances under which I'd vote for it. In the course of the trial, I came to understand—or rather, to experience from within—the morally corrosive effect of the death penalty on everyone it touches; I saw that its existence is ultimately a far more serious threat to society than the deeds of those upon whom it is imposed. As a result, I concluded by the time of deliberations that I could never under any conditions impose the death penalty. But no one could have known that at the outset. Later when I was helping the defense team select a jury in another capital case, we used the assumptions and methods of jury consultants. In the final jury were three people I was *absolutely sure* could never impose the death penalty, both demographically and intuitively (I liked them, I felt they were compassionate people, their jobs and interests were humanistic, and so on). It took that jury less than two hours of deliberation to reach a death verdict. Even as I was horrified and depressed at that outcome, I was cheered that the richness of human nature had yet again eluded the web of the social scientists.

Who Is Chosen

If jury selection is so scientific these days, why do jurors often seem to represent the lowest common denominator? The answer: because jury selection is so scientific. To understand what motivates a lawyer to throw you out or put you in, you have to understand what a trial lawyer wants in a juror and a jury: someone who will return a favorable verdict. Failing that, they want someone who at least will not be able to persuade other jurors to return an unfavorable verdict. So the ideal is twelve jurors sure to vote for you. However, if such prospects are obvious to one side during *voir dire,* they are equally obvious to the judge and to the other side, and will certainly be dismissed for cause or by a peremptory challenge. Therefore the focus shifts. The worst possible juror is one who is on the other side and able to persuade others to it. So a lawyer uses peremptories not only to get rid of obviously prejudiced people, but also to exclude those whose biases are unknown, but who might be dangerous on the wrong side. Anyone with charisma is a danger: one who, even as the selection is occurring, is making friends with the other panelists, one who charms the lawyers as they conduct the questioning. Also risky are those who carry the weight of authority or power: people in professional occupations, people of higher-class background; people in education (teachers and students), who are dangerously liable to be articulate. An additional fear about such people is that they are good "foreman material." In California, any juror can theoretically be chosen, but the most probable choice is someone who is either personally or professionally persuasive. And since the foreperson is the single most influential person on a jury, lawyers will do anything to keep good foreman material off. Since they have limited peremptory challenges and do make mistakes, sometimes members of dangerous groups sneak onto juries.

Voir Dire *as Education*

The major function of the *voir dire* is to assemble a jury. But it also serves to provide a bit of pre-trial education. Lawyers want jurors to come into a trial with some understanding of legal process and basic constitutional assumptions: "innocent until proven guilty," "beyond a reasonable doubt." These concepts will not be prominently mentioned in the trial itself, probably not surfacing until the judge charges the jury, if then. But it is better if jurors have those ideas in mind from the start, and also some understanding of how they ought to work as jurors: vote according to your own beliefs, don't be buffaloed by the more powerful, listen to others. So along with the questioning, or in the guise of questions ("Do you understand the concept of *burden of proof?*"), they slip in a little education. In a capital case, the defense wants a jury containing as many people as possible who have qualms about the death penalty. Those who declare unequivocal opposition will be dismissed for cause. But before the judge makes this ruling, the attorney gets a chance to question the prospective juror to show that he or she *might* vote for death under some conditions; feels scruples rather than the all-out opposition that is grounds for dismissal under *Witherspoon.* (The prosecutor has the opposite interests.) So the defense attorney attempts to break down the panelist's strong position—a process called *rehabilitation.* I have seen videotape demonstrations showing defense attorneys how to shame panelists out of Wither-spooning out: "You understand that jury service is a duty you owe your government? (Yes.) You wouldn't consider it moral to evade your duty? (No.) But if you refuse to even *consider* the death penalty, you will be unable to serve in this case, right? (Yes.) So won't you think a little more . . . ?" It is at least arguable that a moral dilemma is posed by rehabilitation: if a juror rejects the death penalty on moral grounds (as most Witherspooners do), is it ethical to force them to reconsider by shaming them and suggesting that their stand is immoral?

The Judge's Role in Voir Dire

Judges have considerable say in all phases of the conduct of *voir dire,* along with the statutes of a particular jurisdiction. The process itself has come under considerable criticism from judges because it takes so long. It is often pointed out that English courts get by with an attenuated *voir dire* with few challenges for any reason and only brief questioning. At the same time, American appellate decisions mandate or make desirable extensive questioning and many grounds for dismissal. In some courtrooms, judges conduct the entire *voir dire:* attorneys can challenge but cannot themselves ask the questions. (Sometimes they are allowed to submit questions, which the judge either may or must ask.) In other courtrooms, as in Alameda, the lawyers control most of the process.

With the hurdle of *voir dire* over, the court has chosen itself a jury. They are instructed to appear at the beginning of the trial, and the process of becoming a jury begins. Twelve disparate individuals must constitute themselves into a body, a group that can reach consensus while preserving each member's rights and self-respect. Their work can be complicated by certain selection strategies. Sometimes a lawyer, despairing of a favorable verdict, prefers a hung jury to the alternative. One way to hang a jury is to have at least one person on it who is likely to raise the hackles of at least one of the others. Then during the trial and deliberations, the jury will split into factions; and if the lawyer is lucky, animosity will override the jurors' determination to do a good job and reach a fair verdict.

A JUROR'S LIFE

The daily constraints on jurors are a mixture of solemn and silly, literal and symbolic. The jury, after all, is an institution whose functions have come together over more than a millennium. Deeply conservative, the law is loath to break precedent. The adversarial system makes innovation harder, since any conventional form of behavior is apt to have positive repercussions for one side (and therefore negative ones for the other). So any moves to change the jury system— make *voir dire* less time consuming, allow jurors more freedom to ask questions during trials, minimize the long waits that characterize jury service—are likely to run into intractable opposition. As time goes by, and the original reasons for making juries work the way they do become shrouded in antiquity, requirements that once had real practical worth turn into encrusted rituals, sometimes useful for their symbolic value, but always inhospitable to change. So it is with the rules that require jurors to be segregated from the world outside the courtroom.

These constraints have a rational basis: if jurors are free to move about the community, talking to others and sampling the media, they will be exposed to two serious dangers. First, a juror's conclusions in a trial must be based solely on the evidence presented. Therefore jurors must not talk to others (whose beliefs might come from less reliable sources than the jurors') or be influenced by media speculation. Nor are jurors allowed to do their own detective work: going to the scene of the crime, interviewing friends of those involved, and so on. That, too, would subject them to biased perspectives. Second, there are people with an interest in the verdict. Jurors must be protected from "tampering," whether in the form of threats or bribes or merely arguments. So it is important that somehow juries be sealed off from the world. It is also symbolically important, because their separation from ordinary life signifies to jurors that their thinking in the courtroom and jury room must be qualitatively different from that of their daily lives.

Ideally, then, a jury should be hermetically sealed off from the outside world from selection to verdict. Sometimes this is, in fact, done: the jury is sequestered. But this brings its own problems. Sequestration is expensive for the state. Jurors generally resent it, especially for long periods, and may well blame the people who made it necessary—specifically the defendant. People will also exercise every means at their disposal to avoid serving on a jury that is to be sequestered. Long sequestration is a hardship, and tales are told of jurors cracking under the strain, leading to dubious verdicts and mistrials. So as a practical matter, long-term sequestration is rare, used only in notorious cases where jurors would otherwise be highly subject to outside influence. Yet there are real advantages to a jury's feeling set apart, and even realer ones to its actually being set apart.

The dilemma is often resolved by means of partial or symbolic sequestration, for various periods of the jury's service. For instance, there is the practice of having the jury assemble in its room as a body before it is summoned into the courtroom. This signifies to all, jurors and observers, that the jury is a cohesive unit; it provides a buffer between the outside world and the courtroom, allowing the jurors a place to become "the jury" before they must function officially as such. It sets them apart before others and themselves. Another sort of symbolic sequestration is regularly used in Alameda County, where juries are almost never literally sequestered. Until the end of closing arguments, jurors are free to do as they will, not only overnight and on weekends but at lunch. Theoretically they could be tampered with singly and collectively in every way. But throughout their deliberations, they experience symbolic sequestration during lunch. After each morning session, they are collected from the jury room by two bailiffs. (The alternates waiting in the Juror Assembly Room are collected as well.) They all pile into county paddy wagons and are transported to any of several restaurants. The practice is silly taken literally: jurors are being saved from interference during lunch, only to be open to it after they are dismissed for the day. But as a way of emphasizing the symbolic privacy and solemnity of the deliberations, it has meaning.

In the Courtroom

The jurors sit in the courtroom each day trying to learn what they will need to know, trying to get a sense of the *dramatis personae* of the courtroom and how they are connected to one another. The jurors' overriding task—constructing a narrative, finding a single, coherent and plausible story in the conflicting accounts given by the two sides—begins with making sense of the courtroom discourse. At first everything is awesome and mysterious. By the end, it had better be lucid. Analogies to the familiar can help. There is a powerful temptation for jurors to see the courtroom as one big scrappy family: the judge as Father (at least if he's male); the court clerk as Mommy, who takes care of the judge's personal needs (answers the phone, organizes exhibits, arranges schedules); the lawyers as rival-rous older siblings, fighting to look good in front of Father, who knows best. Father often shows favoritism, teasing one of the offspring more than the other, giving one more privileges (such as sustaining objections). Only the judge gets to tease, and he or she can tease everyone else—a form of humor that typically is used by the more powerful against subordinates. Often the prosecutor looks like the competent older sibling, Father's favorite; and the defense attorney, the ne'er-do-well younger kid who has to get set straight by prosecutor and judge together. Defense attorneys often adopt a style that, within the narrow confines of courtroom proprieties, is just a bit more unkempt than that of the prosecutor: a rumpled shirt, a wilder tie, hair just a fraction of an inch longer, a bushier mustache. Sometimes the defense attorney attempts an alliance with the jury on the basis of "us-common-folk," and will deliberately try to appear casual or even incompetent, uncomfortable with the decorum of the courtroom: dropping notes, wandering around the room, forgetting the requisite formalities. In *Delgado*, the defense attorney did all of these at one time or another. At one point the prosecutor even was moved to ask the judge to admonish his adversary for distracting everyone else, and the judge (who had been trying in all possible ways to get the defense attorney to straighten up and fly straight) gladly complied. The defense lawyer tried some five times to make the same objection, each time being overruled by the judge. His insistence (improper behavior by itself) was compounded by his asking the judge explicitly why his objections were being overruled. The judge replied, "The educational seminar will commence at 4:15, when the jury is dismissed." Messages were thus sent to everyone: To the attorney, Clean up your act, or I'll humiliate you again. To the jury, Don't take this guy too seriously, he doesn't know what he's doing. The judge was providing the subtext for the jury's developing narrative.

Especially since these contretemps occurred in a capital case, the jury was nonplused. They were disconcerted at the attorney's behavior. His informality did not strike the "spectrum of the community" as laid-back good-guy camaraderie; rather, it was perceived as either gross incompetence or arrogant insouciance, probably both. The jurors, who took the trial and their role in it seriously, were insulted. They weren't sure who besides the lawyer was at fault: the Public Defender's office, which seemed to have assigned a capital case to this man as his first trial experience (in fact untrue, but that was the only way the jurors could make sense of his inability to approximate the court's expectations of demeanor)?

But even so (or especially so), why wasn't he *trying* harder? They cared—why didn't he?

Jurors are in many ways like the little kids in a family, fussed over when present, but criticized out of earshot. Jurors are told time and again by each side how important their job is and how intelligent they are (as in, "I'm sure you ladies and gentlemen of the jury are too intelligent to believe the statement you heard from Mr.——. . ."). But out of their hearing, lawyers and judges heap scorn on the nonprofessionals, first for not understanding what's going on; second for being of lower social classes and less educated than they are; third for sometimes being bored and inattentive.

Jurors are like children of an earlier age while they are in the courtroom: they must be seen and not heard. (They will be heard from later, but that day may be far in the future.) Their seats are assigned. They are warned each day, several times a day, not to tell tales out of school. There are vague threats and admonitions that they could be punished for doing things wrong that they haven't even been warned explicitly against doing. As in many families there are secrets, things you don't tell the outside world, don't even talk about with one another, for reasons you don't know, just you'll be in big trouble if you do and Father finds out. Like small children, jurors may have questions about what the grownups mean, but either are not permitted to ask or don't have the linguistic sophistication to form the right questions. Like children, they play a dual role in the family dynamic: much is expected of them (eventually); but for now, they're a burden, needing to be kept in order and cajoled or coerced into proper deportment.

In the Jury Room

What makes a group of twelve disparate individuals coalesce into a cohesive jury? For one thing, especially in trials of serious crimes and of long duration, most jurors want to do a good job and be part of a good jury. They want to please the judge, who they assume wants a good jury. (One of my fellow jurors overheard the court clerk say that ours was the best jury that judge had ever seen, and couldn't wait to get back to the others to report it. We were thrilled.) In a long trial, the time jurors spend alone together in the jury room creates an *esprit de corps*. In such trials, jurors come to feel a little like hostages (all the more so, of course, if they are sequestered): they are removed from many of the routines of their daily lives, they are kept separate from the rest of the world for most of every day, they are in a strange place together trying to figure out strange rules, they don't know how long they'll be there and have no say in that decision, others who are more powerful make decisions that affect their lives. In such situations people form close emotional attachments to others in the same predicament.

Although the lawyers see plenty of the jury in the courtroom, what goes on in the jury room where the members assemble and wait before each session (and when they are sent out of the courtroom) is a mystery to everyone else—one that arouses the greatest curiosity and anxiety, the more because lawyers virtually never serve on juries. (Peremptory challenges see to that.) What is going on, in a trial of any length, is the socialization of the jury: the formation of the body and within it, the creation of alliances and power structure. For juries like other groups create their own leaders. Some of these leaders become forepersons; others exercise influence in other ways. Lawyers are terribly curious about all these processes and scrutinize the jurors in every way they can to get clues. Perhaps they spy three jurors going off to lunch together or two exchanging a joke as they file into the courtroom from the jury room. The lawyers learn that Number Four has given a note to the bailiff: is he becoming a spokesperson, and will he be foreman? Five and Seven live in the same neighborhood: are they commuting to court together? Six seemed to be explaining a point to Three during the morning's testimony: is she emerging as a trusted authority?

Indeed, the jurors are getting to know one another, but the relationships are not like those forged in the outside world: the rules are different. Usually we form close ties with people with whom we share something, and we form them by choice, because we feel solidarity. But the twelve jurors (plus alternates) are thrown together haphazardly and must first discover if they share anything at all. Normally you begin to get to know someone by discussing the situation in which you find yourselves. But jurors are warned not to discuss their situation with one another until deliberations. (They do nonetheless, very often, but furtively and guiltily.) So they can't talk about what has brought them together, the one thing they have in common and about which they are all most concerned.

Once people begin to form an alliance, they generally want to learn more about one another. After several encounters, they begin, however delicately, to broach tricky matters: life-style, religion, politics. While these are not the stuff of casual small talk with acquaintances, they are necessary in cementing a true friendship. With casual acquaintances, we don't expect to have many meetings in a short period, so small talk can be the basis of all conversation. But jurors may spend two or more hours a day in each other's company, around a table in a small room, four or even five days a week for many weeks, doing little other than being there together. In other circumstances, only the most intimate of friends or family are so physically close for so long. Contiguity leads them to want and expect intimacy, yet their real-life unconnectedness discourages it. They run out of small talk and are reluctant to try the big talk. There is another reason, too, for reticence. They know that eventually they will have to work together to craft a compromise. Usually people avoid dangerous topics unless and until they can count on trust and intimacy, since up to that time controversy may drive people apart. If your opinions on important issues are very different from mine, I may decide I dislike you before I've really gotten to know you. This is equally and even more significantly true for jurors. If in ordinary life people decide they don't want to be friends because they don't share values, it may be a pity, but otherwise there's no harm done: they just part coolly, and that's the end of it. But if jurors conceive a loathing for one another because of imprudent disclosures (or anything else), the jury's very reason for existence, the ability to reach a verdict, is jeopardized. Jurors may not think through these dangers explicitly, but they do seem instinctively to avoid dangerous topics.

Despite these constraints, juries structure themselves.[5] A jury room waiting for the courtroom day to begin is, in feeling, not unlike a dinner party with twelve or fifteen seated around the table. Some read the papers; others bring books or knitting. But conversations begin. In any group of more than three or four, it is difficult for a single conversation to go on for any time and include all parties. Often what happens is that there is first, for a few minutes, a desultory attempt at general conversation around the table; then it breaks down into smaller groups. These group and regroup but seldom involve more than four to six at once and more often break into twos and threes. The combining and recombining is a wonderfully intricate process, somehow orchestrated so that no one is left out for any length of time. A jury is not dissimilar, except that everyone is not expected to be involved in group activity at all times: one can opt out for a while to do something on one's own. A jury is also different from a dinner party in that it keeps regrouping, day after day. In this it is a bit more like a college classroom, especially a graduate seminar (though those don't meet nearly so often). In school, seats are not assigned, yet students tend to sit in the same seats or nearly the same each time, and sometimes feel vaguely resentful if someone else gets there first and takes "their" seat. Juries tend to behave in the same way. Students have preferences and invest seating arrangements with symbolic meaning. Some like to sit right up front, where they can catch the teacher's eye; others, in the back, where they can read the paper undisturbed and unnoticed (they think); some in the middle, where they'll make no impression of any kind. In the same way, some jurors at the long, narrow table try to sit at an end, and others in the middle. Others take seats away from the table, especially alternates, who tend to feel like poor stepchildren in the family, people with ambiguous roles or no role at all.

Relationships begin to develop, based in part on seating preference (and vice versa) and partly on commonalities that are uncovered over time. People talk about their work, their families, their amusements, their annoyances at their current situation. Not much is exchanged by way of real-life problems or long-term goals. People seem to be actively avoiding the signs of true intimacy. They also talk about the case—at least some do, while others pretend not to hear or look on in disapproval ("the judge told us not to"). Jurors tend to go to lunch together in pairs or trios, and sometimes commute together. Alliances may eventually affect the verdict, either because close associates tend to vote together, or one may bring another to a compromise that otherwise would be untenable. Alliances may also affect the choice of foreperson, the first important decision a jury must make, and one with some impact on all subsequent decisions.

Finding a Foreperson

Lawyers and social scientists have all sorts of opinions, based variously on superstition and research, about how juries select forepersons. In some jurisdictions, the foreperson is automatically the first juror selected. When the jury does its own selecting, the choice is made differently depending on the length of the trial and how much time jurors have spent together before deliberations. Especially in a short trial, when they know little about one another and not too much rides on the choice, the choice may be based on a purely external factor: a juror seated at the end of the table is more apt to be chosen than one in the middle. The head and foot of the table have always been (not only in jury rooms) the power positions. (Juries never seem to sit at round tables—probably because these would require larger rooms.) Other important factors, in trials of any length, are sex (males are forepersons much more often than females); age (the middle-aged are more likely than either the very young or very old); occupation (professional and managerial are favored); and the well educated are more apt to be chosen. The favored groups are those whose members are viewed as articulate and intelligent. They come into the jury room with intrinsic power, which the job of foreperson enhances.

The foreperson officially has no more power than any other juror but can exercise a good deal of control over the proceedings. The duties of the foreperson are: to moderate discussion, to oversee the voting, to summarize discussions and decisions, to sign the verdict form, and to announce to the judge that a verdict has been reached. How the foreperson does each of these jobs will have a significant effect on the deliberations, perhaps affecting whether a verdict is reached at all, and which one is reached, not to mention how the other jurors feel about the verdict, the experience, and one another afterward.

A good foreperson is, above all, solicitous of the opinions of the others, not only giving all a chance to speak, but encouraging the more reticent members. Often the deliberation begins with each person stating his or her views. A straw vote may be taken at this time (voting is generally by secret ballot). The court provides for the jurors' needs: lots of sharpened pencils and yellow lined pads. There is usually a blackboard, on which issues and/or votes may be recorded. The foreperson should be able to summarize the range of opinions at significant points, without distorting anyone's position or putting words into anyone's mouth. He or she should know when to call for a vote (when discussion is beginning to lag) and suggest compromises or present those of others. The foreperson is also responsible for asking the bailiff for pieces of evidence when the jury feels it is necessary.

If deliberations go well, a verdict is reached that feels right to every juror. All may not have gotten what they desired, but all can see the justice of the final outcome. People will not feel put upon or put down by others—even if their choices did not win out, they respect the thinking of the prevailing majority. Even though there may have been sharp and even acrimonious disagreements at times in the deliberations, even though the weeks of jury duty have involved discomfort and deprivation, there is a bittersweet feeling as they leave the jury room for the last time. The courtroom personnel, the judge and lawyers, and their fellow jurors have been for all this time a part of their lives, more salient perhaps than family and friends. They are glad to be returning to their normal existences, yet sad to go, sad the excitement is ending, sorry they won't get to know the others better. Often, in juries that have worked well together, after the verdict is signed and as they wait to be called into court, they will pass around a list of names and phone numbers, vowing to meet again. They probably won't, but at this moment they mean it.

If deliberations go badly, a hung jury is likely; in this case or in case a verdict is reached by intimidation of any kind, some jurors will feel resentful, and most will feel that the experience as a whole was not a good one. There will be no fond farewells nor exchange of phone numbers.

The foreperson's conduct of the deliberations is important in a number of ways: to bring about a verdict truly representative of the feelings of the whole group; and to create good feelings about jury service. As jury duty is the only direct experience most of us will ever have of the workings of government and the bases of American democracy, it is crucial for the survival of the republic that the experience be positive for the majority of people exposed to it.

At the start of the trial, I had looked around at my fellow jurors and seen a motley crew, the mythic spectrum of the community, everything from laborers to professionals, all colors, both genders, a wide range of education and articulateness. I couldn't see how some of the group could grasp the complexities of the decisions they would have to make, much less argue persuasively for any position. People seemed to misunderstand a lot, to jump to conclusions, and to be unable to make a valid case for their beliefs.

During the six weeks, alliances formed, groups of two or three. Two of the group seemed from the start to be emerging, by design or chance, as candidates for foreperson. One was a young woman (let's call her Heather), who worked as a secretary and was the mother of a two-year-old boy, whose accent marked her as a New Yorker, lively and voluble. Ordinarily someone with her demographic profile would be a poor candidate for foreperson; but Heather had qualities. The jury had been selected over a two-hour process that ended in late afternoon, when they were dismissed by the judge and told to reassemble the next morning.

During the selection process, candidates took seats in the jury box and were replaced with dispatch: in capital cases, it will be recalled, there is no questioning of panelists after the sequestered *voir dire*.

We were supposed to be present by 10:00 A.M. each morning, but by 10:10 one of the fifteen (jurors plus three alternates) was still missing. I certainly had no idea who it was. Heather looked around and identified the missing member as an alternate, mentioning other relevant details about him, and her identification proved correct as he walked through the door a couple of minutes later. I was impressed, as I am sure my colleagues were at this extraordinary feat. It augured well for her candidacy, suggesting as it did an interest in other people and a flattering ability to remember things about them.

The other contender was a man in his late thirties, whom I'll call Bob, in a managerial position at a local newspaper, tall, blond and quintessentially Californian, and like Heather married with a small child. Both he and Heather, from the start of the six-week process, zealously took to forming alliances and connections. Heather already slightly knew one of the other jurors. She and Bob (none of the others) brought in photos of their children and showed them around. Heather collected around her three or four adherents, all of whom would disappear into an empty jury room across the hall (strictly speaking, illegal), while the rest of us wondered what they were up to. Bob formed connections principally with two of the men: they were all interested in hunting and fishing, which they would discuss at length. One weekend Bob went duck hunting, and on Monday brought two ducks in a pail for one of his companions.

It was clear that both were emerging as candidates—whether by conscious design or not. Bob was clearly the stronger, because of his sex, age, and occupation, and was eventually chosen, though Heather was in contention.

I had wondered at the outset whether this group of people could function appropriately in a life-or-death decision. As we began to deliberate, Bob had everyone state their feelings, going around the table. I was stunned: even—perhaps especially—those I had been most worried about expressed their thoughts articulately and persuasively; and their words, intelligent and compassionate, made deep sense. People on both sides argued their cases well, respectfully listened to one another, and debated generously and kindly. I felt that people genuinely had learned to like one another, that consensus was as important for most as victory. Especially when the argument grew heated, Bob was careful that the reticent expressed themselves, that no one got run over by the stronger speakers, that all the options and positions got discussed and their merits compared. Heather made a list on the board of the arguments in mitigation and aggravation contributed by each of us. Several ballots were taken.

The principal argument in mitigation was, as I said in chapter 5, post-traumatic stress disorder (PTSD: the defendant was a Vietnam veteran). Most of us agreed that PTSD was plausible, that such things could have happened to someone who fought in that war. But a couple of the younger jurors had come to maturity after the war was over, and had no memory of the anguish of those times. The idea of PTSD was improbable to them; or at least, the defendant's own description of his war experience didn't seem sufficient to justify mitigation.

Then Bob spoke. He said that he had been in Vietnam at the same time as the defendant; and if you hadn't been there, you just couldn't know how it was. While he hadn't committed murder, while his life was much more successful than the defendant's had been, it had not been without suffering and misjudgments. He had had many advantages the defendant hadn't—a close, loving family, good education, majority ethnic status, and so on; and yet, after he had returned, he had come close to self-destruction more than once. The defendant had come home to no one; had no skills, no education. Bob had a family who made sure, for a year after he returned, that he was never alone; medical care; education; jobs. Yet he had drifted, gotten into trouble with drugs and alcohol, smashed up a couple of cars, destroyed a marriage, lost a succession of jobs. Only in the last few years had he gotten his life back together again. Vietnam had done something to him, he hadn't gotten over it yet. He showed us two pictures, one of himself as a high school student before he went off to war: good-looking, cheerful, athletic, confident. And one a year later, after his tour of duty. It was recognizable as the same person, but only barely. There were hollows in his cheeks, and something behind his eyes—black, haunted. He was noticeably thinner—the word you'd use was "gaunt."

Then people began, spontaneously, to talk. They talked of family members, lovers, friends who'd gone off to that war healthy and competent, and come back—somehow, horribly, different. Husbands and lovers had become abusive; friends had drifted away; relatives had become unreachable, sullen, unpredictable and dangerous. A litany went around the table, "I never realized until now what happened to him"—an epiphany.

There was a silence. We took a break. We deliberated again. It was clear that there was a new understanding. The verdict was emerging: life. We still needed to hammer out some of the details, but there was a feeling of trust in the room, so that eventual consensus was a certainty. It was, perhaps, not so much that everyone was totally persuaded of the correctness of the verdict, but that everyone wanted to do something positive, to make a statement that affirmed life and hope and trust, however that could be constructed from the grim body of evidence we had to deal with. When it was all over, we passed around a list of names and numbers. I don't know whether any of us are still in touch, but we felt at that moment that we wanted to be.

OTHER JURIES, OTHER ENDINGS

Other juries reach other conclusions. In the first of the two capital trials I worked on, the jury deliberated for twenty-one days before it was allowed to hang. Later I interviewed those members who would speak to me, and heard—under the concrete statements about votes, sides, and procedure—a subtext that was starkly different. The jurors distrusted one another's motives and disliked one another. Those who were for death (the majority) believed that the reasons given by the pro-life minority were invalid and illegal, and were bitter that they had made a verdict impossible. The foreman apparently had strong pro-death views from the moment of the *voir dire* and was unwilling to consider anything else seriously—a view he communicated to his fellow jurors. The jury never really constituted itself as a jury but remained a loose aggregate of twelve separate factions. There are various reasons that juries hang, some better than others; in this one, it seemed (as far as I could tell from the interviews, which tended toward taciturnity) that the problem was in the air from the start: there was no striving for consensus, no desire to cooperate, no trust.

The jury's task in deliberation is, essentially, the collaborative construction of a narrative, which incorporates bits of both sides, and maybe some of its own—the narrative that *really* hangs together and avoids the embarrassing gaps and leaps of faith that necessarily characterize those of the adversaries. It must evaluate the stories of witnesses on the basis of real-world practical plausibility (juries as the triers of fact) and shear through wishful thinking. Each of the twelve who deliberate comes to the task with his or her own concoction, a narrative that is whole or fragmented, sensible or not. It is the job of the jury to make those twelve parts into one seamless whole, just as the twelve individuals must make themselves, for that length of time, into a single entity. A jury that can make itself cohesive can construct a coherent story—that is, reach a verdict by consensus. One which cannot do the first will be unable to do the second. The verdict the jurors reach (if they do) will not be consensual but obtained by pressure of one kind or another. Such verdicts, while probably not infrequent, are clearly undesirable: they subvert the purpose of the jury system.

I have no prescriptions nor ways to make sure that juries act more like the first than the second. People are too complex and various to allow easy solutions. But everyone involved in the process of jury selection and trial procedure needs to remember how hard the jury's job is, and treat panelists and jurors with real and deep respect. The power of the jury is great, for good or evil, and respectful treatment and careful education of jurors is the surest way I know to make a jury a force for good.

CHAPTER SEVEN

Therapy and the Law: Blurring the Lines

THE problem of abuse cannot be avoided in any discussion of institutional language. If we agree that language is powerful, that it can be used to create and enhance one speaker's power over others, then the abusive potential of communicative strategies becomes clearly apparent. And everyone who hopes to lessen that potential must ask what characteristics of the linguistic form or the discourse context favor abuse, and how that potential can be mitigated.

A power imbalance, overt or covert, strongly favors abuse. An overt power imbalance is found, as I have said, in therapy, classrooms, and courtrooms. But ordinary conversation is not without hazards just because it is conventionally egalitarian. In fact, the covert properties of language are most likely to make trouble, because their workings go unrecognized and unquestioned. As long as a form of discourse is recognized as involving stronger and weaker parties, there is at least the possibility that safeguards will be developed (though there will always be opposition from the stronger side, which hates the thought of relinquishing any of its power almost as much as it hates to be forced to acknowledge the possession of that power). But if the imbalance is secret, then its potential for abuse will go underground; and victims will blame themselves and their incompetence rather than seeing their participation in the abusive discourse as, at least in part, involuntary.

A power imbalance *enables* abuse to exist but does not by itself create abuse or specify the form it will take. The particular characteristics of a discourse type dictate the form for its abuse. Abuses in the courtroom are of one sort; in the classroom, another. In a sense, all are equivalent in that all render the weaker participant unable to achieve full expression, to get his or her needs met, to come out of the communication having used it as it was intended to be used. Abuse in the classroom results most critically in nontransmission of true knowledge; in the courtroom, of the non-administration of justice; in therapy, in the non-achievement of autonomy. All, though, leave the weaker party feeling incompetent and despairing—and sometimes much worse.

There is, then, an intrinsic relation between the function a discourse type is designed to serve; the power relations between participants it engenders or makes use of; and the interpersonal and larger social problems its misuse brings in its train. But as long as we confine our observations—as the previous chapters in this section have done—to a single discourse type, it is hard to see how the specific characteristics of a genre contribute to specific kinds of abuse.

In chapters 4, 5, and 6, I looked closely at two kinds of discourse, both somewhat familiar to members of our culture, though at the same time a little exotic to nonprofessionals (and therefore mysterious). Both possess a rich potential for abuse; but otherwise, if we were asked to compare courtroom and therapeutic discourse, our first response might be that they were incomparable. On the continuum of genres, these two seem at first glance to be far apart. Many of their distinctive formal attributes are not shared. Yet, especially among less superficially observable functional properties, there are curious connections and similarities, which are not accidental: courtroom and consulting room have deep affinities.

Ambiguities in discourse structure or function—whether in therapy or the law—are breeding grounds for abuse. Sometimes the confusion arises because the discourse moves between two genres, masquerading as one while actually working like the other. Sometimes it occurs within a single genre, because definitions or understandings of the meanings of speech acts are vague or ambiguous. But any lack of clarity on the part of any participant is an invitation to danger.

Perhaps the threat is most potent in genre crossing—the bringing of the assumptions, rules, forms, or intentions of one discourse type illegitimately and inexplicitly into another. The types discussed at length in the last three chapters serve as particularly cogent examples of the problem. On the face of it, the claim that two forms of abuse involve confusion between the conventions of the courtroom and the consulting room might seem implausible, few discourse types seeming as dissimilar as these. Yet that confusion lies at the root of at least some of the most critical abuses of both systems, and upon inspection, deep analogies emerge between them. While I could draw examples from many discourse types, I choose these two not only because of my own special interest in both, but also because both can do extraordinary amounts of harm to the less powerful participant in the discourse.

Courtroom and Consulting Room: Differences

A list of the differences between forensic and therapeutic discourse covers the style, aims, and underlying assumptions of each form:

Therapeutic Discourse	*Courtroom Discourse*
private	public
collaborative	adversarial
understanding (forgiving)	blaming
informal	formal
spontaneous	ritualistic
allusive	literal
implicit	explicit
"play"	"real"
continuous, overdetermined	dichotomous

I have discussed many of these earlier but will summarize here:

1. *Private/Public.* Therapeutic discourse is maximally private, entailing the development of "private" language between participants: shared allusions, jointly created metaphors, telegraphic references. This privacy both creates and utilizes trust, which itself is in turn symbolically connected with intimacy. The proceedings of the consulting room are closed to everyone but therapist and client.

Courtroom discourse on the other hand is maximally public: everything must be expressed in ways that everyone can understand.[1] It is concrete, since participants cannot count on shared allusions. Since all proceedings are open to everyone, there is no assumption of trust.

2. *Collaborative/Adversarial.* Therapeutic discourse is a collaboration between trusting partners, the development of a shared narrative.[2] Both therapist and client win by a successful outcome. The adversarial elements of therapeutic discourse ideally are muted.

Courtroom discourse is adversarial.[3] The aim of each side is to discredit the other: if one wins, the other loses. One creates a narrative which the other destroys.

3. *Understanding/Blaming.* These categories reflect the stance taken by participants toward the events or thoughts under discussion. In both therapy and courtroom, much that is described may be reprehensible. But in therapy both participants attempt to understand the client's behavior and (where necessary) forgive it as part of the human condition.

In the courtroom, reprehensible actions receive blame—from the world at large, the jury, and eventually the judge, as well as the prosecutor. These actions are often seen as bizarre and inhuman. One function of a trial is to assert to the larger community that aberrant behavior will not be tolerated.

4. *Informal/Formal.*   Behavior in the consulting room is largely informal: colloquial language, first-name address, relaxed posture (comfortable chairs or even a couch), some touching or at least nonverbal gestures. The individuality of each participant is recognized, and the treatment is geared to each client.

In the courtroom, formality is the rule: impersonal, frozen linguistic forms; title-alone or title-last name address; formal posture; no touching, restrained nonverbal expression; formal dress.[4] Participants are not treated as individuals, and the law at least purports to treat each case in terms of generalities and precedents: "the law" applies to all, for all time.

5. *Spontaneous/Ritualistic.*   The behavior of both participants in therapy is ideally spontaneous: the direct expression of emotions, the unconstrained response. The therapist should not recycle allusions or other special language from one client to another.

There is much use of ritual and ceremony to set the courtroom apart from the outside world. There are repeated formulas at the start and close of each session, and fixed ways to do and say many things.

6. *Allusive/Literal.*   Therapeutic discourse, having as its subject the mind, which is not directly accessible to observation, works indirectly—by parable, allegory, metaphor—and thus tends to strengthen the bonds of trust and intimacy between client and therapist.

Courtroom discourse is literal. It deals with concrete events in direct language.

7. *Implicit/Explicit.*   Therapeutic discourse talks *around* dangerous ideas; much is hinted at, by both participants. The reason is partly that the ideas are frightening, partly that leaps of intuition strengthen trust. Sentences are unfinished, questions substitute for declaratives, injunctions are hedged.

In the courtroom, everything (ideally) is said directly. Questions are questions; declaratives, declaratives. Witnesses are required to be explicit even in responses deemed superfluous. Replies are often overexplicit. Everything must be clear for the record.

8. *"Play"/"Real."*   Therapy, in one sense, is "play," a "game": it is not a real-life relationship, but practice for it; it has no real-world consequences.[5] So it is safer to take risks in therapy than outside. Then, too, the subject matter is often not real but "fantasy": it is not of the world in which we live.

Courtroom discourse is "real." More than anywhere else, every utterance has serious repercussions for someone: life, for at least one participant, will be unalterably changed by the outcome. The subject matter is what is alleged to have actually taken place.

9. *Continuous/Dichotomous.*   Therapeutic discourse at least recognizes the possibility that things may belong to more than one category at once, be

subject to several interpretations ("overdetermination," "the principle of multiple function").6 Ambiguity is necessary and often unresolvable. A symbol in a dream, or a symptom in an illness, may refer at the same time to several sources. Even diagnostic categories (the area where therapy tries to be scientific and rigorous) blur into one another. What line separates neurosis from psychosis? When is a client manic, when hypomanic? That schizophrenia is diagnosed with much greater frequency in some societies than in others implies that there are no universally agreed-upon standards for diagnosis.

The courtroom demands precision and dichotomy. Murder is murder, and manslaughter is manslaughter: the jury must decide. A defendant who has committed homicide must be found to have done so intentionally or not; no middle ground is possible. A jury in a criminal case must return a unanimous verdict. A difference of opinion is a mistrial—a failure.

This is one reason psychiatry and the law can be uneasy partners. In the courtroom, an attorney demands of a psychiatric witness: Is the defendant sane or insane? One or the other? An honest psychiatrist most often prefers to hedge: Well, the defendant's grasp of reality is poor in this way and that; but in other aspects of behavior and cognition, his mind works much like anyone else's.

Courtroom and Consulting Room: Similarities

On the other hand, the courtroom and the consulting room share certain properties:

need for expertise
expertise linked to power
power imbalance
purpose-directed discourse
significant interpretability
nonreciprocity
narrative construction
adversarial aspect
discussion of responsibility
truth as an issue
people as "cases"
the use of confessions
transference/infantilization

1. *The Need for Expertise.* In both discourse types, certain participants know a special language, inaccessible to non-initiates. This linguistic expertise is linked to special knowledge of other kinds.

2. *Expertise Linked to Power.*   Knowing how to speak, what words mean, and what should and should not be said, gives speakers control over their own utterances as well as the ability to interpret others unilaterally and thus to make use of others' language in ways others may not have foreseen. Knowing the language, having special skills, allows the professional participant to define the situation.

3. *Power Imbalance.*   In both genres, the expert, through prior experience and training in the language, has more power than the neophyte. The latter tends therefore to be in awe of the former and to take the former's word as unassailable authority. In both genres, however, there is (or should be) at least a partial reversal of the power imbalance by the end of the total discourse: ideally in therapy, necessarily in the courtroom.

4. *Purpose-Directed Discourse.*   Ordinary conversation is, in general and by convention, undertaken for its own sake: there is no ulterior motive. But therapy and courtroom discourse exist in order to accomplish something: the language is designed to affect the real world in a discernible way.

5. *Significant Interpretability.*   While interpretation functions in different ways in the two genres, in both it plays an important role. In many forms of therapy, it is a crucial agent of change. In this role it is unilateral, though the client certainly does indulge in covert interpretation of the therapist. In the courtroom, all the participants interpret one another, since much significant behavior is hidden. But the jury is allowed unilateral overt interpretation of witnesses, especially of the defendant.

6. *Nonreciprocity.*   In both genres, participants are restricted in their roles, in terms both of how they may speak, and of what they may do, as well as in the determination of what their speech and actions mean.

7. *Narrative Construction.*   In both types, engagement in the production and/or evaluation of a plausible narrative is a major task. In the courtroom, one side destroys what the other constructs; in therapy, both collaborate to create a single viable construction.

8. *Adversarial Stance.*   The American courtroom is necessarily and thoroughly adversarial: one party wins and the other loses. Therapy, too, though ideally principally collaborative, has its adversarial aspect upon which its success depends.

9. *Discussion of Responsibility.*   In both genres, the subject's responsibility for actions is a major focus; while in other kinds of discourse it is taken for granted. An aim of therapy is to increase clients' ability to recognize and accept responsibility for who they are and what they have done; in a trial, one aim is to expose to the outside world the defendant's responsibility for wrongdoing. Sometimes, in court, the two senses of *responsibility* clash: a defendant may admit performing an action, but may claim nonresponsibility for it because of inability (on psychological grounds) to form an

intention ("diminished capacity") or to recognize that the action was wrong ("legal insanity").

10. *Truth as an Issue.*   In both genres, the discovery of "truth" is an important part of the process. In both, it is recognized that the truth may be complicated and ambiguous. In the courtroom, though, it is necessary for the fact-finding body to determine which truth is salient; in therapy, participants may decide that there are several competing truths, each with its own validity.

11. *People as "Cases."*   Arguably this connection is no more than a linguistic coincidence. But calling persons "cases" is one form of *reification* (thing making). People are depersonalized, seen as objects to be mastered and manipulated. The metaphor fits well with the generalizing attitude of the law: "cases" as specific instances of a general phenomenon. Since therapy declares itself to be concerned with individual behavior, with seeing each client as a unique aggregate of behavior and perceptions, the terminology fits it less well.

12. *The Use of Confession.*   The surest way to see into people's minds and discern their actions and motives is to encourage them to talk: when actions and motives are felt to be discreditable, this talk is called "confession." But why confess? It must be worth the confessor's while, there must be some return for the shame incurred, or else there must be some prevailing outside force to compel it. We don't expect confessions in ordinary conversation (and may be as embarrassed on the receiving as on the producing end). But in discourse where truth and responsibility are critical, it is not surprising to find confession, by that name or others, playing a prominent role. The *locus classicus* of confession is, of course, the church; and both therapy and court have symbolic affinities to that institution. In therapy as in church, one confesses in order to receive absolution or relief: guilt is traded for shame. Nothing is done with the confession by its hearer; it is not (or should not ever be) used against the confessor. Hence, the doctrine in both institutions of strict confidentiality.

When a suspect is apprehended, a principal desideratum of the apprehenders is to secure a confession; as long as this is done according to the rules, it is admissible at trial and therefore becomes totally public. A confession in a criminal trial is damaging to the defendant, indeed sometimes lethal; so there must be some strong motive to compel it, while a therapeutic confession is intrinsically motivated. So the two uses of "confession" are different, but both genres are still dependent upon confession to accomplish their aims.

13. *Transference/Infantilization.*   In both courtrooms and therapy, there is a powerful tendency for the nonprofessional participants to develop, more or less consciously, fantasies about the professionals and their relation-

ships with the former. In therapy, it has long been known that clients attribute to therapists the behavior and attitudes of the clients' parents, and therefore respond irrationally toward them. This is the *transference.* At the same time, clients tend to see themselves as children relative to adult therapists and regress in various ways to behavior and attitudes appropriate to childhood. Thus, in therapy, alongside the realistic relationship between the two adults, there develop fantasy relations (in the minds of both) between parent and child, symbolic understandings of what is occurring and what is being said. While transference can create difficulties in the therapeutic process (particularly if it is not recognized and made explicit via interpretation), it is also the premier tool of analytic therapy, the basis of insight, and as such indispensable.

In courtrooms, a parallel process occurs. Not only do jurors (the nonprofessionals) tend, as I have said, to cast the professionals as members of a family in which they are the children,[7] but the very requirements of the courtroom act to infantilize jurors and make them develop a peculiar dependence on at least one of the professionals—the judge. But transference is both more covert in the courtroom and more dangerous. For one thing, it has no necessary function. As in therapy, it is an artifact of the discourse form itself but does not serve to enhance anyone's true understanding of what is going on. As in therapy, it can be misused (a form of abuse) by the object(s) of the transference to encourage overdependence and misunderstanding on the part of jurors.

These similarities encourage a dangerous tendency to confuse the two genres—and not only in the lay mind. The danger is serious: the function of therapy is (ideally) to help the client, even if this involves doing a disservice to the client's community (for instance, by making the client less dependent or more rebellious); but the function of courtroom discourse is to help or succor the larger society by removing convicted criminals from its midst. (Helping a defendant is never the point in a criminal trial.) So confusing courtroom and consulting room is always an opening for abuse, and always to be zealously guarded against: to mix them is to guarantee that someone's interests (usually the weakest person's, the client's or the defendant's) will be misrepresented.

The Therapist as Prosecutor

Consider the case of Dora, summarized in chapter 4, in which the courtroom intrudes upon the consulting room.[8] The therapist, in pressing the client, in urging confession or at least exposure of what the latter would suppress, must attack at least some part of the client, urge the healthy part to cast out the sick or to override its demands. Since it is not the therapist's job to make excuses for troublesome behavior or rationalize unproductive habits of thinking, he or she must, at times, be stern, even harsh, a demanding master. But it is incumbent upon the therapist always to see his or her role as an ally of the client, to believe in the client's essential worth, goodness, capacity for honesty. (Childhood experience teaches us all the difference between criticism administered lovingly and that given in anger.) The aim in therapy must be to teach, to give the client tools for autonomy. It is not the vindication of the therapist's theories, whether about the human psyche or the client's past. Any sign that the therapist delights in the client's discomfiture, or has scored points off the client, indicates an abusive relationship. And that Freud revealed, in his own testimony in his account of Dora.

Freud's is the language of the courtroom, not the consulting room: He "force[s] her to admit." He cannot "in general dispute Dora's characterization of her father" (and thus suggests he saw it as his task to try). Dora "persisted in her denial"; "admitted that she might have been in love with Herr K."; her "reproaches recoiled upon her own head." And on, and on. It is impossible to miss the note of triumph in the prosecutor's—pardon, the analyst's—tone. It isn't so much what Freud says to Dora that is scandalously abusive, but how he says it, and with what intention, as his descriptions of his speech acts make plain. Freud construes the discourse as adversarial: for him to win, Dora must lose, and lose she does, as she prematurely breaks off the treatment in "revenge." The attribution of revenge makes sense only in a win-lose model. So we can conclude that whatever is going on in this history, it is not psychotherapy. On the surface, it looks like it: the patient on the couch, the analyst in the chair, the shared exploration of dreams and symptoms. But in intention, both over all and in detail, therapy is not going on. Freud aims to prove Dora guilty, to "bring her to reason" according to someone else's (her father's) definition of "reason." Her assessment of "reason" is not on the floor for discussion, any more than a court is interested in the "reasons" a defendant felt like committing a crime. Rather than constructing a narrative together of Dora's past life and current vicissitudes, Freud at every turn is showing Dora why her construction won't hold water, is not the real truth but a misunderstanding born of neurosis: he destroys and discredits her narrative, and has no discernible interest in mutual discovery. He accuses, delivers the verdict, sets the sentence. Her imprisonment continues.

The Prosecutor as Therapist

The other examples are the reverse: confusions of legal discourse with psychotherapy. Both occurred in Alameda County in the late 1980s—a community in which the values of therapy have penetrated deeply. Neither is strictly a courtroom episode, as both have to do with the elicitation of confessions preliminary to trial. But since the confession is sought largely because of its effect on a jury in court, there is a connection; and both the interrogation of a suspect and the trial of a defendant are part of the discourse of the legal system.

The first I observed at a preliminary hearing in a story told by a defendant charged with murder. He had, he said, been quarreling with his wife, and went out for a while, had a few drinks, and returned to find her asleep on the sofa. He decided to play a little joke on her. Going to a closet, he got out his shotgun (which he was *sure* was not loaded) and aimed it at her in point-blank range. She woke up. Playfully, because he *knew* the gun wasn't loaded, he pulled the trigger. The gun was loaded, and she was killed instantly. A relative called the police, and the husband was apprehended, full of remorse. After several hours in a holding cell, he was brought to an interrogation room late at night (the usual procedure). He was asked whether he wanted to make a confession. His reply: "Oh yes! I want to confess! I really need to talk to someone!" His confession was considered voluntary and consequently admissible in court.

Certainly he volunteered to talk. But did he understand the full consequences of what he was volunteering to do? Did he, that is, understand the meaning of the term *confession* in that context? For it is ambiguous, depending upon where it is done, to whom, and for what purpose. A suspect does not produce a confession because he "needs to talk to someone"—that is, for relief; that is a therapeutic or a religious, not a legal, confession. A suspect confesses to get a better deal, a lesser charge or more lenient sentence. (Psychological pressures may move him toward confessing, but these are not explicitly acknowledged as motivations, though interrogators know how to evoke and use them.) My interpretation of his outburst is that he confused contexts: the consulting room (or perhaps the church confessional) and the interrogation cell. No one attempted to correct him, and I would suggest that that silence was abusive. It is at least arguable that his confession was not voluntary, however it was legally defined.

Next consider a case in which a young man was accused of killing his fiancée in a wooded park. For a month she had been the object of searches, and finally her body had been found, a few feet away from where the two of them were last seen together. At that juncture he was brought in for questioning. As an undergraduate at a prestigious university, from a middle-class home, he might have been expected to be a little more sophisticated than the previous defendant and refuse to speak without a lawyer present. But the interrogators suggested that, if he insisted on a lawyer, he might show that he had something to hide, so he waived his Miranda rights. The interrogation was protracted; at one point, after repeated denials (according to his court testimony) the interrogator finally said, "Well, *suppose* you had done it. Just fantasy: How would you have done it? What did you do afterward?"

One difference between legal discourse and therapy is that the first deals in "reality," the second in fantasy or "play." The truth of the interrogation and the witness stand is supposed to be the real-world truth, not the truth of the psyche. It is unconscionable for professionals, those who understand and control the discourse, to knowingly confound the two, as they did here. The suspect, probably totally bewildered, cooperated by producing the requested narrative. This was then identified by law enforcement officials as a voluntarily elicited confession, admissible at trial. The defendant argued on the witness stand that he had thought he was just producing a fantasy. The prosecution rejoined that he could not have fantasied such a detailed and horrible story: it must be a true confession. We cannot know; but the deliberate confusion of the two by those who should have known better was abusive, and the reluctance of the law to admit the possibility of intermediate categories between "purely voluntary and cognizant" and "involuntary, coerced or manipulated" enables prosecutors to create the abuse.

How Abuse Happens

Every discourse genre has rules and definitions. As long as these are adhered to, the potential for abuse is absent or at least mitigated. But crossing lines blurs distinctions and leads inevitably to misunderstanding and confusion, and ultimately to abuse of the weaker and noncompetent language user by the stronger professional. Each of the special uses of language discussed here has a legitimate and essential function in the discourse type for which it has been developed. But it becomes abusive by being carried from one genre into another with different expectations, relations, and purposes.

As responsible institutions, both psychotherapy and the law recognize the inherent possibilities for abuse. Both have made attempts to lessen that likelihood or, at least, to discover cases of abuse and take action against the perpetrators. In both, these laudable steps are generally recognized by critics (mostly outside the profession) as less than totally successful: opportunities for abusive behavior continue to exist, and neither discovery nor censure is foolproof or automatic. But of the two, it seems clear that the law has been more successful in policing itself than has therapy, which only recently has begun—under pressure from outside—to take reluctant halfway measures to eradicate some of the most glaring forms of abuse (while remaining generally oblivious of the less apparent, and perhaps more damaging, forms).[9]

One reason therapy has more problems than the courtroom in this area is that the discourse of the former is amorphous; the relationships as well as topics of discourse are ambiguous; and the most likely whistle blowers, the clients, are seen by professionals as being in that role *because* they misperceive reality and have trouble with relationships. Suppose a nonprofessional reports to a therapist that a colleague has behaved in a nontherapeutic way. Too commonly (particularly if the client is female) the accusation is cavalierly dismissed as "fantasy." And since there is no public record, no one to overhear the conversation, it is the client's word against the therapist's: the claim of the weak, untrained, and needy against the strong, knowledgeable, healthy colleague—perhaps the very person from whom the hearer of the complaint gets regular referrals. And since the discourse of therapy is private and intimate, where precisely is one to draw the line between permissible, indeed essential, intimacy and gross impropriety? At worst, a kiss is just a kiss, a caress a slight misjudgment.

In the courtroom, there are legally mandated checks and balances, as well as safeguards arising from the public nature of the discourse, the presence of witnesses. Yet abuse occurs: one has only to think back to the trial of the Chicago Seven in 1969. If the judge oversteps his or her role, the appeals court will see at least some of the misbehavior in the trial transcript, and may reverse all or part of the verdict—as indeed happened in that notorious case. (But this outcome is not guaranteed, and the kinship between trial- and appellate-court judges might make the latter more willing to overlook the peccadillos of the former.) Because the courtroom is known to be adversarial, because it is evident that someone stands to lose, it is easily understood that one player might try to take advantage of another's weakness, and it is recognized that that temptation is inimical to the administration of justice. Hence the elaborate system of juror qualification; the mandated trial procedures and ceremonials; the strict rules of evidence; the possibility of appellate review. True, all of these may be misused or circumvented, but they do exist and often do their job.

Abuse is most likely to sneak into the courtroom where there exist built-in, covert ambiguities. As long as trial procedure is truly concerned with real-world events rather than mental imagery, we can be fairly confident that the safeguards will protect the weak. But too often those strict requirements are breached, often imperceptibly, and then trouble begins.

One case, the special use of "confession," is discussed earlier. Another fuzzy line is that between "intentional" and "unintentional" behavior. Though crucial in homicide decisions, it is not as clear as one might think. Yet the law demands that jurors settle on one or the other. When deciding whether an action was performed, or whether a particular person performed it (decisions based on physically observable reality), dichotomy makes sense: something is done or is not done; A has done it or B has done it. But in respect to mental states, a sharp dichotomy becomes untenable. Particularly in the case of reprehensible deeds, people may intend and not intend at once: Part of them wants to do it; another part blots that desire from conscious awareness. They absent-mindedly pick up a gun as they go to confront someone they don't like. Not that they "plan" to kill, but . . . what if . . . in the course of heated discussion, the pistol finds its way into the hand, the finger squeezes the trigger? What if they are "sure" it was not loaded? A jury will, most probably, eventually come down on one side of the dichotomy or the other, but the verdict may not reflect psychological accuracy. Yet the law does not recognize "sorta meant to" or "almost positive."

So suppose—as in *Delgado,* summarized in chapter 5—two men are riding in a car, and one tells the other that he is in trouble at home. His wife has left him—he thinks, because he is out of a job and cannot buy her "nice things." Here's what he'll do: he'll look in the paper to find someone selling a late-model expensive car; offer to buy it; go to meet that person, kill him or her, take the pink slip, and sell the car himself. *Voilà*— "nice things." Two months later, he does just as he said he would.

The forecasting provides, for the purposes of the law, evidence of premeditation, which permits a finding of first-degree murder, itself a precursor to a possible death-penalty verdict. So life or death may hang on the decision that the remarks I have paraphrased constitute evidence of premeditation. Legally, beyond question, they do. But is that really what was going on?

The problem with accepting this statement as evidence of true premeditation (in the sense of announcing a fully formed intention to act) is that it is senseless. Certainly, I think, if *I* were planning a major crime, I wouldn't spread word around to casual acquaintances (the other guy, who eventually told the police the story, wasn't really a friend). As testimony piles up, the hearer begins to form a picture of an isolated and desperate man who in his heart doesn't want to kill. He wants love—from his wife, from friends—but he can't say that, any more than he can get it. What he wants from his companion is some evidence that he cares: wants him, maybe, to say, "Stop it! I don't want you to destroy your life! Let's do something to fix it." Maybe not consciously, but what looks like a threat is, in truth, a plea for help. The other guy does offer a little support; he's the one who, as reported in chapter 5, said, "Are you crazy?", an attempt at dissuasion. But he doesn't want to get involved. The defendant then proceeds, over the next two months, bit by bit, to put the plan in action: steal the gun, get the paper, call the number, and so on. It certainly looks like premeditated murder, and yet it doesn't make sense that way or, better, only partly makes sense. If premeditation involves the intention and expectation of carrying out the crime, then this is not an example of it. The defendant has told the story not to boast, but in the hope that someone will care enough to make the act unnecessary. The killing was premeditated, but at the same time it wasn't. A therapist could say that, but a defense attorney can't, not credibly, anyway.

I am not sure what the remedy is, or even if there should be one. I am certainly not recommending that the courtroom reconstitute itself as a therapeutic consulting room, alert for nuance and ambiguity at all levels. That would surely lead to the proliferation in court of psychiatric expert witnesses, whose understanding of motive and predictions of future behavior have been shown to be worse, if anything, than that of the average juror. Nor, I think, would it help to complicate the legal definitions of crimes that judges provide jurors and use in their sentencing considerations. In general, the law does well to insist upon certainties and dichotomies. It is only when internal states of mind impinge on external validable reality that these criteria falter. Intention and motive are not, really, the business of the law—and yet they must be if justice is to be tempered with mercy. The law is caught up in a confusion of discourse genres, as well as multiple ambiguities of speech act categories; and the more precise it tries to get about psychic states, the deeper it digs itself into the hole. Abuse arises at points of confusion, as always: the cleverer attorney manages to manipulate the non-professionals (the jurors) into misperceiving the place where the line should be drawn. If the prosecutor plays the better game, the defendant is punished too severely; if the defense, responsibility is insufficiently acknowledged and censured, and society as a whole becomes more insecure: the social contract is threatened.

Rather, we are all going to have to become more vigilant than we now are, in both our professional and our nonprofessional capacities. Clients in therapy and jurors must learn the dangers of mixed genres; know the rules and assumptions of the discourse they propose to take part in; know where the lines blur, and how to discern improper manipulation at those points. Whenever we find ourselves in any form of discourse, we should know, or get informed, from the start:

1. The purpose of the discourse: what constitutes success or failure.
2. The rules: what behavior is proper for each participant.
3. The meaning of each utterance: what is the particular discourse context in which it is used (as opposed, for instance, to its likely meaning in ordinary conversation).
4. The signs of abuse: what steps can be taken to prevent it or punish it.

Of course amateurs should not be expected to come into special forms of discourse (say, courtrooms or therapy) knowing all of this. Yet professionals have always assumed that they should, and have variously taken advantage of ignorance or ridiculed it—but have done little to end it. After all (they reason), it is their possession of the language that makes them professionals, makes them efficacious, and leads others to employ them. Does it make sense to initiate outsiders into the arcana?

But they must, at least enough so that outsiders know what is necessary in order to function properly. Dependent and confused clients or jurors do not enable their respective systems to work well, and as individuals or as members of their society do damage to themselves and others.

It is a hard job, to be sure, to assume responsibility for our communication. But if we do not, we will—individually and as a society—lose our power and our rights. Professional language is too important to be abandoned to professionals.

CHAPTER EIGHT

The Grooves of Academe

MY department is at it again.

Every five years or so we go through it, only to undo our work, like Penelope, with perfect regularity some five years later. We are fighting about revamping the department's graduate program: how many courses, and which, and in what order, are to be required for the Ph.D. It always turns out to be a long-drawn-out process, entailing almost as much internecine acrimony as our all-time favorite fighting issue—hiring of new colleagues. And the real conflicts, the things that fill a simple process with dissension, are never brought out into the light of day: they remain covert, while we debate superficialities.

The Curriculum Committee (and academics do love committees, almost as much as we love subcommittees! they allow us to postpone the inevitable moment of climax, the decision) has proposed a new course, to be required of all graduate students in their first semester of residence, for one unit (most courses are three or four), meeting for one and a half hours, once a week—a very small commitment.

Ordinarily, such small fish don't attract a great deal of discussion, pro or con. We reserve our verbal ammunition for the bigger stuff. But the proposed course is largely concerned with the underpinnings of the field, its ineffable mystique. It would cover, for instance, how to get articles published; how to write abstracts; where to look for bibliography; which journals are geared toward which subfields; the professional interests of the various faculty members of the department.

And more, and worse: how power is allocated in the field of linguistics; who has it, why, and how to get it. And why linguists are such a contentious group, why we can't listen to one another across theoretical boundaries, why scholarly arguments too often turn into personal vendettas.

Everyone agrees that, to receive a Ph.D. in linguistics from the University of California at Berkeley, a student must demonstrate knowledge in a variety of topics: sounds and sound-systems; word-formation and lexical semantics; syntax and sentence-level semantics; processes of historical change; methodology of various types; the claims of competing theories; and, of course, much much more. All this is the explicit and overt knowledge of the field, our public culture, as it were—what we transmit openly to the young and expect them to demonstrate proof of mastering. But that knowledge alone, however broad and deep, does not a competent professional linguist make.

To be one, you not only have to know facts, theories, and methods, you have to know how to be a linguist, how to play by the rules. You have to know how to cite sources and which sources to cite; how to talk and how to write, in terms of style; how to talk and how to write, in terms of which questions may legitimately be raised and which (apparently equally attractive) may not, and what constitutes an "answer." You have to know something about the history of the field, which in turn explains the politics of the field: who likes who and who hates who, who invites contributions from who in the volume who is editing, who is not invited (though working in the same area) and why. You must master the forms, in terms of length, topic, and style: the *abstract,* the *paper* (or *article*), the *monograph,* the *book,* in writing; the *talk,* the *job talk,* the *lecture,* the *panel contribution,* among oral forms. These requirements exist in all academic fields, but each field does them differently and values them differently. In determining tenurability, some departments rank a single book higher than several articles with about the same number of pages; others, the reverse. It's useful to know these things—in fact, often vital for survival in an increasingly competitive business. But no one will tell you this—certainly not spontaneously. Some students know how to pick up a lot of underground stuff by judicious looking and listening; others are sophisticated and brash enough to frame the questions and insist on answers from diffident mentors. But many are not, and it takes them years of agonizing in pre-tenure positions before they understand—too often, too late.

We would be scandalized at a department that refused to tell its students about sentence-construction or typological differences among languages. But we are, some of us, equally scandalized at a proposal to provide the second kind of information openly to all, in the guise of formal course work. When the Curriculum Committee had submitted its lengthy proposal, the first and bitterest fight erupted over this peripheral one-unit course: whether, as "non-intellectual subject matter" it should be taught at all.

Now curricular fights regularly break out over threats to hegemony and relative status. A professor who teaches syntax (for example) will bristle at any proposal to reduce a student's required load in that area: it diminishes the importance of the subfield and, hence, its practitioners' real and symbolic power. People fight over the number and kinds of proficiency examinations required: orals and written papers, at the M.A., Ph.D., and postdissertation levels. These fights are about control. We must make it hard on our students to impress on them that a future in this field is worth struggling for, that the field is legitimate, that we take ourselves seriously. All of these decisions seriously affect a student's graduate career and, perhaps, ultimate success. It is understandable that sides are taken, arguments arise. But a one-hour fight about a one-unit course that threatens no one's preserve?

Well, of course, there are reasons and they are complex. One is simple: university people love to talk. We spew opinions at the slightest provocation; we argue just because it gets the blood flowing (reminding us that we have blood). But we do let some things pass, and this issue might have seemed fit for a bypass.

We are, in fact, fighting about something much bigger than a proposed Linguistics-200 requirement, but no one says so: that would be vulgar. We are fighting about mystique. We are elders in the tribal sweathouse, discussing the rites of initiation the next generation is to undergo. We went through them once, that's how we achieved our present esteemed status. They must, too, in their turn. We all agree on that, and we also agree pretty much that there are certain explicit skills the youth must know before they are deemed ready to take their place in adult society. But someone has raised an unheard-of question: Should they be told the secrets—what happens during the ordeal, what is done and why it is done? It would make it easier for them; the suffering (which we all agree is essential) would make sense; it would be coherent, all the fasting, mutilation, deprivation. Why not enlighten them?

But the oldest of the elders demurs indignantly. Don't we understand *anything?* The whole point is in the mystery. The very senselessness gives the experience a special meaning, a curious depth, makes tribal membership of greater value. If they have to figure it out themselves, by vague hints and overheard whispers, through trial and error, with pain and suffering, they will prize full membership, when it is conferred, all the more. The elders of the tribe must keep its mysteries holy.

Any anthropologically sophisticated Westerner can understand that reasoning in a primitive tribe. But it's a little disconcerting to encounter ourselves at it—ourselves, not only sophisticated Westerners, but intellectuals to boot and, more, intellectuals in an institution which claims as its territory the pursuit of knowledge by reason alone. Mystique has a place, but it is not the stuff of which scholarship is made. But reason alone cannot explain the passions of the argument over Linguistics 200.

Like any other institution, the university has a complex mission, only some of which is supposed to be overtly visible, even to insiders. Therefore, its power relations are complex, and its communications—to outsiders, and to and among its members—are more often than not obscure and ambiguous. In fact, the discourse of academe seems (and not only to non-initiates) especially designed for incomprehensibility. This is demonstrably true. But many of its ambiguities and eccentricities are intentional and intrinsic to the institution, not (as sometimes argued) mere side effects of the university's main communicative purpose.

TRUTH IN LANGUAGE: MISSION IMPOSSIBLE?

Every institution has a public mission, its reason for being, generally couched in benign and even lofty language. The mission of psychotherapy is *change* or *understanding;* of the law, *justice;* of the military, *protection* or *defense;* of government, *order.* In this semantic of noble purpose, we can define the university's mission as the production of *truth,* or *knowledge,* a virtuous enterprise if ever there was one. Unlike the others, it would seem to have no dark side, no hidden risk to anyone. There would seem to be nothing to hide or dissemble.

But for all its virtuousness, the university is an institution, like the others. As such, it must ensure its own survival and the enhancement of the status of itself and its members. It must appear to the outside world, and to its own personnel, as benevolent and useful: it must have something the outside world needs enough to pay for, to support the institution and guarantee its survival. It must be awesome, to convince others of its value; and more, it must seem *good.*

This is a lot to ask of anyone, individual or institution. It is hard to require both love and respect, to retain power and yet radiate benevolence, to get from outsiders scarce resources against strong competition—even more for an institution whose product is abstract, often inscrutable, of no immediate use. We can see why we have to support the government and the military (well, some of us can, some of the time); if we are in pain, we can justify giving money to the medical or psychotherapeutic establishments; if we are legally entangled, we appreciate the necessity of supporting the representatives of the law. But the university has to persuade society that knowledge per se is worthy of support.

Institutions, then, like individuals, have interests at stake; they must compete for resources. But at the same time, to succeed in getting their needs met, they must convince others of their benevolence and disinterestedness. We know what individuals do in such a quandary: they lie. Institutions are no different. Unless the lies become too outrageous or harmful, we mostly accept them. Watergate was intolerable, but Iran-Contragate was within bounds. We know Freud lied, or at least engaged in self-deception, about "infantile seduction," but psychoanalysis retains society's respect. The university, as an institution, can be expected to lie to protect its power and authority.

Cases are not hard to come by. For example, universities are known to reinvent their history when convenient. In 1964, the University of California at Berkeley was shaken by the Free Speech Movement. Popular among students, it was anathema to the administration and many of the faculty, who did everything they could to stamp it out and remove its ringleaders from influence. But life goes on, times change, and what was once a dire threat to institutional business as usual is seen nostalgically, twenty years later, as the shot heard 'round the world, the opening statement of the sixties. It was *important*, it was *historic*, it put the university on the cultural map.

Therefore, in 1984, it seemed appropriate to the university administration—heirs to the men who had called armed deputies in to their rescue—to celebrate the twentieth anniversary of the Free Speech Movement with a plethora of university-sponsored activities stressing the Movement's historic role and the university's participation therein. There were speeches by the powerful and influential, publications, retrospective photography shows, colloquia, everything that can be trotted out to say, This was history and we were a part of it—we made it happen. Lost in the hoopla is the fact that the university was involved, all right—against its will and as a force in opposition. The administration never (that I am aware of) said in so many words: We supported the FSM. But the inviting of celebrities, the holding of public festivities, said as much and, by saying it implicitly, said it more potently, as the message could not easily be contradicted. Nowadays we see the willful distortion of history as evil when it is done by a government or the media. Should it be viewed any differently as an act of the benevolent university?

In fact, it's more troubling. Since it is an institution, it might seem unfair to hold the university to a standard of truthfulness higher than we demand of others. But there is a reason we must. The success of an institution is linked to its efficacy in turning out a well-functioning product. Any institution-internal uncertainty about that product, any hesitation or self-contradiction in the institution, will vitiate the product and, ultimately, eviscerate the institution itself. It may live on (institutions are survivors), but its influence will be much diminished.

Imagine if the military proved unable to protect the people, or if a government allowed rioting to go on unchecked. Those institutions would become objects of ridicule, and be either overthrown or ineffectual, because they were not fulfilling their mission, not producing the goods that they were created and supported in order to produce. Even a partial falling off, a single instance of failure of mission, will weaken an institution's legitimacy, though it probably takes either an egregious example or repeated lesser abuses to actually bring it down.

To catch any institution in a lie is disconcerting, but seldom deeply damaging. The member who lied may be punished, and the institution close over the injury, essentially untouched. Its mission is not compromised. But the mission of the university *is* truth, or knowledge: so when the university lies, it is precisely as if the government dissolved in chaos. To lie is to contravene the mission of the university directly. Therefore, when the university lies (or rather, is lied for by its representatives), it necessarily contributes in a serious way to its loss of legitimacy as an institution.

Unlike other institutions, then, the university has discourse of a particular sort as its mission and its sole product. Some institutions use language just peripherally: the military gets its job done via the giving of orders; but it is weapons that actually do the job, and the job is not intrinsically communicative in nature. The courts and psychotherapy are somewhat different, in that they use particular forms of language specifically to create specific real-world situations; the choice of language influences their result, so that communicative efficacy is crucial for their members, more than in less linguistically oriented institutions.

But the university alone trades only in language, discourse, communication. The university's only acts are speech acts, in Austin's sense.[1] Truth and knowledge are linguistic entities, existing only through and in language. Only for the university is language an end in itself. Therefore (one might argue) the members of the university ought to be especially skillful communicators, since that is all they have to offer, and that is solely how they achieve their effects.

Well, but. . . .

Surely the members of the university community produce a lot of language, in a lot of forms, oral and written, public and private, formal and informal. But by any stylistic standards, the university's prose is inelegant. Indeed, some would call it abysmal—turgid, pompous, inflated, impenetrable, closing off understanding rather than furthering it. The conventional view is that this is a by-product of our mission. We are here to educate and inform, not to entertain. Therefore there is no need for the product to be delightful, amusing, or pleasurable. But "no need" does not begin to express the prevailing attitude toward stylistic amenity. Those who write relatively accessibly are often the recipients of barely veiled hostility, in the form of scholarly disdain: "Just a popular piece." The idea is, if more than three people can understand it, it can't be worth much. In fact, the distress clarity arouses is oddly reminiscent of the discomfiture, at the faculty meeting described earlier at the breaching of the mystique. It's not that there's no need to be intelligible. It's that there is a need not to. Our power, our authority, is intertwined with our ability to maintain secrets even as we seem to dispense them. We write and speak, but we do not communicate. That is our art.

There are other possibilities. In chapter 9, I discuss Elinor Ochs Keenan's work among the Malagasy. In that culture, new information is scarce and precious, hoarded by those who come into possession of any. So when members of the group are asked for information, their tendency is to equivocate and circumlocute, even in giving answers that we would give freely (since information is not in short supply in this culture). The Malagasy value roundabout style as a sign that the speaker knows the value of what is being conveyed, and is therefore a competent member of the culture.

Once academics had no cause to hoard their knowledge, as it had little but intrinsic value. But nowadays things are different: the one who arrives at knowledge first, publishes or patents it before the others get there, will be rewarded with money and prestige. The mission of the university is becoming recognized as (in some of its manifestations) useful in the real world. As a result, that knowledge becomes precious and, therefore, hoarded, as among the Malagasy. The next step is obvious: communication becomes constricted and convoluted, to guarantee that the precious hoard will not get into the wrong hands.

So academese like any linguistic form exists to fulfill the needs of its speakers, who have a peculiar job: while overtly maintaining a pose of egalitarianism and collaborativeness, their intra-institutional relations are really based on hierarchy and adversariality. Trying to maintain those several kinds of relations, overt and covert, drives academics to the turgidities of academese.

HORIZONTAL COMMUNICATION

The university and its members must speak with many voices to fit their many functions—no easy task. First, the university as an institution communicates with the outside world, to show that it is doing a valuable job well. Most universities have public relations offices to send out items to the media on the accomplishments of the university and its members: awards won, public works performed, research completed. It arranges interviews with the media—if a reporter needs a semanticist in a hurry, it will provide one. The university also puts out informational pamphlets: how to apply for admission, the availability of financial aid, and so on. There are publications produced by and about the university intended for the outside world, often alumni, to solicit financial contributions. In all of these contacts, the university presents itself as "the University," a faceless monolith rather than the assortment of diverse interests that it is.

Individuals within the university sometimes communicate, in their identities as university personnel, with the world at large or at least non-academic institutions. They carry from the university, as part of the presuppositions underlying their discourse, the intellectual legitimacy that comes of being a member of that community: expertise is implicitly, if not always legitimately, transferable. In these roles, members consult for industry and government, serve on the panels of government and private granting agencies, serve as expert witnesses in the courtroom. In these roles almost uniquely, professors are addressed and referred to as "Professor" and "Doctor." Within the university, these titles are dispensed with; their use is a mark of naïveté, outsidership (and so is mostly reserved for undergraduates, who are neither members nor even potential members).

More often, and more significantly, members of the university community, especially faculty, communicate as individuals to individuals. Faculty status brings with it membership in several constituencies. First, one is a member of a discipline, a relatively egalitarian relationship. At the same time, one is a member of a department, entailing some hierarchical distinctions; and of one's university's cross-disciplinary community, entailing status distinctions of a different kind. A linguist keeps in contact with other linguists, through publication, professional society meetings, and other conferences, as well as letters and visits. We exchange letters of recommendation for our students and junior colleagues; we review one another's grant applications and submissions for publication.

Within disciplines, we develop special languages. Like any linguistic code, these play two roles. Toward the outside world, they are élitist: we know, you cannot understand, you may not enter. But for insiders they are a secret handshake. When I encounter my profession's terms of art in a piece of writing or a talk, I am obscurely comforted: I am at home among friends. True, "ethnomethodology" and "equi-noun-phrase deletion" are not the friends everyone would choose, but when I find them, I know I am welcome. An article submitted for publication in a professional journal may contain useful and significant information; but if it has been submitted (as occasionally happens) by someone outside the field who does not know the communicative conventions, the reviewer will immediately sense that something is amiss from the absence of the secret wink. In all probability the paper will be rejected. It isn't just that we are being snobbish (we are, of course); but over time we become attuned to our special form of discourse, and literally become unable to understand anything labeled "linguistics" that is not expressed as "linguistics" is supposed to be. The form must match the context, or understanding fails.

A significant part of a graduate student's education consists of learning this language. Part of becoming worthy of the Ph.D., the certificate of membership, is the demonstration that one knows and can use the language.

We do less communicating with colleagues in other fields at our own institutions. Most such discourse is oral, in the form of committee meetings, by which most universities are run. As is typical of oral interchange among the professorate, it tends to go on. The unspoken rule (just about the only thing that *is* unspoken) is that everyone gets to say as much as he or she wants, on whatever topic the speaker desires, as long as it is vaguely relevant. The simplest matters can take a year (or a generation) to solve, by which time most often the original problem has become obsolete. Hence universities are conservative; they move so slowly.

There are recognizable power ploys in academic discourse, often lost on outsiders. In intradisciplinary prose, the footnote is wielded as cavemen wielded clubs, a blunt but effective weapon. The footnote (nowadays, to save printing expenses, more often the end note) says: I know everything about this topic. I could go on forever. Maybe I will. In any case, don't think you can overwhelm me with obscure information. I said it first, here. I control the scholarship, I've read everything, *this is my turf.* The conscientious reader of academic prose must break concentration to read the footnote, another secret signal between writer and reader: We are serious professionals. This communication is not for entertainment. It is *supposed* to be obnoxious.[2]

In interdisciplinary, intramural oral rendezvous, extent of floor-holding is often a sign of clout or a play for it. Since there is often little useful in what is being said, nothing would be said at all if the utterance itself did not fulfill some communicative need.

When I first arrived here many years ago, I quickly found myself serving on a host of academic senate committees, not because I had swiftly distinguished myself as a super politico, but because I was one of a rare and precious breed. Universities were then being threatened with affirmative action suits because women and minorities were underrepresented at all levels of faculty and administration. To demonstrate its lack of bias, the university wished to spotlight women and minorities in positions of governance. But committee positions tend to be assigned to tenured faculty (as they ought to be, since assistant professors should be spending their time publishing). Since I was one of a handful of people with both tenure and two X chromosomes, my presence was exceedingly valuable. I dutifully attended meetings for years, leaving each session with the growing certainty that I was exceptionally stupid or inept. Here I was at one of the world's great universities, in the company of distinguished colleagues, and after listening to the latter for two hours or so, could not recall a single thing of substance that had been said. Worse, it would sometimes occur to me that my respected confrères (almost always men) were spending hours on a point that could be summarized and concluded in a sentence or two. I would attempt to provide that sentence. But once I had spoken, the discourse would close over me like the ocean enveloping a pebble. It was as if I had not spoken—in fact, did not exist. What did it mean?

After a while I figured it out. My colleagues were playing by men's rules: what was important was to gain turf, control territory. That goal was achieved by spreading words around. As an ostensibly egalitarian institution, the university requires that everyone be given equal opportunity to do this. And that is all most people were interested in. If the committee's stated agenda got done, well and good; but if it didn't, what the hell. Next year would bring a new committee, which could start again. The university had been around for a hundred years, what was the hurry? What was important was that everyone had his say, sometimes several of them. I kept running into this wall of words until I learned (*a*) to just say no to committee assignments, on the grounds that they were demeaningly sexist (it is sexist to make appointments to committees purely on the basis of gender); (*b*) when forced to serve, to say nothing.

VERTICAL COMMUNICATION

Within universities, members also communicate vertically: that is, up and down, rather than horizontally across, the hierarchy. The university superficially appears as a community of equal collaborators, equal because engaged in fulfilling a shared mission. No one, inside or outside, believes that. But unlike most institutions, the hierarchy is hidden. Therefore outsiders don't know what signs to look for and, when they come to write about the university, they almost always get it wrong, a problem compounded by the perverse fascination felt by those outside the university about the institution's power structure, manifested in the writing of fiction.[3] Curiously, even many of the fictional works by academics distort or otherwise misrepresent academic power relations as well as the mission of the university.

As with most institutions, much of the university's lore and even *raison d'être* is implicit, passed on to initiates but hidden from the outside world (including undergraduates). The latter therefore form a distorted picture of the institution: the business of the university is teaching; power is assigned according to job title, with "Dean" outranking "Department Chair" outranking "Professor." Sounds plausible, as a guess, but far from the reality. There exist novels in which the plot turns around murders committed by the lowly untitled in order to achieve the chairmanship, or out of vengeance for being passed over. But if murder disturbs the tranquillity of academia, this is an unlikely motive.

Hierarchical power within the university is not based on titles. At Berkeley, and most universities of like stature, chairs, deans, and most other administrators are members of the faculty who assume those positions for a brief period (commonly three to five years) and then return to their former status. Since they have been ordinary faculty and will be again, they are not viewed as particularly lofty, nor are they likely, drunk with power, to appropriate perks not due them: if they tried, they'd be in trouble when they returned to their former rank. Administrators perform a useful, painful, and difficult function—that of saying no when others come to ask for money or favors. For this, they get some extra salary, relief from teaching, an office a cut above the standard, and their own secretary. They also get, depending on their point of view, an excuse to do no research for the duration, or temporary forced retirement from the work they long for.

The real power distinction has to do, above all, with money. In the university as elsewhere, money talks. Not in terms of salary: there are fixed pay scales (there are exceptions, but no one talks much about them). But if power is the ability to get what you want, extra perks and scarce goodies, then it is given to those people or departments who bring money from outside (the government, through grants, or industry) into the university. They are rewarded with more space (buildings), the ability to admit more students, reduced teaching loads, and extra staff support.

Nobel laureates are also powerful, in that they are recipients of perhaps the campus's most coveted and rare privilege: they get a parking space with their name on it.

Otherwise, all tenured faculty are essentially equal within the university. Within each discipline, of course, there are rankings based on reputation: amount of publication, status of publication, achievements of students, and so forth. But the greatest power disparity has to do with the magic word: *tenure.*

Within the university, power and status ascend according to position: at the grossest level, students versus faculty. But a finer breakdown is possible, despite surface appearances of equality like mutual first-naming of all above the level of undergraduates. Undergraduates seem to be at the bottom; or, more accurately they aren't in the running at all; they are outsiders, interlopers. Graduate students, the apprentices, are at the bottom. Then come nonladder teaching personnel, those whose positions mean they will never even be considered for tenure: instructors and lecturers. They have a heavier teaching load than ladder faculty and are paid less, and are disproportionately female. Next on the scale are the nontenured ladder positions, at Berkeley only assistant professors, since tenure comes with associate professorship. (This is not the case everywhere.) Finally, at the pinnacle, are the tenured faculty (there is no significant status difference between associate and full professor).

Any observer at a department meeting can tell who is what. One need only watch and listen, see who speaks, what is said, and what is not. The graduate student representatives generally remain silent unless explicitly asked their opinions. Then they speak briefly, softly, and uncontroversially. Assistant professors may speak on their own initiative, but are generally pretty circumspect. They usually speak only to second the opinions of their particular mentors or allies in the department, and must do so without offending tenured members with opposing viewpoints. They tend to hedge, hem, and haw a lot (even more than academics do in general): a lot of "Of course, what X said sounds really good, but I was just, y'know, wondering . . . ," and "I know a lot less about this than most of you, but do you think it makes sense if . . .?" They are walking a tightrope without a net. Should they antagonize too many tenured faculty (who alone will vote on their promotion to tenure), their days are numbered. On the other hand, if they don't support those elders who are supporting them, their future is apt to be bleak.

The tenured have no such constraints. They say what they want for as long as they want, come what may. Not quite: there are normally implicit rules in effect that specify that everyone will behave nicely, that there will be no obvious name calling or demeaning, or direct confrontation. After all, we will all have to spend many long years together. Tenure is forever. But tenured faculty are constrained only by basic civility, not the need for survival, so they are much more forthright, both in expressing controversial opinions and in expressing them relatively directly.

This power hierarchy makes sense in terms of the mission and function of the institution. The faculty as a whole has the most power, because it is the group that produces and disseminates the product that fulfills the mission: knowledge. Administrators, in this view, merely facilitate this function, so they are but helpful adjuncts. Lecturers and instructors, as the titles imply, dispense knowledge but are not themselves expected to produce it, and so are of lesser value. Graduate students are apprentices, learning how to produce as well as disseminate, meanwhile relieving the producers of their most onerous duties in order to maximize their productivity. And, finally, the undergraduates are the consumers of the product, not directly involved with its creation and therefore irrelevant to the true concerns of the institution. Hence, it makes sense to herd them into large classes, as opposed to the smaller classes and seminars of the graduate level; to restrict their access to professors, who ought not to be distracted from their real work. Likewise, the faculty take pains to socialize graduate students into the profession:[4] detailed critiques of their writings, lengthy oral examinations, close contact; but they typically have no such contacts with undergraduates. This analysis will undoubtedly seem heartless to those whose focus is undergraduate education. The university, it is said, has a moral obligation to produce good teaching in return for undergraduate tuition fees. Yes; just as General Motors has a moral obligation to produce a safe and nonpolluting car. They will do so as long as the institution's real mission is not imperiled, or only in case they are legally compelled to. Graduate education, on the other hand, is more than a moral desideratum: it is imperative for the institution's survival and therefore is done with real solicitude. I'm not defending the system: it *is* heartless, and a large research university can be a cheerless and frightening place for an undergraduate. But this is an artifact of the function of the university, unlikely to change beyond surface cosmetic repairs. The undergraduate who wants continuous personal attention should consider the liberal arts college.

TEACHING VERSUS RESEARCH

The problem of undergraduate teaching raises the specter of another favorite dichotomy and inaccurate perception by outsiders: that there is a sharp distinction between the two major duties of the professorate, teaching and research. The myth has it that we vastly prefer the latter to the former, and (although we are assumed to be paid for teaching alone) sneakily steal as much time from teaching as we can to give to the research monster, to increase our fame and glory. As with many myths, there are grains of truth, but the perception is essentially erroneous.

First, our salaries are paid with the understanding that half our time will be devoted to teaching, the other half to research. Nor do we get away with a ridiculously small number of hours of teaching. True, the number of "contact hours" (hours spent in classes) for ladder faculty at UCB is six per week. That is much less than is the norm at many other public universities and private colleges, because we are expected to devote half the work week to research. "Contact hours" are the tip of the academic iceberg. I calculate that for every hour in class, I spend two preparing: reading, making up lectures, preparing and grading exams, homework and papers, seeing students in and out of office hours— so those six are actually at least eighteen. Then there are meetings (two to four hours weekly), books and journals to keep up with, discussions with colleagues, and so on. We have to struggle to get time for research during the semester, and we mostly spend our vacations writing.

Second, and more important, I always find that teaching deepens and enriches the research I do, and the fact that I'm doing research (I hope) makes my teaching more interesting. I don't find it a dichotomy, but a unity. True, if I'm trying to figure something out, or desperate to finish a piece of writing, I will begrudge the time I have to spend preparing classes and lecturing; but there's a pretty good possibility that something will happen in one of those classes that couldn't have happened if I had remained at the computer—a new synthesis, a new question, a new perplexity.

For instance, the chapter you are reading is not the version I originally submitted to the publisher. All the other chapters in this book were the outcome of years of tryouts: class lectures, professional talks, articles, discussions with colleagues, and so on. This one alone was written for the book without any opportunity for prior discussion. I thought it was satisfactory when I sent it in. But this semester I am teaching a seminar on discourse types, one focus of which is the discourse of the university. I intended merely to cover the material in the original chapter 8. As I was preparing for last week's class, and actually conducting it, my perspective suddenly shifted and I saw an entirely different vision of what the chapter should be about—what you are reading now. I like this one much better. But it never would have come into being if I hadn't had to gather my thoughts into shape for presentation to a class, and respond to my students' questions and objections.

THE RECIPROCITY OF THE STUDENT-TEACHER RELATIONSHIP

The relationship between professors and graduate students is the core of university business, in terms of both mission and politics. It is also perhaps the most complex relationship in the institution, and as such, fraught with pitfalls and potential abuses.

It is obvious that professors have much to give graduate students. Students need so much from us, from the abstract and symbolic—knowledge, training, encouragement—to the more concrete—financial aid during their graduate careers, and later jobs and letters urging promotion. We provide entrée into their chosen world: without our support, at many points and of many kinds, they could not succeed. Therefore, it befits students to be solicitous of professors' needs and whims.

All too often they are not, and not out of malice. Rather, students see faculty as small children see their parents: beings who are above the fray, secure, and beyond needing anything from anyone. Students talk to their mentors like six-year-olds with advanced vocabularies: I need this, do that for me quick, why weren't you there? They don't see the relationship as reciprocal. It is not, in fact, literally reciprocal as I have been using the term (students and faculty play different roles), but in its nontechnical sense, reciprocity exists: they must provide for us, as we do for them.

Students give their mentors one thing only, immortality, as children do their parents. In this case, the immortality is intellectual rather than genetic, but immortality it is. Each of us in the university community today traces some fraction of our thought, our intellectual legitimacy, back to the University of Bologna in the Middle Ages, or to the Socratic circle more than a millennium earlier. Naturally, much has changed: it is the nature of knowledge to evolve. But some fraction is passed on. The job of students is to learn what we have to teach, change it to make it their own, while leaving something of our influence, and pass that on. If we have students, we do not die. Therefore we are happy to teach them, talk to them, read their papers, write letters for them, cheer them in their triumphs, and comfort them in adversity. It's the least we can do, and students should realize it's barely a *quid pro quo*.

POWER IMBALANCE IN THE EGALITARIAN COMMUNITY

In its day-to-day life, the university is a community of unequals, as manifested throughout in its communicative structures. Easy interaction is a concomitant of equality (thus, ordinary conversation is both interactive and conventionally egalitarian); therefore it is to be expected that, as the power disparity decreases throughout the process of academic training, the sharing of discourse power increases equivalently. This process is especially apparent in the university's most prevalent oral mode—the classroom.

There are a few basic forms of class structure, and many variants within each. The large lecture class (over fifty) can be contrasted with the small class (twenty to fifty) and the seminar (under twenty). The major distinction is the possibility of active interaction between lecturer and students. For both mechanical and psychological reasons, the likelihood of any real give and take lessens as class size increases. The chance that any one student in the class will get to make a contribution is even more seriously decreased as class size increases.

The large lecture class makes sense for basic undergraduate courses, even as it has symbolic political implications. It is, as administrators like to remark, "cost-effective": one expensive professor is amortized over maybe several hundred tuitions in a freshman introductory course, as opposed to ten graduate students in a seminar. It also makes sense because, at this basic level, it is improbable that any student has much to contribute to knowledge. Yes, it will aid the student's learning process to be able to ask questions and venture ideas: but that can happen in sections, taught by cheap graduate labor. On the other hand, graduate students often have genuine contributions to make, and should have the chance to be heard by those who can make use of them. Only the boldest undergraduates venture to raise their hands in a large lecture class. That is often as well, since the subject matter is not such as to lend itself to argumentation and debate, consisting largely of what Bateson[5] refers to as *proto-learning,* the learning of facts and methods. Hence, examinations are often of the short-answer, even true-false, variety: you know "the answer," or you don't. Papers, if required at all, are intended to demonstrate basic comprehension of what has been read, rather than an ability to contrast different theoretical perspectives on those readings, much less arrive at an original interpretation. Topics tend to be set by the instructor, rather than discovered by students through their own interests. This is the bottom rung of knowledge, knowing *that* rather than knowing *how,* or knowing how to find out.

As the student progresses, classes tend to become smaller, in the twenty-to-fifty student range. At this size, there is still no real possibility of true reciprocal conversation, but at least it is less intimidating to speak up in class, so students are apt to say more. These classes are intended for advanced undergraduates and beginning graduate students who have mastered the rudiments and are ready to work analytically, coming to independent conclusions (though generally with a lot of preparation and help from faculty). They still take examinations, but these are more and more composed of essays in which students must show their ability to recall theoretical positions and compare and contrast these abstractions in terms of how well they handle data. This is the beginning of what Bateson called *deutero-learning,* or learning to learn: students are becoming able to decide between competing versions of "knowledge." Some, generally undergraduates, are unhappy at the responsibility and rebel, asking questions like, "Is that theory right?" hoping for a clue toward passing the final. Some still persist in asking, "Will that be on the exam?" as beginning students do too often when invited to ask questions in class. But some are becoming more sophisticated, many of these the graduate students of tomorrow.

As classwork puts more and more abstract demands on students, it is gradually and concomitantly decreasing the power imbalance. The analogy to the therapeutic process is real: the more you know, the more power you have in a knowledge-based discourse. The more abstractly you understand, the more you can see knowledge in general not as a set of facts someone provides for you, but as ways of relating facts that you figure out on your own, the more control you have: people are less likely to be able to put things over on you; you have the means to evaluate, more background against which to assess what you hear. The university is a force for conservatism at its lower levels, where it encourages blind acquiescence and regimentation, but becomes subversive later on, when students are encouraged to learn how to learn. No wonder politicians are of two minds about the institution! (And how fortunate for those in power that so many students fall by the wayside before the danger point is reached.)

Still later, principally in advanced graduate courses with low enrollment, the process shifts from unidirectional informing to a collaborative discussion. Topics are often at the cutting edge of the field, where the professor has the advantage of knowing more basic facts, being more in control of theory, but no one has any answers: participants are in it together to get closer to some. Where earlier the instructor set the agenda, now often the class sets it together based on mutual interests, and topics may change as the course develops. Knowledge becomes protean: what you discover one week changes the complexion of next week's meeting. The relationship is still by no means egalitarian. The professor still grades, sets the basic structure, and does much of the holding forth; but increasingly as the course goes on, more and more of the work is done by the students. Students are still respectful of the professor; teasing goes only one way. But disagreement is not only permissible but expected, *as long as it is done right.* There are no exams at this level: exams imply, "learning the material," but here what is to be learned is less the material than an approach to it, pure deutero-learning. Paper topics are initiated by students, loosely based on the course topic, and are expected to demonstrate independent thinking and mastery not only of facts and methods but of responsible conjecture.

So even the instructional process of the university demonstrates its commitment to knowledge and symbolically represents to learners that the achievement of knowledge is of several sorts, with the harder kinds associated with power in the institution. The different sorts of classes are more than an administrative convenience: they demonstrate a succession of steps, incremental mastery; each form is appropriate to its intended function in the overall process; each entails a discourse of its own sort.

HOW TO WRITE LIKE A PROFESSOR

The written style of the university, too, has its own separate formats, each justified by function. This is especially true of intradisciplinary scholarly writing. A significant part of a student's training involves learning these procedures, learning how to sound right as well as how to make valid contributions. I spoke earlier of the relation between the traditional convoluted style of academia and the academic's need for signals of solidarity and acceptance by peers. But turgidity does not come naturally. It must be acquired by slow degrees. Deviation in any direction is punishable.

Neophytes must learn both correct surface form and deeper matters of style and content. They must, first and most obviously, learn how to juggle the technical terminology of their field: the secret handshake *par excellence.* They must learn what each special term means, who introduced it, and therefore its political significance. (While *scenario, frame,* and *schema* may, in discourse semantics and pragmatics, be mutually interchangeable, students who study with the scholars responsible for each term will use that term rather than the others in their own writing.) They will learn what ideas justify the postulation of special terminology: how revolutionary, how important they must be. They will read enough of the literature to know, when they have thought of an idea, whether a term already exists for it, to avoid duplication. They will also learn that creating a term, and offering it to the world, is an act of power best left to the established members of the field. It takes some gall for graduate students to propose terms for their own ideas; for an undergraduate to attempt this borders on the treasonable. And of course, to propose a term when one already exists exposes one to ridicule; and to misuse someone else's terminology, worse.

Undergraduates (and beginning graduate students) are not encouraged to play the same game as their betters. It does not become an undergraduate to sound like a professor. Moreover, since the undergraduate does not have sufficient experience or knowledge, the attempt is apt to be risible. As students progress through graduate school, they are expected to acquire academic style, a little in course papers, more in qualifying papers. But the usage must grow gradually, sparingly, avoiding the appearance of presumptuousness, the accusations of usurpation of territory that belongs to the elders. The pinnacle is reached with the dissertation, wherein a student demonstrates worthiness to become a full-fledged member of the society, having passed all the ordeals the elders have to provide. The dissertation shows not only that the student has mastered the knowledge of the field and its methods; not only that the student has something original to add to that store of knowledge; but that the student knows the rules, knows how to behave like a member of the culture. So the dissertation must be couched in the finest and most etiolated of academese, redolent of footnotes, stylistically impenetrable, bristling with jargon. Only thus can proper deportment be demonstrated.

Indeed, never again is it expected to this extent. For the next several years, through the assistant professorship and until tenure, caution is recommended: style should be academic, though a little relaxation is permissible. The dissertation showed one could take direction: now one must show an ability to be on one's own. Tenure decisions involve the assessment of "collegiality": practically speaking, that means, Do nothing that might offend the thinnest-skinned colleague. Only after the granting of tenure is it safe to abandon the style for something snappier; and even then, obloquy is a probable outcome. But tenure smiles at obloquy.

If academic style were merely the result of carelessness or unconcern for the graces, it would increase as its user advanced in the field, in a straight upward direction; and if undergraduates were capable of using the style, it would be deemed an unmixed sign of competence, not a little off-color. But we find instead the parabolic curve of figure 8.1, which suggests that the style is connected to notions of privilege and power. You are *allowed* to use academese when you have convinced the elders that you are a serious apprentice, no longer an outsider (who is not allowed knowledge of the mysteries). You *must* use academese to prove your worthiness of acceptance and your ability to submit to discipline. You *may* abandon academese, wholly or more likely in part, when you are the gatekeeper and need no longer worry about being excluded from the society.

Over the course of an academic career, writing gradually becomes more overtly territorial, assumes more power for its producer, by achieving more length and broader topical scope. Undergraduate and early graduate course papers are unseemly if they exceed twenty pages or so. They deal with small and concrete topics: no total solutions, no metatheoretical debate. Later, through qualifying papers and other predissertation work, length increases to a maximum of fifty to one hundred pages, and topics become more abstract, more cutting-edge, and of broader scope, as the student demonstrates the desire to achieve full maturity and the ability to understand what the territorial battles are about. The dissertation

FIGURE 8.1
Privilege and Power in Academia

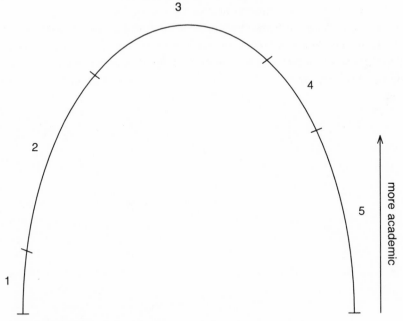

1. Undergraduates and beginning graduate students
2. Advanced graduate students
3. Students writing dissertations
4. Nontenured faculty
5. Tenured faculty

stakes a claim. The writer takes a theoretical stance, either adapting a mentor's theory or inventing a modest theoretical innovation; applies it to a fairly broad swath of language; and tests it against the best that the field has to offer, engaging in conflict with established members of the group (but always respectfully). A dissertation is longer, too, around three hundred pages. Much more than that, though, or too grandiose a proposal marks the writer as hubristic. The assistant professor is allowed a larger swath of territory. But because of the pressure to publish, the tendency is to stick to only mildly controversial topics that can be handled in a relatively short space, in a relatively short time. Later, with tenure, the sky's the limit—on length, breadth, and self-assurance, as well as interpersonal obnoxiousness.

The discourse style of academia turns out not to be solely a by-product of the knowledge factory. It is also the language of a society with complex and covert power and territorial assumptions, often in conflict with its express mission. As an institution, the university is relatively but not totally benign. As a society it is hierarchical and authoritarian, yet necessarily egalitarian and collaborative in its creation of a product. That it does so often produce products of value, that it protects its members from evaluation by the crass standards of the outside, make it an unusually benevolent institution. But that fact should not blind observers to its shortcomings, or cause them to overlook the ways in which those who have power in the university, as in any other institution, misuse it and abuse its weaker members.

III

LANGUAGE ACROSS
CULTURES

CHAPTER NINE

You Say Tom*ay*to, I Say Tom*ah*to

T HE scene is (once again) a California courtroom. A judge is holding sentencing hearings. Before him now is a young man of Asian descent, his last name not one of any of the forms familiar to Americans. The defendant is speaking through the interpreter at his side.

"You call it courtship, we call it kidnapping," says the judge. The interpreter whispers to his client. "Don't let it happen again. I will tolerate one culture clash, no more. Do you understand?"

The interpreter and the defendant confer briefly. The defendant signifies his understanding and compliance with a nod. The judge gives him probation; the case is closed.

The text itself is easy enough to comprehend. The youth has pleaded guilty to kidnapping, and the judge has given him probation. But the subtext is more complex; and what underlies that, more troublesome still.

In some cultures, marriages are arranged by ritual kidnapping: the man, or members of his group (family, clan, tribe), abducts a suitable young woman and holds her incommunicado until she and her kinspeople agree to a marriage. Sometimes the ritual is prearranged (the young woman and her people are in on it); sometimes not. But as long as it is the way marriage is contracted, as long as before too long everything is settled to the satisfaction of all parties who need to be satisfied (which may or may not include the woman), the matter is laid to rest. No crime has been committed; it is just the way things are done—and have been done since time immemorial. It is inconceivable that anything could be wrong with the tradition, or that marriages could be properly contracted in any other way.

In other cultures, marriages are arranged by the couple themselves, after a period of courtship in which both are seen as free agents, able to come and go, choose or not choose. The families play a subordinate role, if any. The contract is licit only in case both parties testify that they have entered into it freely, without even the appearance of coercion. To force someone into marriage through coercive means is a crime. (And, if revealed, the marriage is null and void.)

Within each culture, the local tradition works well, and any other options seem bizarre and unreasonable. No problems arise as long as each culture keeps to itself. But the preceding vignette illustrates what can happen when cultures confront one another without making their assumptions and rules fully explicit. Evidently (I witnessed only the final scene of the drama), the young man was a relative newcomer, probably a Hmong tribesman. The young woman may have been a more assimilated member of the same group or a member of a different culture with other marital traditions. He had kidnapped her (or had her kidnapped) with the intent of marrying her. (We don't know what prior contact they might have had.) In any case, she (or her family) had objected and taken legal steps to voice that objection. The young man, whose aim was, as the judge said, "courtship," was charged in an American court of law with kidnapping, a felony.

From the young man's perspective, things have become surreal. He is in a strange place, like nothing he has ever seen, nothing he can imagine. (It is unlikely his tribe back home had formal courtrooms like this one.) People are speaking a language he cannot understand; all he knows is that he is in trouble, big trouble. If he remembers back to the time he was forced to leave his own country, "big trouble" may have even more frightening ramifications for him than it would for us. He has been warned by his lawyer (through the interpreter) to be obedient, just say yes and no where prompted. He has been told to wear his best clothing (or a passable suit has been found for him)—more signs that something portentous and strange is in the works. But he doesn't have the language to get his questions answered, doesn't even know how to form them, or doesn't dare. (The interpreter is undoubtedly doing his best, but he himself may not be fully fluent—in English, Hmong, or both—or may not fully understand all that is going on.)

Then how can we imagine a translation of the judge's English into Hmong? And how can what the interpreter says possibly be meaningful—in any way equivalent to the judge's intention—to the defendant? The judge is wise and caring, but helpless because of the constraints imposed on him by the legal system and the language barrier. His solution is compassionate and legally correct, but he cannot communicate his reasoning to the person who needs most to understand it.

CULTURE MEETS THE CLASH

Culture clash, a phrase intelligible to most Americans, presupposes a society conversant with the idea of multiple cultures coexisting uneasily. What sense would it make, even without the language difficulty, to a man just recently torn from a society that knew only itself and its own ways? Do the words *culture* and *clash* exist in Hmong? And if they do, does the literal translation convey a meaning anything like that of the original? The defendant nods at the judge, but does he comprehend what he was told? Even if he knows he'd *better not do it again,* does he fully understand what "it" was, or why he shouldn't? And how to translate "you call it courtship, we call it kidnapping" into the language of a culture in which courtship *is* kidnapping?

This is an extreme case of cross-cultural misunderstanding, as it is always the extreme cases that show up in courtrooms. But, the same sort of thing happens to each of us from time to time, sometimes so subtly that we don't realize that it's happening, or so ambiguously that we don't recognize our discomfiture as resulting from a culture clash. We ascribe it to personality differences, conflicts of interest, sheer obtuseness, or perversity and decide that the troublemaker is a bad human being. We will not deal with him or her in the future, or if we do, we will go forearmed, determined that we won't get screwed again. But, in fact, we may be the victims not of misbehavior but of misunderstanding.

Often, too, we notice that people different from ourselves (in race, nationality, or gender, or example) behave in ways we do not expect, as we would not behave in a given context. If we went to another country and noted that its inhabitants wore a special, colorful form of dress, we'd be able to see it as a distinctive national characteristic and would say that the inhabitants of Country X dress "differently" from us, not that they dress "wrong." If we tasted their food, we would also say that it was "different," and if we're at all sophisticated, we do not equate that with "bad." But when people behave differently from the standards we are accustomed to, we don't just say that it's "different": we're apt to think of the behavior as "wrong," "weird," or "bad."

We make little effort to understand it on its own terms, from the other person's point of view. We see all behavior from our own internal perspective: what would that mean if *I* did it? And, of course, if I, as a member of my own group, did what that person did in the presence of other members of my own group, it would be strange or bad: it would have specific meaning in that context. We don't usually extrapolate; we don't say, "Yes, but in *his* frame of reference, what would it mean?" We assume the possibility of direct transfer of meaning, that a gesture or act in culture A can be understood in the same way by members of culture B. Often this is true: there are universals of behavior, but as often that is a dangerous assumption; and by cavalierly ignoring the need for translation, we are making misunderstanding inevitable.

We are fully aware that the linguistic repertoires of societies differ in vocabulary, syntax, and sounds. But it is less readily apparent that the more abstract components of communication, the pragmatic structures, are rule-governed and therefore potentially different from group to group. This variability is one way in which people are different from animals. When a dog wags its tail, it always means the same thing, no matter what breed of dog it is, no matter where it was raised. But a human gesture may have different meanings depending on who uses it and where it is used. The cheerful American "OK" sign (thumb and forefinger in a circle, other fingers extended) is obscene in Brazil.

These differences show up both in fine detail (a wink means one thing to one group, something else to another) and in larger and more abstract structures. For every culture develops a set of overarching strategies for communication. When it is appropriate to be direct and to the point, and when not? When indirectness is proper, what form should it take? What kinds of joking—teasing, kidding, or irony—are expected, between whom? Every culture has a notion of "politeness" and therefore, of its opposite. But sometimes politeness is essential; sometimes, optional or even inappropriate. Sometimes, too, impoliteness is the best response. Cultures also differ on what form politeness should take. Members of two cultures may intend to be polite to each other. But if each culture has different politeness strategies, they may unwittingly offend each other with the best intentions in the world. And because no one considers it good manners to talk about a person's behavior to his or her face, these questions don't get discussed, and misunderstandings fester.

Other kinds of decision affect speakers' cross-cultural effectiveness—that is, become political in multicultural contexts. How should one present oneself in public and in private? How are different kinds of discourse transacted? Whose job is it to ensure that understanding takes place—speaker's or hearer's? Does the speaker compliment the hearer by being direct and to the point, or will that seem boorishly offensive or incompetent?[1] Mostly we are unconscious of the fact that our culture has made all these decisions for us and imposed them upon us as part of our upbringing and education; but when confronted with the radically different assumptions of another culture, we are forced to realize that ours is not the only way, that decisions have in fact been made and can be made differently. In cross-cultural communication, our political efficacy depends on our flexibility and our ability to see our own choices as just that—choices. Some ways of approaching these issues can be found by looking at one branch of pragmatic theory, the area of conversational logic, which deals with strategies and choices of directness and indirectness.

CONVERSATIONAL LOGIC

The theory of *conversational logic* was developed in the 1960s by the philosopher of language H. Paul Grice,[2] to counter the claims of formal logicians that ordinary language, being imprecise and ambiguous, could not be used as the basis of a system of logic. He argued that, with certain assumptions, ordinary conversational usage could be rendered rigorous and therefore logical. Linguists took Grice's outline and fleshed it out, trying to make it into a complete model for people's understanding of one another's indirect utterances.

The theory posits the *Cooperative Principle* as underlying the understanding of all human discourse: speakers engage in conversation with the intent and expectation of exchanging information. Therefore, any piece of discourse is normally assumed to be as informative as it can be, under the circumstances, and as informative as it needs to be in order that the other person may derive from it the requisite information. In theory, then, the best and most typical form of communication would be direct and to the point. Four *Maxims of Conversation* direct a contribution into this optimal form.

Quantity: Say just as much as is necessary.
Quality: Be truthful.
Relevance: Be relevant.
Manner: Be direct, succinct, and clear.

The ideal communication envisioned by the theory is just that, an ideal seldom actually encountered in real conversations. Indeed, if speakers were to adhere strictly to the Maxims, their utterances would grow tediously predictable, and hearers would quickly become insulted or bored. So Grice proposes another mechanism, *conversational implicature,* which interprets utterances that deviate from the Maxims. By means of implicature, speakers can understand even highly oblique and ambiguous utterances, in the right context. (Grice doesn't talk about when implicature is used, or how it is understood in general, or what the difference is between implicatures that successfully communicate their speakers' intentions and those that create confusion. He does distinguish "violations" of the Maxims, which utilize lawful implicature, from "floutings," which go beyond the boundaries of the system and create chaos, but he doesn't provide general pointers to tell whether a given instance is one or the other.) What is useful about this system is its underlying insistence on cooperation: the assumptions that speakers do (mostly) intend their contributions to be meaningful; and that, when meaning is not directly discernible, there are reasons for it and ways to discover the intended meaning. We make allowances for imperfect communication because we believe in one another's essential goodwill.

Grice's major points are these: the basic purpose of talking (of all kinds) is the transmission of information; any departure from that is a violation in the sense that it requires special explanatory devices, whereas adherence to perfect logic does not; logical communication is defined in terms of supplying just as much information, no more and no less, as the occasion requires, of being truthful, and of being relevant both to the perceived purpose of the discourse and to what has been said previously. If an utterance does not meet the logical standards set up by the Maxims, participants can still understand it by performing inferencing operations, the conversational implicatures. Further (since logical communication is an ideal), for implicature to be properly used, speakers must recognize a pressing external reason: it must make more overall sense to be illogical under certain conditions. Participants must determine what makes sense within the confines of the discourse itself, in terms of linguistic structure. But even before they speak (or interpret as hearers), they take inventory of all the other business going on around the speech act itself: the context, social and psychological, in which they are talking, the interactive framework into which the linguistic utterance fits. It makes no sense in this larger sphere to be perfectly logical if that is going to interfere with the purpose of the communication—to accomplish something in the real world; to achieve persuasion, cooperation, success as a human being. So they find themselves, in most discourse contexts, negotiating between two equally pertinent interests: to be clear, get the message across unambiguously so that the other can respond to it without uncertainty; and to be socially responsive, aware of their own and another's needs as human beings, to be treated as competent and likeable, and to feel that way themselves.[3] The second strategy, *rapport,* may conflict with the first, *clarity;* and when it does, in most kinds of discourse the second prevails. This makes sense, because all the logic and intelligibility in the world won't get others to cooperate unless they see it as worth their while.

In contexts where the linguistic message itself, or the impersonal business at hand, is defined as the important issue, clarity may take precedence over rapport, and the relationship between participants will be secondary if it exists at all. So in a lecture designed purely to impart information that the hearers need for their own purposes, the speaker may not spend time showing goodwill or interest in the hearers: no joking, no indications of personal interest, just making the point. But even in a strictly business phone call, speakers often feel that a bit of rapport is called for, and begin and end the conversation with personal questions and remarks: "How's the family?" "Been good talking to you . . . let's do lunch." In other kinds of talking, like conversations among friends just for the sake of talking, the rapport-based contributions may greatly out-weigh the clarity, or information-based, ones. The extreme occurs when people really have nothing to say to one another but social convention demands that they say something: the small talk at a cocktail party, which is virtually all rapport, with information tossed in like mayonnaise to hold the conversational salad together.

Within friendly conversation, the proportion of Maxim-related utterances to violations depends upon a number of factors. For one, the more "risky" the topic, or the more uncomfortable the participants with one another, the less direct a contribution is apt to be, and the more use will be made of implicature. So if participants are to be able to understand implicatures in terms of the Maxim-based statements which they are intended to convey, they must agree about these factors.[4]

THE USE AND ABUSE OF IMPLICATURE

Suppose one speaker (Alice) at a party feels that a polite conversational gambit is asking what another (Bob) does for a living. Because it's a safe ploy to her, her question will be direct, and she will expect an explicit reply. But now imagine that Bob has been out of work and disconsolately looking for a job. To him, Alice's innocent bit of small talk may seem loaded and dangerous, and he will try to fend it off (while remaining polite) by saying as little as possible while seemingly answering the question:

> ALICE: So, Bob, what do you do for a living?
> BOB: Oh, you know, a little of this and that.

Alice will be put off by Bob's (to her) inexplicable dodging, as Bob was by Alice's (apparent) prying. Their relationship is not apt to prosper.

Indirectness is used both to protect the speaker and to salvage the hearer's feelings, as in this sample conversation:

> CARL: Say, Dick, did you finish that book you borrowed?
> DICK: Well, y'know, I've been so busy lately. . . . Things have been frantic around here.

Both speakers are utilizing implicature, each for different reasons. Carl probably means by his question a request or demand: "Give my book back." But direct injunctions are often unsafe: they put participants into a power conflict, at least potentially, and are therefore avoided if possible. Carl is in fact protecting both himself and Dick from encroachment by the other. If Carl were to make a direct demand and be put off, he'd lose face; but if he frames it as an information-seeking question, the refusal isn't nearly as confrontational. The indirectness reassures Dick that Carl doesn't mean to intrude or confront, so Dick doesn't get upset. Dick, in turn, frames his refusal as a statement of inability, meaning something like, "I would give it to you if I could, but I can't." The refusal is framed not as a confrontation: "Make me," "I won't," "I don't want to," but as the result of circumstances out of Dick's control. Dick protects Carl's self-esteem and, at the same time, avoids the responsibility for causing him dissatisfaction. It becomes clear why direct confrontations like the following seldom occur in friendly conversation:

> CARL: Give me my book back.
> DICK: No, I don't want to.

Usually speakers are more than willing to entangle themselves in the complexities of interpretation in order to avoid encroachment, territorial competition, and assignment of blame. But if the conversation were on a completely risk-free topic, indirectness would be much more puzzling (and much less likely). Try to imagine, for instance:

> ELLA: I wonder if that's a watch on your wrist?
> FRANK: It's just about when the news is on TV.

as a way of saying:

> ELLA: Can you give me the time?
> FRANK: It's 6:00.

Since there is nothing normally threatening in either of the original statements, the indirectness of the participants is puzzling, to them as to us; and even though each speaker's utterance would be interpretable by the use of implicature, neither could do the translation because the reason for implicature is not apparent.

But politeness (that is, the avoidance of conflict) is not the only reason for indirect communication. Often we are a little indirect when no threat is involved. So for instance:

> GLORIA: My car's out of gas.
> HARRIET: There's a garage around the corner.

At first glance, this appears to be a perfectly logical dialogue. But closer inspection shows that there are pieces missing that must be supplied by the hearer via implicature. Gloria's apparently informative declarative statement is really a request for help or information: "Tell me where I can get gas for my car." (Hence, it would be inappropriate for Harriet to respond directly: "Is that so? Then you can't go anywhere." In fact, it would be rude.) And Harriet's response is technically incomplete: Gloria must supply information: "Gas is available at garages." But since this information is assumed to be known to all members of the culture, adding it would be strange or insulting and would convey: "I know you aren't one of us." So even though the direct information isn't threatening in itself, providing it would be anomalous and would make troublesome assumptions.

Sometimes the use of implicature is normal, though there is no discernible motive for indirectness:

IRENE: How was your evening?
JOE: Not bad at all.

If Joe means "very good," as he probably does, his statement violates the Maxim of Quantity. What's the advantage of it? We assume that there must be some sort of reward to induce speakers to go through complicated byways when a direct route is available. But pure communicative efficiency (getting the point across in the shortest time) is not always necessarily the desired goal. Verbal playfulness is *fun*, an undervalued commodity. Just as you don't always take the most direct route when driving, but choose one that is more interesting or beautiful, you might well choose a verbal strategy that is more indirect just because it is more interesting, making both participants test their conversational mettle and use their intelligence more fully. In the previous example—admittedly a trivial case— Joe *could* have said, "Very good," but that would have been even more banal than what he actually did say. Indirect communication can be understood as a compliment implying that the hearer is intelligent enough to figure it out, as well as a suggestion that the participants share a cultural background, a powerful unifying influence and a good way to achieve cooperation. So strict adherence to the Maxims is likely just in case the transmission of information is recognized by all participants as the sole reason for the communication. Under other conditions, it is likely that at least a few small violations will occur as a way of achieving rapport, thereby increasing the chances that the communication will achieve its goal. The more interpersonally risky that goal, the greater the likelihood, and extent, of violations. As part of their cultural background, members of a society share an understanding of what utterances are dangerous, and of the best ways to avert the danger; as well as what forms of implicature are apt to be understood, in general or in particular cases; and what kinds of indirectness are complimentary.

CROSS-CULTURAL MISUNDERSTANDING

Cultures do not make these distinctions in the same way. Research suggests that all cultures have ways to be indirect, and recognize conditions under which indirectness is desirable. But the circumstances and forms can differ considerably from one society to another or even from one group in a society to another. Elinor Ochs Keenan[5] discusses the practices of the Malagasy, a group on the island of Madagascar. Theirs is a closed society, in which relatively little happens; there isn't much news, so that what there is becomes a treasured commodity. (In this they are unlike us, who are inundated continually with more new information than we can possibly handle.) Like any valued commodity, information among the Malagasy is hoarded, given out only grudgingly (because once you give it to someone, you don't own it any more). But it's rude, for them as for us, to refuse point-blank to answer information-seeking questions. When someone asks such a question, its recipient is expected to be evasive, even in response to questions that we would normally answer directly. We would see the direct transmission of this sort of information as not threatening in any way, and therefore as not needing to be disguised; but for them, *any* sharing of facts is problematic. So the following might be a normal interchange:

A: Is X at home?
B [*who knows that X is, in fact, there*]: Y says X wasn't in the market today.

From B's response and other things A knows, A can figure out the correct answer, but must work for what, for us, would be given for free.

Irony: Britain versus the United States

Even otherwise similar cultures, like the United States and Great Britain, can differ about the kinds of implicature that are permissible. The British have always regarded themselves, somewhat idealistically, as a homogeneous society in which everyone shares the same basic values and knowledge. Americans, on the other hand, recognize their country as a "melting pot" into which have been thrown people of many disparate cultures, with different values and assumptions: Americans do not count on sharing as the British do.

Irony is a form of implicature which requires an underlying assumption of basic understanding. it is a violation of the Maxim of Quality: the speaker is saying something known not to be true. It can be recognized as a playful gambit, not a lie or a bizarre statement, only when participants are sure that they share basic beliefs. If I want you to understand "John's a real genius" as "John's stupid," I must have reason to believe that you already share my low opinion of John's intelligence. So irony both makes use of presumptive homogeneity and reinforces it: understanding irony communicates, "You and I are the same." But if it isn't understood on its own terms, the result can be disastrous.

The British are skilled ironists; most Americans have trouble with irony, sometimes failing to see it at all, often perceiving it as sarcasm—something completely different in function. In 1964, the Beatles were riding a wave of immense popularity in both Britain and the United States. One of them, John Lennon, made the statement, "The Beatles are more popular than Jesus." As a Briton, and as John Lennon, he clearly intended his statement to be ironic—not a boast, not a statement of literal comparison, but intended to convey something like, "Isn't this attention somewhat ridiculous? We really aren't in the same class as Jesus at all, but people are acting as if we were." He could have said just that, but then the statement would have been banal rather than clever—not at all Lennon's style. In England, his remark was taken as intended and not given a great deal of attention. But in America, there was an explosion of righteous indignation. The comment was taken literally: Lennon boasting that his group had outdistanced the founder of Christianity. Disk jockeys refused to play Beatles music on the air; many communities held public burnings of Beatles records, along with appropriate sermons delivered with utter seriousness by religious leaders. We might say that this example proves the truth of the epigram that England and the United States are two countries divided by a common language. The purely linguistic grammars, for this utterance at least, are identical; but the understanding of the rules and use of irony is part of the grammar of British, not American, English.

The Mysterious East

Evidence exists that in some societies, such as Japan, the very definition of conversational logic is profoundly different from ours. Among the Malagasy, implicature is more widespread than here; the British use forms of implicature different from American usage. But these cultures recognize the primacy of the Cooperative Principle: the transmission of information is the point of communication; and the ideal utterance, the one that does not require special explanation, is the one that emphasizes informative content and is thus in keeping with the Maxims. But this primacy appears to be questionable in Japan in many discourse contexts (or rather, in many more discourse types than is true for us, for we do have types of discourse in which information is more or less irrelevant: small talk and poetry, for two). Expository prose in Japanese requires much more work on the part of its reader than does its English equivalent. In fact, to the Westerner, a great deal of Japanese discourse seems frustratingly ambiguous or vague. It is not even that diligence will allow one to figure out the one intended meaning (which might suggest that the Cooperative Principle is still in effect, but with implicature accorded a wider scope), but that often there is no single intended meaning discernible, just a kind of general sense of what one needs to know. A paraphrase is not available for clarification, as it would be for us. Clarity plays a greatly reduced role in Japanese communicative values—even at a purely linguistic level. Personal pronouns are omitted in contexts where (to a Westerner) they are necessary to disambiguate; tense is often not explicitly expressed in places where European languages usually require it. Intended relationships between clauses in a sentence are much less explicit than their English translations have to be. On the other hand, Japanese requires great explicitness about rapport-based strategies, where English often permits or requires vagueness. While most Western cultures are *speaker-based* in their communicative strategies (the job of determining what an utterance is to mean is up to the speaker, who bears the responsibility for the meaning), the Japanese strategy is *hearer-based:* the meaning resides in the hearer's mind, and it's the hearer's job to extract the point of what is said, not the speaker's to be clear about it.[6]

The linguist Yoshiko Matsumoto has discussed the differences between Japanese and Western understandings of *informativeness.*[7] For Westerners, there is a sharp discrepancy between those aspects of communication that are informative—that is, are in keeping with the Maxims of the Cooperative Principle and exist for the sake of transmitting factual data about reality—and those that are interactive, designed to create or express the feelings of the participants about their relationship. For the Japanese, there is no such distinction. The interactive relation is encoded and understood as an integral part of the information content of the message. Therefore it is impossible, in Japanese, to select a neutral form, one that avoids any interactive component, as is easily done in English. For instance, the speaker of English can choose forms like: "The cat is on the mat," which provides only factual information. Indeed, it is easier and in many contexts more normal to select "neutral" forms like this than those that do encode interactive relations. We can choose the latter if there is good reason, for instance, by saying: "That cat is on the mat." The choice of *that* tells the hearer that the feline is spatially distant from the conversational participants, or expresses the speaker's emotional distance from or disdain for the cat. Or we can say: "The kitty is on the mat," to convey affectionate feelings for the animal, as well, perhaps, as intimacy with the hearer.

In other words, English is capable of encoding interactive information, but often avoids it. In Japanese, on the other hand, the avoidance of rapport creates anomalous utterances. Matsumoto presents two possible ways to express the verb *is* in the sentence, "The cat is on the mat" in Japanese. Each has implications beyond the simple denotative meaning; there is no neutral choice:

Plain Form

Neko	-	wa	matto	-	no	ue	-	ni	*iru.*
cat (topic)		mat	possessive		topic	locative			be (exist)

Polite Form

Neko	-	wa	matto	-	no	ue	-	ni	*imasu.*
cat (topic)		mat	possessive		topic	locative			be (exist)

Although the first form might appear in a logic text, in which there is no implied relationship between writer and reader, its range of occurrence would be severely limited. It could not be used to convey information to one's superior in a conversation, to a non-intimate equal, or to an inferior. The polite form is also constrained: it could not appear as an example in a logic text, nor is it likely to be used between speakers who are equal and intimate.

Westerners see clarity and rapport as opposite strategies. There are circumstances where each one is preferred. To the Japanese speaker, on the other hand, the two are inseparably interrelated parts of every communication. What we in the West dismiss as extraneous and optional are to the Japanese intrinsic parts of the communication, both psychologically and grammatically.

We are often compelled to make a stark decision: to be direct and informative, and risk dangerous confrontation and conflict; or to be delicate and tactful, salvage the relationship, but risk misunderstanding. When a clash arises between rapport and clarity, we normally resolve our indecision in favor of rapport. Unclarity, we feel, can usually be repaired later; but the damaging of a relationship by the failure to be polite is frequently irreparable.

THE POLITICS OF IMPLICATURE

Not only can speakers provide differential amounts of information depending on cultural and contextual expectations; hearers, too, can evaluate utterances for the relative amounts of rapport and clarity they contain using similar criteria. A communication that would ordinarily be interpreted in a perfectly straightforward way (as fully in keeping with the Maxims) if its recipient had no reason to believe that information was purposely being withheld, might be subjected to convoluted interpretation with extraordinary use of implicature if there were grounds for suspicion. There must be ample reason for recipients to use this strategy—a widespread belief that a government or the media are withholding information. Otherwise, we have a name for unjustified presumptions of the need for implicature: *paranoia.*

Citizens of and outsiders with interests in the activities of totalitarian countries often have good reason to resort to these tactics. Indeed, over the forty years of the Cold War, specializations have sprung up in this country's government and media, whose mission is specifically to develop strategies of reading meaning into apparently meaningless data culled from controlled sources in those countries. Among the most prominent have been the Sovietologists and China watchers. Seemingly trivial or irrelevant data (apparent violations of Quantity or Relevance) are interpreted to reveal their "true" meaning, via implicature.

Thus *Newsweek* reports that, during the student demonstrations in Beijing in the spring of 1989, the Chinese government kept a tight rein on the outflow of information. As a result, both the Chinese themselves and outside observers had to make use of convoluted implicatures.

> For Jim Lilley, the new U.S. ambassador to China, it must seem like old times. As sources on Beijing's leadership struggle dry up, the arcane skills of China watching are in demand again. Local papers must be scrutinized for obscure clues: did an item headlined ITALIAN PREMIER RESIGNS contain a suggestion that Prime Minister Li Peng also leave office? Was a reference to "the conspiracy of a small group" the signal of an impending purge of the reformist leaders around Zhao Ziyang?[8]

The United States, on the other hand, makes too much information available to its analysts, so that the Soviet Union's Americologists have the opposite problem from their American counterparts: not only is there too much available for anyone to digest it all, but much of it is contradictory; not all can be true. So a reasonable premise is that any given piece of data is false until corroborated. With the flowering of *glasnost,* American Sovietologists, finding themselves in much the same predicament, are being forced to develop expertise that is the diametric opposite of the skills they had honed over the years of the Cold War. We might say that, where China watchers and old-style Sovietologists were obliged to assume violations of Quantity and Relevance to obtain information, Americologists and new Sovietologists must assume violations of Quality.

GENRE, FUNCTION, AND CLARITY

In discourse genres whose reason for being involves the communication of information, rather than pleasure in the interaction itself, politeness is downplayed or even nonexistent. Thus, in therapy deliberate confrontation by both participants is common, often involving language and ideas that would be downright rude in ordinary conversation. This is just one of the reasons that friendship doesn't mix with therapy: it's hard to move back and forth between a politeness-based system and one based on clarity. It is true that with long-time trusted friends we don't stand on ceremony: many more formal aspects of politeness are discarded. But there are still things we hesitate to say, or apologize for saying, or take care to say in a roundabout way. Client and therapist distort the process if they communicate that way.

While politeness rules exist in all societies, the form politeness takes, and when it should be manifested, may differ, provoking cross-cultural misunderstanding. In chapter 2, I discussed the three basic systems of politeness—distance, deference, and camaraderie. As long as all participants in an interaction use the same system, there will be no difficulty. Otherwise, problems are likely to arise. For instance, one speaker may misunderstand the informative content the other is conveying. If one is speaking according to the rules of distance, impersonally and indirectly, the other, if not a user of the same system, may fail to understand who or what is being discussed. Or one speaker may not understand that the other's usage is conventional rather than intended literally. A user of deference may seem to be leaving all decisions and interpretations up to the hearer. If the hearer responds by taking control rather than negotiating, the deference user may feel slighted. What is intended to bring people together will, if misunderstood, drive them apart.

Although ordinary conversation generally employs rapport-based strategies, every utterance is not necessarily indirect and intelligible only via implicature. Rather, speakers reserve indirectness for times when confrontation threatens or they want to play with words; at other times they obey the Maxims. In fact, there are few pure-rapport or pure-clarity discourses, but mainly mixed types; the issue is how much of each, and when, and how, is normal. People have different views on the appropriate balance in particular contexts, depending on their cultural and personal backgrounds.

Problems arise because we see politeness and indirectness as icing on the communicative cake, not as central to the communication. Americans don't have enough concern for the pragmatic meanings of these choices and are not nearly as conscious of one another's pragmatic intentions as we are of the semantics of our transactions. We make a sharp distinction between style and substance, considering the former trivial or secondary. The Japanese understand better: for them, style *is* substance. Their language does not allow them to make the distinction. (But they misinterpret us as rude or childish, when we are only doing what they're doing: following one particular set of strategies.)

It is essential to see style as an integral part of communication. It is often noted that silence communicates; in the same way, there are no neutral choices even in English. Neutrality conveys a desire for non-involvement, which may be good or bad, but is certainly a statement.

The findings of sociolinguistics and pragmatics imply that (Grice notwithstanding) there is no culture-free universal definition of *logic*. To a Western male with twenty-five hundred years of Aristotelian thought under his belt (or hat), the Japanese way of conveying thoughts allusively is "illogical"; the female style of offering multiple options is "confusing." A serious person (male) knows what he means, says it, and sticks to it. The Gricean ideal is dangerous for us as a culture because Maxim-based utterances can be taken as "ideal" in two senses.

Philosophers of language think of the Maxims as *ideals* in that they represent our ultimate, if unconscious, aim in communicating: the crux of the discourse, the information we need to transmit. But in the other sense of *ideal*, we feel we are inadequate if we are unclear. The logical *ideal* is understood as part of the definition of a good human being in this culture. So we express ourselves dogmatically even when we're not sure what we're saying; we don't allow room for exploration, for the other person's modifications. As a speaker-based culture, we're good talkers but poor listeners and terrible reacters. We define strength in discourse as being "logical," being able to shear off the uncertainties and delicacies that waste time (which is money) and get us nowhere. We feel like clear thinkers; but thinking is not a solitary activity, and we don't know how to mix clarity and rapport so as to achieve a comfortable exchange of ideas.

The Cooperative Principle and politeness strategies exist universally, but their specific forms and range of applicability are aspects of individual cultures and, probably, individual personalities. Using them well and flexibly is knowing how to convey information and receive it. The old Aristotelian understanding of logic is eroding, and not a minute too soon, as the world becomes one community. We have to understand and use not just the rules, but the metarules: to know when to be direct and indirect; how to be polite, and what "logic," conversational and otherwise, really is about.

Cross-cultural variety in itself is a bonus for humanity: it makes us more versatile as a species, more able to respond to novelty. For individuals, it offers the possibility of new experience and flexibility, as well as intellectual challenge. But there is a downside.

Differences between cultures can pose a threat to outsiders. Learning to cope with the demands of a culture different from one's own can raise questions about one's competence; just questioning the necessity of entrenched assumptions may create confusion and doubt. The more shaky a person's own self-esteem, the more troublesome it is to encounter novelty. As the next chapter suggests, the creation of categories and strict boundaries between them is a protection against those threats, as well as an intellectually useful exercise in self- and other-definition. But, pushed too far in the wrong direction, categorial distinctions become divisive forces, *we* versus *they*, an attractive split that poses grave dangers to the species and the individuals within it.

CHAPTER TEN

We First

C ATEGORIZATION is the basis of some of humanity's greatest achievements. It is also one of our most dangerous temptations.

People create categories in order to understand both the physical universe outside themselves and the meaning of being human, belonging to a group. The superordinate categories that we create exist only as psychological ideal forms. We have concrete understanding of specific instances: an oak tree, this red maple. But there is no such thing in nature as a "tree," only specific kinds of trees. Our concept *tree* is a distillation of disparate components that nonetheless our intellectual synthesizing abilities tell us share commonalities. A "maple," an "oak," a "poplar," and an "ailanthus" have more in common than any of them has with "ivy," "snapdragon," or "flagpole." Or so it seems to us, Westerners, speakers of English. For the creation of superordinate categories like *tree*, and the decision about the composition of their membership, are matters of collective determination, not preordained physical realities. Our belief that the category *tree* deserves to exist gives that concept meaning and form, whereas the physical and visible existence of maples and oaks gives them reality. The making of categories is a creative and synthesizing act that allows us to give meaning to our world and definition to the things within it—but is always, to some degree, arbitrary and culturally grounded. The existence in our language of superordinate categories permits us to generalize: to talk about what "trees" are like as well as what "this maple" is like, and thus to understand the universe parsimoniously, with the least amount of effort; and to create abstractions. Our ability to generalize permits us to glimpse the future, to see beyond the here and now. This maple may not be here tomorrow, we cannot tie our belief in the future to it; but maples and, better still, trees will be here forever: one may replace another, one species replace another; but the ideal image, the mental "tree," will always exist; and by grasping the abstract generalization, we build a bridge to the future.[1]

We can also break down larger groups into smaller, creating dichotomies, subordinate categories. Trees can be evergreen or deciduous; deciduous trees, oaks or maples; and oaks, black or white. Then we can observe each type closely to determine its specific properties and contrast them with those of other sorts. If we define categories precisely enough, our observations of specific cases (the only kind of observation anyone can make) will be predictive for all members of the class. By sharp and careful dichotomization, we can accurately taxonomize; by the creation of taxonomies we can develop and test rules, systems of rules, and theories: the basis of science. Then we can test our specific rules on ever-larger general categories to see how far they extend, and come to understand the interrelationships among categories in terms of shared rule systems. Categorization is the basis of science, crucial to human understanding and the growth of our intellect and to our power as a species over the physical universe. It has made us what we are.

Some groups of humans do not construct superordinate categories. They have, as it were, words for "maple," "oak," "ash," or perhaps "red maple" and "sugar maple," but no word for "tree."[2] Such groups function well on a day-to-day basis, they learn and transmit to each new generation the particular properties, uses, and dangers of each kind of tree in their environment. They understand the workings of each separate kind of tree better than we do, in a visceral and direct way, which is the antithesis of abstract ratiocination. Because they cannot abstract (their language does not permit it, not having abstract terms; or rather, their conceptual system does not permit their language to create such terms, since we create only the words for which our perception of reality recognizes a need), they get to know individual cases keenly, where we tend to pass over the specifics in order to get "the big picture." "He can't see the forest for the trees," we say when we want to disparage someone's reasoning ability. Certainly we lose something by our passion for abstracting; but it has given us control over our destiny: perhaps too much control—or, in the end, too little.

CATEGORIZATION AND STEREOTYPING

People have a great intellectual need to categorize. The world is a chaotic and complicated place. If we saw every thing and every person in it as unique, we could not develop predictions or generalizations about the right way to respond in each of the many situations we encounter. We could not make sense of our universe: making sense depends significantly on forming appropriate and useful categories and making proper assignments to them. But that necessary tendency also makes it possible for the propagandist to suggest false and damaging categorizations that, if artfully presented to a willing hearer, can seem to make sense: you can always find a linguistic tie, through metaphor if not literal connection. And when the intellectual pleasure and relief at finding a usable generalization connects with the emotional solace of becoming a member of a larger group (*us* together, *us* against *them*), the power of the categorization to mold attitudes and affect behavior is truly awesome and often terrifying.

Categorization is more than an intellectual game. We do more than assign group membership to the external artifacts of nature. If that were all, it would be an interesting exercise with important intellectual ramifications but would have relatively little to do with how we behave toward each other as human beings. But categorization does not stop with the material universe. Even better than naming trees, we love to name ourselves and one another. Therein lies the peril of categorization as well as perhaps its deepest attraction.

We form hazy and unexamined superordinate categories: we *stereotype*. [3] Men agree that "women are like that," and therefore will interpret all behavior on the part of "women" as being of a piece, interpretable by the same rule. We are told that all six-year-olds learn in similar ways, so we send them indiscriminately into the same first-grade classrooms; and if it turns out that some of them respond better than others to the single way this society believes that classrooms and learning ought to be structured, well, then, the ones that do well are defined as "good" or "smart" six-year-olds, and the others, being "bad" or "dumb," are shunted aside without much distress. They don't fit into our predictive generalizations; their behavior is not only uneconomical but embarrassing. We are only too eager to develop and prove these superordinate categories. Meet two people from Japan and you know what "the Japanese" are like. Then you meet a third Japanese person who behaves differently. But this is intolerable! Either his behavior has to be distorted, in your mind, to match the putative generalization, or he isn't "really" Japanese. (He's lived in the United States for a year, you know what that does.)

We also dichotomize. We devise distinctions, where useful, on the basis of tiny, perhaps even nonexistent differences. In *Gulliver's Travels,* Lilliput was torn between those who broke open their eggs at the big end ("Big-endians") and those who started at the small end ("Small-endians"). To Gulliver and to us that seems a trivial distinction, but Swift was alluding to religious doctrinal differences in eighteenth-century Great Britain that had provoked bloody civil war—and would seem just as minuscule to an outsider. Teenagers are masters of social dichotomy, because they are desperately concerned with defining what it means to belong to a group: minute differences of dress and hair style mark adolescents as "in" or "out," members of one clique or another, and therefore, ultimately, popular or outcast. But when adults play the game, the results are far more deadly. We call it "war," and survival, not popularity, is at stake.

In every war, before, during, and after the actual hostilities, governments prepare their populations. The preparations are not generally explicit, and even those in charge who are getting things ready may not fully realize what they are doing, much less why. But the underpinnings are necessary in order to convince the members of one group that it is permissible or essential to destroy the lives of another group who might, in fact, be much like them. Civil war is the most mysterious case; but even in wars between different ethnic groups, the two sides are infinitely more alike than they are different. How are human beings persuaded to annihilate other human beings?

Linguistic discrimination prepares the ground for other forms. If we can first be persuaded through words that *they* and *we* have little in common, then *we* can go the extra psychological mile and decide that *they* are nonhuman, inhuman, less than *we* are and worse. Every propaganda movie ever made, from the most blatant to the most subtly "artistic," provides that underpinning for hostility, a dichotomization into *we* and *they*. The dichotomization, easy but false, is attractive. *We*-versus-*they* dichotomies have two useful functions for propagandists and those who are seduced by them: they make it easy to hate and mistreat those defined as *they*, and force *us* into tighter and closer union—*us* against the world of *them* out there; "us," the bearers of civilization and all its virtues. Once the basic identity and distinction are forged, the rest is easy. It's like the optimist and the pessimist seeing the same glass as half full and half empty. Any time you look at another human being (for that matter, another living creature) you can see him/her/it either as "like me *except*" or as "unlike me *mostly*." Language choices lend conviction to that decision.

PROPAGANDA

Propaganda. What is it? Does the word have a denotative meaning, or is it just a term of abuse: ours is "information"; theirs is "propaganda"? Scholars who have tried to define it objectively have encountered difficulty because every technique used by the identifiable "propagandist" is also used by trusted public figures and news media.[4] Does that make everyone transmitting "information"—Walter Cronkite, your favorite high school teacher, me—a "propagandist"? (Or make Stalin and Hitler benign educators?) Most of us would say that there is a difference, one not discernible by inspection of surface form. Here as elsewhere we must be able to identify and analyze the relation between form and that abstraction, function, if we are to understand what propaganda is and does.

The propagandist is one with the poet and news writer in constructing categories and dichotomies. Nor is the propagandist alone in making use of stirring words, ringing slogans, and powerful images, verbal or pictorial. Every good writer or television or movie director does. Form alone does not define the genre. A propagandist, unlike a legitimate persuader or informer, is one who encourages slippage: lets one category melt into another, creates distinctions based on little distinction, mixes metaphor promiscuously with literal truth. As long as we're clear on the medium we're working with, we're safe. But the illegitimate persuader works by moving from "safe," self-evident categories and relationships to suggestive, slimy, gossamer connotations. Because we humans derive intellectual and emotional pleasure from being able to make the largest and most daring generalizations we can, we are seduced. The propagandist gives us titillation, which we repay with trust.

WE AND *THEY*

The trick is to see where true connections are being forged and where they are being fuzzed by wordplay or imagistic suggestion. Once the categories of *we* and *they* are, legitimately or not, firmly in place, minds can be manipulated readily in two directions: the creation and bonding of the *we,* and the expulsion of the *they.*

Language often metaphorically equates numbers and power (or prestige). So in several European languages, formal "polite" address is accomplished by enhancing a singular addressee's symbolic status by the second-person plural. *Vous* in French means both "you, more than one," and "you, singular and exalted"; in older English, *ye* and *you,* as opposed to *thou* and *thee,* were both plural and polite. Though not grammatically codified like the second person, the first-person plural can also be used figuratively. The royal *we,* used by kings and queens to refer to themselves, suggests their largeness, their figurative "majesty." Sometimes it turns up in the speech of nonroyals with pretensions to grandeur:

> According to reports in recent British newspapers, Margaret Thatcher, who is in her third term as prime minister, may be getting so sure of herself that she is losing popularity.
>
> Among the nonpolitical bones the press has been picking with Thatcher was her recent public announcement that her son's wife had given birth. "We are a grandmother," she said on the steps of 10 Downing Street.
>
> Thatcher's use of the royal "we" was considered overstepping her bounds. "Watch it, Maggie," wrote columnist George Gale of the Daily Express, a pro-Thatcher newspaper. "No one is indispensable, pride comes before a fall, some modesty and prudence would now become you."[5]

In other words the personal pronouns, those humble and earthly servants of language, can be pressed into service to perform lofty symbolic functions. Their very omnipresence and basic status, the fact that they are so often overlooked and underscrutinized (relative to the more glamorous content words—nouns, verbs, adverbs, and adjectives), make them particularly striking when their special use is, as here, a mite out of line (not only because the prime minister is not a royal, but also because she was speaking of herself in a private, not a public, role.) Note also here the friendly newspaper's familiar address: "Maggie," not only first name but nickname, a deft cutting down to size. But would it have done the same, in analogous circumstances, with a male prime minister ("Watch it, Winnie")? Was Thatcher's hubris more intolerable because it was displayed by a woman?

THE DANGERS OF DICHOTOMIZATION: M/F

We can set individuals apart, as here; but more often it welds them together, throwing them into contrast with another group, explicitly or not. And just as the royal *we* can be used appropriately (by royals, in their role as royals) or inappropriately, so the symbolic functions of truly plural *we* can be used properly or otherwise. The pronoun itself need not be explicitly present to convey the message. An ancient determination by a powerful group that its members were *we,* and all others *they* may linger, unexamined, with damaging consequences, into the present moment. Once it is decided that a powerful *we* are different from *them, we* can decide just which properties *we* share with *them,* and in what ways it is convenient to be different, the perfect opening for the propagandist as well as the usurper of power.

Thus, for instance, ages ago men determined first that they were different from women and then that, because they had more physical strength, they had the right to hold power over women and determine their fate. Because men had distinguished themselves as different, there was no telling just how different they might be: they might claim whatever differences were useful; and over the millennia, many of them were useful. We moderns may dismiss this reconstruction as irrelevant historicism: don't women have the vote, entrée into the professions, all the rights of men? Yes, to a degree, in areas where the *we/they* has been explicit and can therefore be examined and discredited. But when it is implicit in the "scientific" discourse of predominantly male-power assemblages, the misunderstanding (as we may politely term it) lingers into the present moment, into today's news item:

DOCTORS DENYING WOMEN PAIN-KILLERS, RESEARCHER SAYS

Women are half as likely as men to receive painkillers after surgery because doctors often do not take their complaints seriously, according to a University of Rhode Island researcher.

A study of 30 men and 30 women who had coronary bypass surgery indicated a bias against giving painkillers to women, researcher Karen Calderone said.

Calderone, who presented her study during a weekend National Conference for Women in Psychology, said doctors and nurses were twice as likely to give narcotics to men than to women during the first three days after surgery. The study was conducted between January 1985 and August 1986.

"Health care professionals are taught that (narcotics) should be dispensed more conservatively to the expressive patients, who tend to dramatize their pain, and more liberally to stoic patients," said Calderone, who is also an intensive-care nurse at Miriam Hospital in Providence.

Because women often express their feelings more than men, they may be denied pain-killers.[6]

We may translate: American women's typical communicative style is to express emotion openly in an attempt to create a feeling of collaboration; men's is to remain impersonal and distant. Because men are the group with power (in general and even more in medicine), their style is taken as the norm and the proper one: they are understood as expressing *the right amount* of emotion, while women "exaggerate" and are "hysterical," in time-honored fashion. If a man were to be as expressive as women normally are, he might appropriately be seen as being histrionic and overstating the case. So men tend to see women's communicative styles generally as "wrong" and "hysterical" and as "overstatements." They have identified themselves as *we* and women as *they*, whose communications can only be understood as anomalous and wrong versions of *our* ways, rather than in their own terms. Rather than trying to encompass all, men and women alike, within the *we*, and framing the question as, "How much alleviation do people in general need for pain?" or "How are we to learn to understand the normal modes of expression of each group according to a single standard?", we divide the world into "we-normals" and "they-abnormals," whose forms of expression *we* need not even try to understand, because it isn't really "human," and therefore is unintelligible to *us*.

(Women are not the only groups treated this way by the American medical institution. Cultures inculcate in their members various responses to pain and illness, from effusive shows of distress to stoical apathy; these are not indicators of hysteria or bravery, just cultural codes. But Western doctors, seeing their cross-cultural patients through Western eyes, make diagnoses and recommendations for treatment on that basis. If you don't talk, you're in even more danger. Newborn infants who must undergo surgery are given only minimal anesthesia, on the grounds that "they" do not feel pain as "we" do: after all, they can express even the greatest pain only as they express minor inconvenience, by crying, so we reason that they cannot make the same distinctions we do. Language, or its absence, gives us the means and the right to discriminate.)

The covert and symbolic division of *we/they* has been with us for a long time and has been responsible for all manner of great wrongs, from massacres to wars to enslavements. It is arguable that the progress of civilization and enlightenment can be gauged by the extent to which a group has been able to set aside this attractive dichotomy, and see itself and the putative *they* as members of a single *we*, having the same needs and feelings and entitled to the same rights.

Once only the male citizens (often property owners) of the city-state were *we*. No one else could vote. Others could be punished as citizens could not. (In Rome, citizens could not be tortured for information; citizens receiving the death penalty had to be killed relatively humanely, by strangulation rather than crucifixion, a punishment originally reserved for slaves.) Only citizens could hold public office (a rule we still observe). Citizens could not be enslaved in most cultures; a slave was seen as something less than human, therefore able to endure the conditions of servitude that would be intolerable for a human being (Aristotle defined a slave as a "tool with a voice." The loss of humanity was a direct concomitant of servitude. Before enslavement, a slave had the same feelings as any other free person). This definition made it possible for the Athenians to countenance slavery; if they had seen themselves as inflicting on other human beings conditions that would have been intolerable to themselves as human beings, the institution could not have been continued. So the *we* versus *they* dichotomy permits evils to be perpetuated, on the pretense that for *them* they are not evil. *They* do not feel as *we* do.

EXTENSION OF THE *WE*

Over the millennia there has been an ever-so-gradual, but nonetheless observable, erosion of the *we/they* dichotomy. Much of this progress has been made over the last two centuries, as first *we* (white males) began to realize that enslavement did not legitimize mistreatment, and that, in fact, enslavement was itself unjust. At about the same time, some men came to understand that property holding or aristocratic birth did not naturally make for greater delicacy of feeling or fineness of intellect, and that therefore all "men" were entitled to equal rights of self-determination: "all men are created equal." This principle applied, at first, only to "men" like those who framed that ringing declaration—white males. But gradually the understanding was extended, however reluctantly, to nonwhites and women, so that by the end of the twentieth century, those groups are legally recognized as having the same rights *we* have:

they have been, for official purposes at any rate, included in the *we*, making it harder to justify special treatment.

But then an enigma surfaces: How far does the provenance of *we* extend? What groups are fit to be included beyond those already identified? And therein lie some of the most divisive and hate-filled disputations of our times, even as every prior extension of the *we* (and consequent limitation of the *they*) has brought discord and confusion along with progress. Suppose we all agree, however provisionally and reluctantly, that nonwhites and women are included in the officially sanctioned *we*: How much further can the umbrella extend without precipitating political, intellectual, physical, and moral chaos? No one can say. A debate about animal rights is current at many research institutions. The argument is really about whether animals are part of the *we*: we as living creatures coinhabiting the planet, having similar needs and desires, capable of feeling pleasure and pain in similar if not identical ways. For millennia humans could say: animals are different and worse. Whether because the Bible had stated that man was to have dominion over animals; or because it seemed self-evident that animals did not have language, and therefore could not reason as people could, it was considered correct to place them in a lower category and use them for our own purposes. Gradually we have come to realize that it is inappropriate to mistreat them purely for our own self-aggrandizement (hence the development of animal protection laws and organizations in the nineteenth century), but we have not yet resolved whether we have the right to take animal lives to ensure our own self-preservation as individuals or as a species. If we truly believe that animals can suffer as we can, and have a right to pleasure as we do (a position that underlies the protective laws in effect), then we are in a moral quagmire as long as we use animals for research for human ends. What is our relationship to animals? Are they sharers in our *we*, or merely *they?* We do not know, but it's terribly important (and not just for animals, either) that we find out.

Many human groups dichotomize on linguistic terms. Others are named in a group's language by words with meanings like "those who do not speak, those who babble," as the Greeks called foreigners *barbaroi,* "babblers, those who go *bar, bar*"; or "those without minds, who cannot speak or think," as in the Russian word for "German," *Nemets,* related to the verb *nemet',* "to grow dumb" (derived from the Indo-European roots **ne-,* "not," and **ment-,* "mind.") So those who speak (that is, speak so that *we* can understand) are human, with all the rights we enjoy; those who speak differently and therefore unintelligibly are entitled to nothing, whether they be animals, infants, women, or other ethnic groups.

Where do we draw the vital line? What communication, verbal or otherwise, shall we deign to "understand"? Many cultures used to put infants (etymologically "nonspeakers") into the "nonhuman" category, so that they could be exposed and left to die, while it would be punishable to do the same to a member of the official *we*. Now we no longer recognize that distinction legally (though we may medically). But what about the not yet born? Are they virtual human infants, and therefore in the *we*, protected category? Or being not yet endowed with distinctively human attributes, are they *they*, and not protected? If the former, then women who have to carry fetuses against their will are automatically relegated to *they* status: they are not accorded the same rights over their bodies, the same autonomy, as men, the quintessential *we*. So here is a currently insoluble problem: admission of one group to the *we* disenfranchises another. We do not know how to solve this problem: our language gives us no clues. What we once put asunder becomes tricky, in another and morally improved age, to put back together. If these thorny cases give us any guidance, it is to be wary of the temptation to create *we/they* dichotomies. They are seductively easy to create and hellishly hard to undo.

THE USE OF *WE*

Once the dichotomy is created by the propagandist and entrenched in the popular mind, it is capable of no end of ingenious and dangerous uses. The *we* can be appealed to in terms of all men of goodwill, all right-thinking Americans, you and I together, and so on; and any convenient candidate for *they* status is free to be denied rights, mistreated, cast out, because they have no connection to us. A recent example shows how potent a tool the creation of a *we* is in the hand of the propagandist/politician. This speech, only about five minutes long, was delivered on television by Ronald Reagan on 29 January 1984, to announce his decision to run for a second term as President. That was the text; the subtext is an artfully crafted opening campaign speech, one that both cements the President's hold on his constituency and kindles their patriotic fervor and national pride—touchstones of his administration's rhetoric. Much of this is subtly accomplished not by explicit statement, but by the weaving together of several meanings and connotations of *we*. (I have numbered the paragraphs for reference. Otherwise, this is the written version as it appeared in the *San Francisco Chronicle* of 30 January.)

[1] It has been nearly three years since I first spoke to you from this room. Together, we've faced many difficult problems and I've come to feel a bond of kinship with each one of you.

[2] Tonight I'm here for a different reason. I've come to a difficult personal decision as to whether or not I should seek re-election.

[3] When I first addressed you from here, our national defenses were dangerously weak, we had suffered humiliation in Iran and at home, we were adrift possibly because of a failure here in Washington to trust the courage and character of you, the people.

[4] But worst of all, we were on the brink of economic collapse from years of government overindulgence and abusive overtaxation. Thus, I had to report that we were "in the worst economic mess since the Great Depression."

[5] Inflation had risen to over 13 percent in 1979 and to 19 percent in March of 1980. Those back-to-back years of price explosions were the highest in more than 60 years.

[6] In the five years before I came here, taxes had actually doubled. Your cost-of-living pay raises just bumped you into higher tax brackets. Interest rates over 21 percent—the highest in 120 years. Productivity down two consecutive years. Industrial production down. Actual wages and earnings down.

[7] The only things going up were prices, unemployment, taxes and the size of government. While you tightened your belt, the federal government tightened its grip.

[8] Well, things have changed.

[9] This past year, inflation dropped down to 3.2 percent. Interest rates cut nearly in half. Retail sales are surging. Homes are being built and sold. Auto assembly lines are opening up. And in just the last year, 4 million people have found jobs—the greatest employment gain in 33 years.

[10] By beginning to rebuild our defenses, we have restored credible deterrence and can confidently seek a secure and lasting peace, as well as a reduction of arms.

[11] As I said Wednesday night, America is back and standing tall. We've begun to restore great American values: the dignity of work, the warmth of family, the strength of neighborhood and the nourishment of human freedom.

[12] But our work is not finished. We have more to do in creating jobs, achieving control over government spending, returning more autonomy to the states, keeping peace in a more settled world and seeing if we can't find room in our schools for God.

[13] At my inaugural, I quoted words that had been spoken over 200 years ago by Dr. Joseph Warren, president of the Massachusetts Congress.

[14] "On you depend the fortunes of America," he told his fellow Americans. "You are to decide the important question on which rests the happiness and liberty of millions yet unborn." And he added, "Act worthy of yourselves."

[15] Over these last three years, Nancy and I have been sustained by the way you, the real heroes of American democracy, have met Dr. Warren's challenge. You were magnificent as we pulled the nation through the long night of our national calamity. You have, indeed, acted worthy of yourselves.

[16] Your high standards make us remember the central question of public service: Why are we here? Well, we are here to see that government continues to serve you—not the other way around.

[17] We are here to lift the weak, and to build the peace. And, most important, we are here, as Dr. Warren said, to act today for the happiness and liberty of millions yet unborn—to seize the future so that every new child of this beloved republic can dream heroic dreams. If we do less, we betray the memory of those who have given so much.

[18] This historic room and the presidency belong to you. It is your right and responsibility every four years to give someone temporary custody of this office and of the institution of the presidency. You so honored me, and I am grateful—grateful and proud of what together we have accomplished.

[19] We have made a new beginning. Vice President Bush and I would like to have your continued support and cooperation in completing what we began three years ago. I am therefore announcing that I am a candidate and will seek re-election to the office I presently hold.

[20] Thank you for the trust you have placed in me. God bless you, and good night.

Much in this short speech is worthy of comment, and there is not enough space here to do it justice. Most salient are the uses of the pronoun *we*, which occurs in either that form or as *us* or *our*, twenty-five times in this five-minute talk. (That count doesn't include "Nancy and I" in paragraph 15 and "Vice President Bush and I" in 19, both semantically equivalent to *we*.) Most extraordinary is the variety of meanings and connotations it is given throughout. In English, *we* has two major uses: *inclusive* and *exclusive*. In the first, the speaker includes hearers in the scope of the *we*: it is equivalent to "you and I." The second excludes the hearer: it means something like, "I and some others, not you." The royal and editorial *we*'s are developments of the exclusive *we*. Reagan's use of *we* ranges between inclusive and exclusive; a few times it is ambiguous, leaving hearers unsure whether they are being included.

Both the inclusive and the exclusive *we*, in and of themselves, have symbolic senses. Inclusive *we* is a powerful emotional force, bringing speaker and hearer together as one, united and sharing common interests. Exclusive *we* bears the power and authority of numbers: "It's not just I alone who say this, it is *all of us.* So you better believe it." The two would seem to be mutually exclusive in emotional content—one warm, friendly and egalitarian; the other cool, impersonal and authoritarian. But when they are skillfully woven together, the audience experiences both of these effects together, rather than feeling forced to choose. Reagan's administration was often called an "imperial" presidency, one of pomp, distance, and majesty; and as often, commentators noted Reagan's folksy and intimate appeal. Here we get a glimpse of how he (or his speechwriters) achieved that seemingly impossible mixture and managed to satisfy the emotional needs of a remarkable number of the people an amazing amount of the time.

So, for example, inclusive *we* appears in paragraphs 1 and 4 and probably at least parts of 17. Exclusive *we* is found at least in part of paragraphs 12, 17, and 19. The others, and much of 17 and 19, are mixtures or ambiguous, where the skill of the writer is deftly demonstrated. The audience at many points in the speech doesn't quite know who is being referred to, who is to take credit or blame, who has to take the responsibility to get the work done. Who are the "we" whose "work is not finished" in paragraph 12? Is it the administration, Reagan and his cohorts—and are they also the ones referred to in the paragraphs just preceding? It might seem so—the actions described are the work of governments making policy and carrying it out, not the ordinary people who have merely put the reins into their hands. But this policy-making *we* grades imperceptibly into the inclusive "all of us together" *we* at the end of paragraph 12, "seeing if we can't find room in our schools for God." The schools, after all, do belong to all of *us,* not just to the administration in Washington. Along with the switch in reference comes a change in style which also works to suggest subtly, a movement from "government business" to "everyone's business": the first few clauses in the second sentence of paragraph 12 are formal and elevated in diction: the syntactic form ("more to do in . . .") is characteristic of written more than spoken language; there are several Latinate polysyllables: "creating," "achieving," "government," "autonomy": not really formal or high-flown, but suggestive of those formats. Then the last, populist clause makes an abrupt switch. The idiom ("seeing if we can't . . .") is informal, folksy, part of oral talk. Every word in the clause is monosyllabic, with the exception of "seeing," which really is a monosyllable with a simple ending on it. We, the hearers, don't know for sure who is being described, and in what capacity—neighborly regular guy or mover and shaker. Either way it is a form of flattery. On one level, that of the inclusive usage and colloquial talk, the hearer is made to feel like a buddy and confidant. On the other, he or she is being treated to glimpses into the high affairs of state by someone who is privy to secrets. Mixing the two has the effect of making the hearer feel in control of both roles, entrusted with both. And because the "we's" are jumbled, no one has to make embarrassing decisions about actually having done or having to do the controversial and difficult things described. We're left feeling that we can identify with the "we" of the lofty indefinite sentiments (as in paragraph 15), but "we" don't have to do any of the hard work ourselves mentioned in paragraphs 10, 11, and 17: leave that to the President and the big guys.

The exclusive uses are also of several kinds. Some, as noted, are equivalent to "those who run the government"—an impersonal group of importance and authority, but cold and distant. But occasionally the "we" is up close and personal, affording the hearer a surreptitious glimpse into the White House boudoir—"Nancy and I." The use of Mrs. Reagan's first name is telling: the public is invited to think of her, at this moment—and, by extension her spouse—as the neighbors next door with whom we are on first-name terms, privy to their thoughts, hopes, fears. And "Nancy and I" have been sustained—*sustained*—by you! You who "were magnificent as we (who?) pulled the nation through the long night of our national calamity." What calamity? What did "we" do, exactly, to be "magnificent"? Why are "Nancy and I" so grateful as to be proffering intimacies? We don't know, but it does feel nice. After this encomium, and this appeal to our indispensability, how can we do other than to vote for him, since his interests and ours are now inextricably welded together? In paragraph 15, *we* may be "the administration," "Nancy and I" or "you and I," or, probably, all of these together; together we bear the responsibility and take the credit for "magnificence," a magnificent word if ever there was one.

In the next paragraph, the conflation of "we's" does serious work, as the President recalls the burdens of public service. Here the speaker distinctly separates "you" from "us" several times as he talks about the responsibility of the government to "serve." It is useful to remember that this speech was delivered as several of the administration's leading figures were or had been or were about to be under indictment or investigation for something other than "high standards" and public "service." It is a dangerous moment: the President could be revealing his administration's Achilles heel. But the paragraph is sandwiched between two that flatter the hearer, promise to include the hearer in the presidential *we.* So there is a covert invitation to the hearer to take on some of the responsibility for the problems of the *we* of the administration, and to make inclusive the exclusive *we,* thereby relieving the president and his men of some of their culpability, or making it harder to charge them with it—since *they* are now indistinguishable from *us*—not precisely the morally uplifting extension of the *we* discussed earlier.

The exclusive *we* serves another function, too, something close to the royal *we,* for instance in paragraphs 12 and 17. Since the decisions of the administration are taken to be those of the President, to emanate from the Oval Office, if the *we* of these paragraphs is exclusive, it at least calls to mind the royal *we,* the king's prerogative of seeing himself and his decisions as empowered by symbolic numbers and thereby given the force of authority. At the same time, Reagan uses *I* with great frequency. But alongside the whisper of royalty, the mention of himself as *I* makes the President seem accessible, personal and human, even as the use of *we* distances him from controversial decisions.

In many other ways, this little speech demonstrates extraordinary skill in the use of language. There is the persistent flattery of the audience, taking them into the presidential heart and boudoir, involving them in his difficult decisions; reminding them of their magnificence and high standards; connecting them (via the ubiquitous *we*) with the Founding Fathers; and alternating among three distinct rhetorical presences, each in its own way flattering to the audience and evoking their trust in the speaker. There is the folksy Ronnie; the imperial and emotionally stirring Mr. President; and then there is the Chief Executive, in command of facts, technology, statistics, the man you trust to get the job done. This last presence is most apparent in paragraphs 5 through 9, with their numbers and technical (or quasi-technical) terminology: "abusive overtaxation," "price explosions," "higher tax brackets," "interest rates," "productivity," and so on. Paragraph 6 turns into a list, with the last four sentences mere noun phrases. Lists are what organized, important people keep, and having one's lists in order shows one is on top of things. The truncated sentences are businesslike—no nonsense, just the facts. At the same time, the impersonality of the language in these sections is leavened by colloquialisms and jokes: the man is not using this special expertise to frighten us; he's still one of us, Elmer. "Just bumped you" in paragraph 6 is one such; there is a bit of a joke or play on words: "the only things going up. . . . While you tightened your belt, the federal government tightened its grip" (7). In paragraph 4, as Reagan introduces the authoritative statistics, he refers to the situation as a "mess," another colloquialism. These sections are the only ones in which anything like joking occurs, and aside from the suggestion of "seeing if we can't . . ." in paragraph 12, the only colloquialisms in a speech otherwise redolent of high rhetoric.

We might note the prevalence of "you and I," a phrase that occurs several times in the text, is equivalent to an inclusive "we," but perhaps even more strongly inclusive because it makes that sense of "we" explicit. The juxtaposition reminds the hearers again and again of their special relationship with the President. There are two such references in the first paragraph alone, as well as one "we." Sometimes "you" and "I" are together as here; sometimes they're separated by a sentence (6); sometimes one or the other is semantically present but not explicitly present (4): "Thus, I had to report"—that is, "report to you." Also unusually frequent are *deictic references:* explicit linguistic recognitions of the real physical situation of the discourse, words like *this, here, now.* They make what is being said vivid and concrete by reminding the hearers that they and the speaker are involved together in the here-and-now moment of the speech act. Thus we find "this room" (1); "here" (2, 3, 6, and 17); "this historic room" (18) brings the hearer back to the opening, connecting both with the historical references in paragraphs 13 to 15. These concrete references reassure the hearer that the high-flown language in which they occur is not designed to bamboozle; after all, the man is down to earth and right here with us in this room.

The technique works by the continual juxtaposition of ambiguities. Ordinary words—the simplest forms of language, the ones of which we are least on guard— are put to a dazzling range of uses, with no clear boundaries drawn between one use and another. The hearer is variously flattered, threatened, appealed to, and assuaged. Anger, worry and finally gratification and well-being are aroused. Reagan's use of the pronoun *we* is emblematic of his whole technique; and the speech as a whole depends for its effectiveness on its unifying, comforting, and authoritative effect. And the effect works because it is largely subliminal. The symbolic functions of the personal pronouns are not accessible to a hearer's conscious analysis, do not arouse suspicion as nouns and verbs might. They get their power through presupposition and suggestion. If a politician were to say, for instance, "I want to remind you how important you are to me, and how closely connected we are; how you trust me and I trust you; how much authority I have and yet what a nice down-to-earth guy I am; and how you and I together bear all the responsibility for everything and deserve the credit" (the underlying message of the Reagan speech), hearers would be skeptical or alarmed: he's pulling out all the stops, what's he up to, anyway? The American people would see the speech as directly manipulative and make fun of it and turn away in droves. But when all those blandishments are compressed into a few common, unnoticed, everyday pronouns, we assume the emotions stirred in us must be genuine and legitimate. They were inculcated subliminally; they feel like our own ideas. We feel we— and, therefore, politicians and other professional persuaders—have control over nouns, verbs, adjectives, we choose among them with full consciousness; but the nonlexical, grammatical words (pronouns, articles, prepositions) are just *there*, below our consciousness, we don't actively select them. So (we think) there can be no guile in their choice, and we don't think to analyze the emotions evoked by the choice and juxtaposition of pronouns.

TURNING ON *THEM*

The skillful communicator can also choose pronouns or their equivalents to split asunder, as President Reagan used them to bring together. *They* can create fission as well as *we* achieves fusion. The pronoun need not be explicitly invoked: the concept behind the linguistic dichotomy is sufficient.

Lately on television several programs have recalled and examined the Third Reich, including documentaries on Auschwitz. These programs are hard to watch; even still photographs of inmates are painful in showing their emaciation and suffering. So how could the commanders of those death camps, day after day for years, behold that suffering and not only do nothing to end it, not only go on observing dispassionately, but actually and knowingly contribute to the anguish of other human beings, *as they continue to observe the results?* It is imaginable only when the torturers are able to separate themselves emotionally from their victims, see them as something entirely other: *they.*

A peculiar mental image is required, or rather a blank where human connection should be. The linguistic form is the precursor of the psychological construct: *they* permits the denial of commonality. Once the imagistic dichotomy is underscored by the linguistic distinction, it gains power, legitimacy: we believe implicitly that if there are words to describe something, it is real, it is valid. So we start with a vague desire to distinguish some other or others from ourselves; we give it words, whether literal or (often more potent) metaphorical; and then the words themselves evoke new and stronger images, images of dangerous differences and fearful asymmetries. Propagandists skillful in evoking the *we* that binds are often equally good at suggesting the *they* that builds walls. The two are sides of the same counterfeit but glittering coin.

The administration that produced the masterful unifications of Reagan's speech also gave us the image of the *War on Drugs*. *War* is a powerful creator of emotions of all kinds, particularly the invocation of *we* versus *they*. War itself brings two sides into existence—*our* side and *theirs*. Our side is good and theirs is bad; only one can survive. If *we* survive, then we preserve all that is good, true, and lofty, the embodiment of the human ideal. If *they* win, it's back to barbarism and annihilation. There is no room for compromise.

The dichotomies of wartime encourage scapegoating: all that we suspect to be bad in our own character is attributed to the enemy, whom therefore we find it all the more essential to extirpate. The more ruthless we are, the better we will become. Propaganda movies made in times of war depict the other side as being as different from *us* as possible, both physically and mentally: *they* cannot and should not be understood. And not only are they different, their differences necessarily make them worse than we are. Their ways of working, their family relationships, their governmental organization are depicted as not only diametrically opposite to ours, but worse in every way, denials of human rights and possibilities. Before the war, we didn't see them in that light, and after it we won't either, but in order to kill them we must have that picture in our minds. Therefore, stratagems that would, in other circumstances, be questionable or unconscionable become, in war, necessary and right, and anyone who thinks otherwise is a traitor. In fact, war permits and encourages all sorts of dichotomization that would give most people pause in peacetime: every one of *us* is either a patriot or a traitor, and minute differences in attitude demarcate one from the other. Once we patriots identify a traitor, no punishment is too harsh: he or she stands between our survival and oblivion.

A real problem about war, and dichotomy in general, is that as compared with peace and unity, they are exciting. Making fine distinctions tests our intellectual mettle; making real use of them as war requires is a test of our emotional strength, our integrity—so we believe. So while we talk at length about the desirability of peace and unity, it is war and dissension that make us salivate. And any metaphorical appeal to those ideas will be equally attractive.

Some uses of the *war* image are more benign than others: Lyndon Johnson's War on Poverty was benign because a situation, not a group of people, was identified as the enemy to be destroyed. No one was seen as enjoying or profiting from poverty, so the "war" on it threatened damage to no human beings and no human rights. The image encouraged Americans to think of the struggle against poverty as requiring extreme efforts, but it did not appeal to our ruthless urges, our need to dichotomize in order to destroy, to scapegoat in order to feel good. The War against Cancer, similarly, is a relatively safe image, since the adversary is a disease, not a person.

The War on Drugs, on the other hand, is presented to us in the guise of a real war with real villains, deserving of real mistreatment: drug smugglers, pushers, and users. Few of us would deny that the first two, at any rate, are worthy of severe punishment and deterrence. But it does not take the invocation of the *war* metaphor to persuade us of that. The word must be doing additional work. When we look at policy decisions that have been made in this area, we see how much dichotomization can achieve.

In "war," anything that serves to identify and extirpate *them,* the "enemy," is legitimate, in fact, mandatory—even actions that otherwise might be immoral. So, for instance, normally we feel that the family is a valuable institution whose cohesion should be encouraged. The Reagan administration, in fact, stridently adopted "family" values in several arenas. At the same time, the War on Drugs encouraged family members *under some conditions* to betray one another. As we once shuddered to hear, children in Nazi Germany and Stalinist Russia were encouraged to spy on their parents and report on them to governmental authorities, who would then step in and punish the parents, removing them from their children. These examples were presented to Americans during the Second World War and the Cold War as examples of "their" inhumanity, tyranny, and totally un-American values. But during the Reagan administration, several children, who turned their drug-using (not smuggling or dealing) parents in to the police with a phone call, were lionized in the media and treated, indeed, as war heroes. The message was plain. Ordinary moral values are superseded in war, and this is war. But where does that end? Only, presumably, with all-out victory, in which *they* are demolished. But what happens if *they* turn out to be *us,* as our children are encouraged to root around the home in a hopeful quest for drug paraphernalia wherewith to turn Mommy in and get their deserved thirty-second sound bite?

Americans are proud of and generally understand the value of their Constitution with its Bill of Rights. We know that the Fourth Amendment prevents the midnight knock, the search without a warrant or probable cause, the kick of the tyrant's boot against the door or our bodies. We would not want that emblematic image of fascism imposed on us, any of *us*. But in war, the other side is not us, and what happens to *them* is not seen as having anything to do with us. In fact, we must mistreat them to save ourselves: kick the door in first, and ask questions later. So the Bill of Rights gets progressively watered down, decision by decision. Since the Supreme Court's rulings are seen as protecting *us* against *them*, we happily go along. But we do not understand that the strict categorical distinctions of this war are not for all time; once the law, in its magnificent one-size-fits-all generalizing power, gives government the ability to kick in *their* door, at another time, in another "war," it will let them kick in ours. Someday *we* may be *they*. But the potency and excitement of the dichotomization carries the day; and we wouldn't want any of *us* to think we were traitors, would we? And who but a traitor would ask for compassionate, or even fair, treatment of the enemy in a war? Once the linguistic context is provided and accepted, it becomes hard to see reality in any other way than that defined by the chosen terms: *war, survival, us, them*.

The illegitimate uses of *we* and *they* are of value for the propagandist and other dubious persuaders. They create and abet artificial emotions, warm or cold, that interfere with the application of intellectual reasoning and provide apparent justification for questionable decisions and actions. Language can both bring us together and separate us legitimately and otherwise; but the case of "otherwise" is easier and often more readily effective. We cannot legislate against this kind of persuasion, since forms that look identical to it are not only legitimate but even intrinsic to our human capacity for logic and empathy. Besides, even (or especially) in its illegitimate forms this kind of persuasion is seductive, promising intimacy where none exists, excitement in a mundane world. Propaganda of all kinds (both political and the economic propaganda that is advertising) is more interesting than straight talk, more flattering and more stirring. We cannot prevent its use, since we cannot even define it so as to cover all and only the relevant cases. But we can recognize when words, pictures, or music appeal to us in ways that deny our true intellectual and empathic capacities. And, once those manipulative devices are recognized, they can be overridden if we take the responsibility.

Social distinctions, we have seen, often prove dangerous if alluring. But over the history of humanity, none has lasted as long, been as pervasive, or done as much damage as the dichotomy of male versus female—like the other dichotomies, useful and attractive; and also like the others, worth questioning.

CHAPTER ELEVEN

Why Can't a Woman Be Less like a Man?

"But I don't want to go among mad people," Alice remarked.

"Oh, you can't help that," said the Cat; "we're all mad here. I'm mad. You're mad."

"How do you know I'm mad?" said Alice.

"You must be," said the Cat, "or you wouldn't have come here."

Alice didn't think that proved it at all; however, she went on, "And how do you know that you're mad?"

"To begin with," said the Cat, "a dog's not mad. You grant that?"

"I suppose so," said Alice.

"Well, then," the Cat went on, "you see a dog growls when it's angry, and wags its tail when it's pleased. Now *I* growl when I'm pleased, and wag my tail when I'm angry. Therefore I'm mad."

—Lewis Carroll

THE modern women's movement now has behind it some twenty years of theoretical thinking about the many aspects of "the woman question," one of the most important and agonizingly insoluble issues among them being language. From early on, women have recognized the need to take back the language, reclaim it or parts of it, get a right to decide about how to speak and be spoken of and to. But beyond that consensus (or at least as close to a consensus as the movement ever gets) is uncertainty. In what ways do women not have control over or access to language equal to men's? What differences are there, precisely, between men's and women's use of language, and how can these differences be "objectively" demonstrated (if, indeed, that is the right thing to do)? What exactly is the relationship between the way we talk, the way we are, and the way we want to be and are treated? Many of the most vexing questions about language and power come to a head in understanding the situation of women: what it is, what we want, why it is hard to define the one and achieve the other.

I take certain points to be by now self-evident. Men have power, political and social, and have had it since the dawn of recorded history. Women are subservient.[1] I am not much impressed with the argument that women have private power as men have public power, since public power creates and reinforces private power.[2] Those who have public power thereby have power to make language and make definitions—a power that, in turn, enhances and legitimizes their public power. Men have thus had the unquestioned power and authority to define male and female roles, to control language use, and to legitimize nonlinguistic behavior through that control of language. Since men, in control of the words, are defined as *we*, women become by default the quintessential *they*. Women are the other, the outsider: unintelligible and therefore not needing to be heard. They are not, literally and figuratively, part of the conversation, the political discourse. Women's special contributions to discourse (as to everything else) are ignored, disparaged, or—if their value is conclusively demonstrated—co-opted and credited to men. Finally, men enjoy these marks of favor and power and are loath to give them up or even share them. Women over the millennia have learned to use with skill what is left to them. Both men and women, in the short term, have something to gain from things not changing, in not redressing the balance of power, or changing the rules of the game. But for both sexes, in the long run, clinging to old habits is dangerous and, in this world, deadly.

Do women really use language differently from men; and if so, how? And what, in that case, is to be done? Those are the questions we keep getting tangled in, finding no clear answers. Over the years, these questions have been given different amounts of attention and different answers. And since there is no monolithic "women's movement," there are many answers, if few solutions.

One could argue that language differences are old stuff, understood if not solved (and not solved because of reactionary pressure, not lack of doctrinal understanding). But I think rather that the questions surrounding women and language bring together some of the most agonizing, complex, divisive and ultimately insoluble issues facing our society. It is not that we have understood them and can now go on; rather, as one generation succeeds another, as some gender-related problems become ascendant and others recede, we gain new understanding. As we peel the layers of the onion of communicative difficulties between the sexes, more onion emerges: there is no core. The way we understood things twenty years ago is not how we see them now; yet that understanding was fruitful and led to today's deeper understanding. But if we are finally to achieve lasting changes, it is necessary to keep re-examining the same questions, though always from the new and enriched perspectives that come from the experience of many years of trying to achieve change.[3]

At the beginning, it was hard even to find our own voices, our own vision. We had for millennia been accustomed to seeing women, and men, through men's eyes. Therefore, like the cat in the epigraph to this chapter, women have been seen as *the other* and *the worse*. As Carroll implies, the dog is defined as the normal, basic, and unmarked household pet (the superordinate category). Its behavior is interpreted as "normal pet behavior" against which that of the cat, as the "other" pet, is judged. The cat is not seen in its own right as a creature with its own legitimate ways, ways that make sense for it. Rather, when compared with the "normal" dog, everything it does becomes anomalous and unintelligible or, as we put it colloquially, "mad." In the same way, male behavior is taken to be the norm for human beings; and women, seen through that distorting lens, appear not only as "different" but often literally as "mad." At the same time, just as no one wants a barking cat around the house, no one likes a woman who behaves "normally"—that is, as a man does. The imposition of the superordinate category and the assignment of unmarked status to one of its members forces the other into a nearly unwinnable struggle for survival and competence.

When around eighteen years ago I first started to speak, and then write, publicly about women and language, those simple acts aroused considerable distress not only among men but also among women, including myself. Men were unhappy because women were beginning, however politely and academically, to reclaim their rights, to say that the position to which they had been relegated was not justified by stupidity or wickedness, but was an artificial construct developed as a result of male control of political and social power (including language). I can understand their resentment, if I deplore it: who wants to be deprived of privilege; worse, to be told one's group had merely usurped its powers, rather than possessing them by intrinsic right? But it was odd that women were upset: Was some hornet's nest dormant for millennia being stirred up? And what would the consequences be?

The physical artifacts of women's language were pretty apparent to surface inspection (though there was and continues to be plenty of squabbling on that score); more problematic was what the surface differences represented in terms of deeper meaning or intention. In what way (if at all) could it accurately be said that men and women spoke different languages?

In the folklore of some cultures, men and women claim to speak different languages. But on closer inspection, their assertions were less true than they seemed to observers who spoke European languages. Arawak men and women, for example, were said to have mutually unintelligible languages. But then, how could boys communicate with their mothers (who raised them)? To the degree that the claim was valid, one could at most say that men and women *pretended* to be unable to understand one another. In Japanese, there are forms reserved for men, and others for women: to cross over is to invite social disaster. But the forms are nonetheless intelligible to all. So the distinction, to the extent that it exists, is in the *active* use of language; passively, members of these groups understand the forms reserved for the opposite sex.

Linguists and anthropologists had always thought that examples like these represented the curious ways of non-Western groups, that in European societies such distinctions did not occur—as was, on the surface, surely true. In English we can find no words explicitly restricted to members of one sex, or usable only in the presence of one sex or the other, on the basis of form alone. Of course, once we extend our analysis to groups of words based on meaning or function, the case becomes more complicated.

But overtly recognizable differences are not as problematic as covert ones. Misunderstandings don't arise, or if they do, merely occasion the patronizing of one sex by the other. But there are deep and subtle differences that lead to more serious kinds of misunderstanding: both sexes use the same words in the same constructions, *but understand them differently.* This misunderstanding is serious: we think we understand and have been understood, when we really don't and haven't. The differences lie in areas that are not explicitly available for inspection, that require metacommunication to be fully examined. And as we have seen, metacommunication is not something this culture (like most) values or is comfortable doing.

For instance, imagine a couple at home after a day's work. She begins to tell him about a run-in with her boss. He replies: You shouldn't have said X. Next time, try Y. It's always best to do Z. Or worse, he barely looks away from the TV long enough to grunt, "Too bad." In either case, having unburdened herself, she feels worse rather than better and blames him for his insensitivity. She wanted something different from him—reassurance, sympathy, something to the effect that that's happened to him, too, and he just guesses bosses have their off days. But he saw her offering as a more practical communication, a request for advice, and so responded as he felt he was asked to do. Why is she suddenly so irritable?

What neither did was metacommunicate: ask, "What are you really asking for here?" "Is this what you hoped I would say?" If one had used a word totally strange to the other, the latter would likely have felt comfortable requesting a definition: "What do you mean by 'metacommunicate'?" (We do metacommunicate to this extent.) The problem is the form the wife uses to express a request for solicitude. In truth, the language is foreign to the husband: men wouldn't use that form for that function. But it doesn't occur to him to ask for clarification, or to her to try to find out what went wrong. They both speak English, don't they? Besides, if she had resorted to metacommunication ("What I wanted from you just then was a little sympathy. . . ."), it would likely not have helped. It would have made any sympathy thus elicited less than spontaneous, and therefore worthless. Metacommunication is not a guaranteed savior of relationships.

WOMEN'S LANGUAGE

The characteristic ways of communication that have been identified as typical of women range in English over the whole of the linguistic repertoire, from sounds to word choice to syntactic features to pragmatic and conversational options, with the preponderance in the latter categories. In this, gender-related diversity differs from regional and social dialects, whose most noticeable and numerous variations from the standard cluster in the phonology and the lexicon. This difference makes sense because dialects develop in isolation from one another as a result of the instability of linguistic forms and influence from other languages. But gender-related differences have a strong psychological component: they are intimately related to the judgments of members of a culture about how to be and think like a good man or woman. So the characteristic forms cluster at the end of the linguistic spectrum most related to psychological expression. Also anomalous, if we were disposed to consider women's linguistic patterns as one sort of social dialect, is the fact that they persist despite intense and constant fraternization with speakers of the standard; most dialects tend to erode if speakers are constantly exposed to the standard language. Gender differences in language arise not because male and female speakers are isolated from each other, but precisely because they live in close contiguity, which constantly causes comparisons and reinforces the need for polarization—linguistic and otherwise. As is true of many types of dialects and special linguistic forms, some speakers of women's language, but few speakers of the standard (male language), are able to *code-switch*, that is, use the non-standard form in some contexts, the standard in others. Women in business or professional settings often sound indistinguishable from their male counterparts. Speakers of nondominant forms must be bilingual in this way, at least passively, to survive; speakers of the dominant form need not be. (So women don't generally complain that men's communication is impossible to understand, but the battlecry "What do women want?" has echoed in one form or another down the centuries.)

Also striking is that some form of women's language exists in every culture that has been investigated with these questions in mind. The same forms are found in language after language. These special forms may differ from one language to another, but most functional characteristics of women's language are widespread, an unremarkable fact since the language represents behavior supposedly typical of women across the majority of cultures: alleged illogic, submissiveness, sexual utility to men, secondary status.

Reality and Interpretation

As an example of how one form may represent different functions in different cultures, consider again the example in chapter 9 of the Malagasy special use of conversational logic.[4] Because information in that culture is more precious than it is for us, the prudent speaker hoards any that he acquires, to the point of speaking in a way we would consider deliberately misleading, in violation of the rules of conversational logic; although to our eyes, neither a breach of politeness nor self-protection is involved. But this strategy is typical only of male Malagasy speakers. Women do just the reverse: speak directly and to the point (unless there are obvious reasons to do otherwise). As a result, women are considered poor communicators: they just don't know how to behave in a conversation, don't know how to transmit information properly, and are therefore illogical.

In other words, the Malagasy stereotype of women is identical to ours: women don't handle the flow of information properly. But the explicit behavior that gives rise to the stereotype is diametrically opposite in the two cultures. So it cannot be that the basis of the stereotype is a universal Aristotelian logical principle. No one decides what communication is intrinsically "logical," then notices that women don't do it, and therefore rationally determines that women are illogical. It's rather the reverse. The dominant group first notices the ways in which the nondominant differ from themselves. They do not think to attribute such differences to external necessity imposed by themselves, or to differences in cultural expectations. Instead, they assume the difference must be due to some deep intrinsic physical and/or psychological distinction that irrevocably divides the sexes: the need for polarization is very strong. Then they decide that there must be some principled difference between men and women to explain the discrepancy. Women are the other; the other is the worse. (That is already given knowledge.) So there is something about women's minds or bodies that makes them be, think, and speak worse than men. Then what men (ideally) do is called "logical." Therefore women's ideal style is "illogical." Whatever is characteristic of the male in a culture will be defined and identified within that culture as "right" or "logical" behavior. Since women are the other, anything they do that is different will be assigned to the opposite pole. Changing their style will not help. If they change it so as to be the same as that of men, they will be seen not as logical beings in their own newfound right, but as men *manqué* or uppity persons striving for privileges they don't deserve. Anything else they do will be seen as illogical, regardless of its form.

Characteristics of Women's Language

Numerous traits have been said to characterize women's forms of speech in this culture. Not all women use them, and probably no one uses them all the time. (They are, for instance, more likely to show up in informal social circumstances than in business settings.) Men sometimes use them, either with different meanings or for individual special reasons. (Gay men imitate some of them.)[5]

1. Women often seem to hit phonetic points less precisely than men: lisped *s*'s, obscured vowels.
2. Women's intonational contours display more variety than men's.[6]
3. Women use diminutives and euphemisms more than men ("You nickname God's creatures," says Hamlet to Ophelia).
4. Women make more use of expressive forms (adjectives not nouns or verbs and, in that category, those expressing emotional rather than intellectual evaluation) more than men: *lovely, divine.*
5. Women use forms that convey impreciseness: *so, such.*
6. Women use hedges of all kinds more than men.
7. Women use intonation patterns that resemble questions, indicating uncertainty or need for approval.
8. Women's voices are breathier than men's.
9. Women are more indirect and polite than men.
10. Women won't commit themselves to an opinion.
11. In conversation, women are more likely to be interrupted, less likely to introduce successful topics.[7]
12. Women's communicative style tends to be collaborative rather than competitive.[8]
13. More of women's communication is expressed nonverbally (by gesture and intonation) than men's.
14. Women are more careful to be "correct" when they speak, using better grammar and fewer colloquialisms than men.

All of these characteristics can be seen as instantiating one or more of the roles women are supposed to play in this culture. Also notable is the fact that, as suggested by several items on this list, women have communicatively more options than men, more channels legitimately open to them. (That should be seen as a plus, but nonverbal signals are often stigmatized as distracting, and variety in intonation as hysterical.) At the same time, what they may express, and to whom, is more severely limited. This ambivalence is not unique to language: in many ways, it can be said that women are more constrained in their behavior than men (professionally, sexually); yet less in others (dress, home-versus-career options).

Other generalizations: womanly communicative behavior is imprecise and indirect (both characteristic of female deference politeness, actually or symbolically leaving interpretation up to the hearer); nonpowerful or nonseeking of power; and more capable of expressing emotions (a trait scorned by the "logical").

The superficial forms themselves may change slightly over time. The way "ideal" women spoke in 1930s movies (think of Katharine Hepburn or Jean Harlow) is not that of 1950s (Doris Day or Marilyn Monroe), or 1970s (Jane Fonda or Jill Clayburgh) movie heroines. Specific traits shift, but all involve some of the preceding assumptions, for our assessment of their femininity and therefore desirability (and hence ultimately movie bankability) is dependent on stereotypes embedded in the culture.

LANGUAGE, GENDER, AND POWER

Men's language is the language of the powerful. It is meant to be direct, clear, succinct, as would be expected of those who need not fear giving offense, who need not worry about the risks of responsibility. It is the language of people who are in charge of making observable changes in the real world. Women's language developed as a way of surviving and even flourishing without control over economic, physical, or social reality. Then it is necessary to listen more than speak, agree more than confront, be delicate, be indirect, say dangerous things in such a way that their impact will be felt after the speaker is out of range of the hearer's retaliation. It is not that women, because of their smaller brains or Eve-descended wickedness, are intrinsically incapable of direct and forthright communication; rather, we have developed the other type (requiring more finesse and skill) in order to do two impossible things at once: get our needs met, and survive. Moreover, men, busy with the "important" business of the objective universe, came to relegate interpersonal matters to women: nurturance, caring, responsiveness. Lately some men have begun to regret the trade-off, but over the ages women have developed the relevant communicative skills, and most men have not. Again, it isn't because they biologically cannot; but because they have opted out, and now they (and the world) bear the horrific consequences. Those patterns can be unlearned, of course, but millennia of stereotyping and polarization make that a painful task.

Men's discourse is the "important" talk; it is deemed necessary and worthwhile, the stuff of public institutions and public decisions. It is the language of objectivity: science, politics, business. Such is the mythology. The interactive science, business, and politics are left to women to manage, and manage them women always have: women's communicative strategy is the glue that holds society together, keeps it running, a force for conservatism and certainty. We call it "gossip."[9] Unlike men's important talk, it is considered (by the definers, all male) trivial when it is not considered vicious. Usually it is neither. The malice often attributed to women—cattiness, bitchiness—is a direct consequence of being deprived of power and autonomy, rather than an outgrowth of anatomical necessity. (Analogously, academic politics is said to be so vicious because the stakes are so small.)

Women's language was originally defined as language spoken by those without access to power. But it is used by its speakers even with those over whom they do have power: with their children, for instance. And women who have achieved power in business and the professions still use it to some degree. So the relation between the language and its speakers' physical reality is not direct. Moreover, the characteristics of women's language are observed in the speech of children as young as two or three: even at that age, boys and girls talk differently just as they play different games and insist on dressing differently. Women's linguistic traits have arisen out of real-world necessity and actual roles; but over time they have developed symbolic meaning, and therefore are directly connected not with their speakers' actual lack of power, but with their feelings about the possession of power. Women's language becomes a symbolic expression of distance from power, or lack of interest in power. It is a way of showing that the speaker is not someone who wishes to be assertive or have influence—whether, in fact, she does or not. But as a result, when a woman is placed in a position in which being assertive and forceful is necessary, she is faced with a paradox: she can be a good woman but a bad executive or professional; or vice versa. To do both is impossible. As long as a woman stays in "her place," at home and in private, the contradiction does not surface. The dilemma sowed the seeds of the 1980s backlash (which is not to say that policy decisions by male power figures did not play the most significant role in it).

What Is to Be Done?

Thus the superficial traits of women's language all represent a conventional avoidance of even the appearance of holding or desiring power. They arise from a reality but continue, as habits will, even when powerlessness is irrelevant or unrealistic. A trait that developed under physical and political domination has become identified as a defining characteristic of femininity, a mark of the vital polarization of the sexes. To abandon the style would be to renounce femininity, and for what benefit? One does not thereby gain power but merely acquires status as someone outside of the rules and beyond the pale, a nonperson entitled by her behavior neither to the protections (such as they are) accorded to the "weaker sex" as consolation prizes nor to the privileges of the stronger. It is little wonder that even now women feel reluctant to change their ways, linguistic and otherwise; that even women who are otherwise adventurous and brave avoid linguistic risk taking.

In fact, there are points in favor of the conservative position. Nondominance brings with it or encourages the development of other traits, some unequivocally positive. If jockeying for power and getting your directives obeyed are not your major priorities, you might develop a way of talking that stresses collaboration and consensus rather than hierarchical domination. You would have to treat others as individuals, respecting their rights and needs in communication; otherwise, consensual decision is a travesty or an impossibility. Your arts and sciences would devise ways of winning others over to your thinking, cultivating the art of compromise and the science of management. You would have to become extraordinarily skilled in discovering what those you were working with wanted and needed, in order to keep the powerful placated, and your peers cooperative: a sixth sense that can be identified with "women's intuition," although it must be learned, if implicitly, and involves a wide array of complex talents. Women need to be in constant communication in order to keep the consensus stable and preserve feelings of trust ("gossip"). Such communicative communities create bonds among their members and skill in interpersonal relations. The male analogue is the power hierarchy for people, and mastery over things. As with every other difference between the sexes, the masculine prerogative has been exalted at the expense of the feminine. But the latter has always been the cohesive force holding communities together and staving off annihilation, even as men's ways bring us ever closer to the brink.

The ideal would be for both sexes to move their ways of communicating closer to some middle ground. The ideal seldom occurs in nature. This one seems far off—for one thing, because men see little to be gained by changing their style. What would compensate for the loss of that sense of control that the linguistic forms of hierarchy and mastery bring with them? For women, it's not clear that there is a compromise between aggression and deference. That mythic golden mean is sometimes called *assertion*, but it is not clear whether this stylistic category is a possibility for women, or whether, too often, assertive behavior is misidentified as aggression. In fact, any move away from traditional deference is seen by many men (and women) as a threat, as "pushy" or "bitchy." On the other hand, traditional female behavior is also suspect in nontraditional female circumstances. Women's communicative choices, to succeed, must be perceived by others as they are intended.

Playing Boys' Games

In politics it is currently axiomatic that a woman must act, if not speak, more aggressively than a man to convince the electorate that she can be trusted with their country. The Gandhis, Meirs, and Thatchers belie the argument that women should be encouraged in politics in order to make the world a kinder and better place. Women, to succeed, must become honorary men. Those women who have reached the top have done so in parliamentary systems, where they have not had to present themselves directly to the electorate as non-incumbents in order to achieve national office. Once they get into power, they can prove themselves by their pugnacious acts, as all three of the women named here did. Then linguistic style matters less. But in a system of direct presidential election such as ours, a candidate must run on the basis of style, and that style must be appealing to more than 50 percent of the voters. And a woman is automatically damned on that basis, whichever option she chooses. If she talks "like a lady," in a deferential tone and manner, she will seem weak, unable to stand up to the Russians (or whoever the current enemy may be). We cannot "respect" her, we say; she cannot be our commander in chief, her finger will tremble on the button. On the other hand, if she is direct and forthright, if she attacks and ripostes, that behavior doesn't make things better. If a man running for office rips into his opponent, that's politics, that's being tough. But a woman who does the same is not a woman any more, certainly not a lady. And therefore, not a nice person, and we want our chief executive to be (perhaps above all) nice.

We should not be surprised to find that all the hidden agendas, prejudices, and assumptions about role and propriety surface when a woman is on the brink of achieving national office. It has happened only once, in 1984 with Geraldine Ferraro. And she (and her party) were punished so severely for that heresy that it may never happen again. She wasn't even running for president, a position that requires autonomy and leadership ability (traditionally men's domain), but for vice president, which is arguably a perfect position for a woman. The vice president's job is that of an executive's wife. He goes to funerals too minor for the chief executive's attention; he takes on worthwhile social projects, as does the First Lady (drugs, education); he is not supposed to have his own opinions and policies, but must wait for the president to enunciate the official position and then loyally support him. It's true that he retains one masculine prerogative, presiding over the Senate and casting a vote to break ties. But how often does he get that chance?

Nevertheless, the American people were and are leery of a woman one heartbeat from the Oval Office or, rather, were subliminally offended that a woman dared aspire so high. People did virtuously say when interviewed that of course they would be willing to vote for a woman, if they liked the way she talked; but what was unsaid was that they never would. For she could not talk like a woman and like a man at once; not down the middle, but both at the same time. Ferraro tried. In her debates with the Republican vice presidential candidate, George Bush, she presented herself as informed, lucid, and candid (or as candid as a candidate can be). When attacked, as she was much more stridently than a male would have been, she kept her temper but was firm and sometimes sardonic in refutation. Her opponent, on the other hand, acted much more the hysterical lady: his voice rose in indignation in both pitch and volume; he waspishly (no pun intended) reiterated the same charges again and again (he didn't listen); he grew visibly upset and overwrought; his face got red, his voice tense and shrill. He went into his lecture mode. This was not the archetypal male in calm control. Yet the next day pollsters declared Bush the "winner." No one had much to say about why or how. The answer is that Ferraro lost because she dared to speak up in public against a man. The incumbent's wife, Barbara Bush, helped promote stereotypical attitudes in several ways at once by commenting coyly on Ferraro's performance. She was, simpered the Second Lady, "something that rhymes with rich."

The masculine and hierarchical style of at least one other institution, the university, seems likewise resistant to significant change, even as its ranks are leavened by the increasing numbers of women faculty. Faculty rise in administrative ranks (department chair—dean—provost—chancellor) in large measure because their governing style has won the approbation of higher administrators, now and for the foreseeable future mostly male. Since they continue to feel comfortable with their own ways, those women who have learned to code-switch actively—that is, to use male interactive style—will be seen as the most "competent." As in business and politics, and for the same reasons, the rise of individual women does not bring in its train greater appreciation of women's traditional ways in general; nor does it encourage the incorporation of those ways into the prevalent institutional style. One great leap for a woman is not a great leap for womankind, nor is it the opening wedge of a brave new world. The institution changes its nondominant members, not vice versa.

Over the last twenty years, the number of women in tenured and tenurable positions in front-rank universities has increased from essentially zero to—in a few departments—as high as one in four. Feminist scholarship is taken seriously; even male academics espouse "feminist" positions. The result is that women, the quintessential outsiders, have been taken into the inner circle. Feminism, once a stance of radical external critique, can only be compromised by admission to insider status. How can it attack authority when it speaks in the voice of authority? In the academy, there is plenty of evidence that, by gaining a hearing, women are losing their voice.

It is not yet clear whether, or to what degree, power alters women's interactive style in general. Differences between male and female style have been studied for less than twenty years; and in that time, almost all the focus has been on ordinary conversation. Even there the realities have proven difficult to document unambiguously because of the many conflicting environmental variables involved. Ordinary conversation is collaborative, at least ostensibly egalitarian, and not purpose-oriented; these properties encourage the use of collaborative and non-hierarchical strategies. But elsewhere—for instance, faculty department meetings, business conferences, courtroom dialogue, academic lectures—both less is known, and collaborative strategies make less obvious sense. For one thing, unlike ordinary conversation (in which both sexes have always participated), institutional and professional talk has, until recently, been almost totally a male preserve; so the rules of male discourse are not only seen (as in ordinary conversation) as the better way to talk but as the only way. There are no viable alternatives. Secondly, these types are more or less, overtly or covertly non-egalitarian, and the appearance of equality (at least) is necessary for collaboration. Finally, they are purpose-oriented, with focused and formal agendas. In such cases, efficiency counts, and hierarchical style at least looks more efficient, whether or not it actually is.

There is some evidence that in these milieus, at least some women have developed some aspects of collaborative style. But the evidence is sparse, often anecdotal, and therefore inconclusive.[10]

The Razor's Edge

Cases have reached the courts suggesting that in business, too, the thin line along which women must walk is indeed a razor's edge. *Time* magazine discusses two such cases, at least superficially opposites, but basically reinforcing the same point.[11] In one, a woman was denied promotion in an accounting firm despite having brought the firm a great deal of business and having "billed more hours in the preceding year than any other candidate [for partner]." Partners called her "macho," and said she "needed to take a course in charm school." (The first would be a compliment to a male in that position, and the second unthinkable as a criticism of a man.) "One of her biggest supporters [in the firm] advised her that she might improve her chances if she would learn to walk, talk and dress 'more femininely, . . . wear makeup, have her hair styled and wear jewelry.' " None of these, it is worth noting, has anything to do with an accountant's primary responsibilities. And apparently, her "macho" ways did not interfere with her bringing business to the firm. Perhaps the reverse: her businesslike and manlike attitude might imbue a client with confidence in a field such as accounting, which involves many kinds of abilities typically thought of as characteristic of men. Had she changed her ways as advised, she might have lost the confidence of her clients and would have been denied the partnership on those grounds. The case is currently under review by the U.S. Supreme Court.

The other case was then entering litigation in Florida. The plaintiff, an assistant state attorney in Broward County, was reprimanded by her superior because of her choice of clothing: short skirts, spike heels, ornate jewelry—the very accoutrements whose absence was criticized in the first case. (An accompanying photo shows her in a skirt that is short, all right, but no micro-mini.) Her superior told her she looked like a "bimbo." She complained to the federal Equal Employment Opportunity Commission, and shortly thereafter was fired. The message seems clear enough: in business, neither a bitch nor a bimbo be. But in both these cases, it is men who have imposed the definitions on women, both defining the categories and determining when a woman fell into one or the other. Since men don't play the game, it seems unfair that they not only make the rules but apply them.

For these reasons, after twenty years the underlying question remains unanswered. We don't know what a woman should do who wishes to achieve influence in nontraditional fields, neither what is best for her as an individual nor what is ultimately advantageous for women as a class, nor what would most benefit society at large. If we assimilate to men's ways ("when in Rome, etc."), we risk discrimination as too aggressive; we convince the company that women who aspire to high positions are not "womanly" or good people; and we do nothing to change the way male institutions work, nothing to bring better ways of relating to one another to the larger community. Part of the thrust of the women's movement has been, correctly, to ensure that individual women could reach the goals to which they aspired and which they deserved; but another part should surely be (though it seems sometimes that we have lost sight of it) changing the world to a more humane place that works in part by women's communicative rules.

On the other hand, if a woman persists in playing by the age-old feminine rules, she will be seen as unable to win the game. She will become ineffectual, since the characteristics of women's communicative patterns are, in hierarchical settings, unavoidably ineffectual: they complicate decision making, make it difficult to get subordinates to do what they are supposed to do. She will not gain power; she will convince her employers that women are, after all, incompetent, that their place is in the home, and so forth; and since she will not achieve power in her profession, she will be unable to utilize that power to become authoritative in the larger community and become a force to encourage deep changes.

WOMEN'S TALK TODAY

The women's movement expended a lot of effort during the 1970s trying to achieve changes in women's ways of communicating and the ways that society at large communicated to and about women. To what degree were the efforts useful? Where have we come in twenty years, and to what extent does it make a difference?

For one thing, people's awareness of language and the problems its biased use creates has become widespread. True, it is at the expense of twenty years of ridicule, but even ridicule eventually creates familiarity, which in turn leads to acceptance. When *Ms.* was first offered as an alternative to *Miss* and *Mrs.*, the jokes were legion, and traditionalists insisted that the word was unpronounceable (a common indictment of the new and psychologically frightening); of course, it is no more so than *Miss,* and less so than *Mrs.,* on any phonetic basis. It has not achieved the acceptance its proponents hoped for, as a replacement for the latter two terms; but at least it is ensconced in some contexts as a fully acceptable form alongside the others. Similarly with gender-neutral occupational categories. *Firefighter* and *police officer,* for instance, seem to be achieving full acceptance; *chairperson* and its relations less so, probably because such forms explicitly incorporate a noxious reminder that *this is a feminist word.* Increasingly, especially in professional writing, authors use some form of gender neutralization: *he/she* or circumlocutions of various sorts. Even most of those authors who resolutely cling to universal *he* do so apologetically, giving their reasons in a footnote or a preface.

Still, there is an instructive contrast with the linguistic demands of other nondominant groups and their reception by the dominant, related to the nonlinguistic contrasts between the successes of the civil rights movement and the women's movement. Since the 1960s, whenever blacks have suggested changes in the way they were to be spoken of or addressed, society as a whole, including the media, has speedily followed suit. Even the biggest southern redneck has learned to avoid clever pronunciations of "nigger" in public, or risk ostracism; no one calls black men "boys" any more; we don't hear public ridicule or denunciations of black English as nonlanguage, though we used to; and black men and women are considered entitled to terms of address equivalent to those used with whites in the same setting. Racial slurs or ethnic humor by whites is considered crude, and any suggestion of it in public discourse is likely to bring its user instant rebuke and, if he or she is a public figure, immediate and abject disgrace. After a two-decade-long acceptance of *black,* when Jesse Jackson urged its replacement by the cumbersome *African-American* the latter replaced *black* in the media almost at once. I did not hear a whisper from whites about "unpronounceability" or "awkwardness."

Women have not been as successful. It is still considered fair to make fun (albeit "gentle" fun) of the movement's requests, or ignore them completely. Women are still addressed and referred to as "ladies" and "girls," despite ample demonstration of the patronizing or euphemistic character of these "polite" forms. Every move brings equal and opposite backlash: there is still vituperation in the press when a woman requests (not demands) the right to determine her own name. It seemed impossible, in 1984, for the media to recall that Geraldine Ferraro was Ms. Ferraro, not Mrs. Ferraro (her mother) or Mrs. Zaccaro (her mother-in-law); it was as if she didn't have a right to choose her name. *Strident* has achieved nearly formulaic status as an epithet for *feminist,* the two linked in the talk-show audience's mind like *fleet-footed Achilles* or *ox-eyed Hera* in the Homeric audience's. The spectrum of possible ways of talking has widened a bit: women don't lose the same amount of status they did twenty-five years ago should a four-letter word escape their lips. But (as the legal case discussed earlier makes clear) women are not on an even footing with men in this respect.

There is no obviously correct position on how women should talk. (But then, the black community is split on how to deal with black English in the schools and elsewhere.) Much has been written by feminists suggesting attitudes of one sort or another. Women's language is ineffectual: abandon it if you want success in the outside world; women's language is open and collaborative: hold on to it and try to change men's ways. The movement's rhetorical thrust has moved more or less from the first pole to the second over the years. But as fashionable as it is to promote women's ways of speaking and interacting, these suggestions are nearly always couched in men's language—in fact, the extreme form of it characteristic of academic discourse. For the language of the academy displays some of the worst excesses of men's language. It is deliberately and excessively non-interactive: impersonal, non-emotional, objective. All of these make it hard to understand, thus increasing its users' hierarchical power at the expense of those struggling to interpret it: intentional unintelligibility has always been a potent weapon of those seeking to attain and maintain authoritarian power. The discourse style of academe, whether in writing, the classroom, or the meeting, is one of floor-holding, not collaborative reciprocity. That, too, is characteristically masculine. But writing on women's language has come largely out of the academy, and is of the academy. We use their language to tout ours—a bit schizophrenic.

Many women have eliminated the more blatant lexical and syntactic "women's" forms from their speech, but the more subtle and yet more pervasive distinctions of pragmatics persist. The work on conversational interruptability has not documented any shifts over time. Yet women in public positions, in interviews on television, seem to be learning that they don't have to be nice ladies and take it. Not infrequently on interview formats such as the "MacNeil-Lehrer News Hour," women panelists are interrupted by men, while the reverse, though it occurs, is rare. Women seem to be learning to tell the men who interrupt to let them finish, and to be insistent about it should the behavior continue. Women are still touched, first-named, and nicknamed nonreciprocally by men. Women still complain of male sexual harassment, while men profess innocence: what's wrong with a friendly compliment, an affectionate pat on the tush? To dismiss the complaints by saying that, if women did it to men, men wouldn't mind, misses the point. A sexual double standard still exists. Men still use sexuality to assert their power over women, and these "friendly" acts are most often indirect or nonlinguistic expressions of hierarchical dominance. And women are still much more at risk of sexual assault by men than the reverse, even if once in a million years the "rape" of a man by a woman gets wide media play. A "friendly" wolf whistle is, in this context, a threat both physical and psychological. Context determines meaning, so the argument that women shouldn't mind *whatever* form of inequitable treatment because men wouldn't is meaningless as long as differential power creates different interpretations.

Bias persists, alongside of genuine progress in affirmative action and more equitable treatment of women professionally and socially. The power imbalance is still with us, and therefore necessarily linguistic inequity persists. As long as there is a power imbalance, women will be in a double bind communicatively: any way they communicate that differs from the way men do will be stigmatized as different and therefore worse; any attempt they make to approximate the ways of men will be stigmatized as unfeminine, indicative of bad character, and uppity. Yet we have all, as a society, become aware of these discrepancies and alert to possible ways to remedy them. We may not all be ready or able to undertake the deep and sincere changes of attitude that are prerequisite to change in behavior; that will take a long time. But as long as we remain aware and committed, things are likely to continue to get better. We just have to keep the faith.

Gender distinctions are one pervasive form of cross-cultural difference, if we see men and women as separate cultures. But there are many other ways to distinguish cultures from one another. One of the most significant dividers is the answer to the question: What is a good human being? And a subcase of that question, How does one person persuade another to do something? The next two chapters focus on these points: how much of the definition is culture-specific, and what is universal?

De Amicitiis Faciendis et Hominibus Movendis; or, How to Make Friends and Influence People

P OWER is often a product of persuasiveness. People who can use linguistic skills to win others over to a point of view, and get them to act in accordance with their interests, are likely to achieve power. That relationship between power and persuasiveness has been the case as far back as we can see into human history, at least in countries whose inhabitants have some say in political decisions. When power is determined by accident of birth or brute physical force, persuasion plays a more circumscribed role (though even autocrats must get others to do their bidding and fend off attempted takeovers).

We sometimes see the contemporary susceptibility to linguistic persuasion as novel, the result of consumers' incessant exposure to many forms of communication and producers' continual development of ingenious techniques. But the art of persuasion is at least as old as recorded literature: Homeric heroes used and responded to it; and by the period of Athenian democracy, many of its principles had been codified by academic experts and put to the test by practitioners. Rhetoricians specified both the form and the content that were apt to be persuasive for speeches in different public settings: before a deliberative body, before a jury or panel of judges, to an army, to the people, and so forth. Long before the techniques of written style were studied, oral rhetorical tradition flourished. Until comparatively recently, writing was seen as a way to preserve what had been uttered aloud, not as a medium in its own right, with its own rules. The rhetorician, the public speaker, held a position of high honor in democratic Athens and republican Rome. Well into the Roman empire, ambitious fathers sent their sons to study with the greatest rhetoricians in Athens, in order to enable them to take their place in government. Nor is the art of rhetoric valued only in the West; virtually all societies in which persuasion has political power have given special honor to orators of unusual ability. Usually, too, societies have definite ideas about what is persuasive, and how to speak so as to be persuasive.

THE UNIVERSALITY OF PERSUASIVENESS

There are reasons to suppose that the methods of persuasion are universal. After all, persuasiveness is based on two things: emotional appeal and intellectual argument. Both emotions and logical reasoning are assumed to be present in essentially similar forms in all human beings: that universality unites us as a species and enables us to understand and be moved by the artistry (verbal and other) of other cultures in other places and other times. So it seems reasonable to suppose (and if we don't give it much thought, we may well suppose) that rhetorical skill is transferable across cultures. What works for me now, on this page, would have worked for Demosthenes in the Athenian agora two thousand four hundred years ago, and for the Chinese peasant today.

But when we examine the rhetorical practices and theories of other cultures, we find that persuasion is not the same everywhere. It is not that the way to be persuasive in one culture bears no resemblance to the way it is done in another— there are commonalities; but here as often, the differences may strike us first and most profoundly.

The more two cultures are isolated from each other by time, space, or politics, the more different and exotic the rhetorical traditions of each may be to the other. We borrow fashions in rhetoric as in everything else, where there is contact; and whatever culture is currently the most influential politically or economically will tend to export its rhetorical style as well, to some degree. It is often commented that American ways of political campaigning have begun to spread to Europe, along with our language, our music, and "Dallas." But when there is little contact between cultures, and little sympathy, each will cling to its own ways, so that the styles of each appear bizarre and unintelligible to the other.

The political rhetoric of pre-*glasnost* Russia had that effect upon Americans of an earlier epoch. Soviet rhetorical style (like Soviet sartorial fashion) once impressed Americans as heavy, emotional, bombastic and hyperbolic, a throw-back to an earlier era in American politics. In the 1950s when Nikita Khrushchev, to emphasize a point, banged his shoe on the table in a speech at the United Nations, Americans were disconcerted. It seemed overbearing, heavy-handed. True, during this period our own politicians were given to torrents of passion against the Communist menace, but—taking off your *shoe* in public? *Nonverbal* harangue? Barbaric! Rather than seeing Khrushchev's rhetoric as forcefully emphatic, Americans saw it as blustering and overbearing, reaffirming their belief in the Soviet threat, as well as the basic craziness and imperviousness to reason of the entire U.S.S.R. It is unlikely Khrushchev intended his gesture to be read that way.

Chinese Communist rhetoric, in wall posters and elsewhere, also strikes Americans as not persuasive. At one time it was fashionable for competing factions to denounce each other as "running dogs" or "lackeys of capitalism." We understood what they were getting at, but the rhetoric seemed blatant, the metaphors hyperbolic, especially for a culture so venerable and supposedly so subtle. *Newsweek* quotes Deng Xiaoping as saying in 1963: "The old ones occupy the toilets without taking shits. They have to go."[1] Now perhaps politicians in this country talk this way about one another, but not in public. To us Deng's remark seems uncivilized and uncivil. Or, more recently, from the *San Francisco Chronicle's* report about propaganda during the student demonstrations in Beijing, describing a banner hung over the front door of the Beijing branch of Maxim's: *Firmly Take the Socialist Road!*[2] Closer to what we expect, to be sure, but still a bit strident, too much the hard sell. Our campaign posters don't tell us what to do; they only suggest how to feel. The adverb strikes us as especially curious: it seems to demand a precise response from the reader, leaving too little room for initiative. Without it, equivalent slogans could appear on American television. With it, the banner's message is childlike.

But some premises of rhetoric do carry across cultures. We can read a decent translation of Demosthenes' *On the Crown* today and be moved by his appeals. But even as we are carried along by the force of the oratory, we remain aware that no contemporary American would construct a speech like that, and if anyone did, it would be ignored or derided. In the *Peloponnesian Wars,* Thucydides re-creates speeches in which two Athenians, Cleon and Diotus, argue for and against imposing the death penalty on a rebellious colony of Athens. We can respond to the passion and reasoning behind them. But we know that no lawyer today would construct a closing argument in a capital case on those principles. Something has changed, even as some things stay the same. Deep emotions are universal, basic common sense is universal; but how those are appealed to, and mobilized into action, changes. So we cannot really say we understand Chinese wall posters or Demosthenian orations. All men may be created equal, but we are not educated or brought up identical.

In chapter 9, I discussed some of the ways in which the presumably spontaneous and naïve ways of linguistic interaction, our ordinary conversation rules of logic and politeness, differ; our more formal and structured discourse types, in particular persuasive strategies, differ as well. Therefore a translator can never reproduce fully the effect of the original text on its reader or hearer.

Deborah Tannen and I have proposed two concepts that may be useful in this discussion—*pragmatic synonymy* and *pragmatic homonymy*—based on the relations found at the more concrete level of word-formation.[3] Words are synonymous if their forms are different, but their meanings roughly the same: *therapist* and *shrink.* Homonyms are words whose forms are the same, but whose meanings differ: *top* ("summit"), and *top* ("gyroscopic toy"). Pragmatic synonymy occurs when two forms represent essentially the same intention on a speaker's part: for instance, "Won't you come in?" and "How about coming in?" are both politely hedged ways of saying, "Come in!" Pragmatic homonyms are forms that look the same but have two or more distinct interpretations depending on context. A tag question (like those discussed in earlier chapters) such as, "This food is delicious, isn't it?" is pragmatically homonymous, as it might be intended in one context as the speaker's way of avoiding an assertive statement as unladylike; in another, as an attempt to elicit a response from a shy person; in still another, a veiled demand from the cook: "Tell me it's good or I'll be terribly hurt."

Members of two cultures wanting to persuade an audience to the same decision might use different means to achieve that end, on both a large and a small scale: pragmatic synonymy. Or they might use the same form, perhaps by chance, to mean different things, to persuade hearers in different directions: pragmatic homonymy. A third possibility is that the cultures could use the same form to achieve the same effect: *pragmatic equivalence.* Only in the last case can even the most excellent translation affect its readers in the same way as the original affected members of its writer's culture.

DEATH PENALTY ARGUMENTATION: ROMAN AND AMERICAN

Argumentation in capital cases provides an unusually clear window into cross-cultural similarities and differences in rhetorical strategy. Few forms of punishment are perceived universally as equivalent. For identical offenses, one culture prefers incarceration, another corporal punishment, a third the death penalty, another banishment, still another deprivation of property. Especially for cultures separated by time, many items of significance may become incomparable: the relation between currency systems is unclear, improvements in penology make long-term imprisonment possible, and forms of punishment that to one age made logical sense, like the removal of appropriate body parts, to another seem inconceivably barbaric. But the death penalty retains a universal commonality. Everyone experiences life and fears death and understands the stark finality of the latter and the deep significance of depriving another human being of the former. Even in cultures that dispense the death penalty relatively freely, there are hedges and restrictions on its application, whether based on the heinousness of the crime or the position of the criminal in society. Some societies restrict the death penalty to only the most serious crimes; others, only to those who constitute the *they,* or a subclass thereof, to the lawmakers. Moreover, as long as there is an officially recognized tradition of forensic pleading, death penalty cases, because of their seriousness and notoriety, bring out the best (or worst) in an orator and demonstrate a culture's notion of how effective argumentation is done.[4] More than anywhere else, in capital argumentation, pro and con, implicit stereotypes and beliefs held by members of a culture are brought into play. For it is widely and no doubt correctly believed that to convince a sentencing body to kill another human being, strong inhibitions must be broken, so that a culture's most persuasive arguments must be marshaled by the prosecutor. At the same time, a capital crime is apt to instill in the sentencers feelings of alienation and horror, making it easier to kill the defendant, so that, to save that person's life the defense attorney must forge bonds of identity between judge and judged. We are fortunate in having records of one such trial from first century B.C. Rome, a culture that (itself borrowing from the Greeks) is responsible for transmitting much of our current understanding of law and rhetoric. I am basing my discussion on the historian Sallust's description of the argumentation in the Roman senate in 63 B.C. about the penalty to be imposed upon the Catilinarian conspirators.[5]

Lucius Sergius Catilina (Catiline in English) was a well-born man in his mid-forties. Ambitious, he had failed to win election to the state's highest office, the consulship (his political enemy, Cicero, had won one of the two consulships that year). Disgruntled, in financial distress, and apparently upset as well by the chaos, corruption, and mismanagement that characterized the Roman republic of that period, Catiline gathered a band of allies, mostly aristocratic youths like himself, and formed a conspiracy—according to Cicero, to kill government officials, free the slaves, abolish debt, and redistribute property.

After Cicero revealed the conspiracy, Catiline himself slipped away to the group's military camp near modern Florence; there, not long after, the small army was overwhelmed by the forces of the republic. Catiline died, says Sallust, "with all his wounds in front," a death that almost redeemed his life by Roman standards. But before this, two of his fellow conspirators had been captured and were being held prisoner. The debate in the senate was over what to do with them. Two punishments were open: the death penalty; or the equivalent of life imprisonment without possibility of parole, incarceration in whatever Roman municipalities (not the city itself, for reasons of security) were willing to take them.

Rome in this period had stringent constraints on the death penalty. It could not be imposed on Roman citizens without a formal trial, presided over by an elected magistrate (the *praetor*) and decided by an appointed jury. Cicero and his fellow conservatives were, however, uneasy with this option, fearing that the jury could be corrupted to produce an acquittal. In the case of noncitizens it was simpler, and matters were facilitated by the fact that Cicero had terrified the senate, by his predictions of violence and anarchy, into declaring martial law (the *senatus consultum ultimum*). By this decree, the senate was empowered to pronounce sentence of death upon noncitizens by majority vote. The captured conspirators were Roman freeborn males, unquestionably citizens by law. But Cicero, by a bit of convoluted logic he lived to regret, convinced his colleagues that the conspirators' treason rendered them noncitizens, and therefore subject to execution without a trial.

In the debate that followed, liberals led by C. Julius Caesar argued for the option of life without parole. The conservatives urged death. To read Cicero's contemporary and later statements is to perceive him as the leader and the most effective persuader for the death penalty side. But for Sallust, Marcus Porcius Cato was the most persuasive death penalty advocate. Sallust provides in his history of the Catilinarian conspiracy re-creations of the speeches of Caesar and Cato, as well as excerpts of several others on both sides. Cato's arguments, along with Cicero's inflammatory warnings, did the trick. The conspirators were executed by strangulation (considered both the most humane and the most dignified method, short of "voluntary" suicide). A few years later, when Cicero's political enemies were ascendant, he was found guilty of putting Roman citizens to death without a trial, and was forced to spend a year in exile.

The arguments of Caesar and Cato can be compared with analogous portions of the closing arguments in a death penalty trial in Alameda County, California, in 1987. In this case (*People* v. *Wash*), the defendant had been found guilty the year before of multiple murder as well as rape, attempted rape, robbery, and burglary; but that jury hung on the question of penalty. Therefore a second jury was assembled to retry the penalty phase of the case. The only options open to this jury were life without parole, or death. To vote for death, the jury had to be convinced that the factors in aggravation (circumstances that made the crimes or the defendant, in the jury's eyes, more heinous) outweighed those in mitigation. It took the jury approximately two hours of deliberation to return a death verdict. As data I will use the beginning and end of both side's closing arguments in this case. The closing argument is often considered (a little superstitiously) by trial lawyers the pivotal point in jury persuasion, so that it forms a natural focus. In the Alameda County public defender's office, the preparation of closing arguments begins well in advance and is done with great care and reflection, involving as many people—associates, friends, volunteers, whomever—as are willing to help. The Romans had no formal opening and closing arguments, and no presentation of testimony, since the discussion was not a formal trial. Therefore I will use the opening and closing sections of both Caesar's and Cato's speeches, which give the flavor and the distillations of their whole arguments.

In some ways, to be sure, the two debates are different. In one the crime is political, high treason; in the other personal, murder. (But the state is the prosecutor in both.) In the first, the group to be persuaded is a gathering of men of privilege and education, probably the "best and brightest" of the Roman state;

in the other, the typical American "spectrum of the community" jury. In the Catilinarian case, defense and prosecution are volunteers: neither Caesar nor Cato is being paid for his efforts (though both were trained as rhetoricians—that is, lawyers—as was usual for well-born Roman citizens of this period). In the American courtroom, both speakers are lawyers, both government employees, though the prosecutor is explicitly the arm of and defender of the state, and his adversary, a public defender, represents the defendant. But speakers and audiences in both trials are well aware that they are engaged in a solemn and irrevocable decision; that they are being asked to undertake a great responsibility; and they will be judged now and later by their performance.

The task of comparison is complicated by the many comparisons that can be made. First, there are choices of style. How does the orator make his case? How does he present himself to his audience, how does he set forth his argument? Are there cultural presuppositions that make one stylistic choice more appealing to a society than another? Then there are choices in content. What goes into a life versus death argument, now and then? What kinds of facts, what emotional suasion, are considered effective? Deeper than these points of divergence, based on cultural differences, are similarities, based on universal human needs and attributes. People share attitudes toward life and death, and are moved by similar emotions to take or spare a life.

Here, first, is my translation of the opening and closing selections from the Catilinarian speeches, Caesar's in defense and Cato's for the prosecution (Sallust's Latin is in the endnotes): following these, the opening and closing sections of the defense and prosecution final arguments in *Wash.* Caesar's argument, against the death penalty, begins:

It is proper, Senators, for people who must make decisions in the face of confusion to keep their minds free of hatred, friendship, anger, and pity. These emotions interfere with the mind's alertness to truth, and no one can serve his passion and his best interests at once. When you make use of your intelligence, it has power; if passion takes over, it dominates, the mind loses its strength. I recall a great many decisions, Senators, in which kings and populace made bad decisions under the influence of anger or pity. But I would rather speak of what our ancestors did right and properly despite their emotions, in the Macedonian War, which we fought against King Perses. The great and splendid city of Rhodes, which had prospered thanks to the financial help of Rome, acted treacherously against our interests. But once the war was over, when they discussed what to do about Rhodes, our ancestors let them go unpunished, so that no one would say we had started the war for profit rather than to redress a wrong. And, too, in all the Punic Wars, although the Carthaginians had often acted dishonorably both in peace and during truces, the Romans themselves never did the same when they had the opportunity: they were more concerned with acting so as to reflect their decency than harming their enemies—which they had every right to do. And you should take care, Senators, that the crime of P. Lentulus and the others influences you no more than does your own decency, and that you pay less attention to your present anger than to your future reputations. I am in favor of unprecedented measures just in case they are found to be in proportion to the criminals' misdeeds. But unless the enormity of the crime exceeds everyone's imagination, I think we should make use of the penalties prescribed by law.[6]

And it ends:

Should it be enacted, then, that Catiline's army be let go and allowed to multiply? By no means. But this is what I propose: confiscate their money and imprison them in those townships with the most financial resources. Let it be prohibited for anyone to raise the possibility of parole before the senate or the people. Anyone who does otherwise will be considered to be acting against the state and the common welfare.[7]

Cato's argument, for the death penalty, opens:

Senators, I feel altogether differently, when I consider the situation and the dangers we face, and when I weigh various people's opinions. It seems to me that they have talked about the punishments for those men who have made war on their native land, their parents, public and private religion; but reality directs us to be on our guard against the criminals, rather than worrying about what action we should take against them. For with other crimes, we can prosecute them after they are done. If you don't take care that this one does not happen, when it does occur, you will plead for justice in vain: there is no recourse for the vanquished in a conquered city. But, for heaven's sake, I call on you, who have always valued your homes, your estates, your property, above your country: if you want to hold on to whatever it may be that is precious to you, if you want to provide peace and quiet for your amusements, wake up at last and do your duty as citizens. We are not talking about tribute or injuries done by our allies: our very lives and liberty are in jeopardy.[8]

And it closes:

Therefore this is my proposal: the state has been exposed to extreme danger by the unspeakable plot of criminal citizens, and they have been convicted by the testimony of T. Volturcius and the envoys of the Allobroges, and have confessed to planning murder, arson, and other vicious and cruel crimes against fellow citizens and fatherland. The same penalty should be imposed on them, since they have confessed, as would be imposed according to the custom of our ancestors if they had been caught in the act—the death penalty.[9]

In the case of *People* v. *Wash,* the defense's final argument against the death penalty begins:

It was over three years ago that I first received this case. A lot of thoughts go through your mind when you receive a case in which the prosecution is seeking the death penalty. The overwhelming one is a feeling of responsibility. That sense of responsibility became heightened very quickly.

After going through the files and talking with witnesses, I recognized that Jeffrey Wash was responsible for some very tragic events. Jeff never denied that. It became clear that I would at some point be standing in front of a jury, and be responding to an argument by a prosecutor that Jeff Wash should be executed for what he did. A murder is never a pretty crime. Neither is a rape. Both are inflammatory. I knew because of these crimes you would be giving the death penalty serious consideration. But, as I learned more about this case, and most importantly the more I learned about Jeff Wash, and the people who care for him, and the qualities they see in him, and his feelings about what he did, the more I became convinced that imposition of the death penalty would be a mistake. And my job has become one of showing you that.

I anticipated that the prosecutor would do everything he could to play on the inflammatory nature of this case in order to arouse your emotions and make you angry. He did a very effective job of that yesterday. I am sure that you are angry about this crime. You have every right to feel that way. I share it with you. There is nothing wrong with being angry. But my fear is that because of that anger you would not closely examine the flaws in the prosecutor's analysis of what really happened. I am afraid that the anger might render you incapable of looking beyond the crime. I am afraid that you would fail to consider the person before you in your decision.

And it ends:

And so we come down to it. Judge D. will soon instruct you on the principles of law to apply to this case. You have heard the arguments. You should consider them both. And if you agree with me that [the prosecutor] has failed to raise one concern of society that is not met by imposing a penalty of life without possibility of parole, then I trust that you will honor your reverence for life.

The prosecutor's final argument, for the death penalty, begins:

Your Honor, Counsel, ladies and gentlemen:
Thou shalt not kill.
We all know what that means. We all know where it came from. The words have their plain evident English language meaning.
I don't need to explain to you why such a rule ever came into existence or why we even have to have rules like this today.
We have to because people do things like he's done and then the question is: what do we do to them for it?
But before I get to that, before I talk about the case, I think it's important for you all to appreciate how we got to where we are today; starting with religious principles; starting with religious references, Biblical references.
None of you had any religious reservations about serving on a jury like this. But I still feel it is important that you understand that what I'm going to ask you to do is totally in keeping with the spirit of Christ or God or whatever beliefs you have.
Every society has developed a rule like that and it's just been necessary whether they were tribes; whether they were major countries or small clans.
There are references—it is something we could all accept—the Old Testament is full of references to the death penalty, full of references to the types of things that one should, could do and subject him or herself to the death penalty.

And it ends:

I'm telling you why life without parole is not proper for him, and that is because as long as you're alive there is hope, hope that there will be a revolution and that all the prisoners will be freed, hope that this would all be a bad dream.
Well, he shouldn't get that hope. He shouldn't have that hope. Why?
Look at what happened to Erin [one of the victims]. Look at her hope. Look at how he diminished it in her. From the first moment she never, I guarantee you, gave up hope. Even though it was clear from the time he took off the mask that she was dead, I guarantee you she never gave up hope that she was going to live, that somehow she'd survive.
And to only select life without parole for him allows him much more

than he allowed Erin to have at her last moments. He is not entitled to that hope. He has totally given up any right to that hope.

And for all of those reasons, you should find that he deserves the death penalty for what he's done.

ROMAN AND AMERICAN RHETORICAL STRATEGIES

Even upon superficial inspection and through the veil of translation, the Roman passages look different from their contemporary American counterparts. The Roman speeches are arranged in long paragraphs each containing many sentences, each of which is long and syntactically complex. The English speeches are organized in much shorter paragraphs, each containing relatively few sentences. The sentences themselves are mostly syntactically simple or compound rather than complex. It is often said that the Latin language favors convoluted "periodic" structure, because of its dependence upon case endings and complex verb endings, which allow hearers to keep track of the relationships among the items in intricately structured sentences. But English is perfectly capable of periodic style, as a perusal of eighteenth-century prose makes clear. And classical Greek, structurally much like Latin, nevertheless prefers less periodic sentences. So while Latin grammar encourages complex rhetorical arrangement, it does not necessitate it. Rather, there is something in the discourse preferences of speakers of Latin as opposed to English, in their pragmatic system, that makes periodic structures predominate in Caesar's and Cato's arguments.

Indeed, something in the blood, in people's visceral sense tells them how to communicate as good human beings and competent speakers in a particular society. These notions are usually implicit, though formal rhetorical training makes them explicit. We all know what we like to hear, and the rhetorician's (or image consultant's) job is merely to discover and figure out how to teach what everyone intuitively knows.

The Romans, as human beings like ourselves, were responsive to the same stimuli, capable of experiencing similar emotions, with analogous preferences and dislikes. A smile is a smile, a tear a tear. Yet the Romans were different from us. Their cardinal virtues and vices were not always the same as our own. The Romans had a word expressing a constellation of good attitudes and behavior—*pietas*—which is untranslatable for us because the qualities it embodies do not resolve themselves, for us, into a single concept or word. We can paraphrase, to be sure: but the elegance of the Latin becomes awkwardness in English. *Pietas* includes the connection all human beings and divinities should feel for one another by virtue of their basic familial relatedness, their filial and parental devotion: gods to one another, gods to mortals, mortals to gods, parents to children, children to parents, descendants to ancestors. The English derivative, *piety,* is mawkish and weak by comparison. Because Romans were brought up with the idea that *pietas* is a coherent quality and a defining trait of a good human being, they were to that degree different in ethical, intellectual, and emotional makeup from contemporary Americans. For this and other reasons, a good and proper Roman of the first century B.C. would present himself in public—and perhaps in private, too—in a very different manner from an American.

Gravitas and Liteness

Stylistically, the Romans made sharper distinctions between a person's (that is, a man's) public self-presentation and his private self. There were no particular prescriptions for the private person: in intimate circumstances, one could freely be oneself. But in public, something quite different was in order. The mark of a competent human being was the ability to draw the line clearly, to put aside the private self and private needs when in public, and particularly when serving the public. It might be hypocrisy, it was certainly not sincere in our sense, but for the Roman, that was irrelevant.

To the Roman of this period, the public arena was a place where surface propriety counted more than deeper authenticity. One was judged by how successfully one appeared to put aside personal piques, needs, perversities, and personality. In running for office, a man assumed the *toga candida,* a garment whose voluminousness and uniformity hid most of the wearer's physical characteristics. A toga was worn for all official business; the *toga candida* ("shining white") specifically for campaigning (hence our word "candidate"). Besides the connotations of whiteness, the same for the Romans as for us, that uniform reminded the wearer that his official position, not his individual personality, was at issue. The Romans had a word for a man's appropriate public demeanor—*gravitas,* literally "heaviness" or "seriousness." That meant no slippage of the mask, no hints of feelings not for public display. Revelations of personal beliefs or desires were not appropriate, except of course when they were intended as representations of how all good citizens should feel. No idiosyncrasies were tolerated: rhetoricians taught their students specific nonverbal gestures to go with each verbal flourish. Nothing was spontaneous. Indeed, spontaneity of any sort was frowned upon. Distance, predictability, and impersonality kept people safe. Nothing that caused the speaker or hearers to display inappropriate public expression was tolerable: no joking, for instance (though puns were quite acceptable, since no one laughs at them, then or now).

Gravitas manifested itself in everything a Roman did as a public person, down to the syntax of his sentences. Complex sentence structure is a good format for *gravitas.* A speaker must be comfortable with nonspontaneity to move through such structure: he has to know at the beginning where he intends to be at the end, and how each clause is to be explicitly related, syntactically and semantically, to every other. For complex sentences make the relationships between clauses explicit, directing the reader or hearer through them, the endings and particles serving as clear signposts. By contrast, the simpler sentences of contemporary English prose leave much more up to the hearer or reader, who must figure out whether there is a semantic connection between two contiguous clauses, and if so, just what it is. Simple sentence structure makes things easier for the speaker, who doesn't have to have everything settled before leaping in; the responsibility for determining meaning rests with the hearer. But in constructing a complex sentence, the speaker assumes a greater responsibility for meaning, since it must all be explicitly linguistically encoded. So periodic rhetorical structure does not invite the hearer's active participation as much as simple structure does: it keeps participants symbolically distant and discourages spontaneity. This is true not only at the level of the sentence itself but also at higher levels. The longer paragraph of periodic style distances the hearer or reader, expressing the speaker's intention to retain control and discouraging interruption.

Gravitas is territorial and works by the rules of distance politeness. (Today we find complex sentences and long unbroken paragraphs "boring," meaning that we feel shut out, uninvolved. The Romans felt distanced, too, but liked it.) While a persuasive writer or speaker in a *gravitas* society should be able to evoke emotion, he should do it subtly, not by obviously interactive devices. A contemporary novelist can involve readers in the situation being created through the use of direct discourse: conversations are presented as uttered, in quotation marks, giving readers a sense of eavesdropping, not merely getting a second-hand report. The Romans, on the other hand, preferred indirect discourse as cooler. They could and sometimes did use direct discourse, but not often. Another way of directly appealing to a hearer's or reader's feelings is through the use of pragmatic particles—*y'know, I mean, well, really, for sure;* current English is replete with them. Latin, by contrast with English (or classical Greek for that matter), is poor in such particles.

We have evolved a very different style by which to present ourselves. For us, the best person is spontaneous and sincere: what you see is what you get, the same to all comers. We hate any suggestion that someone in public life treats strangers differently from pals: the celebrity we encounter at a restaurant is supposed to stop conversing with table mates and chat with us genially while tirelessly signing autographs for our families in first-name terms. We must present the same face in public as in private. There should be no need for special public display: we are quite fine as we are, "warts and all." And because we are spontaneous, we are supposed to prefer to assert our individuality. It is something of a *faux pas* for two people (especially women) to show up at a gathering in identical dress; we despise uniforms. The sentence and paragraph structure of contemporary American English are ideal for this self-presentation, which we can call *lightness* (by contrast with *gravitas*), or rather *liteness*. (The Romans did in fact have an antonym for *gravitas*—*levitas*—a term of reproach when applied to human demeanor: from the literal meaning "lightness," it connoted frivolity, inconsistency, and unseriousness. In the same way we tell people to "lighten up" when they don't behave according to current requirements. No one ever told Cicero to lighten up.) We present ourselves and our arguments in personal terms: this is *me*, what about *you?* We tell jokes, almost obligatorily, at the start of most public ceremonials, just to convince the audience that we're good guys with something to say that they want to hear. We like to give the impression that we're winging it: if our sentences don't quite parse, so much the better. It shows we're concerned, we're working on it together with *you*, we're not glib. Americans are suspicious of real articulateness, as it suggests aloofness and nonspontaneity. Eloquence, a requisite for Roman statesmen, is suspect for us. In the 1988 election, the one candidate who had ever been described as "eloquent," Joseph Biden, was disposed of early on with the accusation that he had not made up his own campaign speeches (as though other politicians regularly do).

Many if not most of the superficial differences between the rhetoric of the Romans and the Americans in these examples arise out of this deep stylistic discrepancy. Caesar and Cato both write, or speak, in long paragraphs of complex sentences. Both address the issues in generalities: What should *we* as a people or as a deliberative body think and do? How did the conspirators' actions affect *our* state? When they refer to themselves, it is purely in the persona of the orator, not the actor or doer. There are no glimpses of what brought the speaker to his present beliefs, what moral or intellectual torments he suffered. If he did, that information is not shared with his hearers. There is no attempt to bridge identities of speaker and hearers that way, between what *I* think and what *you* might believe. The arguments are rigorously structured: both within each sentence, grammatically, and throughout the paragraph, logically, they are carefully developed, one point leading to the next: hearers are guided. There is, of course, no joking; the circumstances would preclude it in any case.

The liteness of American courtroom rhetoric (even in this most solemn of exercises, the final argument in a capital case) is equally evident. Sentences are short and simple. Paragraphs are short, the prosecutor's coming perilously close to the style of *Fun With Dick and Jane* or magazine advertisements. The vocabulary, too, is remarkably simple, native English (which is more evocative of emotion than formal diction. The Romans, most of whose vocabulary came from native sources, did not have options.) The American speeches, though carefully prepared, rehearsed, and written down, are spoken as though spontaneous, with hesitations and vocalized pauses ("er's" amd "um's"), which do not appear in the transcript and other marks of spontaneity. But most striking, especially in the defense argument, is its personal revelations. From the start, the defense attorney is opening his heart to the jury: he talks about the process of trying a capital case, invites them in to see how the public defender's office functions, and reveals to them his own doubts, despair, dedication. He also makes direct reference to the jurors' emotions (where his counterpart, Caesar, refers to emotions, he does so in general and impersonal terms): "You are angry. . . . I was afraid that you would fail." Neither of the Roman orators juxtaposes the feelings of speaker and hearers, contrasts them, examines them as the American speakers both do. The prosecutor, in his turn, identifies closely with the jurors as people of fellow feeling, far more than Cato does: "What do we do to them for it?" The blunt directness of the sequence of monosyllables suggests visceral arousal, fight-or-flight response. (Compare Cato's last sentence, which is long and extraordinarily complex, and thereby muted in its emotional wallop, though it makes much the same point.)

When we read the Roman excerpts, in the original or in translation, we get a sense of these men and their audience as somehow different from us: more measured, serious, and statesmanly. But that is probably the wrong conclusion to draw, at least if we infer from it that the Romans really possessed those qualities and we do not. Rather, both the Americans and their Roman counterparts had an audience to persuade. But to be persuasive, one must first convince one's audience that one is a good, intelligent, sensible human being who shares their interests. Style is one means by which this is done. The Romans' preference for *gravitas*, like ours for liteness, does not represent deep characterological reality, just a surface representation of self that is, at a particular moment in time, deemed attractive.

It is tempting to distinguish between style and content, considering the first superficial, trivial, or peripheral, the second real. Rather, both convey meaning: the first, pragmatic; the second, semantic. In fact, style is content, content style; no discourse makes use of only one. (Even the absence of "style" is style, and therefore meaningful, as silence is not the absence of communication.) But we can consider the *gravitas*/liteness choice principally stylistic and therefore relatively superficial, while differences in content reflect deeper discrepancies in cultural character.

Guilt and Shame

Anthropologists speak of the difference between *guilt* and *shame* cultures.[10] As with most generalizations, the contrast is not airtight, but it is nonetheless a useful way to epitomize and explain some of the more striking differences between the Roman and the contemporary American world view and rhetorical strategy. The Romans belonged to a shame culture; we, to a guilt culture. In the former, the opinion of the group is paramount: members feel comfortable and competent to the extent that they believe that others approve of their behavior.

And it is behavior observable from the outside, rather than internal thoughts or attitudes, that count. So a person can be adjudged guilty of a crime in a shame culture, but cannot be described as feeling "guilty," since that is a self-assessment. Shame cultures are concerned with reputation: "glory" if it is good *(gloria, laus)*, and "shame" and "dishonor" *(pudor)* if bad. One is judged worthy *(dignus)* to the degree that one's public behavior matches cultural standards of *gravitas* and *pietas:* the public image is what is important. And one is eligible for good repute only if one is a member of the group, in this case Roman citizens, the governors and the governed *(senatus populusque Romanus* "the senate and the people of Rome," or *SPQR*). As long as one's public behavior is meritorious, one can, as a Roman, belong to the group, be granted its privileges, rights, and protections. Group membership identifies the Roman; to lose it is to lose identity, self-esteem, everything. Cicero's misery at his year-long banishment is hardly intelligible to us today: after all, he spent the time in Greece, in whose language he was fully fluent, which he often voluntarily visited, and where he had many friends and admirers. But it was the involuntary withdrawal of group membership that stunned and depressed him. Other members of the group are necessary in a shame culture to give meaning to actions; "What will others think?" is always the first question, when considering a course of action.

In a pure guilt culture, people are their own severest critics. Since we have access to our own internal psychological processes, we judge ourselves first and foremost on that basis: our motives and beliefs determine our virtue in our own eyes. However we may put a good face on our motives for public consumption, whether we can justify our actions to ourselves at 3 A.M. is what really matters. A guilt culture, therefore, makes sharp distinctions between the public and the private self, public and private behavior, and is at heart more concerned with the latter than the former; it cherishes the notion of privacy, for it is important for people to be able to be alone by themselves in order to assess themselves. Members of guilt cultures, of course, can speak of "guilt," meaning internal feelings of inadequacy. When people's recognized motives accord with those the culture values, members feel "self-esteem"; when there is a gap, "guilt." Only members of such cultures can speak of personal responsibility: not what your country expects of you, but what you should expect of yourself. We are not, by any means, a 100-percent guilt culture, as the effectiveness of Kennedy's "Ask not what your country can do for you" speech suggests. But we can often be motivated by appeals to internalized emotions and judgments, as the Romans could not (or, in any event, were not).

Hence, we find both Caesar and Cato appealing to their hearers' concerns about how others would judge them, now and in the future, depending upon their decision. Cato in particular is not above public shaming, of the "I know what you're really like" type: "You who have always valued your homes, estates, property above your country," he sneers—a double insult, not only public shaming, but an accusation against his friends and colleagues of placing individual and private interests above the concerns of the group, the state. Caesar raises the same specter more obliquely when he talks about the ancestors' fear of being thought by others to have acted out of desire for profit, rather than civic outrage. And he remarks, too, that the senators should put their own *dignitas*, "decency" or "honor," above desire for retribution: their reputation counts more than mere emotional gratification. He appeals to their concern about how others, the larger group, will think, and how that will affect their eventual future good name.

Such arguments are not impossible for us, but they seem contrived and bombastic: they don't hit us where we live. So both attorneys in *Wash* appeal to the jurors largely in guilt-culture terms: How will you feel if. . . . What is your responsibility? "I trust that you will honor your reverence for life," says the defense attorney, appealing to an individual, private, and internal state of mind, something not available for outsiders to check. To be right, actions must tally with that internal monitor, not some externally accessible standard of behavior. Likewise, the prosecutor reassures the jury that the death penalty is "totally in keeping with . . . whatever beliefs you have."

Distancing the Defendant

This attitude brings other decisions in its train. One belief held in common is that the death penalty is a heavy decision; and that to get a death verdict, it is necessary to alienate the defendant from the sentencers, to represent him as one of *them*, no longer one of *us*. We have inhibitions against killing our own; the less like oneself the target, the easier it is to kill. Both Roman and American prosecutors therefore have the major task of distancing the sentencers from the defendant; the defense must somehow create an identification between them. But the Romans do both distancing and identification on the basis of shared group membership or its forfeiture; Americans, by appealing to or denying each juror's ability or willingness to find traits in his or her own mind in common with that of the defendant. Where Cato segregates the defendant by a strategy of us/him, the American prosecutor does so by me/him.

Caesar realizes that someone found guilty of high treason cannot be reunited with Roman senators as "we, members of the SPQR," and so spends no time appealing to the Romans for mercy or compassion. Indeed, he discounts these emotions along with others more dangerous to his side (a common disarming tactic in defense arguments: in the same way, the American defense attorney sympathizes with the jury's outrage, remarking, "A murder is never a pretty crime," and "I share [anger] with you"). His efforts are mostly directed toward urging his audience to protect "our" reputation and not to do anything that will disgrace "us" in the future: the conspirators, he implies, aren't worth that humiliation. Cato, on the other hand, devotes a good deal of his argument to inflaming hearers against the conspirators, reminding them of their crimes. The crimes he mentions are those that erode the fabric of society and make a mockery of *pietas:* the overthrow of native land *(patria)*, family structure *(parentes)*, and religion, both public *(arae)* and private *(foci)*. Had the plot succeeded, nothing would have been left of "us": people might survive as individuals, but that, for the Romans, was not survival. Likewise he invokes the picture of a "conquered city," rather than individual destitution as the outcome of the plot.

Identification with the Sentencers

The American attorneys stress individual judgments and response to crimes against individuals. The defense attorney goes through several minutes of autobiographical reflection in the hope of achieving the jury's identification with *him* first, and through him, indirectly, with his client. His speech also provides an opportunity for what psychotherapists call *modeling:* he presents himself as a man much like them, just doing his job, at first horrified (as they are) by the crime; but he has transcended that revulsion and "learned"—that is, gone through an internal process of change. By that action he has come to feel some identity with "Jeff." (The defendant's nickname is typically used by the defense as an intimacy-creating device, one jurors—we learn from postverdict interviews—often discern and resent.) The prosecutor does not refer to the defendant by name at all here (elsewhere he has called him "Mr. Wash"): his aim is to depersonalize and distance. The less precise a picture a juror retains in his mind of the defendant, the easier it will be to kill him. But he does refer to the victim as "Erin," as the defense attorney never does. Finally the defense attorney suggests that the jury's job is to "consider the person before you": the personal empathy is as crucial as an understanding of the crime itself, if a juror is to function properly. He frames that argument (in a subordinate clause, where it is more likely to slip by without arousing the jury's irritation) in a description of himself as personally concerned with the jurors' individual abilities to act appropriately: he forms an alliance with them, the "learner" now the teacher and guide. At the very end, he mentions that the jurors might "agree with me," again creating a personal connection, engaging in one-on-one persuasion with each of the twelve. Both defense and prosecution, as is typical, refer directly or obliquely to "promises" made by jurors to them during *voir dire*, or their "trust" that jurors will act correctly.

The defense likewise brings up "Jeff's" own "feelings about what he did" not only to suggest remorse, but also to remind the jury that they are contemplating executing a fellow human being who has feelings, just as they do. The prosecutor, on the other hand, mentions Jeff's "hope" as a feeling he has no right to have, dwelling instead on the victim's emotions. We are afforded a glimpse into "Erin's" state of mind, but the defendant's "hope" remains a lurid, illegitimate abstraction. Whatever his hope is, it is something that inspires fear in good people: prison revolts, revolutions. His emotions, such as they are, are inhuman: rather than bringing the jurors closer, they repulse them.

Past and Future

One more cultural assumption distinguishes the Roman and American strategies. Americans as a culture are forward-looking. Our ancestors cut themselves off from the past when they came here; we have no past, only a future. Therefore it has always been part of the American myth that the future will be better. We are bound to rise in our careers; our children will do better than we did. If there is a golden age, it is in a future made utopian by science. In our secular myth, progress is taken for granted.

The Roman myth was different. Their golden age was in the past. For them, each generation since that age of demigods and heroes was worse than the last. Their own ancestors were men of stern rectitude and clear intelligence; modern people are corrupt by comparison, but nothing compared to the decadence of posterity. With no public notion of "science," there was no idea of progress, and religion offered only the golden age in the distant past, nothing to come. Rome, too, was a strongly aristocratic society. Most of those in the senate were members of the hereditary nobility, whose ancestors had distinguished themselves by feats still reverently remembered. SPQR gained its legitimacy and its very existence by tracing its descent directly from those heroes whose names current members bore. Indeed, what was perhaps most unforgiveable about Catiline and his group, for men like Cicero, was that they were of noble birth but had spurned their own kind—betrayal on top of betrayal. Cicero, a man of the new middle class wishing more than anything for acceptance by the nobility, was outraged at someone who had it and despised it.

So the Romans appealed to their ancestors, *maiores nostri,* as exemplars and judges of current actions: what would they think if they could see us? How did they behave under similar circumstances? Caesar reminds the senate of the times the ancestors acted mercifully, for whatever reason: that is the right thing to do now. Cato, on the other hand, refers to a different precedent from the *maiores:* "Impose, according to the custom of our ancestors, the death penalty." Elsewhere in his speech Caesar makes another argument against the death penalty. He is not worried, he says, about creating a precedent of this kind in his own time: his contemporaries, good and intelligent people, know what they mean and would not misuse the precedent. But their descendants . . . can they be trusted? Not too likely, he suggests.

It may be that at another time, under another consul who also has control of an army, a falsehood will be taken to be true. When through this precedent the consul is enabled by the senate's decree (of martial law) to draw his sword, who will put an end to it, or who will blunt its force?[11]

For Americans, such arguments are strange, if even meaningful. The prosecutor does make extensive reference to the Bible, but only as a document we can all respect. It is not suggested that Biblical times or people were "better," just that we have the Bible as a compendium of morality to which we can refer for guidance. Not in *Wash*, but in some capital cases, the defense may argue that the death penalty was something people needed at an earlier stage of morality or political sophistication, but we are above that now. We may contrast Caesar's invocation of the ancestors as examples of how to behave with the *Wash* defense attorney's use of himself as model. For us, there is no past to look back upon: if you want a model, look to yourselves.

HOW TO KILL, AND WHY TO SPARE

So both in superficial self-presentation (style) and certain kinds of structure (content), Roman death penalty argumentation differed from ours. These differences, we see, depend upon fundamental differences in social and personality structure between the two cultures. Yet at the same time both groups are human, with human needs, desires, fears, and aspirations, individual and group. Therefore there also exist similarities between the two arguments, which go deeper than the differences and are ultimately more illuminating.

It is often argued that (while aggression may be natural) intraspecies killing is seldom found in nature under ordinary circumstances. Most animals have an inhibitory reflex preventing them from carrying aggression against a member of the same species through to the point of killing. A worsted adversary assumes a posture of submission, and the victor swaggers off content. Something must interfere with the inhibiting reflex to cause killing: one such condition, Konrad Lorenz has suggested, is distance.[12] At a physical distance, for human beings, the subtleties of submission go unnoticed. So it is less painful to kill another person at long range, a gun making it easier than a knife, and a bomb easiest of all. In the same way we make our legal execution procedures "humane"—for the executioner—by setting up a complex series of operations and procedures: a glassed-in death chamber, switches and levers, delayed reaction to a lethal injection; distance in space and time. Psychological distance also makes the job easier; therefore it is useful to distinguish *we* from *they* in war propaganda, as discussed in chapter 10. It removes the killer psychologically from the victim, blunting emotions and defusing the intraspecies inhibition. Our verbal euphemisms for killing likewise separate speaker and doer from what they are doing and the one they do it to: we "do in," "off," "rub out," "waste," "execute," "sacrifice," "euthanize," and many more, the form dependent upon the particular type of killing involved. The words may be vague or misleading—anything to avoid a reference to the stark reality.

Since we find it necessary to euphemize capital punishment, it is not surprising that prosecutors must offer sentencers the opportunity to distance themselves psychologically from their act, as well as from its target. At the same time, they must encourage those bodies to act on the negative emotions their oratory has stirred up before they have a chance to reflect and consider the possibility of future regrets. So theirs is a twofold task—to convince the sentencers that the defendant does not share with them in a common humanity: they cannot empathize with him, they should not even try, he is so monstrously different from them. Second (since the inhibition on killing is so strong that, with reflection, it might assert itself in any event), to compel them to act at once, without reflection, in the heat of passion; to inflame the negative emotions that will separate them from the defendant—anger, fear, revulsion, and vengefulness—so that they will not have the emotional space to think, to consider how they will view their decision in the future.

The prosecutor has one other, more covert and infinitely more dangerous task, one facilitated by the *we/they* split. Just as in war propaganda, the dichotomization encourages scapegoating. The prosecutor will profit if he can convince his audience that, by punishing *that* man's crimes, they can redeem their own, cleanse themselves ritually by sacrificing him. The defendant becomes the symbolic receptacle of all their fears about themselves. By purging him from their midst, they purge themselves of sin. The idea is as old as time and as recent as the latest capital verdict. In the old days, ritual sacrifice was invoked openly; nowadays we're more subtle. The idea is implied in the prosecutor's sharp distinction between *us*, the good citizens, the jurors now as ever doing their duty, and *him*, who has made himself an outcast by his acts. The temptation for the jurors to prove the prosecutor right, to justify the dichotomy by proving themselves fully cleansed and virtuous, is strong in the unconscious.

Another bit of unconscious motivation that prosecutors can play upon is everyone's secret set of humiliations and disappointments at the hands of others. How many times has each of us been hurt or angered by someone else, and thought, in a flash, "I could just kill him!" and at that moment, perhaps, we almost could. But we're civilized, we have inhibitions, and besides we don't have the means or the opportunity and couldn't get away with it. So we put the thought aside. But it lingers. Now we're jurors in a capital case, and now a defendant has come before us whose crimes represent all the misdeeds of everyone in our lives, magnified a zillionfold. How good it would feel, both satisfying and right, to avenge ourselves on everyone, undo the slights of a lifetime, safely, legally, virtuously! The prosecutor's fanning of the flames of anger, ostensibly against the defendant, serves also subliminally to evoke in his audience all the other angers, to tempt them to requite them. The prosecutor speaks as the courtroom moralist; but underneath, his arguments have a disturbingly atavistic, pre-Oedipal coloration.

The defense has the opposite task: to somehow, despite their revulsion at the crimes, convince the sentencers that the defendant is still a member of humanity, linked by whatever tenuous threads to them. To kill him is to kill one of *you*. As the defense attorney does in *Wash*, when all else fails this connection can be attempted by a more complex three-way linkage: defendant—attorney—jury. That way the jury need not (symbolically) "touch" the outcast but can still allow compassion to penetrate as long as they are in sympathy with the lawyer. (As *Wash* shows, however, this tactic need not be successful.) The second part of the defense's job is to try to create in the sentencers a state of calm, a distancing from negative passions. It is the business of the defense to persuade the sentencers to think before they act: consider other options, consider the consequences, consider future opinion. If the defense can penetrate the haze of passion, the inhibition against killing may triumph after all.

So Cato, speaking for the prosecution, reminds his hearers of the conspirators' monstrous plans—schemes that took them beyond the scope of the definition of "Roman citizen" and, hence, by the Roman definition, of human being. Their crimes are *foeda atque crudelia*, vicious and cruel; they are not acting as humans act to one another. He warns against wasting time in reflection, "worrying about what to do," rather than being on guard: developing the right emotions and acting upon them. He arouses anger and fear by his image of the conquered city, its citizens (his hearers) pleading ignominiously for justice (his audience undoubtedly had a vision of the fall of Troy). "Our very lives and liberty are in jeopardy," he warns. He stirs up his audience's rage by humiliating them publicly: they are hapless victims. That anger can be readily turned against the perpetrators. And the senators, by imposing the death penalty, would be acting according to the highest standards of morality, *more maiorum*, "according to the custom of our ancestors."

In much the same vein, the prosecutor in *Wash* reminds the jurors that the defendant, by his acts, has renounced any right to ordinary human emotions or the compassion of others: "He has totally given up any right to that hope." Elsewhere the prosecutor has commented to the jury that he doesn't think they should try to understand the defendant; he doesn't think the defendant can be understood. He has contrasted the victim's understandable hope for life with Wash's frightening and irrational hopes for revolution and the freeing of all prisoners. By going over, again and again, the details of the crime (earlier in the trial he had played the defendant's tape-recorded confession while showing slides of the victims' mutilated bodies in a darkened courtroom), he reminds the jurors of the defendant's viciousness, his difference from them, his willful choice to set himself apart from them. By suggesting the kinds of hope Jeffrey Wash cherishes, before reinvoking his horrible crimes, the prosecutor inflames the jury's anger, fear, and revulsion, just before they are to embark upon their deliberations. By choosing the death penalty, the jury will be not only following the precepts of the Bible, but also strengthening the moral principles of their society ("why we . . . have to have rules like this today"). And, in fact, it isn't even their choice, they aren't the real executioners: rather, it is the defendant's own doing ("the types of things one should, could do and subject him or herself to the death penalty"). So they can feel not only virtuous for protecting their society and upholding its most sacred precepts, but also in no way responsible for killing another human being. The prosecutor has freed them from that responsibility.

In both these cases, the defense is working against great odds. Caesar urges restraint, the putting aside of all emotions, even those ("friendship and pity") that might help his case, in order to make use of pure reason. He argues that such reasonable and dispassionate thinking ultimately works in one's own self-interest; the "ancestors" came out looking better to the world by their forebearance, and so, he says, will you. There exist laws that cover this situation, and it is dangerous to undertake extralegal actions unless there is no recourse. He makes no attempt to convince his hearers to identify directly with the conspirators, though he may hope to suggest, tacitly indeed, that they still are Roman citizens (and therefore still humans and part of the *we*) with all his references to Romans and their history. Catiline, like Caesar himself, came of very distinguished ancestry; and in a class-conscious society like that of Rome, any reminder of long-standing aristocratic connections counted on someone's side, and created, in the aristocratic senate, feelings of identification. He avoids all direct reference to the crimes, concentrating on the decision to be made; in this way, too, he hopes to deflect emotion. Finally, he proposes a solution that links him (and therefore his argument) to the interests of all good citizens: those who do not follow his proposal as specified will be "considered to be acting against the state and the common welfare"—and the senate can, in the future, look forward to venting its pent-up rage against those people then, not the conspirators now.

The defense attorney in *Wash* shares some of these tactics. He tries to create identification through a link from "Jeff" to himself to the jury. The defendant is called by a nickname. The attorney suggests, by his "learning" process, a course of reflective action that the jury might emulate. (It is considered, in today's death-prone atmosphere, indelicate and very risky for the defense to suggest that the death penalty is in any way immoral or ill considered. But the point can be made subtly, as here.) He refers to "the people who care for [Jeff]," reminding the jury that it is possible to be human and compassionate and care for a man like the defendant, another means to an emotional link. A couple of the defendant's character witnesses were articulate and engaging. By this indirect reference to them, the defense attorney hopes to forge a sympathetic bond: jury—nice people—Jeff. Like Caesar, the defense attorney avoids direct reference to the crimes themselves, concentrating on his and the jury's responses to them. He also attempts to segregate the jury from the prosecutor, to cut off his possibility of modeling an appropriate response for them: "I anticipated that the prosecutor would do everything he could to play on the inflammatory nature of this case in order to make you angry." The prosecutor, he hints, is manipulating the jury, not treating them like competent adults. To feel "angry," then, is to be bamboozled, to do less than a competent job. So here, too, reflection is the right response, the response of someone who is a good juror, a good custodian of society's trust. And the defense attorney will help the jury to do that, he is on their side: "I am afraid that that anger might render you incapable. . . ." He is *afraid* for the jurors, so he must share their interests. Their (shared) interest require "close examination, . . . looking beyond the crime, . . . consider[ing] the person before you." And finally, an appeal to a higher duty still: "I trust that you will honor your reverence for life." Here, too, there is a veiled reference to another moral point that defense attorneys are chary of bringing up explicitly: that it is self-contradictory to try to express reverence for life by the legalized murder that is execution. You can, he says, do your duty to society *and* to a higher authority at once if you vote for life. He offers the jurors the chance to feel really good about themselves and their job and their role in society, thereby perhaps deflecting some need for scapegoating and vengeful actions.

Human cultures have multitudes of ways to persuade, as they have many ways to build houses and raise children. The totality of those choices is what we mean by *culture:* it defines people as a cohesive group and gives meaning to their lives. With diligence and goodwill, members of one culture can gain some understanding of the ways of another, may even come to admire them, but can never hope to have the same visceral, empathic response to the structures of other cultures that they have to their own. Roman death penalty argumentation makes sense to us, but at a distance: we don't find it persuasive as we do the American counterpart. Roman and American rhetorical strategies are pragmatic synonyms, not equivalents. But by bringing the Roman case together with the contemporary American, we can get a better sense of the variety of ways people have of expressing themselves and being persuasive, and of the underlying identity we all share by virtue of being human.

CHAPTER THIRTEEN

Winning Hearts and Minds: Pragmatic Homonymy and Beyond

I N *pragmatic synonymy,* two dissimilar surface forms are used with similar meaning or intention. The other side of the coin is *pragmatic homonymy,* in which two instances of persuasion that look superficially similar turn out on deeper inspection not to be equivalent but to have different meanings or intentions. To see its workings, we can contrast a Roman (once again Julius Caesar, who was ubiquitous in that period of history) with a contemporary American, another military man, Lieutenant Colonel Oliver North.

I happened upon this seemingly unlikely pairing while watching North's testimony before Congress during the summer of 1987.[1] All of America had its attention riveted on the blue-eyed patriot for several weeks; not so much what he said, but how he said it, marked Oliver North as a man of extraordinary charisma. Where previous witnesses faced the interrogating lawyers or legislators, he looked toward the camera yet above it, a clear-eyed yet misty focus, down-to-earth but idealistic. His gaze told us he was directing his speech beyond its apparent addressees in the chamber; to us, the American people, his eyes said, *You* are my judges, not these corrupt or uncaring civilians. But beyond us, up there, a still higher judge was, though never invoked directly, reflected in the azure eyes. Through weeks of grueling Q-and-A in the heat of midsummer (the chamber was air-conditioned, but others present were clearly feeling the effects of the heat), his military uniform remained crisp, his lip unbeaded by sweat. Only toward the end did stubble begin to show on his chin and his eyes turn red and bleary. Comparisons with Jimmy Stewart in *Mr. Smith Goes to Washington* became irresistible. Shorn of the extra- and paralinguistics, divested of its rhetorical razzle-dazzle, what the marine lieutenant colonel was saying could be read as subversive, bizarre, or irrelevant. But few heard the substance; everyone was too much beguiled by the style. Commentators speculated on North's political future; for a while, at least, the betting was that he could have the presidency any time he wanted it. Ollie North haircuts were all the rage (among men, at any rate), and not because they were aesthetically pleasing.

Interpreters of the public pulse fell over each other trying to determine just what gave North that compelling quality. One characteristic was frequently noted: North's proclivity for third-person self-reference (referring to himself not as "I," but as "Ollie North," or any of several other appropriate identifications: "this marine lieutenant colonel," and "this American citizen" were two that recurred often). The pundits noted that third-person self-reference is not uncommon among those in the public eye, but that North seemed somehow to be going beyond the norm, or doing something different in his use of it.

THE ROMAN GENERAL

Caius Julius Caesar was a Roman of patrician birth, splendid and diverse talents, and high ambition. Although an aristocrat, he joined the plebeian political party, thereby incurring the odium and contempt of many of his noble contemporaries. He was one of the few people of his age to understand how ungovernable Rome had become by the first century B.C., and how necessary profound political changes were to salvage the system. He determined to achieve high political office through military victories, which then as now appealed to the electorate. (The money gained from plundering conquered countries also helped with campaign expenses.) In 58 B.C., Caesar was sent by the Roman senate as proconsul (governor) of Gallia Cisalpina, the part of Gaul nearest to Italy. His mandate was simple: keep Cisalpine Gaul in order. It was then a confusion of tribes at various levels of civilization, speaking many languages, and generally at war with one another. At the beginning of his term of command, Caesar followed instructions; and in that and each subsequent year, sent back to the Roman senate a narrative of his exploits, intended to reach beyond the senate to the people, as the opening salvo of a campaign for the consulship to be formally undertaken upon his return. His commentaries, *De Bello Gallico (On the Gallic War)*, were written in clear, direct, but disengaged prose, as though the reports of a later uninvolved historian rather than of the principal actor himself. Among the stylistic choices that produce this impersonal effect is his invariable use of the third person (always only "Caesar" or a pronoun, never analogues of North's rhetorical flourishes) to refer to himself.

Watching North, I began to wonder what he was trying to accomplish with his third-person self-reference, and whether his use had anything in common with Caesar's. The two were different in form and perhaps in function as well. North

used it only occasionally; Caesar invariably. The two offer an example of pragmatic homonymy: the marked and special morphological choice of third-person
self-reference has disparate functions.

On one level, Caesar and North were doing the same thing (using third-
person self-reference); at the next deeper level, something different (Caesar's
forms as well as intended function were not the same as North's); but deeper still,
the two turn into an instance of pragmatic equivalence on a larger scale (Caesar
and North were using their discourse for similar ends; and their discourse itself,
or at least significant parts of it, were on remarkably similar topics). So Caesar's
war commentaries and North's congressional testimony are rhetorically similar
documents with similar ultimate purposes. For these reasons, examination of
portions of the texts of both men proves illuminating for our understanding of
persuasion. For both are, beneath the didactic function of Caesar's *Commentaries* and the explanatory character of North's testimony, strongly persuasive
documents in both intention and effect. But since neither makes its persuasive
mission overt, both, in essence, are works of propaganda: each purports to be
something that it is not, and moves fluidly between two distinct kinds of discourse.

Consider first Caesar's situation. He was performing dazzling exploits in
Gaul, just what he needed for future political success. He had pacified his territory
and enriched Rome's treasury with tribute. Good, yes, but not spectacular. What
could he do for an encore? How could he convince his fellow countrymen that
he was not only a good general and a great leader but the man Rome needed in
its highest office?

A solution proposed itself in the form of a German chieftain, Ariovistus.
Now that Caesar had pacified the tribes of Gaul, Rome owed them protection
from outside aggression. Ariovistus had for some time been harassing those tribes
nearest to his own territory. Now they appealed to Caesar. Caesar's story follows:

> On learning this, Caesar gave the Gauls verbal encouragement, and prom-
> ised that he would bear in mind what he had heard. He had great hope,
> he said, that Ariovistus would stop making trouble once he was persuaded
> that it was to his advantage. After his speech he dismissed the council.
> Subsequent to these events, many factors compelled his consideration of
> and action on the problem. First, the fact that he saw that the Aedui, whom
> the Roman senate had often called "blood-brothers," were enslaved under
> German rule, and he understood that hostages (from the Aedui) were living
> with Ariovistus and the Sequani. He deemed this a great disgrace to himself
> and the Republic, considering the tremendous power of Rome. Besides, he
> saw that it would be dangerous to Rome if the Germans were gradually to
> get used to crossing the Rhine and coming to Gaul in large numbers. He
> did not feel able to keep the savage barbarians from going into Provence

and then into Italy, once they had occupied all Gaul—as the Cimbri and Teutons had done in the past—especially as only the Rhone separated the Sequani from Provence. He thought he should take preventive action at the earliest opportunity. Ariovistus himself had become so headstrong and arrogant as to be beyond endurance.

Therefore he decided to send envoys to Ariovistus to ask him to choose a neutral place for a conference, since Caesar wished to discuss with him affairs of state and matters of the greatest consequence for them both. Ariovistus replied to the legation that if he had needed anything from Caesar, he would have gone to Caesar. If Caesar wanted anything of him, Caesar should come to him. Besides, he did not dare to venture without an army into those parts of Gaul under Caesar's control, and he could not bring his army into one place without ample provisions and a great deal of trouble. Moreover, he could not imagine what business Caesar, or the Roman people in general, had in his part of Gaul, which he had conquered in war.

When Caesar received this reply, he sent envoys back to Ariovistus with instructions to say: Ariovistus, who had been the recipient of so many favors from Rome—during Caesar's consulship he had been named king and friend by the senate—was showing his appreciation by hesitating to come to a conference to which he had been invited, and not feeling an obligation to learn of or discuss concerns common to both parties. Therefore, Caesar was making this request of him: first, he was not to lead any more men across the Rhine into Gaul; next, he should return the hostages to the Aedui, and permit the Sequani to return those hostages whom they held, with Ariovistus' blessing; lastly, he should not harm the Aedui nor make war against them or their allies. If he did as advised, he would have the eternal gratitude and friendship of the Roman people. If Caesar's wishes were not respected (since the senate, in the consulship of M. Messala and M. Piso, had decreed that anyone who received the province of Gaul as a service to Rome, would be obliged to defend the Aedui and other friends of Rome), he would not overlook any injuries to the Aedui.

To this Ariovistus replied: It was the rule in war that the victors could impose their will on the vanquished. Besides, Rome was wont to exercise power over those it had conquered not according to the losers' demands, but following its own judgment. If he himself was not telling the Roman people how to run their government, his running of his own public affairs should not be interfered with by Rome. Since the Aedui had risked the fortunes of war, had met him in arms and been conquered, they had become his tributaries. Caesar was doing him great injury, since his arrival had caused a reduction in Ariovistus' income from taxes. He was not about to return the hostages to the Aedui, but he would not make war on them or their allies to avenge any injury as long as they kept to the agreement and paid a yearly tribute. Otherwise, the title "brothers of the Roman people" would be of no use to them. As for Caesar's statement that he would not overlook injuries to the Aedui: Nobody had ever attacked Ariovistus except to their ruin. When Caesar wished, Ariovistus would meet him. Then Caesar would learn what the unconquered Germans, a people most proficient in arms, who had not lived under a roof in fourteen years, could accomplish by their valor.[2]

NORTH'S TESTIMONY

North, too, has a story to tell.

And I realize that it—that this hearing is a difficult thing. Believe me, gentlemen, it isn't as difficult for you as it is for a guy that's got to come up here and tell the truth, and that's what I'm trying to do. And I want to make it very clear that when you put up things like "Parklane Hosiery" and you all snicker at it, and you know that I've got a beautiful secretary, and the good Lord gave her the gift of beauty, and the people snicker that Ollie North might have been doing a little hanky-panky with his secretary, Ollie North has been loyal to his wife since the day he married her. And the fact is, I went to my best friend and I asked her, "Did I ever go to Parklane Hosiery?" And you know what she said to me? "Of course you did, you old buffoon, you went there to buy leotards for our two little girls." And the reason I wrote the check to Parklane Hosiery, just like the checks at Giant, is because I was owed money for what I had spent pursuing that covert operation.

You gentlemen may not agree that we should have been pursuing covert operations at the NSC [National Security Council], but we were. We had an operational account and we used the money for legitimate purposes within that covert operation. Does that answer your question, sir?[3]

Let me—let me just make one thing very clear, counsel. This Lieutenant Colonel is not going to challenge a decision of the Commander in Chief, for whom I still work. And I am proud to work for that Commander in Chief. And if the Commander in Chief tells this Lieutenant Colonel to go stand in the corner and sit on his head, I will do so. And if the Commander in Chief decides to dismiss me from the NSC staff, this Lieutenant Colonel will proudly salute and say, "Thank you for the opportunity to have served," and go. And I am not going to criticize his decision, no matter how he relieves me, sir.[4]

DEIXIS

Language represents two kinds of relations: the one involved in the outside event or situation being referred to, and the one involving the connection between speaker and hearer. Both of these are invoked in most communications, but usually one is predominant at any given moment. *Deixis* is that aspect of language that indicates, mentions, or makes implicit use of the second relation: the reality in which the speech event occurs: the spatial, temporal, emotional, and social connections between participants and between them and the subjects under discussion.[5] Deictic forms include time and space adverbs *(now, then; here, there);* and first- and second-person pronouns *(I, you).* They also include verbal tenses, which locate an action or event in time relative to the time of the utterance. Nondeictic forms, on the other hand, make no overt reference to the connection between the real-world situation and the participants in the discourse. Among personal pronouns the third person *(he, she, it, they)* is nondeictic. Articles *(a, the)* are nondeictic, while demonstratives *(this, that)* are deictic in that they specify the location of a referent relative to the location of speaker and hearer.

Because they explicitly invoke the participants and their relationship to one another, deictic forms often acquire symbolic emotional function.[6] Their original spatial or temporal connection is figuratively realized as emotional closeness or distance. So compare:

Bill Jones had better watch out!

and

That Bill Jones had better watch out!

The second is emotionally more involved and involving, its meaning something like, "Bill Jones (and you know how I feel about him) had better watch out." *You* and *I* become (implicitly) part of the message, not just bystanders.

The closer to the participants in the speech act a referent is, the more emotionally vivid it is apt to be. First- and second-person references, even when literal, tend to be livelier than third-person ones. Some therapists used to tell clients (and some may still do) to "make *I*-statements," meaning to frame references in terms of the speaker's own experience or feelings: "I'm feeling confused at what I'm hearing from you," rather than, "That's confusing." The idea was to give the speaker's words more conviction, more of a feeling of genuineness, than the third person conveys; and to render them less quarrelsome than the second person, which would attribute motives to the hearer (vivid all right, but dangerously so: "You're confusing me"). The use of first or second person creates excitement and involvement but can, for that reason, arouse suspicion. First- or second-person pronouns make it harder for a speaker to look coolly uninterested.

Skillful users of language find ways around potential embarrassments even as they enhance their advantages. Symbolic emotional deixis can make speech more vivid; by the same token, equally symbolic emotional nondeixis—that is, third-person self-reference—can make it more politic. Academics, well aware of this, like to write sentences like, "It will be demonstrated by the authors of this monograph that bats eat cats only under adverse circumstances," fooling no one, but unquestionably proper in displaying our prized objectivity.

Caesar's Third Person

Now we have a motive for both authors' use of third-person self-reference: It's a way for speakers to distance themselves and their interests from the discourse, suggesting that whatever is being talked about is of no consequence to them. Caesar uses the technique simply and straightforwardly to suggest that he is a historian who has nothing to gain or lose from the actions described, who is as unbiased as he is dispassionate. Caesar wants to communicate to his readers, and through them ultimately to his electorate, the simple message of every politician: TRUST ME. Trust me, says Caesar, because I can manage a war, I have waged this campaign for the benefit of you, SPQR, not myself. And you can trust this report because it is written by a disinterested author, someone with no axe to grind. Readers know in their hearts that this isn't so, but the third-person references lull them into the belief that his is disinterested reportage, rather than the personal self-aggrandizement that first-person reference would suggest. And because he uses it invariably, the authorial voice that readers hear is almost that of a nonperson whose identity is eclipsed and is almost imperceptible; we lose track of the connection between the subject and the reporter.

Because Caesar the commentator becomes divorced in the reader's mind from Caesar the general, it is easier to accept the reportage as fact and also to accept the presupposed message as valid. Of course, we can TRUST HIM: a disinterested party is telling us how Caesar is acting in our interests, risking his life for his country (THAT'S US!). Even if we might not otherwise be willing to applaud his actions and believe his stated motives, when they are voiced by the disinterested outside source, they become plausible. So the simple superficial stylistic decision has deep implications about how the reportage itself will be received, how carefully it will be evaluated. We are smart enough to be skeptical of reports in the first person, but we bury our doubts for the third: the facts have, we assume, already been vetted for us. The author who is aware of this habit of mind can play on it with profit, as Caesar did.

North's Third Person

And North as well. But in a much more complicated and ingenious way, as befits one who has twenty more centuries of rhetorical sophistication to draw upon. For one thing, while Caesar is consistent, North is not. He usually refers to himself in the first person, so his switches to third are striking rather than lulling like Caesar's invariable third. In North's testimony, the third person is intended for special effect; it is marked. Secondly, the reference shifts: now "he" is "Ollie North"; now, "this Lieutenant Colonel"; now, "this American." In one sense they are synonyms, because they all refer to the same person. But each portrays that person in a different role; and in this presumably "spontaneous" discourse, each form of third-person self-reference is used under different pragmatic circumstances. "Ollie North" shows up in the first passage cited: the speaker is presenting himself as a regular guy, the "loyal" husband to his "best friend." He projects himself as a homebody, your next-door neighbor, a little perplexed because Father doesn't always know best. He's "Ollie," the diminutive inviting intimacy like the rest of the passage: Come into my house, come into my life, sympathize with me, know me. He reports his conversation with his wife in direct discourse (in reality it is unlikely that real conversation is being reported, but hearers get a feeling of being privy to the actual interchange). It is purportedly egalitarian: Call me Ollie, don't act like these stuffed shirts I'm trying to talk past to reach you.

In the next passage, he appears as "this Lieutenant Colonel," a very different role. Here he is defending his decision to follow the President's orders. That works best if he can be seen as someone who is in a position where obedience to orders is a life-and-death matter, whose position makes it requisite. Plain old Ollie has no clout here: his decision not to challenge the President could be wrong. But North casts the vignette in military terms: he is "this Lieutenant Colonel," speaking not to the President of the United States, not to Ronald Reagan, but to the Commander in Chief of the Armed Forces. We sit up straighter as he talks: *This is the Army!* And in the Army, orders are orders! A hearer with a military background will reflexively stiffen to attention and fall into that hierarchical no-questions mode of thinking; one without any will be too embarrassed at that deficiency to pry deeply into the Lieutenant Colonel's reasoning, and besides, won't be part of the conversation. North not only goes between personae but, within single sentences, switches from first to third person and back again. Each time our emotions are engaged anew, we react viscerally to the implications once again, back and forth, back and forth. It is dazzling. It is confusing. It has distinct affinities to the techniques of brainwashing.

North accomplishes several propagandistic maneuvers in these short passages. First, the third-person reference itself suggests his disinterest, the trustworthiness of his testimony and of the subject's motives (just like Caesar's). But since each such reference is highly colored, casting the speaker in an emotionally gripping role, the hearer is subliminally kept in a state of involvement with the subject. (If North had kept the first person all through, we would be directly moved to sympathy but also be put on guard. By his switches to the third, we are apparently distanced but actually manipulated.) And by switching back and forth between first and third, North keeps us emotionally as well as cognitively off-balance, vulnerable, feeling the lump in the throat (or, alternatively, the rising gorge). Both Caesar and North are playing on our unconscious assumptions and implicit conventions about deixis and its symbolism, but North goes far beyond Caesar in stretching the device to its limit.

The Making of "Ariovistus"

Beyond pronoun choice, other similarities are revealed in the two documents. Though at first glance their purposes seem distant, they turn out to have much in common. Both Caesar and North are military heroes, hoping to parlay the glory of their wartime exploits into something bigger. In Caesar's case, the goal is clear, at least from the vantage point of two thousand years later. We do not yet know the full history of Oliver North. Both have produced documents— one originally written (though its gist no doubt was filtered orally to many prospective voters), the other originally oral, though the transcript was published and sold well. Both documents were directed ostensibly to one audience (the Roman senate, the U.S. Congress) but really intended for another, whose opinion was deemed more important in the long run.

Furthermore, both heroes are engaged—beyond self-aggrandizement—in self-justification. Both were entrusted with mandates by governments they had sworn to serve. Both exceeded their mandates. The documents can be read in part as justifications for their authors' defiance of their government.

In most of *De Bello Gallico,* this message is not obvious. Caesar comes, he sees, he conquers, and there is not much for any Roman to complain about, as long as he confines his conquests to Gaul. But occasionally the reader gets a glimpse of bigger ambitions, of Caesar trying on the boots of Alexander the Great: how much of the world can he conquer by way of keeping his province under control? And if he oversteps his territory, how can he justify it to his constituency, and even make them happy that he did?

The passage I have cited is perhaps the clearest revelation of that larger goal. Ariovistus, for Caesar, was nothing short of a godsend: if he had not existed, he would have had to be created (as, in fact, he largely may have been). Without an aggressor insolently defying the Romans on their own turf, Caesar would have no reason to exceed his mandate. We can probably accept the basic truthfulness of the facts reported: a German chieftain had been straying with his army into Gaul and had refused to retreat at the behest of the Romans. The situation had apparently been going on for some time before Caesar's arrival on the scene, without causing other Roman governors too much distress. The Germans were not their business, and they had no higher plans.

We must remember that the Caesar-Ariovistus encounter is reported by only one of the participants: the Romans get just one side of the story. And there certainly are aspects of Caesar's narrative that give cause for suspicion. For one thing, we don't know how well the two understood each other. While unusually willing for a Roman to learn languages other than Latin and Greek, Caesar almost certainly did not know proto-Germanic. On his side, Ariovistus, at least from the evidence before us, was not a man of broad education (or any at all). Probably illiterate, he almost certainly knew no Latin or very little. So any discourse between the two must have been conducted through interpreters of uncertain competence. Distortions and misunderstandings were more than possible.

That fact highlights one questionable aspect of the communication. Suppose Ariovistus was as presented—a rough-and-ready frontiersman sort, not someone with an education in any way commensurate with Caesar's. Assume, too, that, while he was aware of the existence of Rome and its magnitude as a city, he hadn't spent any time in Rome talking to its citizens, nor had word of the Roman life-style reached his ears. Yet he engaged Caesar in a sophisticated debate; his style is eerily similar to that of his adversary, demonstrating in fact the typical mode of argumentation taught by the foremost rhetoricians of Rome and Greece (by whom Caesar had been trained from boyhood and Ariovistus hadn't). As a man who had not lived under a roof in fourteen years, Ariovistus might be expected to have a personal style more like Rambo's—grunts and monosyllables rather than periodic sentences. So there is at least the suspicion, on grounds of style alone, that much of the Ariovistus we glimpse in *De Bello Gallico* is the creation of Caesar.

But Ariovistus is not just the mouthpiece of Caesar the *auteur*. Caesar presents the two as men of different molds (even if they are both similar debaters). Caesar is calm, tolerant, disengaged, as he is throughout his whole work. He makes reasonable requests that are flung back in his face; he remains calm through insults; he keeps trying to be nice and Ariovistus keeps behaving obnoxiously, by anyone's standards. At just one or two points, Caesar lets his pique show through the veneer of civility, as though to say, "Of course I'm trying to be patient, but when that barbarian shakes his fist at *you*, the Roman people

. . . !" "Ariovistus himself had become headstrong and arrogant beyond endurance," he sighs at the end of the first paragraph. But in keeping with *gravitas* and with the Caesar he is showing to his audience, he frames his exasperation impersonally: not "Ariovistus was driving Caesar crazy," but "his behavior was beyond (anyone's) endurance." (What Caesar literally says is even more impersonal: "so arrogant . . . that he seemed not to be endurable.") The line stands out from the cool distance of the rest of Caesar's prose as a glimpse of the real man beneath the public image of glacial reserve.

Caesar presents the styles of both adversaries as in keeping with Roman rhetorical expectations: Ariovistus is stylistically to be taken seriously, not a mere babbling barbarian. But in substance, he is still a barbarian, dangerous and unpredictable, unresponsive to civil entreaty and reasonable offer. Style and substance together make him a clear and present danger to Rome. First, he insults Rome and SPQR: how dare the hairy savage refuse to meet Caesar's terms? How dare he suggest an equality between them? ("If I needed something from Caesar, I would go to him; if he wants something from me, he should come to me.") He offends Rome's allies. Then Caesar offers further arguments in his own voice, some of which have a decidedly contemporary ring. There is the domino theory: it is dangerous for the Germans to get used to coming to Gaul in large numbers. Once they start, there will be no stopping them. Finally there is the two days' drive from Harlingen, Texas theory: if the Germans overrun Gaul, next they'll be in Italy, and next thing you know they'll be at the gates of Rome. (Which eventually did happen, as a matter of fact, but not for a few hundred years.) So Caesar scares the Romans by an artful mix of style and substance, first giving them a glimpse of the mind of a wily barbarian, and then his own interpretation of what it means. All this is done in a style that communicates to its Roman readers: This is a person who knows our rules. We must take him seriously. But Caesar's trump card is saved for the end.

The Romans of this period share numerous affinities in life-style with contemporary Americans, a taste for indoor plumbing being the least of them. They saw themselves as the rulers of a worldwide empire, but always in danger of losing it and becoming a pitiful helpless giant. For the Romans as for us, this decline would happen because they had fallen into decadence, life had become too easy and pleasant, vice had replaced the old-time virtues. Cato and Cicero had much (too much for almost everyone) to say about that; Caesar, on the other hand, was the leader of the vice squad, his sexual activities and financial extravagance were notorious even in a society dedicated to *la dolce vita.* So Caesar, knowing his public image at home, adroitly sets up the adversarial discourse between himself and Ariovistus to evoke his fellow citizens' greatest fear: that of loss of selves and empire through decadence. He cannot twit them in his own persona, of course: they would laugh at that. But he gives the lines to Ariovistus: "Then Caesar would learn what the unconquered Germans, a people most proficient in arms, who had not lived under a roof in fourteen years, could accomplish by their valor." As opposed, naturally, to the Romans, a people once capable of winning wars, who had gone soft. If—the unspoken message goes—Caesar and the Romans leave this challenge unavenged, they prove Ariovistus correct, and their decadence and helplessness become a reality. Caesar alone can save them. And he does. In the very next section he describes his attack upon Ariovistus, his pursuit, the eventual victory of the Romans and the German's defeat and death. John Wayne would be proud.

Caesar framed the encounter with Ariovistus so that the Romans could not reproach him with exceeding his mandate; had he not taken the initiative, the document implies, Rome would be shamed, the Germans would be at the gates of the city, SPQR would be publicly unmanned and an object of ridicule to all the barbarians of the world. Caesar never says this in so many words: his method is rhetorically superior. He lets Ariovistus—or rather, "Ariovistus"—do the talking, and for a savage barbarian the man is deadly persuasive. Caesar was not so much forgiven as lionized for taking the law into his own hands. And if the senate grumbled, as some of its members undoubtedly did, Caesar had become a hero to the people, who wanted empire *and* indoor plumbing (along with bread and circuses).

The Creation of "Ollie"

Parallels with Lieutenant Colonel Oliver North suggest themselves at once. Like Caesar, he is in a tricky position, maybe even more so than Caesar. He stands accused of two sorts of malfeasances: of misspending public moneys and of exceeding the congressional mandate by arranging trades of arms and hostages with Iran and giving the money from that deal to the Nicaraguan Contras ("Freedom Fighters"). He has to convince his hearers (not so much the committee as the people watching the contretemps on television) that he is an honorable man whose every act is for their benefit. Unlike Caesar's, his audience is accustomed to liteness in its rhetoric, so his self-justification will necessarily be more (apparently) revelatory of his self than was Caesar's. We see, in fact, two selves—"Ollie," or regular good guy, and "Lieutenant Colonel Oliver North," or intrepid yet dutiful soldier. In neither persona, has he, he says, violated the public trust or gone beyond his orders. As Caesar creates both a striking "Ariovistus" and a bland "Caesar," North creates for his hearers both "Ollie North and His Family," and "Lieutenant Colonel North and his Commanding Officer," two compelling mini-dramas. Each of his two roles is designed to showcase one facet of the American ideal male. There is no reason to believe these are any less fictional than Caesar's creation.

North represents Ollie as an ordinary guy, a good hand with John Wayne-style colloquialism: "a guy that's got to come up here and tell the truth," "snicker," "hanky-panky." He provides a heart-warming evocation of Ollie's home life: "my best friend," "Of course you did, you old buffoon," "our two little girls." Unlike Caesar, whose public stylistic constraints require his reporting the colloquy between himself and Ariovistus exclusively in indirect discourse, North here opts for a direct version, giving the hearer the thrill of eavesdropping on the gallant colonel's cozy home life. *This is absolutely accurate,* the quotation marks imply. *This is just what happened. You can trust me on this, as on everything else.* But as we listen entranced, a nagging doubt intrudes. Almost every glimpse of the "real" Ollie, on second thought, rings vaguely false. He never gets the idioms quite right. "The people snicker that . . ." isn't exactly grammatical. One doesn't, in English, "snicker that something," one "snickers at something." "Doing a little hanky-panky" isn't quite right either, besides sounding a tad archaic. "There was a little hanky-panky going on," we'd be more apt to say, if we talked that way at all. It's not garishly unidiomatic, just a degree or two off. He then refers to himself as "loyal" to his wife, where most people would say "faithful." He goes on: "I went to my best friend." He means here to telescope, "I went to my wife," and the old canard, "my wife is my best friend," but the telescoping is a little startling, as if he's bitten off too much at once. The dialogue, too, has its surreal moments. "You old buffoon," his best friend says. But we don't believe it: who talks like that outside of slapstick comedy? Even Lucy didn't call Ricky "you old buffoon." And what about the *pièce de résistance,* "our two little girls"? Heart-tugging, yes, like "my best friend," but also like it, not quite right. One might refer to one's children in those terms publicly to strangers. But if a wife is speaking to her best-friend husband about the children they share, this is hardly the way she'd do it. She'd say, rather, "Susie and Mary," or whatever their names are. We're invited into Ollie's house, all right, but we gradually realize we must eavesdrop through a fun-house mirror. Or rather, we are still outside with the press corps, disillusioned as soon as we realize we've been had.

The second passage offers North in a different role, This Marine Lieutenant Colonel. No longer onstage is the regular guy in the bosom of his family. This is a figure of authority, a man who understands the importance of following orders, who knows his place in the chain of command. The hearer must accept North's characterization of events: he's a military officer who is there to give his life to protect us. If he unquestioningly stands in the corner and sits on his head (no easy task) at the behest of his Commander in Chief, can we do less for him?

We are drawn into his re-enactment of events first because we identify with "Ollie" and therefore trust him; then, because we stand in awe of "this Lieutenant Colonel," and obey his orders. "Stand on your head," says the Commander in Chief, and the Lieutenant Colonel does. "Trust me," says the Lieutenant Colonel, and we do.

North is not unique in his discovery of the manipulative power of the emotion-tugging, if entirely irrelevant, appeal of the family, especially inter-twined with syrupy patriotic rhetoric. Compare a description of Imelda Marcos's unhappiness about her exile in Hawaii and her daughter's family's in Casablanca: "The little boy called me and said, 'Why does beloved Uncle Sam not allow me to see beloved Grandpa?' "[7]

THE SHOW MUST GO ON

Ultimately, then, Caesar and North are up to the same tricks, using the same strategies. They want to justify their basically illegal actions by presenting them-selves as decent people concerned with their hearers' best interests; both dis-courses are devised to convey the message: TRUST ME. Both appeal to their real intended hearers through the veil of apparent addressees, official persons who are, at the same time, implicitly being warned: I have my real audience where I want them. You'd better go along, even if you're too sophisticated to believe me. They are the ones who keep you in power. And now I control them. North and Caesar share an ability to utilize the hopes, fears, and fantasies of their true audience, to play with them. They share certain stylistic characteristics, though they may mean different things by them. Both Caesar's and North's third person self-references derive their effects through their violation of normal deictic refer-ence. Where Caesar remains mostly aloof, as befits *gravitas*, North moves in closer, in keeping with the demands of liteness. Caesar's is close to an ideal *gravitas* style: complex sentences, impersonal devices, indirect discourse; North's is lite. Both spin gripping narratives, purportedly true and first-person vivid, but only the naïve would believe either as it is presented.

Finally both men are first-rate propagandists, moving between genres and styles, meeting the needs of all hearers, appealing to emotions while seemingly telling it straight, being informative in an informational setting. Caesar's Ariovis-tus narrative is embedded in a work whose almost unbearably didactic first sentence was once known to generations of schoolchildren:

> *Gallia est omnis divisa in partes tres, quarum unam incolunt Belgae, aliam*
> *Aquitani, et tertiam qui ipsorum lingua Celtae, nostra Galli, appellantur.*
> [Gaul is as a whole divided into three parts, of which one is inhabited by
> the Belgians, the second by the Aquitanians, and the third by those called
> "Celts" in their own language, and "Gauls" in ours.][8]

Likewise, North often interlards his narrative pyrotechnics with bone-dry excur-sions into history, geography, and geopolitics. Such men, and such tricks, are dangerous—entertaining and convincing. Both North and Caesar are attempting to do two things by their testimony: retrospectively justify dubious past actions, and create dazzling personae for future use. To accomplish these ends, both resort to the creation of fictional characters tangentially linked to real ones. The device is reminiscent of *faction,* the technique of writers like Norman Mailer (in *The Executioner's Song*) or Truman Capote *(In Cold Blood):* the attribution to real persons of dialogue, thoughts, or motives that are the invention of the novelist, a blend of fact and fiction. But North and Caesar create characters with the names of real people but fictitious words and motives.

Ironically, for these dramatists the use of third person self-reference comes full circle. A device that is ostensibly distancing is utilized to create exciting drama. The third person allows the creation of characters; the connection with the first person provides an aura of authority and verisimilitude. Together they weave a spell, first catching the audience's attention, then gaining its trust.

On one level, the use by North and Caesar of third-person self-reference exemplifies pragmatic homonymy: the former uses it to create emotional identification; the latter, detachment. But the positive impact of intimacy in a liteness style precisely parallels that of aloofness for a *gravitas* culture. The impact of each on its intended audience is similar. Both engender trust: *this is a good person.* So more deeply, pragmatic homonymy, under different social circumstances, becomes pragmatic equivalence. Caesar and North may be scripting dramas with different casts of characters, but the plots are the same for both, and both shows are smash hits.

IV

THE LANGUAGE OF POWER

CHAPTER FOURTEEN

Projecting an Image:
Ronald Reagan and George Bush

L ANGUAGE is an intrinsic component of personality. Linguistic style is an outgrowth of psychological style, and a diagnostic of it as well. We assume that the way people talk tells the truth about them.

But early in the history of our species, we learned that it was possible, and often advantageous, to separate the word from the thought on the one hand and the deed on the other. Once concepts like *insincerity* and *lying* become available, we can make promises we don't intend to carry out, report deeds in distorted fashion, and represent our thoughts in words that have little to do with what we think or feel.[1] We have come to accept the idea, if not to like it, that politics and truthfulness do not go hand in hand: that smart politicians will talk out of both sides of their mouths, and that those who won't or can't will not succeed.

We expect politicians to be untruthful, but we also expect them to be too smart to be caught at it: that is the crime we cannot forgive. And, indeed, we don't precisely expect them to *lie*—that is, make statements that directly misrepresent a discoverable reality. That wouldn't be smart, because that can be checked. We have become, of late, less interested in the way politicians represent or misrepresent the external world to their constituents, than we are in their presentation of their inner realities, of themselves. Our major interest as voters would appear from recent evidence to be "What kind of a guy is he?" We go for style, in other words—not style versus substance, but style *as* substance.

So it was in the 1988 presidential campaign. Both sides relied heavily on image consultants and spin doctors. The Democratic candidate was faulted for not appearing "spontaneous" in a campaign in which every syllable uttered by every candidate had been subjected to hours of in-depth preanalysis. We meant, of course, that he didn't sculpt his image so as to appear spontaneous, as is demanded in a liteness culture. He seemed to lack "passion," the expression of appropriate feeling that a camaraderie society likes to see displayed. No one asked what anyone really felt. For one thing, there was no way to tell; for another, it didn't matter. The good guy was the one who wore the right heart on his sleeve, who knew how to look spontaneous and impassioned. Anyone who couldn't play the game didn't deserve to win it.

So Michael Dukakis was asked, in one of the televised "debates," given his opposition to the death penalty, how he would respond if his wife were raped and murdered. No one seriously questioned the propriety of such a question: by now we take for granted the intrusion into someone's most private life, the forced public exploration of unspeakable horror, the microphone thrust into the face of the survivor of tragedy, as appropriate media occurrences. The question was not viewed as a rape in its own right because questioner and hearers knew that the anticipated response wasn't supposed to be heartfelt, just "spontaneously impassioned." A carefully tailored facial expression of dismay; some words about the horror and the anger unleashed; then, perhaps, a precisely crafted statement about not letting rage get the better of one's civilized instincts, was called for: the show of feeling and properly controlled passion. Dukakis—probably interpreting the question as seeking a literal, and hence publicly wholly inappropriate, response—replied tangentially, avoiding the issue and the called-for response entirely. Score: zero. Had he responded with real passion, with appropriate anger at the questioner for raising such a question in public, or at all, his score would have been lower still. He got a zero not so much for the quality of his answer, but as a result of his inability to recognize and play the game.

THE WORD AND THE PICTURE

Maybe once the electorate sincerely wanted to know candidates' positions on the "issues"—though that is debatable, few U.S. political campaigns having been conducted on a high intellectual level. But television makes things worse. First, it encourages a short attention span: the thirty-second sound bite (I understand it is now edging closer to ten seconds) is the candidate's chance to communicate; no one hears the speeches as a whole, not even the live audience to whom they are delivered. They are too busy cheering and chanting slogans for the television news reporters, so that the "event" will get on the 6:00 P.M. news—to hell with the words themselves. Candidates are more concerned for the laugh lines, the applause lines, the chant lines, than with getting ideas across anyhow. Besides, ideas are dangerous. Someone might disagree with them.

Then, the immediacy and pictorial quality of television encourage speakers to go for the emotions, rather than the mind. Pictures go directly to the heart or the gut; words must be digested at least partially through cognitive means.

How the candidate looks, how he stands, whether he smiles or cries, is what matters: the camera gets it all, at once; and the unanalyzable package is presented to the viewer to process in a split second and then—on to the next sound bite! No time to reflect. We don't do that any more. It's antithetical to liteness.

Words still count, to be sure, as long as they help us get the emotional message we are primed to hear. A snappy slogan wins over a thoughtful analysis every time. We are eager for charisma, for candidates who make us feel good, excited, part of a larger group, part of success, upbeat. (It is no accident that the word *charisma* came into modern use with the accession of John Kennedy, our first television president.) It doesn't matter a great deal what message the candidate is sending out, as long as his main message is a believable TRUST ME, the signal of the charismatic. That message must be transmitted subtly, yet via every channel available—verbally, yes, though mutedly; but mainly nonverbally via intonation, facial expression, gesture, stance, dress, and all the other ways we have of tacitly telling others who we are. All channels must be saying the same thing. No mixed messages will be tolerated. We tend to assume that we choose our words, but the other channels are reflections of our inner reality, which cannot be hidden or counterfeited. So there is some evidence that we are better at catching verbal than nonverbal lies.[2] Similarly we assume that what a speaker is doing nonverbally is not subject to his control or censorship and therefore cannot be a lie: it represents the real person. Then if a person seems to be a good guy (or a bad guy) because of the way he or she moves or sweats (or doesn't) or gestures or smiles, we take that as unvarnished reality. Sure, politicians lie when they get a chance, but (we believe) they cannot lie nonverbally, they have no control over that.

Unfortunately, here as so often science, or at least technology, has out-stripped our human instincts. Actors have for centuries intuitively known how to counterfeit emotions, and more recently their techniques have been made precise and encoded in ways that can be taught readily to the apt pupil. Image consultants teach politicians to create themselves as we wish they were with a subtle gesture, a half-smile, a cocked head. Not every politician is so malleable, but those who are not have no future at the highest levels of elective office. The rest of us have not yet quite caught on to it: to us, rhetorical training is what we learned in high school debating club, if at all: the planned flamboyant gesture, the clever phrase, the ringing slogan. If we encounter these, we think, "Fake!" The successful candidate knows this well, and that such techniques fall flat on television anyhow, and has gone on to subtler stratagems.

We must learn to protect ourselves, to perceive the effects of new tech-niques, to recognize when our ancient strategies break down. We have to become able to dissect the feelings that flood our hearts as we watch candidates posturing on the tube. Because their actions and words are artful syntheses of what someone thinks we want to hear, we must develop methods of analysis, to become able to take them apart and reduce them to their basic elements. The more exciting a speaker is, the more crucial it is to countermand that emotion, to discover what elements compose it, and how they work together.

I may seem to be suggesting that the words don't count any more: we have learned to be so suspicious of the deliberate verbal message that the propagandist is forced to go underground. True to a degree, but language still matters. For the wink and the head toss go only to the gut. Since we're not fully aware of them, since they aren't "intentional," we cannot claim to base intellectual decisions on them or use them to persuade someone else to our position. The media cannot take a half-smile and subject it to interpretation. This is in one sense an advantage, but in another not really: nonverbal messages die with their immediate reception; they do not resound, getting more and more potent with repetition and reflection. But well-chosen words, jests, slogans, linger in the mind and can be recalled to oneself or others to justify one's electoral decisions. Words are still potent.

Saying the Right Thing

It is important, though, to find the right words, no small task in a pluralistic society. The aim is to say what everyone wants to hear, and nothing that they don't want to hear: to convey all things to all people, to tell each individual to TRUST ME. But my ringing inspiration is your insipid platitude and someone else's vile slander. No one wants the obvious emptiness of "just rhetoric"; but neither does anyone want a message they don't like, and everybody doesn't like something, as the commercial of a few years ago had it. How to be both safe and persuasive?

George Orwell had one idea how it might be done. In an appendix to *Nineteen Eighty-Four*, he described the forms and intended function of the language of the dictatorship, Newspeak. Traditional totalitarian states, Orwell suggested, attempt to achieve control over their citizens by brute force, by controlling their actions or overt words. If the repression is brutal enough, it can work, at least for a time. But ultimately repression from outside is counterproductive. It's expensive: there must be constant surveillance. And it creates resentment, as people remain aware that they must speak and behave in ways that do not reflect what is going on in their minds. But suppose, he says, that a totalitarian government learns to control dangerous ideas at their source, the mind itself? Then the task becomes much simpler. People believe that they are speaking and behaving properly because they want to; they love the government. There is no desire to rebel; those few renegades who are not fully "educated" can be found out readily, as everyone else will be glad to turn them in. They will find it almost impossible to infect others. Then they, too, can be re-educated to think properly, as Winston Smith, at the end of the book, "loved Big Brother."[3]

Orwell thought that this could be achieved by manipulating the language, since it is language that gives form to thought. If the words, the means of expression, are lacking, ideas cannot be entertained at all, much less communicated to others. To this end Newspeak was created, not a new language but a revamping of English, less a creation than a destruction: the elimination of a great many words, and the restriction of the meaning of many more. What was destroyed was essentially the emotional and evocative force of language, its figurative capacity. What remained were concrete words in their literal meanings:

> Newspeak was designed not to extend but to *diminish* the range of thought, and this purpose was indirectly assisted by cutting the choice of words down to a minimum. . . . All ambiguities had been purged out of them.[4]

Orwell thought that the way to ensure obedience and continued trust in authority was to make all other emotions nonexistent or at least inexpressible. And if the emotions no longer existed, intellectual ideation, which draws upon emotion, cannot exist either. People become like animals, able to discuss the here and now, concrete facts, but not abstract ideas and needs, future desires, or past pleasures. They become unable to discuss them, or even to experience them.

Our current political style offers another route to the same end. Orwellian Newspeak is not represented in the rhetorical spectrum of the last several campaigns. Rather than the suppression of emotion, we find effusions of it, wallowing in sentimentality, with no cognitive linkage—emotion out of control. Political rhetoric has become a plethora of gut-grabbing metaphors and similes. It hardly matters that these are flung out without much regard for their reference, an odd linguistic reflex since figurative language normally derives its power from the implicit link between the figure and the reality it invokes. In current political style, the good feeling aroused by the figure is sufficient. No one asks where it is leading; that would be unsportsmanlike. The Republicans do much better than the Democrats in this kind of language. Their platforms are studded with evocative entries; they appeal to the gut, where the Democrats go to the mind. For instance:

Democrat	*Republican*
choice	life
competence	"a kinder, gentler America"

All of these are good words. But the Democrats' good words are good in the head: we have to think to realize what they mean and why they are good. We don't respond with visceral cheers at the very mention of *choice* or *competence*. We do not get carried away. But we want to get carried away, we want the trance induced by being part of a cheering throng. Words like *life* have instantaneous and profound resonance. We don't have to explain, to ourselves or anyone else, what they mean or why we like them. You have to like them; more, you have to love them. In a world where more and more experiences are synthetic, plastic, manufactured, those feelings evoked in the gut are all we have that we know for sure are real. They feel like the genuine experiences we believe our ancestors had. Nothing comes between us and our gut emotions. We trust them, and gladly give our allegiance to anyone who evokes them.

The gripping words do not have to have any real referent, need not refer specifically to a plan of action or a political theory. All the better if they don't. Once the hearer is won over, seduced, it doesn't matter what the real meaning is, what platform it represents. *Go for the gusto!*—that's all. It would be ungrateful, inhuman, to ask questions. On its side, the Democratic rhetoric leaves the mind open to ask: What does he mean by that? What's in it for me? The words don't bind adherents; people are left free. An admirable thing in a free election in a free country, you say. But count the votes.

RONALD REAGAN, THE GREAT COMMUNICATOR

Our two most recent successful presidential candidates furnish illuminating examples of variants of these techniques at work. Both Ronald Reagan and George Bush can be seen as the creations of other people—and as successful creations in that both achieved the presidency. Reagan especially has been canonized; suggestions have been made to chisel his likeness on Mount Rushmore.

Early in his administration, Ronald Reagan was dubbed by the media "the Great Communicator," at first a little tongue in cheek, though by now any original irony has been forgotten. *Communicator* has an ironic cast, in part because it represents a new category of human skill; it's a word whose current sense could not have been coined until recently. Reagan is no *orator*, nor is he renowned as a *raconteur* or a *lecturer*. All of those are precise terms of art, each describing a skill in a particular kind of discourse, each currently more or less obsolescent. All describe someone who produces a nonspontaneous set piece, explicitly demonstrating hard-won and practiced rhetorical techniques. Hearers were flattered that special skills were being put to work for *them*. But a *communicator*, great or otherwise, is in a different category. The word is longer than the others, less a part of everyday language. And like many recent Latinate borrowings, it has not had a chance to acquire the emotional overtones and connotations that give a word specificity. It is vague. We know what an orator or a lecturer does, we can identify their sphere of expertise, but we don't quite know what skills might belong to a communicator or distinguish the great communicator from the good, the good from the poor. We are not alert to that kind of technical polish and therefore not apt to be suspicious that special skills are being utilized for dubious effect. *Communication* places more stress on its effect on the audience than do the older words in this category, less on just what a speaker is doing. In referring to a "great orator" (Demosthenes or William Jennings Bryan), we focus on his or her pyrotechnics, see the speaker at the lectern; the audience is just a dim blur, the recipient of the action, not truly participating. But by referring to a "great communicator," we impute to the audience more of a role. They are not only listening, but also appreciating, comprehending. In general, then, the creation of the category *communicator,* along with the increased frequency of occurrence of the related verb, are artifacts of a liteness and camaraderie culture. To be a *communicator* is first, to be spontaneous: no special learned and rehearsed skills are in evidence. Second, it is to be involved with others in the activity, not solitary or élite, but egalitarian: to communicate you need the audience as much as they need you. And the very vagueness of the word suggests that there's nothing special or underhanded going on: just easy talk among friends perhaps, or someone trying to get a point across to you because he cares for you enough to make the effort.

And Reagan is the first man in history to be accorded this epithet. What, exactly, does he do to merit it? He convinces his hearers to TRUST HIM, all that is required or desired of a politician. Where others try to achieve that end by explaining who they are or what they intend to do, Reagan just is himself: that is his communication. I didn't say "his real self." His talent is the actor's: the ability to project to each member of the audience the particular "Ronald Reagan"—and at the same time, "President of the United States"—that they want, everyone's private fantasy of the man in that role. What the President intends to do in that role, why he did what he did, what he knew and when he knew it, are purely secondary concerns in the heart of the electorate. They will settle for an examination of such questions as a last resort if the person entrusted with their vote will not give them the glimpse into "himself" that they really want: Richard Nixon's error. But give them *communication,* and they'll be more than content. Let them eat words.

Control by Ambiguity

Reagan's genius as a communicator lies in his use of ambiguity. A politician's job is to be all things to all people, to please everyone and offend no one. This cannot be done by proposing specific programs and explicitly describing intentions and actions. On the other hand, a politician cannot say nothing, cannot hole up in the Oval Office or the Rose Garden and avoid controversy entirely. Then the people would know he was up to no good, or, worse, didn't like them and didn't want to be with them. Well! They wouldn't want to be with him any more either, and that is easily arranged in early November. So someone in that position walks a narrow line requiring consummate skill to negotiate. Once, before the time of incessant media coverage and instant access, it was possible for the president to stay out of the sight, or earshot, of most of the people, much of the time. But now the Chief Executive must know how to be in the spotlight and before the microphones continually, yet say nothing that could antagonize any significant segment of the electorate.

Ambiguity is the politician's best friend in these straits. An *ambiguous* utterance is one that has more than one possible meaning, or understanding. But each of those possibilities is precise and definable, in a given context. Linguists have talked a lot about ambiguities that are resolved by changes in their syntactic ambience, as is the case with a famous specimen: "Visiting relatives can be a nuisance."[5] This sentence is ambiguous only when taken out of context, when it is cited in isolation, as it is here. In actual discourse, depending upon what else has been said (its context), it will be understood in either of two ways:

1. To visit one's relatives is a nuisance (for one).
2. For one's relatives to visit one is a nuisance.

In the first meaning, *relatives* is the direct object of *visiting;* in the second, its subject. The syntactic properties of the clause and the sentence in which it occurs permit two interpretations. But once we know, for instance, that the previous speaker has just said something like, "I'm depressed because I have to go to New York to see my uncle," on the one hand, or "My brother-in-law came over last night and ate all the Dove Bars in the freezer," on the other, we will understand the sentence as unambiguous.

The context that disambiguates linguistic forms need not be linguistic. It can involve any of a hearer's previous life experience, attitudes, education, and so forth—everything that makes that person unique. In one person's context, a skillful politician's utterance can mean one thing; in another's, something else. But to each one some meaning is perfectly clear, so one feels no need to check it out, and therefore doesn't discover the ambiguity. It is meaningful to everyone, and for each means what that person wants to hear. From each according to his context; to each according to his need.

This is Reagan's consummate skill. I gave an example of it in chapter 10, where his use of *we* in one short speech was multiply ambiguous. A hearer had a range of choices, depending on what was desired. That speech demonstrates a virtue of ambiguity: its user is freed of the responsibility for assigning meaning. Ambiguous utterances are left to the hearer to interpret. But the speaker, as a person with power, retains the right to provide an exegesis when that is desirable—and to maintain a sphinxlike silence when it is not. If one, because of life experience, settles on a problematic interpretation, well, that's the hearer's fault, not the speaker's, who can claim to have meant something perfectly innocent. *Honi soit qui mal y pense.* Ambiguity is the mother of Teflon.

Let us worry but let us not sneer. Ambiguity is a difficult technique to master, especially hard to control under continual scrutiny for a long period of time. It requires the skill of a great communicator deserving of our respect if not our admiration. The construction of the *we* speech (in chapter 10) displays its complexity and the abilities of both writer and speaker. That speech is not alone in showcasing Reagan's credentials.

The Right to Flippancy

One notorious case could have made a great deal of trouble for a first-term president, and almost certainly would have for any other. Yet the President's remarks—which could have been interpreted as snide and biased, and as having racist and McCarthyite overtones—had no lasting repercussions. After a squawk or two in the media for a few days, the matter died, only enhancing the image of the "Teflon president."

In 1983, Congress passed legislation to make the birthday of the Reverend Dr. Martin Luther King a national holiday. Several conservatives urged the president to veto the bill. Reagan said he would sign it because of its "symbolic" importance, but then went on record at a press conference with a cryptic remark. The story follows:

> President Reagan telephoned the widow of Martin Luther King yesterday and asked her not to be offended by his press conference comment that "We'll know in about 35 years, won't we?" whether King was a Communist sympathizer.
>
> "He apologized to me," Coretta Scott King said after the phone conversation. "He said it was a flippant remark made in response to what he considered a flippant question."
>
> White House aides, however, denied that the president had apologized. "It was an explanation," assistant press secretary Anson Franklin said. "He didn't mean the remarks the way they sounded."
>
> . . . White House senior officials, who had convinced Reagan to support the holiday as a friendly gesture to blacks—the voting bloc most adamantly opposed to his policies—were taken aback by the president's response when he was asked whether he agreed with Senator Jesse Helms, R-N.C., that King had Communist associations and was a Communist sympathizer.

"We'll know in about 35 years, won't we?" Reagan replied, apparently referring to when FBI wiretap files on King will be unsealed.[6]

Three items in the article are especially pertinent. First, there is Reagan's initial remark, both its form and its substance. Second, there is Reagan's comment to Mrs. King, that the remark was "flippant." And finally, there is the question of what that disclaimer meant in speech-act terms: was it an "apology" or an "explanation," and what is the difference? Why did the President's men insist so strongly that it was the latter rather than the former? (The newspaper headline over the page-1 beginning of the story is: "President 'Apologizes' to Mrs. King." The continuation of the article is headlined simply, "Reagan's Apology," without quotes.)

Illustrated here are many of the salient features of the Reagan technique. The initiating utterance is ambiguous in several ways: we don't know its illocutionary force (whether as a sincere statement in keeping with the Maxim of Quality, or as irony or "flippancy," which are not); beyond this, we don't know how to interpret its syntactic form, a tag question.[7] If it is an information-seeking question, it has no truth function, and the issue of its compliance with Quality is irrelevant. But tags, as we have already seen, are exceptionally versatile forms, which can be used in many different senses: they are ambiguous. Moreover, Reagan's use of "we" here is interesting; while not ambiguous itself, it contributes to the possibilities for confusion.

The major uncertainties are these: (1) Is Reagan saying (hinting, suggesting) that King was a Communist sympathizer? If Reagan was serious, probably yes; if "flippant," probably not—at least technically. (2) Is the tag question rhetorical or sincere (that is, expects an informative response)? If the former, Reagan implies he knows the answer (see 1); if not, it's left open.

If the sentence is taken in isolation, there is no way of answering those questions: the utterance is truly ambiguous in several directions. And as long as hearers (including members of the press corps) don't press the Great Communicator on questions of speech act theory (an infrequent occurrence), he will not be forced to supply his intended context, and everyone, reporters and readers alike, can each derive their own preferred conclusions. Teflon time.

But if we make use of what pragmaticists know about conversational logic and speech acts,[8] the possibilities for interpretation are severely circumscribed—provided we can take account of extralinguistic context in constructing meaning. In the first place, this is the utterance of a man in power. That means that he can afford to be inexplicit or ambiguous: others will do the work of interpretation. But power also brings constraints, or should—in part because of the tendency of others to delve deep into interpretation. The exercise of power does not work well within a liteness/camaraderie style. Power is most easily wielded in a hierarchical society, where there are explicitly followed distancing conventions, where linguistic pomp and solemnity can safely and effectively be used to reinforce physical power. But such was not the America and the presidency of the 1980s. There are, however, certain rules for the powerful; and even if they collide with that person's desire to be seen as a nice guy, they must be followed if chaos is not to be the ultimate result. Powerful people must be more literal than the rest of us. They cannot ordinarily violate Quality and retain legitimacy and trust. Since their most indirect utterances are bound to be given specific interpretations, flippancy is a real danger in the powerful; even if they intend it, that will not be the understanding. *Flippancy* is saying something with the expectation that it will not be taken seriously. But everything a powerful person says is taken seriously. So the powerful person is powerless in this respect: he or she *cannot* be flippant, since that requires cooperation by the hearer, and the hearer in this case is unlikely (and unable) to be cooperative. There is also a more general question about the appropriateness of flippancy in the public media, since its interpretation usually requires a degree of intimacy: you have to know someone rather well to tell if they're kidding. At best, the President was here confusing elaborated and restricted code communication—never a good idea. And finally, it is usually normal to be flippant about trivia (another reason why the powerful can't be flippant, since their every pronouncement is fraught with significance), and the attribution to a man of King's stature of Communist sympathies is not an occasion for light-hearted badinage. For all these reasons, then, the normally competent speaker, given this context, is unlikely to arrive at Anson Franklin's interpretation. Out of context it's perfectly plausible. In this context, you'd have to be a Martian, or at least a grossly inept communicator, to understand the remark as flippant. However Reagan meant it, its effect has to be serious.

But perhaps, by the use of a tag question, Reagan meant to leave the conclusion open? To suggest sincere doubt? Improbable. First, recall that a tag is a special kind of question, not pragmatically equivalent to a simple yes-no question. (And, in fact, even the latter, by merely raising the point, makes an implication. So if I say to you, "Is the president a crook?" I am not leaving things completely open. I have raised the possibility; and again, by the rules of conversational logic—this time the Maxim of Quantity—if the question weren't interesting or informative, or rather didn't allow for an answer with those properties, it couldn't be asked.) If the President had phrased his question differently ("I ask you, could M. L. King be a Communist?"), it could be taken as a rhetorical question anticipating a negative response. But although (as we shall see in a moment), the question undoubtedly *was* rhetorical, it anticipated a positive answer.

By framing his question as a tag, Reagan precluded the possibility that he was uncertain about the answer he expected, since tags strongly presuppose one answer (in this case, like all positive tags, "yes") rather than the other. And since it was delivered to a large audience at a press conference, it is improbable in any case that he intended it as a sincere question requiring an informative answer. The tag is, then, semantically (but not pragmatically) equivalent to a simple declarative: We'll know in thirty-five years. The tag form itself creates a sense of participation and camaraderie: we (that *we* again) are all in this together, we share the same point of view on this as on other things, *we* do. The tag implies: I *could* ask you for a real answer, and if I did, I know you'd be on my wavelength, so I don't even have to. The speaker creates a climate of good feeling and shared beliefs, not by any explicit appeal, which would make people do some searching and maybe question what they were hearing, but implicitly, by an identification-inducing syntactic construction, an appeal to the gut that circumvents the mind.

But what is the semantic content of the remark? Literally, it seems to say that the matter is still open, since "We'll know in 35 years" presupposes, "We don't know now." Here again conversational logic offers an interpretation. The tag is less a true question than a declarative statement plus a suggestion of camaraderie. The statement is, in effect, a promise that if the hearers will but retain their interest for thirty-five years or so, their attention will be rewarded: something *interesting* will turn up at the end of the vigil. Otherwise, if nothing new surfaces, who would want to wait around? The Maxim of Quantity states that an utterance should be informative—say what a hearer needs to know. So there is at least a tacit suggestion that what will emerge will be the more exciting outcome, which in this case is *yes, he was* rather than (ho hum) *no, he wasn't.* Nothing is said in so many words, to be sure, but anyone who knows how to navigate the shoals of pragmatics knows what is glittering beneath the surface. Finally, too, if just anyone were to drop into a conversation the suggestion that King was a Communist sympathizer, a hearer might well display skepticism and ask for evidence. But the speaker here is the President of the United States. If anyone has access to secrets like these, he does. When he draws us into his confidence with the tag question, the *we* is accompanied by a covert wink: maybe *you* won't know for thirty-five years, but. . . . So overall, a hearer has every right and every likelihood of drawing from the question the implication that the President of the United States believes that King is guilty as charged. There are other interpretations of the utterance in isolation, to be sure. But in this context, that understanding is heavily favored.

Power to the Flippant

Then there is the conversation with Mrs. King. It is odd that Reagan tries to use flippancy as a way out: "I didn't mean anything by it." But a man of his stature doesn't have that out. Ambiguously, he wants it both ways: to be an ordinary guy who can be flippant, and the president, who doesn't have to apologize for being offensive. The latter is apparently important, since Reagan's spin doctors go out of their way to deny that the attribution of "flippancy" was intended as an "apology," even at the cost of perhaps annoying Mrs. King all over again. Here, too, the surface form is ambiguous. There is no way to tell whether the statement was intended as apology, explanation, or something else. But it makes a difference how it was *received*. To give and receive an apology, both parties must agree on certain facts:

1. The utterer (apologizer), or someone under the apologizer's control, performed the act in question.
2. The act was injurious to the receiver of the apology.
3. The utterer needs forgiveness from the hearer.

Each of these puts the speaker in a position of relative powerlessness or loss of authority, vis-à-vis the receiver: the apologizer is in the wrong and obliged to make redress. The receiver can accept the apology and forgive, or not. Therefore apologies are delicate speech acts, and none too popular. Therefore, too, we tend to perform apologies ambiguously and indirectly: we do not come right out and say, "I apologize for X," but say, "I'm sorry that X happened to you," which avoids any mention of fact number 1, the speaker's responsibility. The ingenious apologist can even avoid a direct statement of (anyone's) wrongdoing ("Oh, was that your foot?") which, if done right, can convey the impression that the injured one was at fault in having a foot in the wrong place, and perhaps even wring an apology from him or her. Or, as in this case, the speech act can be framed as an "explanation," which differs from an apology in significant ways, chiefly that no wrongdoing is implied on the part of the speaker: if the hearer is upset, it is because there was something she or he didn't know; the explanation will repair this ignorance and thus the hurt. So an explanation of this type occurs in situations analogous to those requiring apologies (hence the possibility of ambiguous understanding); but it puts the hearer in the one-down position as the one who didn't understand, and the speaker retains the power: not only did he or she do no wrong, but that person knows something the hearer doesn't and will help the latter by imparting it, thereby doing him or her a favor. For this reason it was important that Reagan as a powerful person not be seen "apologizing" in public, but an "explanation" was fine. Ambiguity piles on ambiguity; but in the end, the man with the power (and the communication skills) comes up smelling like he'd had a roll in the Rose Garden.

The Joke's on Us

Nor is this an isolated case of milking ambiguities for all they're worth. Flippancy is not the only form of permissible conversational logic Maxim violation. Joking is another, by no means unrelated; and Reagan's "joking" is notorious.

On several occasions during his presidency, Reagan joked with his audience, not, that is, told a formal, setpiece joke, but bantered or kidded spontaneously—

as is characteristic of both liteness and camaraderie. JFK was noted for his wit; but wit is pointed and ultimately distancing. Kidding in the Reagan mold is more egalitarian in feeling, less "admire my cleverness" than "we both feel the same way." Joking of this kind is a violation of the conversational Maxim of Quality: the point of the joke is something that is not literally true; but if it is properly interpreted (as with irony), a deeper truth emerges. Since the surface communication itself is patently not really true, the teller can claim to have been "just joking"—a disclaimer not only on the content itself but on the speaker's intentions: "I meant no harm, you weren't supposed to take it or me seriously." So by couching controversial ideas as jokes, the joker can have it both ways. Those who wish to go for the deeper truth can recognize the speaker's real feelings, and increase their solidarity and camaraderie with the speaker by concluding not only that the two share the deeper attitude; but also, because the hearer got the joke, the two share cultural affinities. At the same time, saying serious things "in jest" both creates camaraderie and allows the speaker to avoid responsibility for anything controversial in the message: It's "just a joke," after all—"Can't you take a joke?" The teller might be in trouble if a joke is heard as racist or mean-spirited; but often a critic who would be quick to point that out about serious statements is loath to criticize a joke on those grounds: in a lite and camaraderie society, worse than being racist or mean-spirited is not getting a joke or being unable to take one.

So like flippancy, joking provides an escape hatch, a *double entendre*, particularly for the powerful, whose words will be taken seriously no matter how they are intended. By the same token, a powerful person must beware of jokes: more is apt to be made of them than of the jokes of others. Power gives its possessor many privileges and advantages, but it does carry the disadvantage of circumscribing one's interpretive possibilities: you can't get away with too much, or you shouldn't.

Yet Reagan managed to have his illocutionary cake and eat it, too. Each of his little "jokes" produced a momentary *frisson* of horror and disbelief in the media: Did he really *say* that? Did he really mean *that?* Did he have any idea that that was what he *meant?* But his image specialists would invariably drop a few comments about people not getting or being unable to take a joke, and the commentators would retreat in confusion.

Example: Reagan is about to make a speech, and is standing in front of a microphone that is supposed to be dead. As if he were making a real speech before a live mike, he announces that we have just dropped a bomb on the Soviet Union. It turns out the mike was live, and his remarks have been picked up by the media—our own and everyone else's. Just a joke, of course: but even if the mike were dead, is it appropriate for the President of the United States to joke publicly about a topic like that?

Here as in other similar cases, Reagan enjoyed a dual advantage. When criticism came, it was brushed aside because the remark was "just a joke." But the critics' feelings of distress arose in part because they perceived the hidden serious message: "It would be good (right, fun, and so on) to actually bomb the Soviet Union." Those who applaud such sentiments felt that the joke revealed Reagan's real sentiments, marking him as one of their own. True, in his serious moments, he had to pretend to be moderate, but the joke was like a secret hand signal, conservative to conservative, a wink: *we know.*

Or another: During the 1988 campaign, a rumor was floated that Michael Dukakis had been treated for depression many years earlier. Although it was supposed to have happened under circumstances that would have plunged any normal person into depression, it negatively affected Dukakis's approval rating. Republicans virtuously opined before the media that they had no comment on the rumor—with every mention reviving it and spreading it further. At a press conference, Reagan was asked an unrelated question about Dukakis. "I won't answer that," he said. "I wouldn't want to upset an invalid."

This is really quite ingenious. The meat of the jest, the word *invalid,* is presupposed because of its syntactic role as direct object. Reagan isn't asserting, "Dukakis is an invalid"; he is just referring obliquely to a story that is old news to everyone—an ethically unassailable gambit. At the same time, the old-stuff quality subtly underscores its presumptive truthfulness: if everyone already knows about it, it must be so; if the President already knows everyone knows, it's surely factual. As a presupposition, it can't be questioned or scrutinized any further: it's embedded in the sentence and in our consciousness. Thus, presenting the utterance as a joke places it beyond criticism, and the framing of the gist of its content as a presupposition puts it beyond scrutiny. And then, because it's a "joke," you can't fault its teller, or you have "no sense of humor." But the deeper message remains, discernible to those who want to discern it: Dukakis is a sick man, the rumors are true, he is incompetent. But shielded by its status as a joke, a Quality violation, the accusation cannot be called into question and therefore assumes the status of self-evident truth. And because any throat-clearing by the President receives wide media play, everyone hears the remark, and the rumor is spread by innuendo. But it's a joke, so the President need assume no responsibility for its consequences. The ambiguity of joking has the same benefits as any other type of ambiguity for the powerful.

GEORGE BUSH, THE AMERICAN TIRESIAS

George Bush is also a politician, and by any standards a successful one. Not that he is in line for the "Great Communicator" mantle. Indeed, however Bush has gotten to be where he currently is, it isn't by the deft use of language demonstrated by his predecessor. But his language nevertheless has something in common with Reagan's.

Anyone who nowadays aspires to high national office must be willing and able to submit to a head-to-toe makeover by image specialists of every kind. A prospective candidate is groomed inch by inch, literally and figuratively: his positions and opinions are brushed and combed till they gleam with superficial splendor if little depth; but more attention is focused on appearance and style. The candidate's hair is carefully tousled; gray is obliterated (unless it's Donahue-gorgeous); eyebrows may be darkened; facelifts are not unheard of; cosmetics are a must on television since Nixon's 1960 television debacle. Clothing is scrutinized, and the candidate taught to wear it well. But most of all, the candidate's speaking style is reinvented. What may have worked at the local level won't do any more. Traces of real personality, rough edges, uncertainty are obliterated; every word the candidate might imaginably be called upon to utter to anyone on any occasion is gone over and critiqued; by the time of the convention, any spontaneous utterance is unthinkable (but "spontaneous" off-the-cuff remarks are painstakingly drafted by the speechwriters and rehearsed by the candidate). From the primaries till Election Day, no word escapes the candidate's lips unvetted by a team of experts. Once the election is over (until the next election), the speechwriters, spin doctors, and image consultants tend to drift away or at least give the president a little slack. He tends to backslide into his old ways, at least some of the time. But the power of the experts to remake personality while it counts gives the machinations in *The Manchurian Candidate* the innocence of training by a high-school debate coach.

With George Bush, expertise achieved its apogee. The team was skilled, the candidate a man who had gotten as far as he had by his willingness and ability to be whatever those in charge wanted him to be—to be all things to all people. Dukakis, his people said, ran into trouble because he was stubborn: he wouldn't change his ways, refused to (or couldn't) become someone else. If his shoulders naturally drooped, they stayed drooped; if his intonation fell at the ends of his sentences, there it remained. One might think his hearers, the electorate, would be gratified at a glimpse of a man with a true center, a man who wouldn't bend with every wind; but that isn't the way it worked.

Most extraordinary of all the Bush transformations was one of gender. It recalls the ancient myth of Tiresias, the blind seer. In one version of his story, Zeus and Hera are arguing, as they often do. This time it's about who enjoys sex more. Zeus says women; Hera, men. With Olympian wisdom, they determine that the argument can only be resolved empirically. They find a young man on earth, Tiresias, and change him into a woman. After seven years, they bring him (her) up to Olympus and change her (him) back into a man. They then put the question to him. He replies, It's better for women. Infuriated, Hera strikes him blind. But as a reward, Zeus gives him the ability to foresee the future.

We are not privy to the details of the procedure the deities used to effect the sex change; but we can surmise that it was bloodless and non-intrusive, as they say. Much the same must have been the operation his doctors performed upon Bush—or, at least, on his style of self-presentation. I am, of course, not claiming that Bush ever was literally a woman; just that prior to the 1988 Republican convention, his style was that of one, by all the diagnostics anyone ever offered.

As described in chapter 11, the underlying characteristics of women's speech are, first, an avoidance of competition for power; second, and as a result, deferential or noncommittal style. But the surface traits that result from that feminine socialization could also come into someone's repertoire for other reasons. If a man is born into a social position that brings with it automatic power or influence, he will not have to compete for it. Such a man, if he has a sufficiently uncombative personality, will be apt to have many if not all of the traits of women's style, because he shares with women the lack of a desire to, or a need to, compete for power. The man's reasons are very different from the woman's: one has it because she will be unsexed by competition; the other, because he need not compete at all, having come into power by birth. But the superficial patterns are similar: pragmatic homonymy.

Until the convention, Bush talked like a stereotypical woman. His advisers were reported to be in despair: how to make him into a man (since America was not about to elect a woman president)? He smiled too much and too broadly. He tended to avoid eye contact. His gestures were those of a woman: graceful flutters of the hands, fingers apart, rounded, soft. His voice tended to trail off at the ends of sentences, if his sentences ever ended. Often they didn't: they turned into vague ellipses, sometimes capped with a giggle. His utterances were full of hedges: speech act hedges ("y'know," "I guess"); lexical hedges ("sorta," "kinda," "the . . . thing"). All of these are forms of deference, letting the other participant determine the speaker's meaning and conversational intent, opting out of decisions and thereby avoiding confrontation. Bush had them all.

By the election, all that had vanished. The new President may have opted for a kinder, gentler America, but a sharper, more confrontative George Bush. He stopped smiling. His staff had tried to get him to stop gesturing; failing that, they remade his gestures. Now they were chopping, stabbing, or pointing—aggressive masculine moves. His voice no longer trailed off but became tense and demanding. It still tends to rise in pitch as its owner's passions mount. The noncommittal grammar improved, though fuzz is still much in evidence.

Fuzz in High Places

Among Bush's more endearing communicative traits is an inability to get the idiom quite right, whether in form or in appropriate context. (It's reminiscent of North's problem: one more thing they have in common. Neither is quite comfortable with the image he is seeking to project.) He tries to be a casual guy with the colloquialisms, just as he affects a baseball cap and eats pork rinds. But it never quite feels right. *Newsweek* reports some older examples:

> In Indianapolis he said he'd like to drive in the Indy 500 as "a macho man going around the bank at 130 miles an hour." But later he defended the administration's Panama policy against Dukakis by saying, ". . . we don't want to set that back by some kind of macho statement out of Harvard."
>
> At a St. Louis rally, Bush said he would not be afraid to "hit a lick for peace." At a New Hampshire truck stop, he asked for "a splash more coffee." Flying home from a visit to China in 1985, he said some Chinese leaders were doing things that might previously have gotten them in "deep doo-doo."[9]

At the 1988 Republican convention, Dan Quayle told the media how he had learned of his selection as Bush's running mate. Returning Bush's phone call, he heard on the other end, "Now, about this vice-presidential thing. . . ."

More recently Bush seems to have curbed his idiomatic exuberance, but still retains an affection for hedges in the form of sentences that go nowhere:

> "And I tell you," he said, "one of the things that has been marvelous about this summit is the understanding that our values, that alliance's values—but our values are winning the battle around the world.
>
> "There's no longer a question of whether we've been on the right side on democracy and freedom and those things."[10]

The style is quintessentially feminine, in the old stereotypical sense, in its preference for backing away from anything resounding, anything likely to have a clear impact. In fact, utterances like these demonstrate both the similarities and the differences in style between the Great Communicator and the American Tiresias.

Both, as consummately successful politicians, necessarily have mastered the basic political strategy: being all things to all people. Reagan, I have argued, achieves that end by ambiguity: his utterances have several possible distinct meanings, and each hearer can disambiguate them according to his or her desires. He seems, to each hearer, to be saying precisely and only what that person hopes to hear, and hence gets the hearer's trust.

Bush's way is different. He attempts trustworthiness via vagueness: what he says tends to have no clear discoverable meaning. Hearers are left not knowing just what was said. This can be a safety device: if there's no meaning, no one can be offended by it. But it is a negative kind of reassurance. With Reagan's ambiguity, each hearer could find a positive meaning; with Bush's vagueness, all anyone can abstract is the lack of anything negative. His words sound good; they are soothing, even nurturant—but when you ask what real-world action or position they describe or promise, you are left with scarcely the air required to pronounce them. A lot of political rhetoric is fuzz and bombast, to be sure; but Bush rhetoric offers little else.

It does sound good, a tasty mix of metaphor and emotional suasion so evocative that we are sure it means something real, because it sounds too good not to. But what binds the formal rhetoric is not a coherency of principle or vision or program, but an artful intertwining of figurative motifs. It is what makes a brilliant poem. But an administration is not a poem, any more than a revolution is a tea party.

The New Breeze

Consider one of Bush's writers' finest productions, his inaugural address.[11] It touches many bases, many points of common concern. It seems to promise a concerned president who is committed to acting so as to bring results. But take the rhetoric apart and not much of substance is left. Where an inaugural should be—besides an invocation of common national purpose and rededication—a call to action with an explicit promise for action, this one rings the patriotic bells but makes no promises. An inaugural address should be evocative, should catch the imagination, but it should also be grounded in reality.

A potent metaphor runs through the speech: "a new breeze."

> For a new breeze is blowing, and a world refreshed by freedom seems reborn; . . . the totalitarian era is passing, its old ideas blown away like leaves from an ancient lifeless tree.
>
> A new breeze is blowing—and a nation refreshed by freedom stands ready to push on: . . .
>
> There are times when the future seems thick as a fog. . . .
>
> But this is a time when the future seems a door you can walk right through—into a room called Tomorrow.

All this is near the top of the speech. It turns to other topics, but at the very end reverts to this defining metaphor:

> The new breeze blows, a page turns, the story unfolds—and so today a chapter begins: a small and stately story of unity, diversity, and generosity— shared, and written, together.

That passage picks up the "history as book" metaphor from the preceding paragraph, uniting that static and pedantic image with the basic motif, outdoorsy and (that ultra-good word in the current lexicon) natural: a breeze. The breeze ruffles the pages of the book, all themes are united in an orgy of alliteration ("breeze blows"; "small and stately story") and assonance ("unity, diversity, and generosity"). Indeed, rhetorically the passage brings it all "together," the underlying message. But what is "it"? Here, as at several points in the speech, the grandiloquent rhetoric falters if subjected to logical explication. There is something wrong with "a small and stately story": the phrase jangles semantically, gorgeous as it sounds. Stories aren't "stately"; and even if one is, how can something be "small and stately"? That's having it both ways: the aw-shucks modesty of the first uneasily wed to the pompous sweep of the second. Is that the "unity" called for here? Is this a glimmer of the real George (Tiresias) Bush, peeping through his speechwriters' spellbinding?

There is more to be uneasy about in the rhetorical structure of the speech as a whole. The concatenated metaphors and reiterated emotion tuggers that permeate it provide its only cohesion. A truly cohesive and therefore meaningful discourse achieves textual unity at least in part on the basis of a developing theme: what I am going to do, what we must do together, how things are going to change, what programs I am going to institute, in the prototypical inaugural address. But beyond passing references, none of those themes is in any way explicitly developed. Mentions of the fact that things must be done, sacrifices made, ideas explored fall from the speaker's tongue—to be dropped almost as soon as they appear. The suggestion of positive steps is further belied by the fact that virtually every such reference is vague: impersonal, passive without agent, or otherwise syntactically and semantically hedged.

> My friends, we have work to do. There are the homeless, lost and roaming—there are the children who have nothing, no love, no normalcy—there are those who cannot free themselves of enslavement to whatever addiction—drugs, welfare, demoralization that rules the slums. There is crime to be conquered. There are young women to be helped who are about to become mothers of children they can't care for and might not love. They need our care, our guidance, and education; though we bless them for choosing life.

The passage sounds, as it is engineered to, warm and compassionate: emotionally potent words are laid out one by one: "lost and roaming"; "love" (let us pass silently over the clunker "normalcy"); "enslavement"; "crime"; "conquered"; "care, guidance, education"; "bless"; and the clincher, to a roar of applause, the code word "life." Here is the President at his Bushiest. Never does he express directly the intended sense of the last two, and most potent, sentences: "I am opposed to abortion, even when the woman is unwilling and unable to be a mother." To utter those words is to invite disharmony, risk someone's disapproval. Bush is afraid to do so, yet he must curry favor on the other side. His reference here is vaguer than vague: the real message comes in via implication and entailment, where it cannot be confronted, questioned, debated. This is the rhetoric of the propagandist, offering concord, sowing confusion. The first and last sentences in the passage are the only ones in which he (and unnamed others) are the explicit actors. The others are all either impersonal *there* constructions or agentless passives. The first sentence, while it sounds good, is empty of specific suggestion; the last, seemingly benign and soothing, actually contains the only positive statement of action or position, but in highly disguised form. The compassion and concern wither, in this context, into little in terms of real benevolence on the part of anyone who could actually do anything.

Matters don't improve in subsequent passages (these from the middle portion of the text):

> We will make the hard choices, looking at what we have, perhaps allocating it differently, making our decisions based on honest need and prudent safety.
>
> And then, we will do the wisest thing of all: we will turn to the only resource we have that in times of need always grows: the goodness and the courage of the American people.

In other words, we have real problems, and we will solve them. But Bush seems here to be taking a leaf from Reagan's book (to borrow a metaphor): the "we" is imprecise and slippery. The "we" who will make the hard choices seems at first to be the totality—Bush and the American people, the audience; but in the second paragraph, it shifts to Bush, or his administration, alone, as the decision makers, shearing off "the American people" as a separate unit (as the explicit reference at the end shows). Bush makes the hard decision: let someone other than George do it. The point is not made explicitly but slipped in between the lines. One has the sense of having been volunteered for something while one was out of the room, and it's too late to refuse, especially since it is unclear what one has been volunteered for. Vagueness triumphs again; but the result of the fuzz is that nothing gets done since no one has been explicitly entrusted with the responsibility.

Here as elsewhere in this twenty-one-minute speech, the images are upbeat, happy, sentimental; they invoke nature, health, freshness, and at the same time the good old days, our fathers and mothers, when things were as they should have been:

> And we can't turn back clocks, and I don't want to. But when our fathers were young, Mr. Speaker, our differences ended at the water's edge. And we don't wish to turn back time. But when our mothers were young, Mr.

Majority Leader, the Congress and the executive were capable of working together to produce a budget on which this nation could live.

In this passage we see many of the techniques that inform the speech as a whole. First, the profusion of metaphor and other figures: turn back clocks (as often, the idiom not quite right); the water's edge (what water?). We notice, if we are not lulled into agreement by, the incantatory, fairy-tale quality of the prose, the simple language, the repetitions ("turn back"; "when our fathers were young . . . when our mothers were young"). Bush is here setting up a Just-So Story, a creation myth about the Golden Age: here, as throughout the speech, there is almost a religious quality to the prose, the resonant simplicity of the King James Bible. Why does Bush use those ringing phrases, "when our mothers/fathers were young"? He could have said, "Long ago" or even "Once upon a time." But the mention of our parents has an emotional resonance, suggesting not only the youth of the Republic but our own one-time youth and innocence along with it, and bathing the former in sentiment appropriate to the latter. The "we" slips around again: are "our" parents those of all participants, all Americans? Or only those in the immediate quasi-conversation: Bush's and the congressional leaders'? We cannot tell. We do not know whether the cohesive unit to which he is appealing includes us or not. The "we" at the beginning of the passage surely includes all Americans. But in the next paragraph, "Let us negotiate soon," the pronoun includes only himself and the Congress.

Finally, what about his explicit use of the title-alone address? We know, first of all, that this is the most formal way to address someone whose name is known. It is formal because it depersonalizes: it isn't explicitly addressed to Mr. Jim Wright (at that time Speaker of the House), or Mr. George Mitchell (the Senate Majority Leader), but to *anyone* who happens to occupy that position at that moment. Sometimes this use can indicate respect, but usually only when the addressee's status is higher than the speaker's. In short, it's a way of suggesting (covertly) that the addressee bears the responsibility for some sort of negative situation. So by his courtly use of the titles, Bush manages both to imply that the bipartisan effort he's suggesting is really the responsibility of the Democrats; and to mitigate the sting by the use of titles of respect.

Thus both Bush and Reagan use tricks to convince the majority of their hearers that their interests are shared. Reagan does it through ambiguity: for each hearer there is a precise message, but (as we used to say) different strokes for different folks. Bush uses vagueness: it sounds as though he's saying something, and the emotional undercurrents make it seem like something we want to hear; the metaphors are warm, outdoorsy, folksy—so their referents must be equally virtuous. Themes develop via intertwined and reinvoked figures of speech, so it feels as if there is a development of ideas, movement toward progress, connections, cohesion—when, in fact, the cohesion is totally formal and not functional.

There's no there there. Perhaps the comic strip in figure 14.1 best captures the curiosities of the Bush message.

NONVERBAL TACTICS: ILLUSTRATORS AND REGULATORS

My examination has thus far been confined to one channel in the rhetorical stream—the verbal. Nonverbal behavior conveys as much meaning, though in a more indirect and inaccessible way. Reagan and Bush are as distinct in their nonverbal repertoires as in their verbal style.

The advent of television as the principal campaigning medium has necessitated great changes in how a candidate for public office communicates nonverbally. On stage or at the lectern a person is truly a *public* speaker, speaking to everyone assembled there at once. The cohesion of the crowd, the creation of group emotion and consensus, are highly significant. Physically, to reach the crowd, large gestures and a loud voice are essential; to go with these, inflated rhetoric and overblown oratory make sense. But television comes into our living room, and a speaker on television is sitting in the armchair across from us, just visiting. It's one on one. For the visitor to gesticulate, or roar, or thunder, to bang on the arm of the chair, would be distressing: What's the matter with him, anyway? (And he's spilled his drink.) He loses credibility, since he doesn't even know how to behave.

Ronald Reagan was the first politician to know deeply and instinctively how to behave on television. (As well he should, having worked in that medium since its infancy—and his middle age.) His mastery of the medium added to his luster as the "Great Communicator." We saw him sitting there, nodding, grinning a bit, twinkling. We trusted him. He didn't have to ask for our trust. His nonverbal behavior, which we took to be unintended and therefore fully genuine, won us over.

Compare the technique with Jimmy Carter's. Carter, like everyone running for president, needed to say TRUST ME. He did—in so many words:

> There are lots of things I would not do to be elected, listen to me. I'll never tell a lie. I'll never make a misleading statement. I'll never betray the confidence any of you has in me. . . . Watch TV. Listen to the radio. If you ever see me do any of those things, don't support me, because I would not be worthy to be President of this country. But I don't intend to do any of those things.[12]

Carter won in 1976 (when this speech was made) by the slenderest of margins, in an election he should have swept, after Watergate and against an unelected

incumbent who had pardoned an unindicted co-conspirator. But this blatantly direct appeal aroused his hearers' suspicions, by the Maxim of Quantity: if he has to say it in so many words, there must be grounds to believe something else. He is telling us more than we ought to need to know. Direct promises of good behavior, unsolicited, arouse suspicion. Reagan knew that indirect (and presumably unconscious) signals to the same effect reinforce trust.

Bush, too, makes much use of nonlinguistic communicative devices, but of different kinds and with different results. The psychologists Paul Ekman and Wallace Friesen have produced a taxonomy of nonverbal communicative devices.[13] They classified nonverbal behavior into five types, based on their intentionality, relation to the verbal message, and conditions of use, among other factors. Two of their categories are *Illustrators* and *Regulators*.

Illustrators and Regulators supplement the verbal message: make it more precise or modulate it in some way. (In this they are both distinct from a third category, *Emblems,* such as the thumbs-up sign, which replace words and have distinct semantic reference in their own right.) *Illustrators,* as the name implies, illustrate the illocutionary force of the message: the pointing finger says, "This is instruction! Notice this!" The fist on the table says, "This is important! I am putting all my weight behind this!" We assume that speakers are aware of making these gestures, but not so much as with verbal choices or emblems. In general, Illustrators say, "I am serious about this. I want you to listen to me and pay attention."

Regulators work at a less conscious level. They are frequent in informal dyadic conversation (where illustrators tend to occur in formal, floor-holding speech). Often they serve to signal that a turn is ending, or that a hearer wants the floor. They can convey subtleties of emotion: "I am sincere," or "Don't you agree?" A little flutter of the hand at the wrist, a slight nod of the head are examples. They convey overall: "I want you to understand. We are in this together."

Reagan used regulators almost exclusively, but Bush relies to a far greater extent on illustrators: the jabbing finger, the chopping hand, the balled fist. It is a curious turnabout: verbally Reagan is the more precise, but Bush relies on nonverbal signals to punctuate and specify his verbal rhetoric. It is an interesting technique, an attempt to achieve definition and clarity, but using the nonverbal channel, for which the speaker won't be held responsible. Reagan's combination said: "I'm a nice guy (the nonverbal message). Therefore you owe it to me to choose that meaning of my verbal message that, in your eyes, a nice guy would intend." So we did. Bush, on the other hand, says: "I'm not sure what I'm saying at all . . . but you better believe it. Speak fuzzily but carry a big stick." We feel, at a subliminal level, coerced or manipulated, but to do what?

Bush's paralinguistics and extralinguistics remind me of some of my less beloved grade school teachers. Now, being older and maybe more compassionate, and having spent years as a teacher with the usual complement of frustrations, I appreciate their difficulty: how to get entirely too many fractious kids with infinitesimal attention spans to be quiet and pay attention. It was often a losing battle. The teachers resorted to communicative bludgeoning. Corporal punishment was forbidden, but they did all they could to coerce in other ways. As we squirmed and whispered, their voices rose in volume and pitch, and were strained by tension. They knew we weren't listening, so just to be sure we got the message, they'd repeat it several times. They'd name names. "SOME OF US AREN'T PAYING ATTENTION, FREDDY!" They knew we weren't paying attention, so they would over-articulate, Sounding.Out.Each.Word to make sure it would get across. They'd point fingers, saw the air with their hands, to make sure we got the point. We got the point. But we knew it wasn't worth hearing.

In Bush, I sense a distillation of those well-meaning schoolteachers. He really wants us to get the point, pass the test, learn to read and write. But in his heart he knows we'd rather put one another's braids in the inkwell. The attitude is a mixture of desperation and condescension. His job (like theirs) depends on getting us to pay attention and do our work. But he (like them) knows we're just dumb little kids, needing more motivation than he (or they) can provide. He'll keep trying, but he'd better dodge the spitballs.

Every candidate must find and develop a personal style that the electorate will take to its collective heart. In an ideal world, that would bear some connection to the candidate's real self. But since the voters don't demand a match, candidates go for surface sheen: it's easier and pleasanter, especially since deep changes require soul searching, and soul searching is best done via psychotherapy, and an admission of having experienced psychotherapy is an electoral kiss of death. Therefore, it is up to us, the voters, to learn to cut through the paint job to the rust below, or we will find ourselves before too long in Room 101 with Winston Smith. We must take control of language—not of everyone else's, as the bosses we look at next would do, but at our own, our understanding as much as our use.

CHAPTER FIFTEEN

Language Bosses

DO YOU MAKE ANY OF THESE EMBARRASSING MISTAKES?

1. Hopefully, the A's will win the pennant.
2. Prescriptivism is something I won't put up with.
3. Their mission is to boldly go where no man has gone before.
4. Who did you say Bill resembles?
5. He hasn't done nothing all day.

Years ago full-page advertisements similar to this used to appear in magazines. Even as a child they made me nervous, as though my grammar-school teachers weren't doing enough toward that end. Undoubtedly they worked for other readers too, since the ads appeared for years. Don't try to deny the twinge of apprehension you felt as you began to read this chapter.

If you are an average speaker of English, the Language Bosses have you where they want you. If you are a Language Boss yourself, there are bigger bosses and they have you even better.

OR, FOR THAT MATTER, HOW ABOUT THESE?

1. I will give this candy to whomever asks nicely.
2. It is the job of we professors to tell you how to talk.
3. John thinks as a good American.
4. The problem was solved by Mary and myself.
5. I feel badly about what happened.

Some of these sentences may seem fine to you; some may cause uncertainty; others may seem downright wrong. What all have in common is that none is strictly correct English, and all result from the efforts of the Language Bosses.

Who are the Language Bosses, what do they do, and why do they do it? Simply put, a Language Boss is anyone who finds it necessary to tell others how to talk; feels some words, pronunciations, or constructions are "bad," "ungrammatical," "degenerate," "illogical," or "corrupt" (or any of several other terms of abuse); and fears that the prevalence of such errors presages not only a decline in the culture's linguistic prowess, but also its cognitive ability and probably its political freedom. Language Bosses like to announce that the corruption of their language is a sign of the times, evidence of their society's decadence, and argue that in the past, things—linguistic things, anyway—were immeasurably better.[1]

Language Bosses tend to be better at picking out problems than at solving them: most of the bugbears on the first list would have been on their ancestors' lists over the last century. Their solutions, when they offer them, aren't overly practical: Pass laws against the use of certain expressions by the media, come down harder on your adolescent children (who are to blame for much of the miasma), have more drills in school, don't allow nonprescriptive dictionaries to be published. But abominations continue to fester as the Bosses fulminate.

A BRIEF HISTORY OF PRESCRIPTIVE GRAMMAR

Lists like the first, and their compilers, have been with us forever. The fear that current language usage is "corrupt" or "degenerate," and that that condition is somehow connected as cause, effect, or both, to the decline of other aspects of one's society goes back at least to the golden age of Athens, where we find Thucydides musing on the reasons behind the decline of the Athenian Empire:

> The ordinary acceptation of words in their relation to things was changed as men thought fit. Reckless audacity came to be regarded as courageous loyalty to party, prudent hesitation as specious cowardice, moderation as a cloak for unmanly weakness, and to be clever in everything was to do naught in anything.[2]

By the early Roman Empire, with diverse ethnic groups coming to Rome and influencing Latin, the literati were actively concerned with what they viewed as corruption and decadence—in the language as in the populace. The poet Horace has some words of comfort and advice:

> Many words that have long since vanished will be reborn, and those which are now held in esteem will vanish, if custom wills it—custom, which controls the authority and the laws and rules of speaking.[3]

A few hundred years later, with Rome even more visibly in dire straits, grammarians worried even more strenuously about preserving the language and restoring it to its pristine state—even as the Goths howled at the gates of the city. They compiled *Indices Probi,* lists of proper words and forms, as opposed to what they heard around them every day. But there is an odd fact about those lists. In the majority of cases, where one form survives in the modern Romance languages, it is the "bad" one, despite the efforts of the grammarians. Nor would most of us claim that modern French, Italian, Spanish, Portuguese, or Rumanian suffers as a result. Language changes whether speakers know it or not; whether "authorities" will it or not. It changes for various reasons, sometimes faster, sometimes slower; sometimes in one direction, sometimes in another. But always it changes. And nothing terrible ever comes of it. No case is known of a society that fell apart because its language ceased to be a fit vehicle for communication. In fact, no case is known of a language ceasing to work; we can't even imagine what that would mean in practical terms. So linguists tend not to worry about the decline of language and, in fact, refuse to take an active role in staving it off, to the Bosses' frequent disgust. John Simon, a frequent commentator on the state of language and culture in America, expresses the Bosses' feelings eloquently.

> Two readers . . . have sent me identical clippings from *UC This Week,* a University of Cincinnati faculty and staff newspaper. The May 2 issue summarizes a talk by William Lasher, associate professor of English, chairman of the committee on linguistics, and director of undergraduate studies in English. Professor Lasher adduced two sentences—"we was at the ball game last night" and "Mary had five card"—calling them clear and logical attempts to simplify the language.
> . . . . What this is, masquerading under the euphemism "descriptive linguistics" (and Lasher is far from being an isolated promulgator of it—in fact, he is part of a growing majority), is a benighted and despicable catering to mass ignorance under the supposed aegis of democracy, of being fair to underprivileged minorities, and similar irruptions of politics where it has no business being.[4]

Especially noteworthy is Simon's passion: what does it mean when words like "masquerade," "euphemism," "benighted," "despicable," "catering," and "ignorance"—gut grabbers all—are marshaled in defense of language (empty words, just rhetoric, only semantics)?

Swift's Modest Proposal

It means (we academics like to answer our own questions) that, for some people at least, language is as important as life itself; and language change as threatening as a shift from capitalism to communism, or worse. The map has merged with the territory. Simon's diatribe suggests that things are worse now for the English language than ever, and that this decline is a new phenomenon arising from false promises of equality and democracy for all. But worries of this kind are far from new. English has been teetering on the brink of ruin, according to its self-appointed saviors, at least since the early eighteenth century. Evidence is a proposal made by Jonathan Swift to Robert, Earl of Oxford, Lord High Treasurer, in 1711. In this long missive, Swift suggests that the English language is in danger of corruption or already seriously corrupt. Other countries have protected their languages from corruption by instituting academies to determine which words and usages were to be permitted into the language: the French Academy is one such case that continues to function into the present day (I mean our present day). Swift urges that a similar group be set up in England.

> The persons who are to undertake this work will have the example of the French before them, to imitate where they have proceeded right, and to avoid their mistakes. Besides the grammar part, wherein we are allowed to be very defective, they will observe many gross improprieties, which, however authorized by practice, and grown familiar, ought to be discarded. They will find many words that deserve to be utterly thrown out of our language; many more to be corrected; and perhaps not a few, long since antiquated, which ought to be restored on account of their energy and sound.
>   But what I have most at heart is, that some method should be thought on for ascertaining and fixing our language for ever, after such alterations are made in it as shall be thought requisite. For I am of opinion it is better a language should not be wholly perfect, than that it should be perpetually changing; and we must give over at one time, or at length infallibly change for the worse; as the Romans did, when they began to quit their simplicity of style for affected refinements, such as we meet in Tacitus and other authors; which ended by degrees in many barbarities, even before the Goths had invaded Italy.[5]

What is striking in Swift's essay as a whole is, first, the echoes of his concerns and solutions into the present day; and second, their futility. Curiously, in his essay of some five thousand five hundred words, he gives almost no explicit examples of the "corruptions" that worry him. Almost the only one is this:

> What does your lordship think of the words *drudg'd, disturb'd, rebuk'd, fledg'd,* and a thousand others everywhere to be met with in prose as well as verse? where, by leaving out a vowel to save a syllable, we form so jarring a sound, and so difficult to utter, that I have often wondered how it could ever obtain.[6]

Those barbarous and impossible pronunciations Swift detests are precisely the ones we employ at present; and no contemporary speaker of English has any problem with them. One era's corruption is another's standard.

Reading through the essay, a contemporary reader is struck by the large number of words and constructions that do not exist in modern English or have changed their meanings:

> . . . to *ascertain* our language.
> . . . they think the work very *possible to be compassed* under the protection of a prince.
> . . . faster than the most visionary *projector* can adjust his *schemes.*
> the *pretenders to polish and refine it.*
> I am apt to *doubt whether* the corruptions in our language have *not* at least equalled the refinements of it.

In each of the words or phrases I have italicized, contemporary readers can understand what Swift meant; the language has not changed all that radically in the last three hundred years. Yet each of them sounds strange. *Ascertain* is a word we still use—but when we do, it is followed by a full subordinate clause ("I ascertained that he knew what he was talking about") rather than a simple noun, as here. Moreover, as the change in construction suggests, the meaning has changed, from Swift's "make a thing objectively certain, fix," to our "find out or learn for a certainty."

The second example is more complicated. First, the construction that occurs with *possible* has changed. In Swift's time it worked the way *likely,* a near-synonym, works for us; just as we can say either, "It is likely that your cat has fleas," or, "Your cat is likely to have fleas," with similar meaning Swift could use either of those constructions with *possible.* For us, only the first is grammatical, so that we can say (the asterisk marks an ungrammatical sentence): "It is possible that your cat has fleas," but not *Your cat is possible to have fleas. So Swift could say both: "The work is very possible to be compassed. . . . ," and "It is very possible to compass the work."

Next, what is *compass?* We have a noun of this form, but no such verb; and its closest contemporary relative, *encompass,* doesn't appear to fit into the semantic slot. The *Oxford English Dictionary* provides Swift's meaning: "attain, achieve, accomplish." So the modern English "translation" of Swift's sentence is, "They think it is very possible to accomplish the work under the protection of a prince."

The next sentence also contains two curiosities: *projector* and *schemes.* Both are extant words in contemporary English. But it is immediately obvious that the first is not here the *projector* of "slide projector." It refers to a human being. The *OED* tells us that for Swift the noun was still very closely related to the verb *project,* in one sense in which we still use the latter: "plan, devise." So a *projector* for him is a planner, who thus can quite readily be visionary and have schemes. The use of the latter is also not entirely parallel to our own. For us, *scheme* almost always has a negative sense: "plot, conspiracy." In Swift's time, that was much less likely to be true, so that here the word means little more than "plan" or "idea."

In another phrase, grammatical constructions have changed as well as lexical meaning. *Pretend* for us is a *counterfactive* verb: its use presupposes that the clause that follows it is untrue: "John pretended to be an Armenian" presupposes that John is not an Armenian, and also that John knows he isn't: he is being deliberately deceptive. For Swift, *pretend* is nonfactive, but not counterfactive: it is close in sense to "claim." The people he is talking about presumably *claim* to polish and refine the language—whether they actually do is not known. Swift doesn't seem to be implying that they are knowingly deceiving others, or even that they are in fact *not* polishing and refining the language. Also, apparently, in Swift's time agentive nominalizations like *pretender* were freer in construction than they are today. We can use the verb itself as Swift uses the noun: "They pretended to polish and refine it." But if we want to make the agent noun *pretender* from the verb, its syntactic possibilities are restricted: it must be followed by the preposition *to* and then a noun; in fact, in its most usual sense the verb cannot be directly transmuted into an agentive nominal: "Max pretends to love guacamole," but not, *Max is a pretender to loving guacamole."

We would express Swift's thought as: "Those who claim to polish and refine it." And finally, in Swift's time, *doubt* normally was followed by a negative, to express a meaning closer to the modern *wonder.* Swift's sentence is equivalent in meaning to the contemporary English, "I am inclined to wonder whether the corruptions in our language are to say the least equal to its refinements." To render the sentence fully intelligible to the late twentieth-century reader, it is necessary virtually to translate it.

We might note, too, in passing, that Swift's style is not in current fashion. His opening paragraph contains some 350 words, organized in six sentences. That's about 58 words per sentence—very much longer than our current norm. The sentences themselves are much more complex syntactically than those we are apt to write. Additionally, the essay, addressed to an eminent man, both an aristocrat and a high government figure, is polite and deferential as we would expect in such a case, but to a degree that even the most powerful and aristocratic American statesman would find (probably) fulsome and offensive:

> It will be among the distinguishing marks of your ministry, my lord, that you have a genius above all such regards, and that no reasonable proposal for the honour, the advantage, or the ornament of your country, however foreign to your immediate office, was ever neglected by you. I confess the merit of this candour and condescension is very much lessened, because your lordship hardly leaves us room to offer our good wishes; removing all our difficulties, and supplying our wants, faster than the most visionary projector can adjust his schemes.[7]

At every level, from phonology to syntax to semantics to pragmatics, Swift's English differs substantially from ours. Yet the modern paraphrases of Swiftian periods do not seem "corrupt" or "barbaric" to us. Language change has not destroyed English.

Prescriptivism and Power

There were reasons for the emergence of desire for "purification" of English, and the removal of "corruptions" in the seventeenth and eighteenth centuries. During the Elizabethan period, England first became a world power. Until that time, her citizens looked abroad for culture; the language and literature of a tiny and weak island country could not be taken seriously. But the late sixteenth century brought not only a period of geographical conquest and exploration, but also high achievements in literature; so England emerged from Elizabeth's reign as an important power whose language had to be worthy of her political strength. Therefore attention was turned to perfecting that language to make it a vehicle for the dispersal of English culture over the globe. The best historical model of an influential empire with a language to match was Rome; and in this period, the perfection of the Latin language was still seen as closely connected to the success of Roman political expansion. So (the reasoning went), for England to achieve equivalent political success, its language had to be rendered as "perfect" as Latin—preferably by coaxing it into the model of Latin, making it as much like Latin in form as possible. A tradition of Latinizing grammars arose during this period, remaining influential into the present century.

We realize now that the effort was misguided. There is no intrinsic connection between the form of a language and its potential for worldwide spread and influence. If a country exercises great political and cultural influence, its language will achieve extensive dominance—not because of its form, but because the people of other countries want to learn the language of the dominant nation in order to trade with it, be educated in its schools, or negotiate with it; or because the dominant country colonizes others or compels their obedience, and others must learn its language if they are to survive. During the nineteenth century and through the middle of the twentieth, the British Empire was the most powerful nation in the world. Everyone else wanted to learn English, not because it was especially beautiful or its literature particularly pre-eminent, but because they had to live in a world dominated by speakers of English. The dialect they demanded was British English; American teachers of English as a second language found it hard to get employment abroad: their accents were "wrong." Since then, as the United States has become increasingly dominant, American English, accent and all, is now becoming the prestige form.

Until recently Latinizing grammars tried to make English follow the model of Latin, so that the most correct English was defined as that which was most like Latin. Of course, in many ways English cannot be made to imitate Latin: we have only the most vestigial case system left and nothing like the complex verbal conjugations of Latin. But pedants still tried to impose Latin rules on English. It is for this reason that we are warned against ending sentences with prepositions or splitting infinitives (Embarrassing Mistakes 2 and 3 on page 283). There is no problem in English with either of these. But Latin, like French or German, forms its infinitive by putting an ending on a verbal stem: ending and stem are inseparable. In Latin you *cannot* split an infinitive, however you yearn to do so. Therefore the Latinizers declared that infinitives were not to be "split" in English either, even though our infinitive marker is a word in its own right, perfectly separable. Likewise, the rule about prepositions. In Latin as in other highly inflected languages, prepositions are grammatically associated with the nouns they modify, which have case endings determined in part by the preposition preceding them. Actually it is technically possible to put a preposition to the right of its associated noun in Latin; a few such forms (therefore called *postpositions*) regularly follow their nouns, and others occasionally do in poetic diction, a figure called *anastrophe*. But the ordinary rule is: prepositions precede their noun and are felt to be inextricably bound to them. In English, the binding is less total, in part because there is no case ending on the noun associated with the preposition, so that the two are syntactically independent of each other. So it's less of a problem to move the preposition to the end of the sentence. If it's moved too far away from the noun it semantically modifies, awkwardness may result; but that is no reason for a blanket prohibition.

CHANGE AND CORRUPTION

When prescriptivism is not based on admiration for another language and culture, it arises out of the notion that conservatism is good in itself. Any change in the way a language works—lexical or grammatical—is a "corruption," a loss of strength, logic, or intelligibility. The old form is taken as the standard: any difference from it is *ipso facto* a worsening. It is sometimes true that, viewed in isolation, an innovation may seem illogical or bring with it an apparent loss of meaning. But it is necessary to look at the language as a whole before wringing one's hands over lost glories. Normally, meaning is lost only in case it is gained somewhere else: a new word, a new strategy. Language evolves like any living thing, and like evolution in biological creatures can be prevented only by killing off the organism. Latin serves as a comforting model for the Language Bosses because it has stayed stable and invariable for so many years. But it has done so because it has not been anyone's primary mode of communication for centuries. Change is a mark of a vital and influential language stretching and developing in order to serve the needs of an evolving society, and a language flexible enough to be a useful vehicle of communication for other cultures to which it has been transported. In some fairy-tale world, perhaps, if all the Bosses pooled their influence, we could keep English stable, even roll back the clock. But at what cost? And to what end?

If linguistic conservatism has no justification in reality, why is it so attractive? For one thing, conservatism in general is attractive. But many people who in their political views are liberal or even radical share the terror of political conservatives at the idea of changes in their language. They see social change as necessary evolution, political change as healthy, but language change as worsening our communication and thinking and leaving us more vulnerable to political takeover. Language Bosses' hysteria (as in John Simon's remarks) about decline and fall far exceeds any evidence they have to offer. Ordinary speakers follow suit; advice columnists are implored to dispense wisdom on linguistic matters almost as often as they must adjudicate family quarrels or etiquette snafus:

Dear Ann Landers:

My husband recently ran for public office. He went to the local radio station to record an ad to be read on the air. The copy was written by someone at the station.

One of the sentences was, "Me and my family will be moving to (this town)." When I heard it on the air, I was shocked. My husband said, "That's the way they wrote it. It didn't sound right to me, either."

I immediately went to the station and challenged them. They said,

"You are wrong." We then telephoned a graduate of Northwestern University who was an English major. He said it could be either "I" or "me."

Am I an ignoramus? I was taught to diagram sentences when in doubt. It comes out, *"Me* will be moving." Does this sound like correct English to you? Please settle it.—Feeling Like a Fool.
Dear Feeling:

You are right, but let us not tarnish the name of Northwestern. I checked with Edith Skom, a lecturer in the Department of English there, and she said, " 'Me and my family' is incorrect. 'Me' is a pronoun and is always used as the object of a preposition. Since the person is referring to himself as the subject of the sentence, 'I' is called for."

Some authorities may argue that "me" is acceptable colloquial usage, but it pierces my ear like a needle. Me don't like it.[8]

All sorts of anguish, along with attempts to dispel it, ooze from the exchange above. The writer of the letter was so upset that she *"immediately* went to the station": the case of the pronoun was a life-or-death matter. She *challenged* them, and they riposted: "You are *wrong."* Duels have been fought with less animus. The writer makes a covert assumption that the problem can be immediately and simply solved, that it is an open-and-shut case of right or wrong. As a last resort the writer consults an expert, someone with a degree *in English* from a reputable university. (Actually most English majors have minimal contact with linguistics, even English linguistics.) He doesn't provide a satisfactory answer, if he is correctly quoted. But Ann Landers's research only confuses things further.

She then goes to an even bigger expert, a *lecturer in English,* who gives not only an oversimplified answer but one based on incorrect reasoning. *Me* is not restricted to being the "object of a preposition": it can also be the direct or indirect object of a verb in even the most highly prescriptive grammar. She, or someone, should have expatiated further (but since they didn't, I will).

The Logic of Change

Once upon a time, English like Latin was a case language. All nouns and pronouns had endings; one, if they functioned as the subject of a sentence; others, if they showed possession or were the direct object of a verb, the object of a preposition, and so on. Over time, and heavily influenced by the imposition of Old French with the Norman invasion, English nouns lost their case endings. But case distinctions were retained by the pronouns, leading to an imbalance or anomaly in the system. In a perfectly logical system, all nominals would have case, or would not; for the last eight hundred years or so, the system in English has been in a state of imbalance. Under such conditions, there is a tendency for a language to change, most likely in the direction of abolishing case distinctions in the pronoun system as well.

In fact, the unbalanced system has been remarkably stable. But there are signs of erosion, of the language striving to reach regularity or entropy. The erosion begins, as erosion does, at the most vulnerable point, with *whom*. *Whom* is problematic for present-day speakers of English on two grounds: it is inflected (has a case ending) and it occurs where pronouns with case endings normally do not: in sentence-initial position, normally reserved for subjects (which are not inflected). (This is because questions of this kind in English move the questioned nominal, a direct object, to initial position, a place normally occupied by the subject of the sentence.) So there is considerable pressure to make *who* invariable, and probably most contemporary speakers of American English do so in informal and spontaneous talk. When they have to write or speak formally they get worried and find themselves thrashing around trying to sound "right" but not sure how that is done; probably, they think, the "right" form is the one they always forget to use, the least natural: *whom*. So they find themselves saying things like "Whom shall I say is calling?" just to be on the safe side. Such desperate measures are known to sociolinguists as *hypercorrections*, or *overcorrections*. All the examples on the second list at the beginning of the chapter fall into this category.

There is also some movement toward regularization elsewhere in the pronoun system, though much subtler and slower. "It's me" has pretty much replaced the technically correct "It's I"—just as, in French centuries ago, *C'est moi* replaced *C'est je*, which in turn replaced *Ce suis je.* And (for some reason that remains mysterious to everyone) while ordinarily (as the writer of the letter correctly notes) pronouns occurring by themselves in subject position take the subject form, when they occur in more complex constructions colloquial or nonstandard forms of English often permit the objective forms:

You and me have always been close. (Never "Me have always been close.")
Us linguists love a good fight. (Never "Us love a good fight.")

No responsible authority would claim forms like these are "correct" without further explanation. They remain informal and probably nonstandard, acceptable for many speakers in spontaneous speech, but anathema elsewhere (including nonspontaneous announcements in the public media). I can't imagine why the writer's husband was given the ad in that form: surely the PR people knew that "me and my family" isn't standard. Perhaps they wanted to sound "folksy," but if so, they went overboard. There's populism and there's overpopulism, and this looks like a case for Planned Language Parenthood. But as a coordinate conjunction, "me and my family" is used in subject position informally by many speakers. It is, however, heavily stigmatized by prescriptive grammarians even in those contexts. As a result, ordinary speakers (who are not aware of the deeper generalization), who have gotten the idea that nonsubject forms of pronouns are *always* suspect in those syntactic circumstances in which someone might use them incorrectly (that is, complex constructions), shun them there even when they are correct.

Sentence 2 on the second list at the beginning of the chapter is a hypercorrection that occurs frequently for this reason. Other examples:

> We'll keep this discussion between you and I.
> I hate to make a fool of myself in front of we, the people.
> Let he who is without guilt cast the first stone.

Hypercorrection is the other side of the prescriptive coin. Both Language Bossism and the hypercorrections of ordinary speakers arise because many of us are passionately afraid of the corruption of the language. We fear that if things go on as they have been going, we risk communicative chaos: mutual unintelligibility, obfuscation, failure to understand one another, inability to speak logically or think clearly. But if any of these fears were rational, we would surely have reached chaos eons ago, since language has been changing constantly since its inception. So, in the absence of proof that Language Bossism is necessary, or even that it works, there must be other reasons people, even those who are otherwise well meaning, intelligent, and open-minded, continue to torment themselves and others.

Language Phobias

One reason is xenophobia. Some societies are resistant to incursion by other cultures and use every means at their disposal to discourage interlopers. They regulate dress, religion, and the arts to discourage outside influence. Often the first target is language. Laws may be passed to make the dominant culture's language the "official language" of the country. This action may have only symbolic value, but it often has practical concomitants: services may not be available to nonspeakers of the standard, and they may be severely disadvantaged educationally and vocationally. One result is increasing resentment and tension between dominant and nondominant groups.

The form of some languages renders them especially resistant to foreign influence. Some languages readily adopt new words from outside, relatively unchanged; others require either extensive changes to fit their grammatical schemes or the finding of native equivalents. English, both structurally and culturally, has always been happy to let newcomers in; as a result, English probably has the largest number of words of any language in the world. Japanese, though structurally more constrained, is nowadays open to additions from without. On the other hand, speakers of French, a language that structurally would have no problem accepting new forms, are culturally averse to doing so and have their Academy to do what it can to prevent it (generally nowadays to little avail). I spoke earlier of the German *Fernsprecher*, formed analogously to its English equivalent, telephone, but of native roots where English borrowed its form from Greek. English seems comfortable enough with borrowing words and even (sometimes) making up words from whole cloth, but its speakers balk at changing words or grammatical structures already part of the language.

Fear of outside takeover is only one force moving Language Bosses to try to control their language. Fear of change itself is another—in fact, the basis of the first. This is a mild paradox. The more exciting and volatile the times, the more quickly language has to change to keep up. New words, contacts with other languages, scientific and geographical discovery, and hunger for innovation in speech combine to spur the natural evolutionary process. But the more the outside world changes, the more daily life and ordinary expectations become unpredictable, the less experience and wisdom seem to count for anything, the more anxious and threatened many people become—especially those who have already achieved some power and prestige in the world as it is, and don't want to be forced to give up what they have acquired, or even to lessen their influence by having to share it with anyone else. In a rapidly changing world, such people feel a deep yearning to move back the clock, or at least stop it. They long for old-fashioned ways, the world as they imagine it used to be. But external reality can never be significantly reversed or even made to stand still. Progress only creates more progress, change forces more change.

As reality speeds up, language spins ever more dizzily to keep up with it. It is then a natural tendency for those fearful of the changes they observe in concrete reality to turn on language and see its evolution as the villain: the cause of their own distress, the motive force behind the threatening changes they encounter in real life (although it is reality change that creates language change, not vice versa). Their rage is directed against language itself: the young are speaking in a code they can't understand, much less use; changes in the way of life they might otherwise be able to ignore leap out at them from every TV commercial in neologisms and slangy verbal combinations. The problem is language, they think. Since the new words lack for them the preciseness and emotional evocative power of the ones with which they have grown up, they naturally conclude that the novelties lack those characteristics. Since the new forms combine concepts in new ways, they conclude that essential boundaries are being breached, necessary clarity smudged. To them, innovations are a barrier to clear thought, since for them clear thought is expressed otherwise. But for those young or flexible enough to adjust their grammars to keep up with innovation, nothing is lost, and the language and its speakers have gained: the language matches its users' reality, as it must if it is to be an effective vehicle of communication. Those who are fearful of real-world change rightly see language change as both a response to changes in the real world, and an augury as well as a creator of further chaos. They cherish the futile hope that, though reality is too immense to control, perhaps if they can have an effect on the language they can at least retain power over something. If they can but stop the shift of nouns to verbs *(impact, contact, input)*; stamp out the use of *hopefully* to mean "I hope" rather than "in a hopeful manner"; criminalize spellings like *lite* and *thru,* they can achieve tranquillity. Time can have a stop. Curiously, often political and social innovators moan the loudest at linguistic innovation. Perhaps even the most fiery radicals need somewhere, some part of the world, they can trust to remain predictable. Let it be language, they say. But it cannot, and should not, be language.

POWER TO THE ARTICULATE

To become a Language Boss out of fear is perhaps not commendable but is certainly understandable. Often, though, another motive lurks behind the wish to keep control of language: by doing so, those already in power (political, intellectual, or social) both justify their possession of power and keep others from getting a piece of the pie. In a meritocracy such as ours, we believe that those who best demonstrate the ability to think and persuade should have the lion's share of power. Articulateness according to the rules goes a long way; and its possessors are assumed to possess intelligence and virtue as inseparable concomitants. People who say things right, who plead their cases well, will be listened to and their suggestions acted upon. They will make the money, win the offices, find love, get all the goodies their society has to give. Those whose linguistic powers are less potent fall by the wayside. As long as we believe (as, in our hearts, we do) that linguistic expertise is the external manifestation of deeper competence, this is as it should be. But the truth of the assumption depends on our definition of linguistic competence. A great deal rests on the speaker's ability to use standard language and to tailor utterances to the physical and social context in which they occur: to know the rules of the culture. Those properties do not have as much to do with intelligence or benevolence as they do with having had a comfortable upbringing and a good education. The well-born and well-educated have always been in positions of influence and have therefore been the people with the power to determine what forms of language count as "articulate" and "persuasive." As long as conservative judgments predominate and no one questions the right of those on top both to determine what is good language and to award society's plums to those judged to command good language, that group will naturally continue to award itself the medals and ribbons and prizes and will claim in all sincerity that it is making those awards on the basis of "merit." It's like the members of the Academy of Motion Picture Arts and Sciences giving out Oscars to each other, but much more serious and dangerous, an unusually self-serving form of peer review. Sticks and stones may break our bones, but in this way at least, words can definitely harm us if they are not the right ones, as judged by someone with a powerful interest in keeping a heavy hand on things.

It is true that we are more readily persuaded to a position presented in fluent, appropriate, and stylish language. I know that what I have said would seem to argue for our dispensing with all that, with reverting to and glorying in the grunt, the linguistic lowest common denominator. I am uneasy with that conclusion, the more so because it seems to me that, in linguistic matters as in others, the most competent and ingenious should get the rewards. But how can that happen in a world subject to the requirements of a linguistic Gresham's Law?

The apparent self-contradiction of my position can be resolved if we realize that expressions like *articulate* and *good English* are used to cover two separate kinds of usage; in one case, the distinctions they posit are justifiable and useful; in the other, not. It is possible to speak nonstandard English, to use the forms stigmatized by the Bosses, and yet be a persuasive and forceful user of the language: witness Jesse Jackson. The logic we strive for in language is not inherent in the standard forms but resides in the arguments we are using those forms to make. No one is as polished and coruscating a speaker of the language as William F. Buckley; never does a solecism escape his lips. But it does not follow that everything he says makes perfect logical sense.

Hypercorrection goes together with Language Bossism. As those who have not had the advantages are made to feel that whatever respect they get hinges on their "correct" use of language; and as "correct" usage is taught (if it is taught at all any more) as a mystery wrapped in an enigma, with rules laid down by rote; people begin to feel more and more frightened and confused: they know they'd better get it right, but since language is creative, they're always saying sentences they've never said or even heard before. They need general principles, but are never provided with true reasons or generalizations, only none too helpful rules of thumb. So, often, they don't know whether they have done it right or not and figure they'd better err on the side of fanciness, since they don't understand the underlying principle. Language Bossism leads to linguistic insecurity, which leads inevitably to hypercorrection. Eventually if society is sufficiently confused and battered by the Bosses, hypercorrect forms become the norm, the correct version. There's nothing wrong with this, of course: it's one means of linguistic change. But it does make the Bosses nervous, being one more thing they can't control, although ironically it has arisen because of their efforts at control. Language takes its little revenge.

The prevalence of hypercorrection indicates the strength of the Bosses' achievements: their very best efforts get people to move from nonstandard to hypercorrect, a dubious gain at best for authority. And the gain is achieved at the expense of making everyone less comfortable communicating and increasing the distrust we already have of ourselves and one another. It has been argued, also by Bosses, that America is becoming increasingly inarticulate, with *y'know* and *I mean* epidemic throughout, along with a serious inability to complete a meaningful sentence, let alone longer units. To the degree that that accusation is true, it is largely a malady of the middle class, which by no coincidence (being the most upwardly mobile) is most prey to linguistic insecurity and most in thrall to the Bosses. The imaginary ailment of linguistic corruption has created the very real one of communicative breakdown. Bosses can take credit for both.

GOVERNMENTAL EUPHEMISM

For change that comes spontaneously from below, or within, our policy should be, Let your language alone, and leave its speakers alone! But other forms of language manipulation have other origins, other motives, other effects, and are far more dangerous. Bosses sometimes conflate the two; but we can do better.

People of middling influence, with no hunger for individual absolute power, want to keep things (linguistic and otherwise) as they are or move them backward. They are conservative or reactionary forces. But real linguistic radicals would use language as a weapon of conquest, making linguistic change a forced concomitant of political repression. This was Orwell's horrific vision in *Nineteen Eighty-Four*. No one has succeeded in matching Orwell's predictions, nor is anyone likely to. Even with control of media more omnipresent and omnipotent than Orwell ever envisioned, ordinary speakers are too strong in their linguistic independence and wedded to their ingrained linguistic habits to be amenable to the imposition of Newspeak. But in smaller ways, piecemeal, people with political axes to grind have had some success in changing language in order to control how we think, or in preventing us from thinking at all.

Most efforts seem directed less toward keeping things out of public attention altogether, or getting them in, than toward putting a particular interpretation, or "spin," on them: this is the business of a whole new group of political geniuses, the *spin doctors* who practice *spin control*. A good way to doctor spin is to furnish the words: whoever first applies a lexical item to a reality defines that reality in the public mind. It becomes increasingly important to control the words behind the scenes: to give people a snappier, zippier way to talk about something, which incidentally happens to make the reality brighter, happier, kinder, or gentler.

Euphemism has achieved the status of a science. A recent rundown of the state of the art provides representatives from all areas of public intercourse with something to hide or prettify. Some examples:

Economics

Revenue enhancement	Tax increase
Negatively impacted	Fired
Nonretained	Fired
Fourth-quarter equity retreat	Stock market crash

Health

Self-deliverance	Suicide
Basic alterations in health status	Illness
Diagnostic malpractice of a high magnitude	Death

Military

Friendly fire	Killing allies
Collateral damage	Civilian casualties
Coercive diplomacy	Bombing

Communication

Creative license	Lie
Terminological inexactitude	Lie
Different version of the facts	Lie[9]

These excursions into creative lexicology are driven by two motives: to conceal an unfortunate situation, and to magnify the power or importance of some involved person. (In the latter capacity, *sanitary engineer* replaces *janitor,* itself once a replacement for *handyman; thanatologist* replaces *mortician,* a replacement for *undertaker.*) As long as we recognize the real meaning of the euphemism or grandiloquence, we can dismiss it as harmless hype. It's only when the usage becomes so pervasive that we lose track of what it substitutes for— forget that these devices are cover-ups, and forget to look for or think about the reasons for the deception—that language becomes dangerous. The terms must be exceptionally ingratiating, their creators determined and influential, the audience stolidly receptive, for them to have the potency of Orwellian Newspeak. I don't mean to urge complacency: the one way to guard against the *Nineteen Eighty-Four*–type of inroads into the mind is to remain alert to changes imposed from above: What do they really mean? Why is the substitute offered? If we don't notice, if we overlook significant developments because they are presented to us as trivial, and because we have better things to worry about than "just words," we have no one but ourselves to blame.

In a totalitarian government that, because of both its own repressive devices and the country's economic organization, has full control of the media, more menacing things occur. For a couple of months in the spring of 1989, America was galvanized by events in China: students demonstrated *en masse* in Beijing and other cities for more democracy. At first the government seemed benevolent and even responsive, but then cracked down brutally, suppressing the demonstrations and eventually tracking down, trying and executing or imprisoning the leaders. The American media reported each development in detail and, by their pictures, analyses, and interviews, enabled Americans to get a sharp and detailed version of events as they developed. The Chinese media were much less reliable, but between what they could report, and what Americans sent to their Chinese counterparts via fax machines, much was available during the demonstrations themselves. But once the government cracked down, all internal reporting ceased. Most chilling were the efforts made by Beijing to suppress not only the movement itself but any record of it in the public memory.

Horrifying to Americans was the thoroughness and speed with which the Chinese government managed to convince its citizens that the events they had seen or heard about had not occurred at all, or had occurred in a much less significant form, or very differently, as in this report:

> In the week since the bloody crackdown on the democracy movement in Beijing, the Chinese propaganda machine has been put into full swing, seeking to transform the event into a heroic operation that saved the country from "a counterrevolutionary plot."
>
> In Shanghai and in every other city in China, the newspapers and television stations have been running film clips, interviews and statements from leaders portraying accounts of the crackdown by diplomats, foreign journalists and witnesses as rumors.
>
> The bloody massacre described in the foreign press—and in the foreign radio broadcasts beamed at China—never took place, Chinese news reports have been saying. According to the official television stations and newspapers, what actually occurred was a largely peaceful operation, vigorously supported by public opinion, aimed at "quelling the turmoil" brought about by "a small number of bad elements."
>
> The campaign is reminiscent of past attempts in China to rewrite history. The difference this time is that the rewriting is taking place within days of the historic event itself.
>
> An extraordinary series of broadcasts over several nights on national television illustrates the tone of the propaganda effort.
>
> For two nights, both the early and late evening news programs broadcast segments of a street interview done by ABC News in Beijing shortly after the army's assaults. A man is shown being interviewed, his voice rising with anger and his arms imitating the motion of a machine

gun, as he describes a scene of terrible carnage committed, he says, by the army.

A caption on the bottom of the screen during the interview identifies the man as "somebody spreading rumors about the cleanup of Tiananmen Square." After the man speaks, the news announcer warns the public to beware of believing such rumors, then says that the man is wanted by the police and appeals to the public to turn him in.

Last night, the national news showed the same man, looking haggard and terrified, in police custody, retracting in front of the cameras what he had said to ABC News. The news announcer says that the man is Xiao Bing, an unemployed 42-year-old factory worker, and that he was turned in one hour after the appeal to the public.

"I never saw anything," Xiao says of the Beijing crackdown. He goes on, his head bowed: "I apologize for bringing great harm to the party and the country."[10]

When a government can manipulate language and communication in so efficient and complex a way, no one can trust what is seen or heard. What is heard is discounted; a class of experts arises capable of reading what is not said between the lines, which is assumed to be the reality:

Last week diplomats and journalists alike found themselves scanning the faces of television newscasters [in Beijing] for telltale gestures; averted eyes during the reading of martial-law decrees were taken as evidence of government pressure on the media. Some even studied vocabulary lists for China's televised English-language lessons. The juxtaposition of *monster, dinosaur,* and *extinct* was an occasion of excitement; some thought it portended the downfall of both Li and Deng.[11]

When no one can trust what they are told, language itself becomes empty and valueless. As with currency, inflation sets in: those in power raise the wattage of their rhetoric, stepping up threats, promises, patriotic calls to duty. No one knows what to believe.

Language Bosses sometimes use the Biblical story of the Tower of Babel to warn us of what will happen if we don't keep our language undefiled, if we let impurities filter into the standard from the masses below. But the real danger—to language, its users, and the world it allows them to understand and exist in—is from above. If those who already hold excessive power wish to consolidate their strength still further, they will seek to do so through control of language at its source: the media. Words will be chosen less for their informative than for their emotionally evocative content. What is said by someone identified as a "rumor-monger" will be automatically discounted; if he is further described offhandedly as "someone spreading rumors" (assuming the original has the same effect in Chinese as the translation does for us), hearers will be even more dismissive: the man is a cipher, a nobody. If enough of the "news" contradicts what people have actually seen or find credible, wide-scale discrediting of all authoritative language may occur, and language will truly lose its meaning as it has lost its function to inform and connect. A society is then indeed in dire straits: manipulated into believing what is not true, and yet moved to discount everything it hears, it lives out the Tower of Babel scenario. Language is shorn of its power, its ability to make reference to the world outside the speaker and hearer and to unite speaker and hearer in a mutually trusting connection. Its use, rather than bringing participants closer because of what it enables them to share, drives them apart through distrust and boredom. Society fragments; nothing is accomplished except through brute force imposed by a repressive government.

The threat of such a debacle demonstrates the ultimate power and yet essential impotence of language. Through the thoughtful and respectful use of language, we increase our wisdom and humanity and function well as a society, achieving our highest competence as human beings. But if we misuse language, it becomes a weapon of social and intellectual death; it cannot save us from ourselves and our destructive motives. We can choose to try to boss language, and one another through it, thereby making a reality of the Orwellian nightmare; or we can understand language as a creative political force, a means of free expression and cooperation.

NOTES

Introduction. The Politics of Language

1. The concept of the linguistic code was introduced in B. Bernstein 1962.

2. As an introduction to the field of structural linguistics, and an illustration of its assumptions and methods, see L. Bloomfield 1933. For the authoritative statement of the "new linguistics"—transformational grammar—see N. Chomsky 1965. And for my favorite among contemporary introductions to the field of linguistics as a whole, see D. Bolinger 1968.

3. For an overview of pragmatics, see S. Levinson 1983; of sociolinguistics, R. Hudson 1980.

Chapter 1. Language, Politics, and Power

1. The concept of the family as politically structured has been given much attention in recent years in several fields. A couple of the seminal works in this area are J. Haley 1963 and R. D. Laing 1967.

2. Lewis Carroll, *Through the Looking-Glass* (n.d.), p. 214.

Chapter 2. Talking about Language

1. The concept of the speech act was originated in J. L. Austin 1962; and developed further in J. Searle 1969.

2. Basic discussions of politeness within pragmatics and sociolinguistics are found in P. Brown and S. Levinson 1987; and in R. Lakoff 1973.

3. For some discussion and illustration, see D. Tannen 1986 and 1990.

Chapter 3. Talking Politics

1. Probably the first major work defining and demonstrating conversation analysis, though not very accessible, is H. Sacks, E. Schegloff, and G. Jefferson 1974.

2. On closings, see H. Sacks and E. Schegloff 1973.

3. For discussion of gender and its role in conversational success, see D. Zimmerman and C. West 1975.

4. See D. Tannen 1984.

5. For discussion of the relative values and functions of literate and oral transmission of culture, see J. Goody and I. Watt 1963; and D. Olson 1977.

6. For discussion of classroom discourse, see J. Cook-Gumperz 1981.

Chapter 4. The Talking Cure

1. This case history is taken from S. Freud [1901] 1905. My discussion here is based in part on work in collaboration with James Coyne.

2. See Bateson 1972 and J. Haley 1963.

3. This position was stated first and perhaps most eloquently in J. Breuer and S. Freud 1893–95.

4. S. Freud [1895] 1950.

5. For a sampling of the discussion, from within the field and outside, of the scientific status of psychoanalysis, see K. Eissler 1969; S. Fisher and R. P. Greenberg 1977; A. Grunbaum 1984; and H. Hartmann 1964.

6. See B. Bettelheim 1983.

7. See K. Menninger 1973.

8. On the technique of psychoanalysis, see S. Freud 1911–15; R. Greenson 1967; and M. Aftel and R. Lakoff 1985.

9. See Greenson, 1967; and E. Zetzel 1956.

10. Freud uses this, or analogous terms, several times in his writings. See especially Freud 1916–17, p. 348.

11. J. Haley 1963.

12. For other discussion, see J. M. Masson 1988.

Chapter 5. Life and Language in Court

1. Examples of trial manuals, which help neophytes through the rigors of courtroom appearances, are P. Bergman (1979); S. H. Goldberg 1982; and F. L. Wellman 1903.

2. For a different perspective on formality, see J. M. Atkinson 1984.

3. On the effect of judges' nonverbal behavior on jurors, see P. D. Blanck, R. Rosenthal, and L. H. Cordell 1985.

4. For assessment of jurors' evaluation of lawyers, see D. Linz, S. Penrod, and E. McDonald 1986.

5. On lawyers' assessment of judges, see D. Suggs and B. Sales 1978.

6. See B. Erickson et al., 1978.

7. For discussion of elaborated and restricted code communication, see B. Bernstein 1962.

8. Actually two decisions are directly relevant—*Furman* v. *Georgia* in 1972, which declares "unguided discretion" statutes unconstitutional under the Eighth Amendment; and *Gregg* v. *Georgia,* of 1976, which declares statutes incorporating juror "guided discretion" constitutional.

9. This is the 1978 California voter initiative mandated Proposition 7.

10. California State Supreme Court, 40 Cal 3d 512, 546 (on *People* v. *Brown* 1985). A recent decision by the U.S. Supreme Court (*Boyde* v. *California*, 90 C.D.O.S. 1558) nullifies this whole discussion, however, by arguing that a *shall* instruction does not excessively interfere with the jury's discretion.

11. Brian St. Pierre, "Merlot Comes of Age," *Focus* magazine, August 1989.

12. *People* v. *Delgado,* Alameda County, California Superior Court No. H-4710 (1984).

Chapter 6. We, the Jury

1. This form of juror questioning is mandated in California by a 1980 decision of the State Supreme Court *Hovey* v. *Superior Court,* 28 Cal 3d 1. It is not required in most other states at present.

2. *Witherspoon* v. *Illinois.* 391 U.S. 510, 20 Ed. L. 2d 796 (1968).

3. *People* v. *Delgado,* Alameda County, California Superior Court No. H-4710 (1984).

4. For instance, see A. Etzioni 1974.

5. For some testimony to this point, there are several books and innumerable articles written by former jurors, most often those who have served in notorious trials, more often than not as forepersons. See for instance, E. Kennebeck 1973; and M. Timothy 1974.

Chapter 7. Therapy and the Law: Blurring the Lines

1. For discussion of public language, see J. Gumperz 1982.

2. On collaboration in therapy, see: R. Greenson 1967 and M. Aftel and R. Lakoff 1985.

3. For descriptions of the adversarial nature of the courtroom, see trial manuals such as P. Bergman 1979; S. H. Goldberg 1982; and F. L. Wellman 1903.

4. For discussion of formality, see J. M. Atkinson 1984.

5. For a discussion of therapy as "deadly serious play," see J. Haley 1963.

6. The concept of "overdetermination" originated with J. Breuer and S. Freud 1893–95. The principle of multiple function is discussed in R. Waelder 1936.

7. For discussion, see R. Lakoff 1985.

8. S. Freud [1901] 1905.

9. For discussion of some particularly striking cases, see J. M. Masson 1988.

Chapter 8. The Grooves of Academe

1. Compare J. L. Austin 1962.

2. See what I mean?

3. For reasons that should be apparent, there exist (to my knowledge) no in-depth, detailed examinations of collegial speech patterns in academia. Perhaps the best written documentation exists in the form of the academic novel, an abundant genre. For a few examples: Mary McCarthy, *The Groves of Academe;* Kingsley Amis, *Lucky Jim;* David Lodge, *Small World* and *Trading Places.*

4. There is not, unsurprisingly, a great deal of literature on this socialization process in academia; but the recent collection of papers edited by J. S. Nelson, A. Megill, and D. C. McCloskey 1987 represents several perspectives on this issue. See also, for relevant insights, C. Bazerman 1981; and L. Brodkey 1988.

5. G. Bateson 1972, especially part III.

Chapter 9. You Say Tom*a*yto, I Say Tom*ah*to

1. For insightful analysis of cross-cultural linguistic confusion, see the videotape produced by J. J. Gumperz, T. Jupp, and C. Roberts, *Crosstalk* (London: Centre for Industrial Language Teaching, 1979).

2. H. P. Grice 1975.

3. See R. Lakoff 1973.

4. See P. Brown and S. Levinson 1987.

5. E. O. Keenan 1976.

6. For discussion of speaker-based and hearer-based strategies, see R. Lakoff 1984.

7. Y. Matsumoto 1989.

8. *Newsweek,* 5 June 1989, p. 34.

Chapter 10. *We* First

1. Discussion within the field of linguistic semantics of the formation of categories in language begins with a famous article that postulates what has come to be called the Sapir-Whorf hypothesis, B. L. Whorf 1940: The language of a culture creates and restricts its perception of reality. Significant contributions to the understanding of categories have been made in psychology by E. Rosch 1973, and in linguistics by G. Lakoff 1987.

2. For discussion of the difference among groups in category formation, see B. Berlin and P. Kay 1969.

3. The concept of the social stereotype was introduced during the 1920s by Walter Lippmann (see W. Lippmann, 1965).

4. One especially thorough and relatively recent study is J. Ellul 1965.

5. *San Francisco Chronicle,* 16 March 1989.

6. *San Francisco Chronicle,* 13 March 1989.

Chapter 11. Why Can't a Woman Be Less like a Man?

1. For especially cogent discussion of the causes and consequences of the power discrepancy between men and women, see C. MacKinnon 1983.

2. As expressed in I. Illich 1982.

3. Some of the most important works in the large and continually expanding body of writings on language and gender are: M. R. Key 1975; B. Thorne and N. Henley 1975; C. Miller and K. Swift 1976; and D. Spender 1980. Also compare R. Lakoff 1975.

4. E. O. Keenan 1976.

5. Some of the claims (such as number 3) go back millennia, without a great deal of substantiation. Others have been the subject of ostensibly "scientific" description. Otto Jespersen, one of the great linguists of the earlier part of this century, is responsible for several 1921.

6. This claim is discussed, for instance, in R. Lakoff 1975, along with numbers 3 through 7.

7. Discussed in D. Zimmerman and C. West 1975.

8. Discussed especially in D. Tannen (forthcoming).

9. Instructive here is a remark made by Allan E. Gotlieb, former U.S. ambassador to Canada: "In Washington, gossip is not gossip. Gossip is intelligence." In other words, it is context rather than content that elevates the utterance to the level of something important. Quoted in *California Monthly,* April 1989, p. 10, in an interview by Harry Kreisler.

10. See the discussion in, for example, R. M. Kanter 1977 and D. Tannen (forthcoming).

11. *Time,* 14 November 1988, p. 98.

Chapter 12. *De Amicitiis Faciendis et Hominibus Movendis;* or, How to Make Friends and Influence People

1. *Newsweek,* 5 June 1989, p. 35.

2. *San Francisco Chronicle,* 3 June 1989.

3. R. Lakoff and D. Tannen 1984.

4. For interesting theoretical and practical discussion of the problems involved on the defense side, see D. Logan (n.d.)

5. C. Sallustius Crispus, *Bellum Catilinae.*

6. Ibid. 51. 1–8. The translation of this and subsequent passages is my own. Omnes homines, patres conscripti, qui de rebus dubiis consultant, ab odio, amicitia, ira atque misericordia vacuos esse decet. Haud facile animus verum providet, ubi illa officiunt, neque quisquam omnium lubidini simul et usui paruit. Ubi intenderis ingenium, valet; si lubido possidet, ea dominatur, animus nihil valet. Magna mihi copia est memorandi, patres conscripti, quae reges atque populi ira aut misericordia impulsi male consuluerint. Sed eo malo dicere, quae maiores nostri contra lubidinem animi sui recte atque ordine fecere bello Macedonico, quod cum rege Perse gessimus. Rhodiorum civitas magna atque magnifica, quae populi Romani opibus creverat, infida et advorsa nobis fuit. Sed postquam bello

confecto de Rhodiis consultum est, maiores nostri, ne quis divitiarum magis quam iniuriae causa bellum inceptum diceret, impunitos eos dimisere. Item bellis Punicis omnibus, quom saepe Carthaginienses et in pace et per indutias multa nefaria facinora fecissent, numquam ipsi per occasionem talia fecere: magis quid se dignum foret, quam quid in illos iure fieri posset, quaerebant. Hoc item vobis providendum est, patres conscripti, ne plus apud vos valeat P. Lentuli et ceterorum scelus quam vostra dignitas, neu magis irae vostrae quam famae consultatis. Nam si digna poena pro factis eorum reperitur, novom consilium adprobo; sin magnitudo sceleris omnium ingenia exuperat, his utendum censeo, quae legibus comparata sunt.

7. Ibid. 51. 43. Placet igitur eos dimitti et augeri exercitum Catilinae? Minime. Sed ita censeo: publicandas eorum pecunias, ipsos in vinculis habendos per municipia, quae maxume opibus valent; neu quis de iis postea ad senatum referat neve cum populo agat; qui aliter fecerit, senatum existumare eum contra rem publicam et salutem omnium facturum.

8. Ibid. 52. 2–6. Longe alia mihi mens est, patres conscripti, quom res atque pericula nostra considero, et quom sententias nonnullorum ipse mecum repeto. Illi mihi disseruisse videntur de poena eorum, qui patriae, parentibus, aris atque focis suis bellum paravere; res autem monet cavere ab illis magis quam quid in eos statuamus consultare. Nam cetera maleficia tum persequare, ubi facta sunt; hoc nisi provideris ne adcidat, ubi evenit, frustra iudicia inplores: capta urbe nihil fit reliqui victis. Sed, per deos inmortalis, vos ego appello, qui semper domos, villas, signa, tabulas vostras pluris quam rem publicam fecistis: si ista, quoiuscumque modi sunt amplexamini, retinere, si voluptatibus vostris otium praebere voltis, expergiscimini aliquando et capessite rem publicam. Non agitur de vectigalibus neque de sociorum iniuriis; libertas et anima nostra in dubio est.

9. Ibid. 52. 36. Quare ita censeo, quom nefario consilio sceleratorum civium res publica in summa pericula venerit, iique indicio T. Volturci et legatorum Allobrogum convicti confessique sint caedem, incendia, aliaque se foeda atque crudelia facinora in civis patriamque paravisse, de confessis, sicuti de manufestis rerum capitalium, more maiorum supplicium sumundum.

10. The concept of guilt and shame cultures is discussed, for example, in R. Benedict 1946; and G. Roheim 1950.

11. See note 5, this chapter.

12. See K. Lorenz, *On Aggression* 1966, for further discussion.

Chapter 13. Winning Hearts and Minds: Pragmatic Homonymy and Beyond

1. The transcripts of his testimony are published as *Taking the Stand,* 1987.

2. Caesar, *De Bello Gallico* 1.33–36. The translation is mine. His responsis ad Caesarem relatis iterum ad eum Caesar legatos cum his mandatis mittit: Quoniam tanto suo populique Romani beneficio affectus, cum in consulatu suo rex atque amicus a senatu appellatus esset, hanc sibi populoque Romano gratiam referret, ut in colloquium venire invitatus gravaretur neque de communi re dicendum sibi et cognoscendum putaret, haec esse, quae ab eo postularet: primum ne quam multitudinem hominum amplius trans Rhenum in Galliam traduceret; deinde obsides, quos haberet ab Aeduis, redderet Sequanisque permitteret, ut, quos illi haberent, voluntate eius reddere illis liceret; neve Aeduos

iniuria lacesseret, neve his sociisque eorum bello inferret. Si ita fecisset, sibi populo Romano perpetuam gratiam atque amicitiam cum eo futuram: si non impetraret, sese, quoniam M. Messala, M. Pisone consulibus senatus censuisset, uti, quicumque Galliam provinciam obtineret, quod commodo rei publicae facere posset, Aeduos ceterosque amicos populi Romani defenderet, se Aeduorum iniurias non neglecturum.

Ad haec Ariovistus respondit: Ius esse belli, ut, qui vicissent, iis, quos vicissent, quemadmodum vellent, imperarent: item populum Romanum victis non ad alterius praescriptum, sed ad suum arbitrium imperare consuesse. Si ipse populo Romano non praescriberet, quemadmodum suo iure uteretur, non oportere se a populo Romano in suo iure impediri. Aeduos sibi, quoniam belli fortunam temptassent et armis congressi ac superati essent, stipendarios esse factor. Magnam Caesarem iniuriam facere, qui suo adventu vectigalia sibi deteriora faceret. Aeduis se obsides redditurum non esse, neque iis neque eorum sociis iniuria bellum illaturum, si in eo manerent, quod convenisset, stipendiumque quotannis penderent; si id non fecissent, longe iis fraternum nomen populi Romani afuturum. Quod sibi Caesar denuntiaret, se Aeduorum iniurias non neglecturum, neminem secum sine sua pernicie contendisse. Cum vellet, congrederetur: intellecturum, quid invicti Germani, exercitatissimi in armis, qui inter annos XIV tectum non subissent, virtute possent.

3. North, *Taking the Stand,* pp. 191ff.

4. Ibid., p. 342.

5. A good description and theoretical discussion of deixis and deictic phenomena is found in C. Fillmore 1975.

6. See, for further discussion, R. Lakoff 1974.

7. *Newsweek,* 8 May 1989, p. 38.

8. Caesar, *De Bello Gallico* 1.1.

Chapter 14. Projecting an Image: Ronald Reagan and George Bush

1. People have always claimed to despise such behavior. Thus Plato, in the *Republic,* banishes poets from his ideal state because they "lie." At the same time, he countenances the philosopher-kings' telling of the "noble lie" in order to keep their subjects obedient.

2. The research underlying this conclusion is described in P. Ekman and W. Friesen 1969.

3. G. Orwell 1949.

4. Ibid., p. 247.

5. This famous example first appears in N. Chomsky 1965.

6. *San Francisco Chronicle,* 22 October 1983.

7. For discussion of illocutionary force and its problems, see J. L. Austin 1962 and J. Searle 1969. For discussion of tag questions and the relation between their form and their function, see R. Lakoff 1985.

8. For discussion of speech act theory, see Austin 1962 and Searle 1969. For the concept of conversational logic, see H. P. Grice 1975.

9. *Newsweek,* 23 May 1989.

10. *San Francisco Chronicle,* 31 May 1989.

11. Printed in the *San Francisco Chronicle,* 21 January 1989.

12. J. Carter, 1976, quoted in T. H. White, *America in Search of Itself* (New York: Warner, 1982), p. 189.

13. P. Ekman and W. Friesen 1968.

Chapter 15. Language Bosses

1. For other discussion of the phenomenon, which he calls "language shamanism," see D. Bolinger 1980. For some history, see E. Finegan 1980.

2. Thucydides, *Peloponnesian Wars* 3.82.4.

3. Horace, *Ars Poetica* 70–72. The translation is mine.

4. J. Simon 1980.

5. Jonathan Swift, "A Proposal for Correcting, Improving, and Ascertaining the English Tongue."

6. Ibid.

7. Ibid.

8. *San Francisco Chronicle,* 8 September 1981.

9. Most of these examples are from the *San Francisco Examiner,* 20 November 1988.

10. In the *San Francisco Chronicle,* 12 June 1989, taken from a story in the *New York Times* by Richard Bernstein.

11. *Newsweek,* 5 June 1989, p. 34.

BIBLIOGRAPHY

Aftel, M.; and Lakoff, R. 1985. *When Talk Is Not Cheap.* New York: Warner.

Atkinson, J. M. 1984. "Understanding Formality: The Categorization and Production of 'Formal' Interaction." *British Journal of Sociology* 33(1): 86–117.

Austin, J. L. 1962. *How to Do Things with Words.* Oxford: Clarendon.

Bateson, G. 1972. *Steps to an Ecology of Mind.* New York: Ballantine.

Bazerman, C. 1981. "What Written Knowledge Does: Three Examples of Scientific Discourse." *Philosophy of the Social Sciences* 2:361–87.

Belenky, M. F.; et al. 1986. *Women's Ways of Knowing.* New York: Basic Books.

Benedict, R. 1946. *The Chrysanthemum and the Sword.* Cambridge, Mass.: Riverside Press.

Bergman, P. 1979. *Trial Advocacy in a Nutshell.* St. Paul, Minn.: West Publishing.

Berlin, B.; and Kay, P. 1969. *Basic Color Terms: Their Universality and Evolution.* Berkeley and Los Angeles: University of California Press.

Bernstein, B. 1962. "Linguistic Codes, Hesitation Phenomena, and Intelligence." *Language and Speech* 5:31–46.

Bettelheim, B. 1983. *Freud and Man's Soul.* New York: Alfred A. Knopf.

Blanck, P. D., Rosenthal, R.; and Cordell, L. H. 1985. "The Appearance of Justice: Judges' Verbal and Nonverbal Behavior in Criminal Jury Trials." *Stanford Law Review* 38(1): 89–164.

Bloomfield, L. 1933. *Language.* New York: Holt, Rinehart & Winston.

Bolinger, D. 1968. *Aspects of Language.* New York: Harcourt, Brace.

Bolinger, D. 1980. *Language: The Loaded Weapon.* London: Longmans.

Breuer, J.; and Freud, S. 1893–95. *Studies on Hysteria.* In J. Strachey and A. Freud, eds., *The Standard Edition of the Complete Psychological Works of Sigmund Freud,* volume II. London: Hogarth.

Brodkey, L. 1988. *Academic Writing as Social Practice.* Philadelphia: Temple University Press.

Brown, P.; and Levinson, S. 1987. *Politeness: Some Universals in Language.* Cambridge: Cambridge University Press.

Caesar, C. Julius. *De Bello Gallico.*

Carroll, L. n.d. *Through the Looking-Glass.* In The Complete Works of Lewis Carroll. New York: Random House.

Chomsky, N. 1965. *Aspects of the Theory of Syntax.* Cambridge, Mass.: M.I.T. Press.

Cook-Gumperz, J. 1981. "Persuasive Talk: The Social Organization of Children's Talk." In J. Green and C. Wallat, eds., *Ethnography and Language in Educational Settings,* pp. 23–50. Norwood, N.J.: Ablex.

Eissler, K. 1969. "Irreverent Remarks about the Future of Psychoanalysis." *International Journal of Psychoanalysis* 50:461–71.

Ekman, P.; and Friesen, W. 1968. "The Repertoire of Nonverbal Behavior: Categories, Origins, Usage, and Coding." *Semiotica* 1:49–97.

Ekman, P.; and Friesen, W. 1969. "Nonverbal Leakage and Clues to Deception." *Psychiatry* 32:88–105.

Ellul, J. 1965. *Propaganda: The Formation of Men's Attitudes.* New York: Alfred A. Knopf.

Erickson, B.; et al. 1978. "Speech Style and Impression Formation in a Court Setting: The Effects of "Powerful" and "Powerless" Language." *Journal of Experimental Social Psychology* 14: 266–79.

Etzioni, A. 1974. "Creating an Imbalance." *Trial* 10:28.

Fillmore, C. 1975. Santa Cruz lectures on deixis. Bloomington, Ind.: Indiana University Linguistics Club. Mimeograph.

Finegan, E. 1980. *Attitudes toward English usage.* New York and London: Teachers College (Columbia University) Press.

Fisher, S.; and Greenberg, R. P. 1977. *The Scientific Credibility of Freud's Theory and Therapy.* New York: Basic Books.

Freud, S. [1895] 1950. *Project for a Scientific Psychology.* In J. Strachey and A. Freud, eds., *The Standard Edition of the Complete Psychological Works of Sigmund Freud,* vol. I, pp. 283–397. London: Hogarth Press.

——— [1901] 1905. *Fragment of an Analysis of a Case of Hysteria.* In J. Strachey and A. Freud, eds., *The Standard Edition of the Complete Psychological Works of Sigmund Freud,* vol. VII, pp. 7–122. London: Hogarth Press.

——— 1911–15. "Papers on Technique." In J. Strachey and A. Freud, eds. *The Standard Edition of the Complete Psychological Works of Sigmund Freud,* vol. XII, pp. 91–171. London: Hogarth Press.

——— Part III. 1916–1917. *Introductory Lectures on Psycho–Analysis,* In J. Strachey and A. Freud, eds., *The Standard Edition of the Complete Psychological Works of Sigmund Freud,* vol. XVI. London: Hogarth Press.

Gilligan, C. 1982. *In a Different Voice.* Cambridge, Mass.: Harvard University Press.

Goldberg, S. H. 1982. *The First Trial.* St. Paul, Minn.: West Publishing.

Goody, J.; and Watt I. 1963. "The Consequences of Literacy." *Comparative Studies in Society* 5:304–45.

Greenson, R. 1967. *The Technique and Practice of Psychoanalysis.* New York: International Universities Press.

Grice, H. P. 1975. "Logic and Conversation." In P. Cole and J. L. Morgan, eds., *Syntax and Semantics 3: Speech Acts,* pp. 41–58. New York: Academic Press.

Grünbaum, A. 1984. *The Foundations of Psychoanalysis.* Berkeley and Los Angeles, California: University of California Press.

Gumperz, J. J. 1982. *Social Identity.* Cambridge: Cambridge University Press.

Haley, J. 1963. *Strategies of Psychotherapy.* New York: Grune & Stratton.

Hartmann, H. 1964. "Psychoanalysis as a Scientific Theory. In *Essays on Ego Psychology.* New York: International Universities Press.

Hudson, R. 1980. *Sociolinguistics.* Cambridge: Cambridge University Press.

Illich, I. 1982. *Gender.* New York: Pantheon.

Jespersen, O. 1921. "The Woman." in *Language: Its Nature, Development, and Origin,* chapter 13. New York: W. W. Norton.

Kanter, R. M. 1977. *Men and Women of the Corporation.* New York: Basic Books.

Keenan, E. O. 1976. "The Universality of Conversational Postulates." *Language in Society* 5:67–80.

Keller, E. F. 1985. *Reflections on Gender and Science.* New Haven and London: Yale University Press.

Kennebeck, E. 1973. *Juror No. 4.* New York: W. W. Norton.

Key, M. R. 1975. *Male/Female Language.* Metuchen, N.J.: Scarecrow Press.

Korzybski, A. 1958. *Science and Sanity.* Lakeville, Conn.: The International Non-Aristotelian Library.

Laing, R. D. 1967. *The Politics of Experience.* New York: Ballantine.

Lakoff, G. 1987. *Women, Fire, and Other Dangerous Things: What Categories Reveal about the Mind.* Chicago: University of Chicago Press.

Lakoff, R. 1973. "The Logic of Politeness; or, Minding Your P's and Q's." In *Papers from the Ninth Regional Meeting of the Chicago Linguistic Society.*

—— 1974. "Remarks on *This* and *That.*" In *Papers from the Tenth Regional Meeting of the Chicago Linguistic Society,* pp. 345–56.

—— 1975. *Language and Woman's Place.* New York: Harper & Row.

—— 1984. "The Pragmatics of Subordination." In *Proceedings of the Tenth Annual Meeting of the Berkeley Linguistic Society,* pp. 481–92.

—— 1985. "The Politics of Language." *CATESOL Occasional Papers,* Fall 1985, pp. 1–15.

—— 1986. "My Life in Court." *Georgetown University Round Table* 85:171–79.

Lakoff, R.; and Tannen, D. 1984. "Communicative Strategies and Metastrategies in a Pragmatic Theory: The Case of *Scenes from a Marriage.*" *Semiotica* 17(3–4): 323–46.

Levinson, S. 1983. *Pragmatics.* Cambridge: Cambridge University Press.

Linz, D.; Penrod, S.; and McDonald, E. 1986. "Attorney Communication and Impression-making in the Courtroom." *Law and Human Behavior* 10(4): 281–302.

Lippmann, W. 1965. *Public Opinion.* New York: Free Press.

Logan, D. (n.d.). Building Penalty Phase Final Arguments. Alameda County (California) Public Defender's Office.

Lorenz, K. 1966. *On Aggression.* New York: Harcourt, Brace.

MacKinnon, C. 1983. "Feminism, Marxism, Method, and the State: Toward Feminist Jurisprudence." *Signs* 8:635.

Masson, J. M. 1988. *Against Therapy.* New York: Atheneum.

Matsumoto, Y. 1989. "Politeness and Conversational Universals: Observations from Japanese." *Multilingua.*

Menninger, K. 1973. *Whatever Became of Sin?* New York: Hawthorn Books.

Miller, C.; and Swift, K. 1977. *Words and Women.* New York: Doubleday (Anchor).

Nelson, J. S.; Megill, A.; and McCloskey, D. C. 1987. *The Rhetoric of the Human Sciences.* Madison, Wis.: University of Wisconsin Press.

North, O. 1987. *Taking the Stand.* New York: Pocket Books.

Olson, D. 1977. "From Utterance to Text: The Bias of Language in Speech and Writing." *Harvard Educational Review* 47(3): 257–81.

Orwell, G. 1949. *Nineteen Eighty-four.* New York: Harcourt Brace Jovanovich.

Packard, V. 1958. *The Hidden Persuaders.* New York: David MacKay.

Roheim, G. 1950. *Psychoanalysis and Anthropology.* New York: International Universities Press.

Rosch, E. 1973, "Natural Categories." *Cognitive Psychology* 4:328–50.

Sacks, H.; and Schegloff, E. 1973. "Opening Up Closings." *Semiotica* 7(4): 289–327.

Sacks, H.; Schegloff, E.; and Jefferson, G. 1974. "A Simplest Systematics for the Analysis of Turn-taking for Conversation." *Language* 50(4): 696–755.

Sallustius Crispus, C. *Bellum Catilinae.*

Searle, J. 1969. *Speech Acts.* Cambridge: Cambridge University Press.

Simon, J. 1980. "The Corruption of English." In L. Michaels and C. Ricks, eds., *The State of the Language,* pp. 35–42. Berkeley and Los Angeles: University of California Press.

Spender, D. 1980. *Man Made Language.* London: Routledge & Kegan Paul.

Suggs, D.; and Sales, B. 1978. "Using Communicative Cues to Evaluate Prospective Jurors during the Voir Dire." *Arizona Law Review* 20:629–42.

Tannen, D. 1984. *Conversational Style.* Norwood, N. J.: Ablex.

———— 1986. *That's Not What I Meant!: How Conversational Style Makes or Breaks Your Relations with Others.* New York: William Morrow.

———— 1990. *You Just Don't Understand: Women and Men in Conversation*. New York: William Morrow.

Thorne, B.; and Henley, N., eds. 1975. *Language and Sex: Differences and Dominance.* Rowley, Mass.: Newberry House.

Thucydides. 1928. *History of the Peloponnesian Wars.* Trans. Charles Forster Smith. Loeb Classical Library. New York: G. P. Putnam.

Timothy, M. 1974. *Jury Woman.* Glide Publications.

Waelder, R. 1936. "The Principle of Multiple Function." *Psychoanalytic Quarterly* 5.

Wellman, F. L. 1903. *The Art of Cross-examination.* New York: Collier-Macmillan.

Whorf, B. L. 1940. "Science and Linguistics." *Technological Review* 42:229–31, 47–48.

Wittgenstein, L. 1958. *Philosophical Investigations.* Oxford: Blackwell.

Zetzel, E. 1956. "Current Concepts of Transference." *International Journal of Psychoanalysis* 37(3): 69–76.

Zimmerman, D.; and West, C. 1975. "Sex Roles, Interruptions and Silences in Conversations." In B. Thorne and N. Henley, eds., *Language and Sex: Difference and Dominance.* Rowley, Mass.: Newbury House.

INDEX